Never Leave an Airman Behind

*How the Air Force Faltered and Failed
in the Wake of the Lackland Sex Scandal*

Craig M. Perry
Lieutenant Colonel, USAF (retired)

Table of Contents

Preface

When I joined the Air Force back in 1994, I never imagined I would one day have the opportunity to command a squadron. Two decades later, I was bewildered to find myself fired from this dream job, my once-promising career destroyed for no good reason. Despite these unexpected setbacks, I remained determined to set the record straight and restore my hard-earned reputation. On the anniversary of my entry into service, I penned this retrospective, which I feel sums up my career quite nicely:

Twenty years ago today, I arrived at Officer Training School to begin my Air Force journey. I had no idea what an amazing adventure this would be! Over the years I've had a dozen different assignments all around the world, from Korea to Germany to Alaska. I was fortunate enough to be selected as an Olmsted Scholar in Russia, and to be trusted with ever-increasing responsibility for my fellow service members with each new promotion. I've been deployed multiple times, in support of air operations over Iraq and the Balkans, and on the ground in Baghdad leading the first-ever Air Force weapons intelligence teams. And sadly, it was my solemn duty to eulogize three of my fallen comrades in Iraq.

I am incredibly proud to have carried on the tradition of my grandfathers, who each retired here in San Antonio after remarkable Air Force careers. One was a B-25 pilot in Italy during World War II, and served in England after the war. The other spent nearly a year in a German POW camp after his B-24 was shot down, then went on to fly fighters in Korea and Vietnam. I wish they could have been there when I assumed squadron command last year. That was definitely a high point of my career.

Six months later, it was all over. I was barred from my squadron, relieved of command, given career-ending punishments, then offered an assignment some felt would induce me to retire. I was officially reprimanded, notified my conduct had brought great discredit to myself and the United States Air Force, and informed it reflected an appalling failure to appreciate what is expected of me as an officer and commander. This was a devastating rebuke: after almost 20 years of distinguished service to my country, suddenly I no longer measured up.

And yet, I have no regrets about my time in command. No doubt I made some mistakes, but I always conducted myself with integrity and tried to foster a climate of dignity and respect in my squadron. After I was fired, the Air Force actually praised my wife, Caroline, and me for successfully engaging in the lives of my subordinates, fostering a healthy Key Spouse program, and demonstrating our commitment to the families in my squadron. "All were good examples of the types of behavior we admire in our commanders and in all Air Force members," they said.

Caroline and I have been overwhelmed by the outpouring of support from senior officers, peers, and former subordinates since I was relieved of command. I've crossed paths with a lot of folks over the last two decades, and it's gratifying to think I made some small difference in even a few of their lives. Ironically, the hardships we've suffered these past nine months have brought us closer to many of these current and former Airmen. And they've definitely taught us the importance of resiliency.

Now that I've done my 20, I'm eligible for retirement. I imagine I could hang up my uniform and walk away from what's left of my career anytime now. And one of these days, sooner or later, I know I will. But not today. Not while there's still hope that the Air Force I've served so faithfully all these years can set the record straight.

This is not over ... and I am not done yet.[1]

A lot has changed since I wrote those words over a year ago. My optimism that Air Force leadership would eventually do the right thing gave way to a more realistic perspective: my

---

[1] Facebook post, August 15, 2014

superiors had no intention of reconsidering my case, or holding those who wronged me accountable. I exhausted all avenues of appeal without result, and many of my friends and coworkers abandoned me and my family. Sadly, my predicament is not at all unique, as dozens of other airmen have suffered similar fates in recent years. Many of their accounts are far more compelling than mine, and maybe someday they will come forward to share their tales as well. As for my story, there was only so much I could say while I remained on active duty, so I faced a dilemma: continue to serve in an Air Force that no longer values my contribution to national security, or hang up my uniform and speak out about the troubling trends jeopardizing the effectiveness of our nation's air arm. In the end, the decision was easy.

I hope my memoir will draw attention to the crisis our Air Force is facing, and bring some comfort to other airmen who've been left behind. I would love to acknowledge all my sources for this book, but many remain on active duty and fear retaliation if their support for me were known. This fear is not unfounded: several airmen have been harassed by their chains of command for merely "liking" the "Team Perry" Facebook page created to advocate for my cause. A handful of folks were nevertheless willing to write character reference letters on my behalf, risking their professional reputations in a futile attempt to exonerate me. Others have provided candid feedback on their experiences at Basic Military Training or elsewhere in the Air Force, either directly to me or by way of the "Team Perry" page. Thankfully, Caroline and I have gained many new friends through our trials and tribulations, who have demonstrated what it means to never leave an airman behind.

I would particularly like to thank Lieutenant Colonel Elisa "Liz" Valenzuela and her wife, Bunny. They have truly been our wingmen, commiserating with us over our nightmarish experiences at Joint Base San Antonio-Lackland. We couldn't ask for truer, more loyal friends, and the Air Force has few officers with as much integrity or selflessness as Liz. I also want to thank Captain Angie "Hellfire" Maldonado, a BMT flight commander, and Melessa Casey, the wife of another, for looking out for Caroline and me during our ordeal, as well as BMT Key Spouses such as Brooke Poole and Melanie Hite who were similarly supportive. Chief Master Sergeant Dave Milne and his wife, Pam, have stood by us in word and in deed, and CMSgt Ken Williams and Senior Master

Sergeant Howie Watkins, both now retired, have provided us invaluable insight into events at BMT.

My "curious case" brought me to the attention of several airmen who've suffered much worse fates than me, including Master Sergeant Jeff Jordan, Major Michael Turpiano, and Master Sergeant Mike Silva, whose fiancé, Lisa Chloros, is a tireless advocate for justice in his case. Of course, I owe my notoriety to those in the media willing to tell my story, particularly Kristin Davis and the prolific Tony Carr. Without their reporting, curiosity about my case never could have reached the level it did – and that interest would not have lasted as long as it has if not for Hamant Kalidas, an administrator of the "Team Perry" page. To the countless others who contributed to this story or provided moral support, I cannot thank you enough.

None of this would have been possible without the love and devotion of my beautiful bride. Caroline sometimes blames herself for my relief of command, but the truth is, she was the best commander's wife I've ever had the pleasure to meet – and I never could have made it this far without her. Indeed, this isn't over until she says it's over!

Introduction

One morning in early January 2014, I received an unexpected e-mail from my boss, Colonel Deborah Liddick, regarding "toxic" leadership in the military. I was very surprised she forwarded this message to me, considering she had removed me from command of the 737th Training Support Squadron just two weeks earlier. At the time, I was the subject of an investigation into unspecified allegations against me, banished to a windowless office in a remote corner of Joint Base San Antonio-Lackland while I awaited news of my fate. Given these circumstances, it came as a shock that the commander of Air Force Basic Military Training had chosen to address this particular topic, as Col. Liddick was among the most toxic leaders my colleagues and I had ever encountered in our Air Force careers.

The e-mail, entitled "Second Order Impacts of Toxic Leadership," was authored by Major General Leonard Patrick, Second Air Force commander. He was forwarding a link to a *National Public Radio* story, prefaced be a brief introduction to his subordinate commanders: "Gang," he began,

> Take a look at this and consider this as we work to create a culture of dignity and respect...I have every confidence in your abilities and I have no issue with how you are running your organizations, but you need to consider this as you evaluate your Group and SQ/CCs, Chiefs, and front line supervisors.

The 37th Training Wing vice commander dutifully shared this message with his group leadership, including Col. Liddick, who in turn passed it on to her squadron commander distribution list – making sure to copy the officer she had placed in charge of my unit in my absence. "Leaders, recommend you take 15 min (that's how long it took me!) to read the attached article on Toxic Leadership. Pls reflect and ensure you are creating a culture of dignity and respect within your organization."[2]

If you listen to the NPR story or read through the transcript, you'll learn how the Army is struggling to address toxic

---

[2] E-mail thread from Maj. Gen. Leonard Patrick, Col. Vincent Fisher, and Col. Deborah Liddick, "Second Order Impacts of Toxic Leadership," January 8-9, 2014

leadership – which the author describes as "the kind of bosses who make their employees miserable" – in its ranks.[3] This is a very real problem, which afflicts all branches of the military. At one point or another, every military member ends up working for a negative leader who relies on his or her positional power to influence followers, and we have all seen the impact this behavior has on individual initiative and unit morale. Unfortunately, most toxic leaders don't recognize these qualities in themselves, even when their subordinates have the courage to call them out. Worse, their superiors often appear to overlook the warning signs about these leaders, allowing a toxic command climate to fester and discouraging those who place their faith in the system.

This phenomenon played out in the e-mail exchange above: the problem, my superiors seemed to be saying, is not at their level, but several echelons down the chain. In the 15 minutes it took Col. Liddick to read this article, how much time did she take to reflect on the leadership climate she herself was creating at BMT?

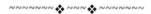

Less than five months later – after I had been formally relieved of command under dubious circumstances – an online article about my "curious case" went viral, sparking discussions across the Air Force about toxic leadership. Squadron commanders wondered if they, too, might be punished for seemingly innocuous interaction with their subordinates. Spouses feared their efforts to improve unit morale or help airmen in need would be taken the wrong way, and end up hurting their sponsor's career. Enlisted members questioned why officers who looked out for them were apparently being targeted. And airmen everywhere wondered how toxic leaders and backstabbing subordinates could get away with ruining an officer's career, while the chain of command stood by and watched.

Lackland had only recently emerged from a sexual misconduct scandal, during which numerous Military Training Instructors – the "drill sergeants" who mold new recruits – were found to have engaged in serious wrongdoing involving BMT

---

[3] Daniel Zwerdling, "Army Takes On Its Own Toxic Leaders," NPR, January 7, 2014

trainees. The Air Force launched an extensive witch-hunt to identify additional victims and perpetrators, and implemented a series of reforms to prevent future transgressions. This is how I ended up back in my hometown of San Antonio: I had been specifically recruited to command a BMT squadron, charged with helping transform this troubled institution in the wake of the crisis. But I would quickly realize these initiatives weren't all they were cracked up to be, and many MTIs were being unfairly punished for increasingly inconsequential misconduct. Little did I know, I would soon join their number.

My removal from command exposed me first-hand to the corruption of Air Force leadership. I was subjected to an amateurish, months-long investigation with no other purpose than to establish a pretext to fire me. Witnesses were found willing to denounce me and a few other folks my boss didn't like, without regard for how they might personally benefit from my removal. But getting me out of the way wasn't enough. The wing commander, Col. Mark Camerer, set out to utterly destroy my career and perhaps force me to retire, over trivial allegations that merited nothing more serious than a talking-to.

Despite these setbacks, however, I remained faithful to my proud Air Force heritage, whose tradition of honor and legacy of valor – in the words of the "Airman's Creed" used to indoctrinate new recruits – actually inspired me throughout my career. I was certain my wrongful punishment would not stand. Yet all my efforts to shine light on this injustice, and hold accountable those who had wronged me, came to nothing. I had tried everything: complaints to inspectors general at several levels of command; a formal request for redress under Article 138 of the Uniform Code of Military Justice; informal pleas for reconsideration to the general in charge of Air Education and Training Command and the Secretary of the Air Force; and inquiries by multiple members of Congress. My wife, Caroline, even filed a lawsuit against my boss for misappropriating her property, and helped expose my plight in the press and social media. Rather than honestly review my case to ensure a fair outcome, senior Air Force leaders closed ranks around the indefensible decisions that cost me my career.

James Baldwin once wrote, "The most dangerous creation of any society is the man who has nothing to lose" – a quote Caroline often paraphrases to describe my situation. I was the second-most senior officer to lose his job at Lackland in the wake of the so-called sex scandal, yet I was offered no opportunity to clear my name or rehabilitate my career. In my struggle to make sense of what happened, I quickly realized my mistreatment was merely the tip of a very large iceberg of toxic leadership, abuse of authority, and institutionalized injustice. It soon became abundantly clear my story was neither unique nor the most egregious, and the problem extended well beyond Lackland.

Despite dedicating over two decades to the service of my country, I was abandoned by Air Force leaders who have utterly failed to live up to the core values they demand of the rest of us. They certainly fell short of the much-maligned "Airman's Creed," whose concluding stanza offers this affirmation:

> *I am an American Airman:*
> *Wingman, Leader Warrior.*
> *I will never leave an Airman behind,*
> *I will never falter, and I will not fail.*

While I am now happily retired, and although the Air Force may never acknowledge the wrong that was done to me and so many other airmen, this is far from over. And I, for one, will never leave an airman behind.

Chapter 1: Assuming Command

By most accounts, my military career was going pretty well back in 2013. After nearly 19 years in the Air Force, I had amassed a fairly decent record: distinguished graduate from multiple military schools; good stratifications at various assignments; numerous overseas postings, including as an Olmsted Scholar and a deployment to a combat zone. I had also served as operations officer in a large squadron and executive officer to a three-star general, and had been a candidate for squadron command within my career field several times over. I had even been selected to attend senior developmental education in residence, placing me among the top 15 percent of my Lieutenant Colonel peers.

As the year began, I was assigned to the United States Cyber Command at Fort Meade, Maryland, working with a great bunch of service members from every military branch in a high-profile, cutting-edge mission area. Nevertheless, I had pretty much resigned myself to never getting the chance to command – so it came as quite a surprise when I received a phone call one evening in January 2013 from Rear Admiral Sean Filipowski, the USCYBERCOM director of intelligence. He was calling to share some good news: I had been selected for command of an Air Force Basic Military Training squadron at Joint Base San Antonio-Lackland..

What I didn't realize at the time was that a very different process had been used to select me for this assignment. After a sexual misconduct scandal rocked the "Gateway to the Air Force" a couple of years earlier, Major General Margaret Woodward issued a comprehensive report in 2012 calling for dozens of changes at Lackland. Finding that most officers were unfamiliar with the unique aspects of this training environment when they took command, she recommended the Air Force "should strive to place officers from among the highest-caliber and best-qualified officers available" into BMT squadron command billets.[4] Rather than selecting from among candidates who had been passed over for command within their own respective disciplines, General Edward Rice, commander of Air Education and Training Command, reportedly requested each career field provide their best

---

[4] Margaret Woodward, "Developing America's Airmen: A Review of Air Force Enlisted Training," *Commander Directed Investigation Report*, August 22, 2012, p. 31

candidates up front, from among whom he would pick the BMT squadron commander "Class of 2013."

Whatever trepidation I felt at the prospect of commanding a squadron whose mission – transforming raw recruits into enlisted airmen – I knew almost nothing about, it was tempered by my excitement about the location of my new assignment. For the first time since I shipped off to Officer Training School from the San Antonio Military Entrance Processing Facility 19 years earlier, I would be returning to my hometown to live and work near friends and family. Most of all, I was humbled to have been selected for command, and determined to make the most of this long-awaited opportunity, wasting no time in mastering my new unit's mission and taking care of the airmen under my charge.

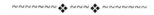

The 737th Training Group commander, Colonel Deborah Liddick, soon contacted me to coordinate a date for my change-of-command ceremony. At the time I was assigned to a sub-unified command, and I hoped to accrue at least 22 months in my position so I could earn joint service credit – an important factor in future promotion. However, Col. Liddick wasn't interested in waiting until after Labor Day for the sake of my career. In early February, she called my bluff:

> *Craig--I received info that you are not is not in a joint billet (not joint encumbered). Right now your RNLTD is 30 Jun 13. Pls let me know if you have any questions.*[5]

This was my first encounter with my future boss – a rather inauspicious beginning to what turned out to be a rocky working relationship.

My wife, Caroline, and I went down to San Antonio for my birthday in March, and selected a site to build our new home on the far west side of town. A few months later, we packed up our house in Maryland, loaded the dogs in a U-Haul, and headed off on our next adventure. After a short turnover with my predecessor, Lt. Col. Jared Granstrom, the big day arrived. On July 2, he relinquished command, and I accepted the squadron guidon from

---

[5] E-mail from Col. Liddick, "joint credit/RNLTD," February 8, 2013

Col. Liddick. She had given me strict instructions to spend no more than a few minutes on my change-of-command speech, so I kept my comments short and sweet:

> *I want to begin by thanking Col. Liddick for her kind words, and for trusting me to lead Basic Military Training support during such an important time. I also want to thank Col. Camerer and the other distinguished guests who took time out if their busy schedules to be here today.*
>
> *I am very excited to be assuming command here in my hometown of San Antonio. Both of my parents were Air Force brats whose fathers were assigned to Kelly Air Force Base back in the day. My dad actually went through BMT more than four decades ago, when I was just a baby, and my Aunt Dee attended Officer Training School not far from here.*
>
> *My wife, Caroline, is also from Texas, and we've known each other since high school. However, she's only been a military spouse for a couple to years now, so it is quite an honor for me that her mother drove all the way from Houston to be here today. I'm so proud my family is here to share this moment with me, and I want to honor them with these tokens of my appreciation.*
> *Thanks as well to my other relatives and friends who have traveled here from as far away as Dallas and Austin – it means so much to me that you could all be here.*
>
> *To the members of the 737th Training Support Squadron, I am humbled by the outpouring of support and confidence you've already shown me. You are an amazing group of Airmen with a critical, no-fail mission, and I'm eager to continue the excellent work of my predecessor as we move forward in the coming years. We have some challenges ahead of us, but let there be no doubt ... you can't miss with the TRSS!*

(That last line was the squadron motto, which I resolved to replace as one of my first orders of business ... right after I overhauled the unit's lackluster mission and vision statements.)

I had my first actual sit-down meeting with Col. Liddick a few days after the change-of-command ceremony. This was an awkward encounter, for which my boss seemed wholly unprepared. Although she had just invested me with the awesome responsibility of command, she seemed utterly confused as to who I was. For example, she didn't know my career field, and thought I had come to BMT from an overseas assignment. She was also surprised to learn my wife and I were building a house, since she assumed all her squadron commanders were considered "key and essential personnel" who must live on base. (Not according to the base housing office.) Most troubling, she didn't realize I had never before been a commander. "I thought all the commanders I hired were prior commanders," she commented, calling her role in my selection into question, as well as her confidence in my ability to do this job.

Nevertheless, Col. Liddick had nothing but good things to say about my new unit. While our support role may not be "glamorous," the group commander described the 737 TRSS as the "heartbeat of BMT" and the "most important squadron," noting "if you guys fail, we're going to fail in BMT." She praised my predecessor as the "best at showing he cared about people," and singled out Mr. Jim Steele, the training support operations flight chief, as my "go-to civilian." My new boss encouraged me to be a "smart leader" who adapts to his environment, rather than being quick to change it. More ominously, she suggested I read the Woodward report, and warned me not to ignore "small stuff," as I needed to "hold folks accountable" and ensure they're "committed to the Core Values."

I spent my first few weeks on the job getting to know my squadron and its people. The unit was organized into four flights spread across eight operating locations at Lackland. We were responsible for many of the "behind the scenes" missions at BMT, from inprocessing raw recruits to facilitating graduation events eight-and-a-half weeks later. Altogether, nearly 100 permanent-party personnel were assigned to the squadron, including more than 30 government civilians and a handful of contractors. In addition, students attending the Military Training Instructor School and recruits facing separation were administratively assigned to my unit.

Col. Liddick called me back to her office for my initial performance feedback session on July 24, to officially document her expectations of me as a commander. The front side of the performance worksheet seemed boilerplate, including her guidance that I listen to my "Chief" on enlisted issues – presumably a reference to my squadron superintendent, one of the few in the group who was not a Chief Master Sergeant. She suggested I not delegate too much to my operations officer – ironic advice, given her testimony against me months later – and I should never talk down to my subordinates about my superiors' decisions. (In another ironic twist, she admonished me that paperwork "needs to be letter perfect" – "if you sign something with mistakes then that shows you don't care" – in a document riddled with at least half a dozen spelling and other errors.) On the back of the form, she offered insights into my professional development, again betraying her ignorance of my career field or the fact that I had previously been selected to attend senior developmental education in residence. She did acknowledge, however, that I might leave BMT as a Colonel, as I would be in the primary zone for promotion in late 2014. She encouraged me to enjoy command through 2015, ominously warning that once it's over, I "may never have an opportunity to command again." On a more positive note, she pledged to help me "grow and develop as a commander": "I will be cheering you on!"[6] I later learned she provided the same awkward words of encouragement to all her subordinates.

One of my first orders of business as a new commander was to lay out my priorities for the squadron. At my first commander's call, held in the same auditorium where I assumed command three weeks earlier, I praised the hard work and dedication of my subordinates, and pledged not to pursue change for change's sake – if it ain't broke, why fix it? As Col. Liddick looked on from the back of the room, I shared with them my boss's impressions about the centrality of the training support squadron to BMT success. I had already noticed a few issues in the unit that deserved more attention, however. First, I pledged to focus on leadership development within the squadron. Second, because our unit consisted of several disparate functions spread out over multiple locations across Lackland, unit cohesion and esprit de corps were a priority. Third, our family support system seemed

---

[6] Col. Liddick, AF Form 724, *Performance Feedback Worksheet (Lt thru Col)*, for Lt. Col. Perry, July 24, 2013

underdeveloped, so I committed to bolstering the Key Spouse program. Finally, there were several "major muscle movements" on the horizon, including an upcoming unit compliance inspection, the construction of a new BMT reception center, and taking on part of the 324th Training Squadron mission when that unit stood down the following summer. I also unveiled our new unit mission and vision statements: "Provide superior operations support, personnel processing, medical response, and instructor development to Basic Military Training ... Absolute professionals supporting the foundational development of world-class Warrior Airmen."

Like most Air Force squadrons, the 737 TRSS was authorized several key leaders to assist the commander in his duties: an operations officer, a superintendent, and a first sergeant. My "DO," Captain Rob Sprouse, was the only other commissioned officer in my squadron (apart from a female Captain who was deployed throughout my short command tour). As a prior-enlisted officer with a line number for promotion to Major, Rob seemed to have the experience and maturity necessary to manage training support operations. Like me, he was originally from San Antonio, and had previously been assigned to Lackland as executive officer for the 37th Training Wing commander.

My senior enlisted leader, Senior Master Sergeant "LG,"[7] was a Master Military Training Instructor, who earned the blue rope she wore on her campaign hat – designating her as among the "best of the best," the top 10 percent of the instructor force – during a previous BMT assignment. (In fact, an old MTI recruiting poster hanging in my office, under the caption, "Join the Elite of the Air Force," featured the future SMSgt "LG" along with several other MTIs who had since returned to Lackland – including SMSgt Lynn Barron, chief of BMT standardization and evaluation, and MSgt Jamie Williams, 342 TRS first sergeant and wife of the incumbent BMT superintendent, CMSgt Ken Williams). SMSgt "LG" was handpicked to return to BMT in 2012 as a squadron superintendent in the 321 TRS, but had been reassigned to my squadron shortly before I arrived. Finally, MSgt Kerry Carr was my first sergeant, with whom I quickly established an excellent rapport on disciplinary and morale issues. I met with all three of these key leaders on a regular basis, including at weekly staff meetings and morning synchronization sessions a few times each week.

---

[7] At her request, I am not identifying my superintendent by name

In addition to these key leaders, I also directly supervised each of the flight chiefs. SMSgt David Milne, commandant of the MTI School, had been selected for promotion to Chief Master Sergeant and would soon depart for a remote tour in Korea. The chief Independent Duty Medical Technician, responsible for on-scene support to BMT trainees, was also scheduled for reassignment to the local medical wing, and was soon replaced by MSgt Thomas Ward, whose wife was an MTI student in my squadron. MSgt Arturo Ayala led the personnel processing flight, while a retired former MTI, Mr. Steele, was responsible for training support operations. I also supervised the unit program coordinator, Ms. Cynthia Coleman, who performed secretarial functions just outside my office. Each of these personnel, along with the managers of the unit deployment, training, and fitness programs, were regular attendees at weekly squadron staff meetings.

As a supervisor, I felt it imperative to get to know the folks I worked with each day. At the same time, with so few fellow officers in my unit, I was careful to avoid any appearance of fraternization – forming personal relationships with enlisted members on terms of military equality – and I steered clear of situations where I might be alone with any female subordinates behind closed doors. Given the hyper-compliant BMT environment, exacerbated by the recent sex scandal at Lackland, I didn't feel comfortable calling even my most senior enlisted subordinates by their first names, for fear of appearing overly familiar. I did, however, make a point of taking several of my key leaders to lunch, and my wife, Caroline, made every effort to get to know their families at official social events. We even invited each member of my leadership team to dinner at our home – but as it turned out, none of them took us up on the invitation before I was relieved of command.

It's often said that showing up is half the battle. As a commander, I was determined to get out from behind my desk and be highly visible around the squadron. I blocked off time throughout the week on my calendar for "walkabouts" in various work centers, both to make myself more accessible to my subordinates and to get a first-hand appreciation of the work they were doing. In addition, Caroline would occasionally schedule luncheons in a particular work center, and bring in a home-cooked meal for everyone to enjoy while we sat around and talked about whatever was on their minds. She and I also welcomed new members of my leadership team with gift baskets, delivered presents for babies born into the squadron, and brought flowers, homemade soup, or other goodies to members in the hospital. With the help of the TRSS Private Organization – a booster club whose membership and leaders were drawn from unit personnel – we also organized a squadron picnic, holiday party, and a civilian appreciation luncheon to welcome back furloughed employees after the 2013 government shutdown. Although we had no kids of our own, Caroline and I also actively supported group-wide children's events.

Caroline was also instrumental in reinvigorating our squadron's Key Spouse program. Designed to enhance readiness and establish a sense of Air Force community, this commander's program was critical to improving family support and unit cohesion. One of our focus areas was the MTI School, where most BMT staff begin their assignments as MTI students, before transitioning to one of the line squadrons. Adjusting to this new environment could be tough, as one MTI later acknowledged to me: "When I got orders to become an MTI I got absolutely no help from a sponsor. The first and only individuals who contacted me and my husband were Mrs. Perry and [one of the key spouses]. My husband was new to the AF way of life and I remember telling him that it was odd that we got support from the SPOUSES group instead of any support whatsoever from the school."

As each new MTI School class kicked off, I would introduce them to the squadron superintendent, first sergeant, and members of the Key Spouse team: Ms. Melanie Hite, wife of one of the MTI School instructors; SMSgt "LG"'s husband, who was himself a former "Blue Rope" MTI; and Caroline, the Key Spouse Mentor who supported their efforts. One MTI later shared her first impression of this program with me. "I remember the day clearly that Mrs. Caroline came to our MTIS class and spoke about the Key Spouse program that the Group had. I was amazed at her apparent passion for the program, but also for the legitimate well-being she portrayed for our spouses. I have sat in mandatory Key Spouse briefings before, and her briefing was like none other. She was sincere. And she projected that sincerity in her message to the class. She was honest about how the MTI career can be hard on spouses and she encouraged us to get our spouses involved so they did not feel alone. I was so moved by her advocating for my spouse that very evening I went home and told my husband all about it and I felt it would be something he could benefit from. I have never advocated for the Key Spouse program until this time. When someone is truly passionate about something, you can tell and it showed in Mrs. Caroline."

Since the vast majority of military members assigned to BMT begin their tours as students in the 737 TRSS, we made an effort to synchronize the MTI recruiting and sponsorship programs with projected manpower requirements, so as to match incoming students with mentors in their gaining line squadrons. Our Key Spouses coordinated closely with their counterparts in the 323d Training Squadron and elsewhere to ensure a smooth handoff through each phase of MTI training and certification. This arrangement proved so successful, Col. Liddick actually selected our Key Spouse team to brief General Robin Rand, commander of Air Education and Training Command, when he and his wife visited BMT in November 2013. Gen. Rand praised the program for its innovative outreach to our hard-working "deployed-in-place" MTIs, and asked Caroline to send him additional information about our program. (The general even made a point of hugging my wife before he boarded his surrey to depart.) It was no wonder when Melanie went on to win 37 TRW Key Spouse of the Year in early 2014.

Unfortunately, Col. Liddick was not always so supportive of my initiatives. When I arrived at BMT, I found Capt. Sprouse and SMSgt "LG" sharing a small office, an awkward space that had once served as a storage closet. Both of them expressed frustration with the arrangement, which did not befit their rank or positions, and afforded them no privacy to counsel subordinates or discuss sensitive issues. I resolved to find each of them their own offices, just as my first sergeant and each of my flight chiefs enjoyed. But because we shared a building with the group staff, Col. Liddick insisted on approving any office moves. Claiming operations officers and superintendents routinely share offices in the maintenance community where she hailed from, Col. Liddick rejected multiple proposals to install these two key leaders in their own spaces. On August 26, she wrote me an e-mail indicating she did not support Capt. Sprouse having his own office: "He and

[SMSgt "LG"] need to be working together (same office)...we can discuss...I'm trying to 'minimize' all of the secret meetings and conversations that take place in BMT...I would like see a more transparent workplace...our Officers need to know/understand the issues with enlisted personnel and work with SNCO's."[8] I found this an odd explanation, as Rob began his career as an enlisted member, and surely had some insight into enlisted personnel issues. Nevertheless, Col. Liddick did allow my operations officer and superintendent to move to a larger, but still shared, office. Disappointed, I reassured my subordinates that we could re-engage on this issue the following summer, once a new group commander was in place.

This wasn't the only instance that Col. Liddick inserted herself into an internal squadron matter despite my objections. When the time came to find a replacement for SMSgt Milne as MTI School commandant, I assembled a board of senior MTIs to help me select his replacement. In addition to SMSgt Milne and SMSgt "LG," I also asked the BMT stan/eval chief, SMSgt Barron, to participate. After interviewing six candidates for the job, our consensus was that SMSgt Howie Watkins, the 331 TRS superintendent, was the most qualified to train the next generation of MTIs. Not only was he senior to the other candidates and an experienced squadron superintendent, he also had a bachelor's degree in psychology. When I mentioned to Col. Liddick that I intended to hire SMSgt Watkins for this job, however, she forbid it, asserting he was not supportive of group initiatives. Instead, she insisted I hire the board's second choice, MSgt Jeremy Pickett, who was then in charge of MTI Recruiting within my squadron. She noted Pickett was stratified as the #1 Master Sergeant in the group, ignoring the fact that the Senior Master Sergeant we selected was higher ranking and more experienced. CMSgt Williams later tried to convince our boss to reconsider this decision, but she was adamant.

While I was disappointed by this encounter, I was not about to let MSgt Pickett think he wasn't my first choice for the job. He was on paternity leave for the birth of his first child at the time, so rather than wait until he returned to work, Caroline and I decided to make the nearly 80-mile round trip to his home in Adkins, Texas, on August 20, to deliver a baby gift and break the good news in person. My impression of this "Blue Rope" MTI was

---

[8] E-mail from Col. Liddick, August 26, 2013

of a by-the-book senior noncommissioned officer, professional in appearance and demeanor but prone to micromanaging his subordinates. I was concerned his leadership style might create friction in the MTI School, which was then staffed exclusively by a cadre of very "squared away" Master MTIs, and with the "Deliberate Development" section, a three-person team charged with cultivating the leadership skills of the MTI corps. When MSgt Pickett returned to duty, I sat him down and laid out my expectations for him as MTI School commandant: "If it ain't broke, don't fix it."

Col. Liddick and I also clashed over my new first sergeant. Soon after I assumed command, I learned that MSgt Carr was being forced to leave BMT, since he had less than a year's worth of experience in this special duty. Col. Liddick hired his replacement, MSgt Jadirra Walls, from a maintenance squadron at Charleston AFB, but this veteran "Shirt" and I initially didn't hit it off so well. As soon as she arrived at Lackland in mid-August, MSgt Walls signed out on house-hunting leave without bothering to introduce herself to me; she then informed MSgt Carr she intended to take the following week off as well. As her supervisor, I was concerned my new first sergeant was making no effort to clear her leave plans with me, and she was further cutting into any turnover time with her predecessor. When she finally reported for duty, she explained her children were starting school the following Monday, so she wanted the entire week off. Unfortunately, there were several important meetings I needed her to attend that week, including a day-and-a-half of mandatory training for commanders and first sergeants put on by the base legal office. In the end, I insisted she attend this training with me, but allowed her to take the rest of the week off.

MSgt Walls found a home on the far north side of town, which meant she had to contend with rush-hour traffic during her daily commute. She resolved this by simply coming into work early, and leaving each afternoon well before the end of the duty day. Unlike her predecessor, however, she wasn't in the habit of checking in with me before she left to ensure there were no time-sensitive issues we needed to discuss. Several times I went looking for her after 3 pm, only to find my "Shirt" had already departed for the day. And I wasn't the only one who had difficulty tracking down MSgt Walls. "While in-processing, it was near impossible to ever find MSgt Walls in her office," an MTI student later informed me. "When I was finally able to corner her in her office, she was quick, direct, and to the point. Her absences of never being in her office almost made me provide feedback in our end of course critique. I wanted to let someone know that it would have been very helpful if she would have had a schedule on the outside of her door stating when she was going to be available, because I wasted a lot of my time tracking her down to get her to sign off on my in-processing checklist. I was scared to make waves and I did not have 100% confidence that my feedback would have been confidential."

Finally, I sat down with MSgt Walls for a mentoring session. I explained that she seemed preoccupied with personal issues, and her modified work schedule made her unavailable for me and other members of the squadron. I suggested she might want to adjust her hours, and circulate more in the work centers to get to know people. Initially she seemed upset, but the next day she came back to my office and thanked me for bringing this to her attention. She admitted she'd been taking it for granted that, as an experienced first sergeant, there was no need for her to prove herself in this new unit.

Still, MSgt Walls remained aloof from squadron activities. While she and her family made a brief appearance at the squadron picnic in September, they did not attend the BMT children's fall festival or the squadron holiday party. She also didn't seem to approve of my wife. When Caroline inadvertently referred to me by my first name while introducing herself to a class of MTI students, MSgt Walls seemed scandalized. She was overheard griping about this to members of the MTI School staff immediately afterward, and even went to the BMT superintendent, CMSgt Williams, to complain about Caroline's unprofessional conduct. She never said a word about it to me, however.

One peculiarity of my position as 737 TRSS commander was that my squadron was responsible for some unit-level functions at the group and wing level as well. I exercised command authority over personnel assigned to the 737 TRG and 37 TRW staffs, and my first sergeant advised their respective commanders – Col. Liddick and Col. Camerer – on disciplinary issues affecting these personnel. It soon became obvious that the loyalty of MSgt Walls was divided between me and my boss. She confessed to me that Col. Liddick would often discuss personnel issues in my squadron with the group commander, but Col. Liddick directed her not to tell me what they talked about. Nevertheless, it soon became obvious that one of the people they were talking about behind my back was me. Not long after I mentored MSgt Walls about gaining the trust of the unit, Col. Liddick lectured me about changing her work hours, and declared my subordinates should trust her simply because she wears a first sergeant "diamond" on her sleeve.

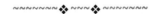

Given my concerns about MSgt Walls and MSgt Pickett, I encouraged my senior enlisted leader, SMSgt "LG," to mentor them in their new positions. I felt this would not only benefit her more junior colleagues, but also offer her a chance to better establish herself in her superintendent role. Although she previously served in this capacity in the 321 TRS, SMSgt "LG" had quickly run afoul of Col. Liddick, who fired her from that position several months before I arrived. While I didn't fully understand the circumstances surrounding these events at the time, it was clear I needed to boost SMSgt "LG"'s confidence after such a devastating career setback – not only for her sake, but to ensure she was effective as my superintendent. Asking her to mentor MSgt Walls and MSgt Pickett would be part of this rehabilitation process.

Meanwhile, her office-mate, Capt. Sprouse, had been conscripted as a project officer for the group staff. The 737 TRG training director, Dr. Laura Munro, enlisted him to help report the results of various "restoring the trust" initiatives intended to transform BMT after the sex scandal. Rob often vented to me during our morning synch meetings about "Doc" Munro's incessant tasks pulling him away from his squadron duties. While I might have resolved this issue by interceding on Rob's behalf with Dr. Munro (who was herself a former 737 TRSS commander), he never actually asked me to intervene, and in any case I felt it important to give this prospective field-grade officer a chance to work through this issue on his own. Besides, the squadron seemed to running smoothly even without my DO's undivided attention, so I saw no need to pick a fight with group leadership over his additional duties.

Still, it seems Capt. Sprouse may have been overly sensitive about the prerogatives of his rank. At a commander's call on October 11, I made an off-hand comment about not having any company-grade officers in the squadron eligible to compete for quarterly awards. During an intermission, Capt. Sprouse confronted me backstage, complaining he had never been so humiliated in his whole life. (He also claimed this was the second time I had publicly belittled him, but didn't elaborate.) I was naturally mortified, and I apologized profusely, reassuring him I meant no disrespect. After the break, I made my apology public, explaining that, as a Major-select, Capt. Sprouse was effectively a field-grade officer, and so was too senior to compete in the CGO category. I assumed this "mea culpa" smoothed over any ruffled feathers, as Rob had me officiate his promotion ceremony three weeks later.

As a new commander, I inherited several ongoing disciplinary issues from my predecessor, including the court-martial of an MTI School instructor, Technical Sergeant Marc Gayden, who went on trial three weeks after I assumed command. Lt. Col. Granstrom had preferred charges of rape and forcible sodomy against this "Blue Rope" MTI for an alleged Christmas Eve 2010 assault, but I was skeptical of these allegations. To begin with, TSgt Gayden's accuser only came forward after agents from the Air Force Office of Special Investigations contacted her multiple times. They then had her send her former MTI a provocative e-mail in hopes of soliciting an incriminating response, but he didn't take the bait. Moreover, several of her former BMT colleagues made statements undermining her credibility. Although his civilian defense attorney was not allowed to call these witnesses to testify or mention the e-mail exchange during the trial,[9] TSgt Gayden was nonetheless acquitted on all charges – the only MTI to be completely exonerated during the so-called Lackland sex scandal.

I was ecstatic about this result. Having reviewed the evidence and sat in on part of the trial, it was clear to me this was a very weak case that never should have gone to court-martial. Unlike several other MTIs who were busted for misconduct, no one had anything bad to say about TSgt Gayden, and SMSgt Milne refused to remove his photo from the MTI School instructor wall during this ordeal. When he was found not guilty, there was no

---

[9] Sig Christenson, "Trainer accused of Christmas Eve sexual assault," *San Antonio Express-News*, July 24, 2013

question in my mind we would restore him to his former position as soon as possible. He quietly returned to work the following week, but the 37 TRW public affairs officer passed off this unprecedented reinstatement as business as usual.[10]

Nevertheless, Col. Liddick remained unconvinced. When CMSgt Williams tried to discuss the implications of TSgt Gayden's innocence with our boss, the group commander corrected him: "Chief, he's not innocent, he was just found not guilty." She said something similar to Caroline the evening the verdict was announced, and repeated this mantra at the group staff meeting the following Monday. (Several of my fellow squadron commanders seemed to agree.) Yet the more I interacted with TSgt Gayden, the more convinced I became that he truly was innocent of these charges. A former MTI student later noted TSgt Gayden was one of only two instructors at the schoolhouse who "consistently remained professional," as opposed to some other members of the staffl; these MTIs "were positive and never ever had ill words to say about anyone or anything. They set the example, and you could believe their actions in that they genuinely cared."

Another former MTI assigned to my squadron, Airman Basic Andrew Lira, wasn't so lucky at trial. Convicted the week before I assumed command, he was serving a six-month sentence for unprofessional relationships he pursued with trainees in a different unit years earlier. MSgt Walls and I visited him in confinement at Lackland's Medina Annex, but she discouraged my wife from bringing him a care package. It was also left to me to take follow-up administrative actions against another MTI, to whom Lt. Col. Granstrom issued a letter of reprimand for an unprofessional relationship and adultery just before he relinquished command. Although these offenses merited nonjudicial punishment under Article 15 of the Uniform Code of Military Justice, I was informed too much time had passed to pursue this disciplinary option. Nevertheless, I red-lined his promotion to E-6 and eliminated him from the MTI career field.

I also found myself reviewing an appeal of nonjudicial punishment my predecessor handed down against the former 37 TRW inspections superintendent for allegedly falsifying her medical records. Her appeal included allegations of reprisal against Lt. Col. Granstrom and the wing command chief, which I

---

[10] Kristin Davis, "Cleared of all charges, blue-rope MTI back on the job," *Air Force Times,* July 31, 2013

immediately passed to the legal office, but she presented no compelling new evidence of her innocence. At the time, I saw no reason to doubt the results of the extensive investigation into her case, and neither did the Second Air Force commander, Major General Patrick, who upheld the punishment. Only later did I learn she had already filed a formal complaint of reprisal, which had been referred to the AETC inspector general for investigation, and Maj. Gen. Patrick ordered a parallel commander-directed investigation into her allegations.[11] Nothing seems to have come of these inquiries, however – an all-too-common occurrence during this period, as I would soon learn.

As the 737 TRSS commander, I had the unique responsibility of reviewing the discharge packages for all recruits who washed out of training. They were administratively reassigned to my squadron, but remained under the operational control of the 324 TRS "operations flight" until they were sent home or returned to training. (The 324 TRS also managed the medical hold and "Get Fit" programs, as well as any holdover airmen awaiting technical training.) Most discharges were for preexisting medical or mental health conditions that disqualified these recruits for military service. Other trainees admitted to previously undisclosed drug use during security investigations.

However, a handful of trainees faced discharge for misconduct committed while at Lackland, and some continued to offend once assigned to my squadron. One notable case involved a female trainee who allegedly sexually assaulted a fellow recruit, then ended up in the psychiatric ward of the San Antonio Military Medical Center. By the time these issues were resolved, she had been in the Air Force for so long she qualified for veterans' benefits. Another trainee falsely accused an MTI of misconduct, then made contradictory statements under oath. Just a week after I assumed command, his case came up in a wing-level discussion of pending disciplinary issues, where Col. Camerer endorsed the idea that I make an example of him. I issued this trainee nonjudicial punishment under Article 15, UCMJ, for making false official statements, then processed his discharge from the service.

---

[11] Kristin Davis, "Master sgt.: 'I've lost faith in the Air Force system'," *Air Force Times*, October 7, 2013

Construction of our house wrapped up in early September 2013, and we were finally able to move out of the 1-bedroom furnished apartment we'd shared with our dogs for over two months. Our new home was spacious and perfect for hosting parties, which I considered one of my social obligations as a squadron commander. Although we couldn't cram my entire 100-person unit into the house at once, we intended to work our way through the squadron systematically, perhaps flight by flight. However, the movers delivered such a ridiculous amount of household goods, it seemed like it going to take us forever to unpack all the boxes and set up the house. What we needed was some sort of deadline to motivate us.

SMSgt Milne's impending departure for Korea provided us the excuse we were looking for. This Chief-select would be leaving his family behind in San Antonio for a year, and we wanted to send him off in style while reassuring him his family would be taken care of during his absence. We decided to co-host a surprise going-away party on September 28, inviting about two-dozen of his friends and family from a guest list his wife provided. A handful of my subordinates attended, including the members of the MTI School's "Deliberate Development" team – MSgt Ricardo Chavez, SSgt Tommy Little, and Hassan Kamel, a contractor – as well as SMSgt "LG" and her children. I also personally extended invitations to my other squadron key leaders, Capt. Sprouse and MSgt Walls, but they were no-shows. We had a great time that night, and Chief Milne was very appreciative of the support we'd shown his family. "The true test of someone's character," he told us, "is how they treat someone they don't need."

The following weekend we had most of the squadron commanders and their wives over to the house for dinner, but we were never again allowed to host a party for members of my squadron. On October 7, Col. Liddick called me into her office and informed me someone had complained they weren't invited to the party. I suspected it might have been MSgt Pickett, whom I had reluctantly hired to replace SMSgt Milne as the MTI School commandant, but she assured me he wasn't the source. She lectured me on how commanders must avoid the appearance of favoritism, and even suggested I shouldn't even have any of my fellow squadron commanders over unless all of them were invited. With her deputy, Lt. Col. Jim Upchurch, present, my boss counseled me not to host any more parties at the house unless I could invite everyone in the unit. As I reflected on this admonishment, it occurred to me Col. Liddick had never hosted a party or had any of us squadron commanders over to her house; our only social interactions with our boss came at mandatory events put on by base or wing leadership at the Gateway Club. Moreover, I'm pretty sure she never instructed any of my colleagues not to host parties for members of their squadrons, as several of them routinely did this sort of thing.

Although we didn't throw any more squadron parties, we did, in fact, have a few more subordinates over to the house. When SSgt Little was admitted to the hospital in early October, his mother flew into town to visit. Caroline and I met her at a luncheon for her son after he was discharged from the hospital, along with several other BMT personnel. Mrs. Little said she had heard Caroline was an excellent chef, so my wife graciously offered to cook for her sometime. Since she would only be in town through the weekend, however, Caroline invited the entire group over to dinner that Saturday, October 12. In the end, only Mrs. Little, her son, and his co-worker, Mr. Kamel, showed up that night.

By a peculiarity of his contract, Mr. Kamel actually reported directly to the 737 TRSS commander. He had been at BMT for about seven years, providing behavioral and organizational development services to MTIs. I consulted with him occasionally on various initiatives, such as offering Myers-Briggs Type Inventory assessments to BMT leadership, while he and Caroline worked out a plan to do the same for MTI spouses. He was assisted in his work by a small "Deliberate Development" team, a pair of "Blue Ropes" embedded in the MTI School. MSgt Chavez, a Reservist administratively assigned to the 433 TRS, was the noncommissioned officer in charge of the team.

SSgt Little was an experienced "DD" instructor who garnered much praise from senior leaders for his poise and professionalism. Col. Liddick often tapped SSgt Little to represent BMT during media engagements, including an appearance on *Texas Public Radio* that aired July 25 and an interview with the *San Antonio Express-News* on August 22. She also routinely scheduled my subordinate to brief distinguished visitors on the "DD" program, without bothering to coordinate through me or his chain of command. As his squadron commander, however, I was responsible for making the tough call when it came time to offer a spot promotion – known in the Air Force as "Stripes for Exceptional

Performers" – to one of my airmen. SMSgt Milne suggested we nominate SSgt Little for this opportunity, but after reviewing his records I declined to pursue it, as he hadn't yet completed his Community College of the Air Force associates degree.

Although I didn't realize it at the time, it was a previous BMT commander, Col. Shane Courville, who was credited with establishing the "DD" program, to provide MTIs additional professional development during their tours. "I think the enlisted leadership of our Air Force has a very high expectation of our MTIs," he said in a 2011 interview. "When the various career fields release an individual for a special duty assignment as an MTI, I think the expectation is that they're going to get a highly trained, even more professional individual when they return. The Deliberate Development Program is the key for that additional training."[12] Courville's successor, Col. Glenn Palmer, also embraced the program, with the goal of better preparing MTIs for career advancement after their BMT special duty assignment.[13] AETC even bolstered BMT manpower by adding three positions to support this program and MTI continuation training requirements.[14] Unfortunately, Col. Liddick seemed much less enthusiastic about "DD," or my oversight of the program as 737 TRSS commander.

By the end of September, I had completed all the mandatory training for my position, including an online AETC squadron commander's course; various 37 TRW and JBSA orientations; and new BMT and 2 AF leadership classes imposed in the wake of the Lackland sex scandal. This indoctrination hammered into us the need to implement the recommendations from Maj. Gen. Woodward's 2012 commander-directed investigation, as well as other AETC-mandated safeguards, to

---

[12] Mike Joseph, "Courville: Leading BMT 'the best'," JBSA official website, June 23, 2011

[13] Mike Joseph, "New AF basic training leader returns to his roots," *San Antonio Express-News*, August 18, 2011

[14] General Edward Rice, "AETC Commander's Report to the Secretary of the Air Force: Review of Major General Woodward's Commander Directed Investigation," November 2, 2012, p. 34

dissuade, deter, detect, and hold accountable individuals who engage in unprofessional conduct. As one of several commanders handpicked to help transform BMT during this challenging time, I saw it as my duty to provide feedback on the implementation of these initiatives, as well as offer suggestions on how to further improve the organization. While it seemed to me that BMT had definitely turned a corner and was quickly getting back on track, I also suspected not all the reforms had been well thought out, nor had the second- and third-order effects of so much change so quickly.

The BMT training director, "Doc" Munro, would often quote General Rice regarding these transformation initiatives, who reportedly told his staff, "I have zero percent confidence we got this 100 percent correct." My fellow squadron commanders and I took that as an invitation to offer constructive criticism, but it quickly became clear Col. Liddick did not share this perspective. For example, when the group commander would raise issues during staff meetings, we soon learned they weren't up for discussion, and she wasn't seeking the input of her subordinate commanders. Rather, she preferred our unquestioning obedience, and seemed to consider those of us who spoke up with our own ideas as disloyal. For his part, Col. Camerer seemed similarly unwilling to reconsider the party line. During a training session in early September, when I asked him whether he thought the pendulum was beginning to swing back regarding disciplinary issues, he seemed annoyed by my unintentionally impertinent question.

Nevertheless, all the discussion of what went wrong and how to fix it got me thinking. I was particularly intrigued to learn how manpower issues may have contributed to the widespread misconduct that occurred at BMT. Back in 2006, as more and more airmen were supporting the wars in Iraq and Afghanistan – often in lieu of soldiers and Marines engaged in combat operations elsewhere – it was clear BMT graduates needed more basic war-fighting skills to operate in a deployed environment. Expanding upon an earlier "Warrior Week" effort, the Air Force established the Basic Expeditionary Airman Skills Training ("BEAST") exercise and increased the length of the basic training course from six-and-a-half to eight-and-a-half weeks, beginning in November 2008.[15] (By comparison, Navy boot camp is eight weeks, Army basic

---

[15] "Air Force Basic Military Training Fact Sheet," AF BMT official website, July 9, 2011

training is 10 weeks, and Marine recruits spend 13 weeks in training.) However, this instantly created a manpower shortage, as trainees were now spending over 30 percent longer at BMT, while the number of instructors hadn't increased accordingly. AETC opted to solve this problem by relaxing MTI recruiting standards, allowing a rapid influx of airmen to quickly fill the instructor ranks. Furthermore, once these new applicants graduated from the MTI School, they completed on-the-job qualification training in their assigned squadrons, which were then facing severe personnel shortages of their own, creating incentives for trainers to sign off quickly on evaluations. Nevertheless, when they met at Lackland in May 2010, the 22nd Basic Military Training Triennial Review Committee was "in awe" and "impressed" at the significant quality improvements in the program achieved by expanding BMT to 8.5 weeks.[16]

While this generation of MTIs no doubt included some remarkable and talented noncommissioned officers, it also featured some instructors who were less qualified and proficient than their colleagues – and in fact, most of the MTIs later caught up in the Lackland sex scandal were recruited and trained during this surge. Yet even after this push to increase MTI production, manning levels still remained below requirements, as filling BMT instructor slots was not then a high priority at AETC. This problem was exacerbated by Program Budget Decision 720, which effectively eliminated operations officer positions from BMT squadrons. Commanders were left to lead these enlisted training units without any commissioned colleagues to offer assistance or counsel. The typical BMT squadron leadership team during this era featured squadron superintendents who had spent much of their careers as MTIs – so long, in fact, that some were no longer even qualified in their primary Air Force career fields. While well versed in the byzantine politics of BMT, they had little insight into the challenges new recruits would face in the operational Air Force. On the other hand, first sergeants tended to be relatively inexperienced, or worse, unqualified E-6s who lacked formal in-residence training for this demanding special duty. While none of these structural factors begin to excuse the behavior of MTIs who abused, had sex with, or even raped trainees under their care, they

---

[16] Mike Joseph, "Review panel praises BMT," AETC official website, May 20, 2010

do help explain how such misconduct could become so widespread yet remain undetected.

One group that remained relatively unscathed by these events was the "Blue Ropes." Established in 1975 to recognize the "best of the best" among the instructor corps, the "Master MTI" program established a competitive process to identify high-performing instructors, who were then authorized to wear a distinctive blue rope on their campaign hats. The MTI monument – which stands prominently between the JBSA-Lackland parade grounds and the 37 TRW headquarters building – features a "Blue Ropes of the Year" plaque, on which are inscribed the following words:

> *A Master Military Training Instructor is one who is a total professional in all phases of Basic Training – the top ten percent of the instructor force.*
> *Is a leader among other instructors and exhibits only the highest characteristics of ethics, morality and integrity.*
> *Fully supports the mission, traditions and esprit de corps of the Basic Military Training School.*
> *Is the "best of the best."*

Not surprisingly, "Blue Rope" MTIs have tended to hold most enlisted leadership positions at BMT over the years, including group superintendent, squadron superintendents, instructor supervisors, and masters of drill and ceremony. Yet this elite cadre was not implicated in the abuses of the Lackland sex scandal. Of the 35 MTIs whose cases were taken to courts-martial, only three (less than ten percent) were "Blue Ropes" – and of these, only one was actually convicted. The Woodward report mentioned Master MTIs only in passing, merely noting "BMT created a culture where the power of a campaign hat or a blue rope trumped the earned authority and respect of an NCO's or a senior noncommissioned officer's (SNCO) rank."[17]

Nevertheless, once Col. Liddick assumed command of the 737 TRG, the Master MTI awards program was suspended, and MTIs were barred from serving as group or line-squadron superintendents. By the time I arrived at BMT, most of the dwindling "Blue Rope" cadre was assigned to my squadron, or on the group staff in the stan/eval shop. In fact, almost every MTI in

---

[17] Woodward report, p. 64

my unit wore a blue rope, including my squadron superintendent, the MTI School commandant and instructors, and the BMT Reception Center chief. Some of these "Blue Ropes" actually earned this honor during a previous Lackland tour, and had since been invited back to BMT as "retreads" after distinguishing themselves in the operational Air Force. I came to see the blue rope as analogous to the patch Air Force weapons officers wear to identify themselves as tactical system experts, master instructors, and leaders in the operational Air Force.[18] These folks clearly weren't part of the problem at BMT – in fact, I felt they ought to be part of the solution.

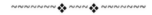

Just a few days after I assumed command, "Doc" Munro copied me on an e-mail regarding how to measure progress towards implementing the Woodward report recommendations. She had grouped the findings into a few overarching themes, as a point of departure for discussing what went wrong at BMT. In response, Col. Liddick praised this list as "a perfect product for our CC's [sic] to use as a cheat sheet!"[19] But I wasn't so sure. For some reason, the BMT training director lumped nine of the 22 findings under the heading "culture gone astray," including those Maj. Gen. Woodward labeled as leadership or selection and manning issues. In fact, only one Woodward report finding referenced "BMT culture,"[20] which the author went out of her way to downplay: "while we necessarily highlighted the negative elements in BMT culture that contributed to misconduct, we must also emphasize that the vast majority of MTIs serve with distinction. They are outstanding role models who work tirelessly to make the next generation of Airmen even stronger than the last."[21]

I found Dr. Munro's approach misleading and inconsistent, and I was concerned BMT leadership may have misdiagnosed the

---

[18] United States Air Force Weapons School fact sheet, August 12, 2015

[19] E-mail response from Col. Liddick to Dr. Munro et al., "CDI Findings and BMT Metrics - Path to Restoring the Trust," July 8, 2013

[20] *Ibid.*, p. 64-65

[21] *Ibid.*, p. 127

problem we were facing. On the other hand, there were some promising signs of progress. I was encouraged when the local medical wing stood up a "Military Training Consult Service" at BMT. This team of psychologists, led by Lt. Col. Alan Ogle, was brought in to provide counseling services to MTIs, offer periodic mental health evaluations, and screen potential candidates for MTI duty. Dr. Ogle also occasionally briefed the group staff and squadron leadership on relevant psychological topics, such as the "behavioral drift" and moral disengagement evidenced in the classic experiments by Stanley Milgram and Philip Zimbardo, and in the real-world interrogations of Abu Ghraib, Iraq. I felt strongly his team was offering an invaluable service – similar to that provided to survival, evasion, resistance, and escape training instructors – which would help prevent the recurrence of abuses at BMT.

On October 3, 2013, I sent Col. Liddick a note summarizing some of the conclusions I had come to during my first three months in command:

> *Ma'am, now that I've completed all my mandatory Sq/CC training, I've turned my attention to how we can better message the lessons learned from our recent history. I think it's important to emphasize that BMT and the MTI corps have a proud heritage and tradition of honor that dates back generations … but we (collectively) got off track several years ago for the reasons clearly spelled out in the Woodward report. Many of the corrective actions we've taken are not new initiatives, but rather "getting back to basics" -- providing proper leadership oversight and staffing levels, emphasizing Core Values, NCO responsibilities, accountability, compliance with established standards, etc. I also think Dr. Ogle's analogy to "bad apples" vs. "bad barrel" is useful: we (collectively) created an environment where a handful of criminals could flourish undetected and unpunished, and influence others to behave inappropriately. However, now that we've removed the bad apples and flushed out the barrel, we're on track to restore BMT to a position of trust and reputation for excellence.*

After a brief discussion of "Doc" Munro's flawed "culture gone astray" taxonomy, I continued:

Now that we've identified and implemented the changes necessary to get BMT "back to basics", I believe we need to focus on building a sense of teamwork and camaraderie both within the MTI corps and between leadership and line MTIs. A key component of this is avoiding the perception that we're blaming the MTIs for all that went wrong. Obviously, there were some bad apples, and far too much behavioral drift among many other MTIs. But the Woodward report only had one finding -- #12 -- which explicitly addressed MTI culture. Virtually everything else can be chalked up to ineffective (non-MTI) leadership, insufficient manpower, inadequate training, and issues related to detection, reporting, and handling of alleged misconduct which are specific to training environments. While the BMT/MTI culture certainly went astray in many respects, this was more a result of these multiple factors/trends than an underlying cause. We can bring in new leadership and impose new policies, but until and unless we have the buy-in of the MTI corps, all our hard work to restore the trust in BMT will not be sustainable. It's time we partner with them more effectively to rehabilitate the MTI brand -- including the Blue Rope program, which only received passing mention in the Woodward report -- and celebrate the great work they do each and every day.

I'm looking forward to partnering with TRG leadership and moving forward here in the TRSS to shape the message of BMT getting "back to basics". Thanks for your time and attention to this important issue! [22]

Ominously, Col. Liddick never responded to this e-mail, which Caroline jokingly referred to as my "manifesto." But it soon became clear I no longer had the trust or confidence of my group commander.

---

[22] E-mail to Col. Liddick, "RE: CDI Findings and BMT Metrics - Path to Restoring the Trust," October 3, 2013

Just a week after I assumed command in July, my squadron facilitated the administration of brand-new surveys developed by the RAND Corporation. We soon began offering graduating trainees a weekly computer-based survey, in fulfillment of a Woodward report recommendation.[23] The survey for MTIs, on the other hand, was never fully implemented. The test poll administered that summer exposed a "post-apocalyptic" culture characterized by deep dissatisfaction among the MTI corps. Instructor duty was generally not considered career enhancing, and MTIs desired greater respect and cooperation from squadron leadership and fellow instructors. They complained of insufficient resources and staffing, as well as constant changes in policy, conflicting job expectations, and inconsistent policy guidance. MTIs feared trainee accusations and disproportionate leadership response, and most were not getting enough sleep.

When these MTI survey results were finally briefed to the BMT squadron commanders at the end of October, Col. Liddick seemed uncharacteristically calm, even reflective. She put a positive spin on the findings, which she acknowledged could have been much worse, and she wrote off the most negative comments as attributable to a handful of disgruntled MTIs. At a commander's call later that week, she adopted an unusually upbeat tone. Was Col. Liddick finally starting to mellow out, we wondered, or had something else happened to lighten her mood?

As it happened, the annual wing commander list – a catalog of officers selected to take charge of large Air Force units the following year – had recently been released, and Col. Liddick's name wasn't on it. For some reason, my boss had confided in my wife, Caroline, that she had planned to retire before coming to Lackland, but she changed her mind when she was selected to command BMT. She hoped her current assignment would serve as a stepping-stone to wing command and eventual promotion to general officer – but now she would have to resign herself to retire after all.

For the moment, at least, Col. Liddick seemed to relax a bit. Perhaps she realized she no longer needed to try so hard to impress her superiors, since she no longer had a shot at promotion. Or maybe she was simply experiencing the after-effects of a vacation she took a couple of weeks earlier, scheduled to coincide with the Military Training Instructor Association convention. This

---

[23] Woodward report, p. 117

annual MTI "love fest" brings together current and former instructors to celebrate their proud heritage and swap BMT war stories. As the MTIA vice president, my superintendent, SMSgt "LG," was involved in planning all these events, including the "Tiger Stripe Ball" (a barbecue at the BMT obstacle course), the MTIA Honors Banquet (a formal ceremony at the Gateway Club), and the "Blue Rope Ball" (another casual event honoring top-10-percenters).

At the banquet on October 17, my superintendent and her husband were seated at the head table, while Caroline and I were assigned to a different table with Mrs. Milne and her youngest daughter; Mr. Kamel; SSgt Little; and a member of the stan/eval team and her husband – the only guests not associated with my squadron. When we realized the "Blue Rope of the Year," SSgt Joshua Hite, and his wife, Melanie (a squadron Key Spouse who was up for an award that evening), were seated elsewhere by themselves, we arranged for them to swap with the odd couple at our table. Then we noticed my first sergeant, MSgt Walls, was also stranded with another group, so we squeezed her in as well.

That week also marked the first visit by the new AETC commander, Gen. Rand, to BMT. I had a great deal of respect for this senior leader, whom I had worked for years earlier during my deployment to Iraq in 2006-07, where he was my wing commander. I had high hopes for the kind of leadership he would bring to AETC. Gen. Rand conducted a commander's call in the BMT Reception Center, where he announced his priorities: mission, airmen, and family. At the end of this presentation, Col. Camerer addressed the audience, and admitted that, when he first stood before the MTI corps shortly after assuming command a year earlier, there were still many among their ranks suspected of misconduct. Now, however, the wing commander was confident they had weeded out the worst offenders, and he was proud of the instructors who remained.

The highlight of the week, however, was the retirement ceremony for CMSgt Williams. Held on Medina Annex in the 342 TRS (where his wife was first sergeant), the Chief's send-off was a well-attended affair officiated by his former boss, Col. Palmer. Now deputy director of operations at Air Force Special Operations Command, this former 737 TRG commander had been relieved in August 2012, collateral damage from the Lackland sex scandal. Inviting such a controversial senior leader to return just a year after his downfall seemed like a watershed event, as if BMT had truly turned a corner and put the dark days of the past behind it. While Col. Camerer and other wing leaders were in attendance, Col. Liddick was noticeably absent at her senior enlisted leader's send-off.

In a strange twist of fate, two photographs taken that week would eventually feature prominently in my own downfall. One was from the Blue Rope Ball, where my superintendent and I joined several other airmen on stage to honor our squadron's newest "Blue Rope of the Year," SSgt Jason Estrada. We were all dressed in civilian clothes, and I was actually wearing a cowboy hat and checkered Western shirt in keeping with the lighthearted theme of the event. I later made a version of this picture – cropped to show only SMSgt "LG," SSgt Hite, and me – as my Facebook profile picture. The other photo, a portrait of Caroline and me dressed up for the MTIA Honors Banquet, ended up plastered on the cover of the *Air Force Times* in June 2014, next to this blockbuster headline: "Officer's wife says his career was derailed because they were too friendly with enlisted. The Air Force says he undermined his boss. The curious case of Lt. Col. Perry."

Chapter 2: BMT in Crisis

On June 25, 2011, a Military Training Instructor named Staff Sergeant Luis Walker was removed from his duties in the 326th Training Squadron at Joint Base San Antonio-Lackland over allegations he had raped a trainee. A week later, Colonel (select) Glenn Palmer assumed command of the 737th Training Group, and began grappling with the largest sexual misconduct scandal in Air Force history. Within a year, the Air Force announced it had removed 35 MTIs from their duties – an alarming eight percent of the 473-person instructor corps – while conceding most were eliminated for something other than sexual misconduct.[24] Almost all of these cases would ultimately end in courts-martial, while the Air Force implemented a dizzying array of reforms intended to prevent a recurrence of such widespread misconduct. Unfortunately, many of these measures turned out to be misguided and counterproductive.

This was not the first time MTIs had been accused of sexual misconduct with trainees at Lackland. Historically, the Air Force addressed two or three such cases per year, and a total of 11 MTIs were held accountable for unprofessional relationships with trainees or students between 2006 and 2010. When the number of MTIs under investigation reached a dozen by April 2012, however, it was clear that the recent phenomenon was different.[25] Moreover, the scale of SSgt Walker's alleged crimes was unprecedented. "In our review of the history, we have not seen any case of this magnitude at Lackland," a JBSA spokesman acknowledged.[26] The Air Force Office of Special Investigations identified 10 of his victims by November 2011, when instructors in a different squadron came forward with allegations of additional MTIs engaging in misconduct with female trainees. OSI agents launched another investigation, but could find no credible evidence of sexual or other misconduct, as none of the alleged victims corroborated the allegations. Unconvinced, the 802nd Mission Support Group staff judge advocate directed the Security Forces Office of Investigations to look into the matter. In January 2012,

---

[24] Sig Christenson, "Number of instructors ousted at Lackland is 'extraordinary'," *San Antonio Express-News*, June 11, 2012
[25] AETC Commander's Report to SecAF, p. 10
[26] Sig Christenson, "Former Lackland instructor accused," San *Antonio Express-News*, December 20, 2011

they found a former female student who admitted to beginning a sexual relationship with SSgt Peter Vega-Maldonado after graduating from BMT, and over the next several months SFOI investigators identified six more MTIs who allegedly engaged in sexual misconduct with trainees and students. In exchange for a sentence cap and testimonial immunity, Vega-Maldonado provided a significant number of investigative leads, and testified against a handful of his fellow MTIs regarding their alleged misconduct with trainees.[27]

"The fact that MTIs stepped forward to identify those suspected of misconduct cannot be overlooked," said Col. Polly Kenny, Second Air Force staff judge advocate. "It demonstrates that these NCOs care about the integrity of the BMT Corps, and are not willing to tolerate behavior that will tarnish a hallowed Air Force institution." Meanwhile, the BMT commander, Col. Palmer, encouraged trainees to come forward as well. "You are my neighborhood watch – each and every one of you," he would announce during initial orientation briefings. "If there is any MTI misconduct going on, report it. If it's happening to you, report it. If you observe it happening, be a good wingman and report it." Trainees also received briefings from chaplains, lawyers, special agents, and sexual assault response coordinators, while the 37th Training Wing surveyed nearly six thousand trainees in March 2012 to identify additional sexual misconduct. For their part, MTIs were ordered to re-read Air Force Instruction 36-2909, *Professional and Unprofessional Relationships*, along with AETC-specific guidance, and then sign an agreement of understanding.[28]

These were among the initiatives implemented as part of the *Basic Military Training Command Climate Optimization Plan*, which the wing commander, Col. Eric Axelbank, authorized in February 2012. It called for fundamental reforms, including identifying all victims of sexual assault; creating an atmosphere where trainees feel free to report misconduct without fear of retribution; employing heightened tracking and trend analysis while vigilantly investigating all misconduct accusations; and deliberately developing MTIs who uphold the "airmen of character" virtue and do not tolerate those who tarnish the reputation of the

---

[27] Woodward report, p. v-vii
[28] Clinton Atkins, "Commander calls for command-wide investigation of inappropriate relationships," Air Education and Training Command official website, June 22, 2012

MTI corps. On July 13, the 737 TRG released an update to the plan, which detailed 30 additional changes, and provided a further progress report in the first week of August. During a parallel commander-directed investigation that summer, Maj. Gen. Woodward found "leaders at the squadron, group, wing, and numbered Air Force levels are actively engaged in reforming BMT in such a way that incoming trainees will find a safe, yet challenging, training environment."[29] In fact, most of the reforms she ultimately recommended were already well underway by the time Col. Palmer was unexpectedly relieved of command that summer.

Criminal proceedings against MTIs accused of sexual misconduct progressed slowly at first. Charges against SSgt Walker were not preferred until late November 2011, and he didn't stand trial until the following July. The first court-martial was actually against SSgt Vega-Maldonado, who pled guilty in April 2012 to an unprofessional relationship in exchange for his testimony against other 331 TRS instructors. This landmark deal turned sour a couple of months later, however, when Vega-Maldonado admitted to much more extensive sexual misconduct during Article 32 evidentiary hearings into allegations against SSgt Craig LeBlanc and SSgt Kwinton Estacio – both of whom were later found not guilty of the most serious charges against them.

Despite these initial setbacks, the wheels of military justice kept slowly turning, and the pace of prosecutions accelerated sharply in early 2013. This effort was aided by the establishment of a so-called "prosecution task force" at Lackland, under the authority of the local staff judge advocate, Col. Adam Oler. OSI resumed its criminal investigations in May 2012, reaching out to thousands of current or former airman to uncover additional allegations of MTI misconduct. More than four-dozen full-time investigators were involved, with additional support from hundreds of criminal analysts, psychologists, and other personnel from 39 different Air Force bases.[30] In October 2012, AETC began its own massive outreach to BMT graduates dating back a decade

---

[29] Woodward report, p. 11-13
[30] AETC Commander's Report to SecAF, p. 11

to make them aware of the new 24/7 sexual assault and response coordinator hotline.[31] Thousands of e-mails were sent out asking current and former airmen to come forward if they knew about or were victims of any unprofessional conduct by MTIs.[32]

This witch-hunt paid dividends in terms of convictions: of the 35 cases brought to courts-martial, all but two resulted in guilty verdicts on at least one charge. On the other hand, only six of these cases involved charges of rape or sexual assault, and the Air Force managed to secure only three convictions on these counts – one of which was later overturned on appeal. In the end, the only MTIs who were proven in a court of law to be rapists were SSgt Walker – whose notorious crimes opened this Pandora's box – and another former instructor accused of dubious charges dating from decades earlier. (I will discuss this case in Chapter 19.)

Then again, it's not terribly surprising the Air Force was able to secure so few sexual assault convictions. Such crimes are notoriously difficult to prove, as there are often no witnesses other than the alleged victim and perpetrator, and any physical evidence is rarely collected at the time of the crime. If the defendant asserts the interaction was consensual, the government must further demonstrate coercion. Moreover, sexual assault victims are often reluctant to report the crime, or to confront their attacker at trial. They often blame themselves for what happened, fear reprisal for coming forward, or simply don't want to relive the trauma of their assault. The outcomes of such courts-martial often hinges on the quality of the defense team, which in military cases often includes civilian attorneys in addition to the uniformed area defense counsel provided at no cost to the defendant. Not surprisingly, the Air Force conviction rate for such cases was only 43 percent in fiscal year 2014.[33]

The military justice system often compounds these difficulties. Decisions about whether to prosecute sexual assault cases are left to the alleged perpetrator's chain of command, posing a potential conflict of interest – made all the more complicated if the victim is in the same unit. If the commander prefers charges, the victim may be called to testify at an Article 32 hearing, a

---

[31] *Ibid.*, p. 38

[32] Eileen Pace, "New Charges At Lackland On 20-Year-Old Case," *Texas Public Radio*, February 24, 2014

[33] The Judge Advocate General's Corps, *Air Force Sexual Assault Court-Martial Summaries, 2010 – March 2015*, p. 2

preliminary examination of the evidence roughly analogous to a civilian grand jury. However, unlike in the civilian system, the Uniform Code of Military Justice allows the defense to question the victim during these hearings, and such Article 32 testimony is typically not sealed. If the case then goes to court-martial, the victim will likely again be subjected to cross-examination. These are real challenges, which prompted various calls for reforms, some of which were enacted by the 2014 National Defense Authorization Act. On the other hand, commanders and prosecutors have come under enormous political pressure in recent years to take a harder line against purported crimes of a sexual nature, no matter the quality of evidence or reliability of the alleged victims.

A review of cases where the prosecution failed to win sexual assault convictions against MTIs is revealing. Accusing these instructors of using their position and authority to force trainees to engage in unwanted sexual acts, they failed to convince judges and juries that coercion was involved. For example, two former trainees testified they felt pressure and a sense of nervousness when a pair of MTIs summoned them from their dorm for a late-night rendezvous. "We promised each other that we weren't going to separate," one said, "and we weren't going to have sex with them." However, she did not tell her MTI to stop, or recall pushing him away from her.[34] In another case, the defense argued that the alleged victim freely engaged in sex with their client on multiple occasions, and only claimed she was sexually assaulted out of embarrassment by what she had done. "I wouldn't trust her," testified another former trainee who admitted to a consensual relationship with the MTI.[35] The credibility of the accuser was also on trial in a case I discussed in the previous chapter, where the prosecution failed to establish the alleged victim had even been alone in the dorm with her MTI on the date in question. Finally, there's the case of an MTI whose sexual assault conviction was later overturned on appeal. "We do not discount ... [the accuser's] testimony, and we recognize she portrayed what could have been a sinister act," the appeals court wrote, and it is possible the MTI "used some combination of his coercive power." Nevertheless, the

---

[34] Sig Christenson, "Call over the intercom led to Lackland sex tryst," *San Antonio Express-News*, June 2, 2012

[35] Sig Christenson, "Trainer to spend 2 years behind bars," *San Antonio Express-News*, June 29, 2013

government's evidence "is too thin to satisfy us beyond a reasonable doubt that [he] used force to cause the sexual conduct."[36]

To be sure, not all MTIs acquitted of these crimes were necessarily innocent, and all but one was found guilty of engaging in unprofessional relationships or other related charges. While prosecutors were unable to prove sexual assault, most of these MTIs clearly engaged in sexual activities involving women with whom they had no business consorting. Still, it's not entirely clear that justice was served in many of these cases.

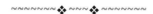

The impacts of this unfolding scandal were felt across the entire Air Force, affecting even its most senior leaders. Senator John Cornyn (R-TX) held up the nomination of General Mark Welsh III to become the next Chief of Staff of the Air Force for a week, until the nominee "demonstrated a genuine resolve to improving Air Force-wide policies to prevent a recurrence of the grossly unacceptable conduct that took place at Lackland" during a personal meeting with the Senator in early August 2012. The incoming CSAF immediately committed to address sexual assault, proclaiming "every commander, every supervisor who isn't actively engaged in being part of the solution of this is part of the problem."[37] Thus began the era of incessant sexual assault prevention and response instruction, featured in countless commander's calls, mandatory computer-based training, and several force-wide operational stand-downs, while service-wide "health and welfare inspections" purged workplaces of any items – magazines, calendars, even family photos – deemed sexually suggestive. The Lackland scandal also ushered in new policies, procedures, personnel, and infrastructure that fundamentally changed Air Education and Training Command.

Other politicians were quick to condemn the seeming epidemic of sexual assault in the military, and at Lackland in particular. Representative Jackie Speier and 77 other members of

---

[36] Kristin Davis, "Air Force appeals court tosses MTI rape conviction," *Air Force Times*, September 29, 2014

[37] Jennifer Svan, "Incoming Air Force chief says eliminating sexual assault a priority," *Stars and Stripes,* August 3, 2012

Congress signed a letter to the leaders of the House Armed Service Committee requesting public hearing on the subject. Senator Kay Bailey Hutchinson initially called for Congressional hearings, but later indicated she wanted Air Force officials to conclude their investigations first. Other members of the Texas congressional delegation also took a wait-and-see attitude. Rep. Mac Thornberry concluded, "My understanding is there is no evidence of a widespread problem," and General Edward Rice, commander of Air Education and Training Command, "seems to be moving out very aggressively to deal with it." However, "If there are indications that the military system has not or cannot deal with it, then [...] we have an obligation to come in." Rep. Mike Conaway, a fellow House Armed Services Committee member, also deferred to the Air Force investigation. "Let's get to the bottom of this horrendous circumstance and get it dealt with and get the victims taken care of," he said, adding he didn't know how helpful "congressional theater" would be.[38]

In April 2012, Gen. Rice directed Maj. Gen. Leonard Patrick, 2 AF commander, to begin an internal review of the BMT environment.[39] Two months later, he appointed Maj. Gen. Margaret Woodward, a senior leader from outside the command, to lead a comprehensive investigation of Air Force accession training. "It's important to look even deeper and wider to identify any systemic issues that may place our youngest airmen at risk in any basic or technical training environment," he announced. "If there are, we need to address them."[40] However, many critics insisted on a more independent inquiry. Under the misleading subheading, "Twelve of the base's instructors have been accused of sexual assault," *The Nation* urged Congressional hearings into "a widespread sexual crime epidemic."[41] The "Protect Our Defenders" advocacy group collected 10,000 signatures on a petition demanding that Congress

---

[38] Trish Choate, "LACKLAND AFB: Senator wants sex scandal hearing in D.C," *San Angelo Standard-Times*, July 9, 2012
[39] AETC Commander's Report to SecAF, p. 11
[40] Clinton Atkins, "Commander calls for command-wide investigation of inappropriate relationships," Air Education and Training Command official website, June 22, 2012
[41] Soumya Karlamangla, "Why Won't Congress Investigate the Sex Abuse Scandal at Lackland Air Force Base?" *The Nation*, July 17, 2012

open a hearing and investigation "about the widening sexual abuse scandal at Lackland."[42]

The editorial board at the *San Antonio Express-News* also concluded the abuses at Lackland called for hearings in Congress. Noting "problems with military instructors engaging in illicit conduct with trainees at Lackland long preceded the scandal that has unfolded this year," the local paper reported 24 instructors faced charges for improper conduct involving trainees between September 2002 and December 2011, when the current scandal made headlines. In 13 of those historical cases, "instructors had sexual relationships with at least one trainee," but many of them were handled in nonjudicial (Article 15) disciplinary channels. "The persistence of this conduct for at least a decade at Lackland should have made clear that nonjudicial proceedings were not curtailing the abuses."[43]

But were these concerns overblown? In Congressional testimony in January 2013, Gen. Rice noted the 32 instructors identified at that point represented less than four percent of the MTIs who had served at BMT since 2009[44] – and not all of them turned out to be guilty of sexual crimes. During this latest scandal, investigators found less than a dozen MTIs who used their position to gain sexual favors from trainees under their control. On the other hand, an even greater number of MTIs was prosecuted for nothing more serious than consensual sex with airmen who had already departed BMT. The *Express-News* editorial highlights a persistent flaw in the reporting on this story: the use of the term "trainee" to apply not only to new recruits subjected to the crucible of BMT, but also to students further along in the technical-training pipeline, over whom MTIs no longer had any authority or unfettered access. While such romantic affairs between MTIs and students barely out of boot camp are certainly unprofessional – and strictly forbidden by Air Force regulations – they are not criminal offenses worthy of jail time. Fully a third of the MTIs prosecuted by

---

[42] Protect Our Defenders, "Washington, DC Press Conference Testimony Demanding Congress Investigate Lackland," *ProtectOurDefenders.com*, August 2, 2012

[43] Express-News Editorial Board, "Abuses at Lackland call for hearings in Congress," *San Antonio Express-News*, September 1, 2012

[44] Molly O'Toole, "Lackland Sex Scandal Gets House Hearing As Air Force Inquiry Continues," *The Huffington Post*, January 23, 2013

courts-martial in 2012-14 deserved nothing harsher than nonjudicial punishment for their transgressions.

The Air Force inadvertently contributed to the hysteria surrounding this so-called sex scandal. Officials initially resisted calls to quantify how many MTIs might be implicated, seemingly recognizing how such quantification can drive public expectations. "We don't want to get stuck on a number," a 37th Training Wing spokesman declared in March 2012, "because it could go up or down day to day."[45] Nevertheless, by late June, the Air Force began providing regular updates on the number of MTIs under investigation, as well as a tally of alleged victims. By the end of the year, they announced 30 instructors had been caught up in the scandal, while the total number of courts-martial steadily climbed towards this target during 2013. This "body count" approach left Air Force leaders few options but to prosecute as many of these MTIs as possible, even if investigations revealed their offenses were merely misdemeanors. Furthermore, AETC insisted on identifying all trainees and students involved in unprofessional relationships as victims, regardless of consent.[46] It was only in January 2013, during the second consecutive court-martial of an MTI for consensual sex with technical-school students, that an Air Force prosecutor noted these women "don't think they're victims and we're not calling them victims."[47] And it took another month before AETC began to more clearly stress the distinction between trainees and students in their press statements.

Meanwhile, pressure for Congressional hearings grew. Secretary of the Air Force Michael Donley provided the House Armed Services Committee a closed-door briefing in early August 2012.[48] The following month, the committee chairman, Rep. Buck McKeon, made an unpublicized trip to Lackland, where he met with Gen. Rice and other leaders, as well as 30 trainees at BMT. He came away from this visit impressed with Air Force efforts to address the scandal, which he suggested was the result of a few bad apples. "Just because a few people go beyond the bounds of propriety and

---

[45] Sig Christenson, "Second Lackland AFB instructor charged in sex case," *San Antonio Express-News*, March 30, 2012

[46] AETC Commander's Report to SecAF, p. 12-13

[47] Sig Christenson, "AF instructor is sentenced to 100 days in jail," *San Antonio Express-News*, January 3, 2013

[48] Philip Ewing, "Congress Approves AF Chief After Sex Scandal Brief," *Military.com*, August 3, 2012

misuse the authority they've been given – a very important authority – that does not mean they can't clean up the problem," he said. "They're working on it and I'm convinced going to do a great job of it."[49] Just days later, however, Rep. McKeon announced his committee would hold another closed-door briefing the following week, and convene a public hearing after the Air Force had concluded its prosecutions.[50]

Ultimately, the House Armed Services Committee did hold open hearings on the Lackland scandal in January 2013. Several members criticized Gen. Welsh and Gen. Rice for a culture that seemingly allowed pervasive sexual abuse of recruits. "In order for changes to really take hold, the culture of the military has to change," said Rep. Nikki Tsongas, co-chairwoman of the House Military Sexual Assault Prevention Caucus. Rep. Susan Davis questioned why Maj. Gen. Woodward failed to meet with MTIs not involved in the scandal during her investigation, while Rep. Speier asked why none of the victims were interviewed. Chairman McKeon again applauded the Air Force's response to the scandal, but said he was troubled by delays in the initial reporting of abuses and lack of prompt action by local leaders. The two Congressmen whose districts encompass the sprawling Lackland complex sounded a more positive note. Rep. Joaquín Castro said the Air Force must learn from the scandal to protect men and women in the military, while Rep. Pete Gallego was hopeful that "lessons have been learned and that action is taken to ensure that something like this never happens again." Still, despite assurances of progress by the generals, Rep. Kristi Noem warned, "every single airman is watching the situation and watching our victims to see how they're being treated."[51]

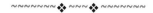

Several Air Force officers saw their careers impacted by this scandal. Col. Axelbank relieved Lt. Col. Michael Paquette of

[49] Jeremy Herb, "McKeon visits Lackland Air Force Base to discuss basic training sex scandal," *The Hill*, September 9, 2012
[50] Express-News Editorial Board, "Set congressional hearings date," *San Antonio Express-News*, September 13, 2012
[51] Gary Martin, "Panel criticizes handling of Lackland abuse complaints," *San Antonio Express-News*, January 24, 2013

command of the 331 TRS on June 20, 2012, just a few days before his scheduled change of command, citing loss of confidence in this commander.[52] Of the dozen MTIs so far implicated for sexual misconduct, nine were assigned to this particular squadron – most implicated by SSgt Vega-Maldonado in exchange for a lighter sentence. In a statement the following week, General Rice noted AETC was "doing a very intensive investigation on that squadron to find out what exactly happened and why," but he deemed it a localized problem: "In my assessment to this point, it is not an issue of an endemic problem throughout basic military training."[53]

However, Gen. Rice offered a slightly different assessment in an interview the following year, just before he retired. Looking back, he claimed no one had any clue at the outset how bad things had become at Lackland, and the Walker case seemed no different than the handful of similar incidents that occurred there every year. But when they learned of three apparently linked allegations – Vega-Maldonado, Estacio, and LeBlanc in the 331 TRS – "a few months later that investigation started to spider, and we went from three to about eight or nine," he recalled. "And at that point, I knew that this was something that was not ordinary, that it was likely going to be extraordinary and our approach to the challenge changed."[54] The very same day that Col. Axelbank fired the 331 TRS commander, Gen. Rice launched a comprehensive investigation of the entire Air Force enlisted training enterprise.

Before Maj. Gen. Woodward could finish her inquiry, however, Col. Axelbank suddenly relieved the BMT commander on August 10. A wing spokeswoman was quick to acknowledge that "Col. Palmer did not create the environment that resulted in the misconduct," but "Col. Axelbank wants a different leader to implement the changes that will be needed in basic military training." She described this step as part of the wing commander's "deliberate effort to fit the right leadership with the 737th Training

[52] Sig Christenson, "Training boss ousted in Lackland sex scandal," *San Antonio Express-News*, June 21, 2012
[53] Chris Carroll, "Air Force has identified 31 alleged victims in Lackland sex abuse scandal," *Stars and Stripes*, June 28, 2012
[54] Sig Christenson, "Edward Rice, AF general who handled Lackland instructor scandals, retires," *San Antonio Express-News*, October 15, 2013

Group in order to move forward in light of the continuing investigation."[55]

There are reasons to doubt how deliberate this effort really was. Just before he fired the BMT commander, Col. Axelbank was notified he would be leaving Lackland earlier than expected, after only a year-and-a-half at the helm of the 37 TRW. Despite public assurances he was not being forced out as a result of the scandal, Col. Axelbank abruptly cancelled an August 15 press engagement, and his change of command on September 4 – held inside the Gateway Club, rather than on the parade grounds – was closed to the media.[56] It seems clear Col. Axelbank was being pushed aside, but why did he take Col. Palmer down with him?

This Special Operations officer was uniquely qualified to lead the 737 TRG. As the first prior-enlisted commander in BMT history, Col. Palmer brought a different perspective to the challenges faced by both trainees and their instructors.[57] For example, soon after he assumed command, an instructor was punished for forcing a trainee to get into a clothes dryer after he screwed up the laundry detail. (The MTI lost a stripe and was eliminated from the career field.) At his next commander's call, the group commander broke the ice by asking, "does anybody know how many dryer sheets it takes to get a trainee fluffy?" For the MTIs in attendance, the message was clear: Do your job – and have fun doing it – but if you break the rules, there will be consequences. Col. Palmer certainly didn't go easy on MTIs implicated in the ongoing sex scandal, which he likened to a cancer. "I've got to get them out," he was quoted as saying. "They don't belong."[58]

By all accounts, Col. Palmer was doing an excellent job leading BMT during troubled times – which makes his sudden relief of command all the more inexplicable. More than one source I've spoken to has suggested Axelbank's motive may have been jealousy. There was apparently no love lost between these two officers, as the charismatic Palmer often seemed to upstage his

---

[55] Sig Christenson, "Lackland training chief is ousted," *San Antonio Express-News*, August 11, 2012

[56] Sig Christenson, "Col. Axelbank exits Lackland for the Pentagon," *San Antonio Express-News*, September 5, 2012

[57] Mike Joseph, "New AF basic training leader returns to his roots," *San Antonio Express-News*, August 18, 2011

[58] Kristin Davis, "Basic training commander sacked amid scandal," *Air Force Times*, August 10, 2012

inept boss, and he was very popular among MTIs for his measured response to the unfolding scandal. Then again, the decision to fire Col. Palmer may have been made at a much higher level. He was relieved of command on the very same day Gen. Welsh was sworn in as Chief of Staff of the Air Force, after Congress had held up his confirmation over the issue of sexual assault. Some have theorized the new CSAF shook up the leadership team down at Lackland to give the appearance of being tough on crime.

Whatever his reasons, Col. Axelbank relieved his subordinate of command early on a Friday morning, less than an hour before the BMT commander was scheduled to officiate the weekly graduation ceremony. The wing commander told Col. Palmer he had done absolutely nothing wrong, and even credited him with accomplishing amazing things during his 13 months in command. However, Col. Axelbank claimed he had lost faith and confidence in the group commander's ability to lead the 737 TRG. This decision clearly wasn't well coordinated, however, as it took another five weeks for Col. Palmer's replacement to be announced.[59]

In his report to the Secretary of the Air Force in November 2012, Gen. Rice acknowledged the leadership accountability actions taken to date. In addition to relieving a BMT group and squadron commander, AETC had served six additional commanders with administrative disciplinary actions: two Letters of Reprimand, and another four Letters of Admonition.[60] The following year, AETC acknowledged only five officers – a former wing commander, group commander and three squadron commanders – plus a senior noncommissioned officer were disciplined.[61] None of these airmen were identified, but we can draw some reasonable inferences.

On the advice of his staff judge advocate, Col. Lisa Turner, Gen. Rice issued LOAs in late 2012 to three former BMT squadron

---

[59] Associated Press, "Woman to lead Air Force training after sex scandal," *USA Today*, September 16, 2012

[60] AETC Commander's Report to SecAF, p. G-1

[61] Sig Christenson, "Ex-Lackland leaders disciplined," *San Antonio Express-News*, May 1, 2013

commanders, and reprimanded another for addressing alleged MTI misconduct with disciplinary action lower than supposedly warranted by the evidence. (That MTI, who later went on to supervise the notorious SSgt Walker, was likely the senior NCO mentioned above.) It doesn't appear Col. Axelbank ever received paperwork, but it's rumored his predecessor as 37 TRW commander, Colonel William Mott V, was reprimanded after he retired. That leaves Col. Palmer's predecessor, Col. Shane Courville, as the probable recipient of the remaining LOA, yet that apparently didn't disqualify him from continued service as Gen. Rice's director of staff.

One senior leader who seems to have completely escaped accountability for his role in this scandal is Maj. Gen. Patrick, who commanded both the 37 TRW and JBSA – when the decisions were made to expand BMT and recruit less qualified candidates as MTIs – before assuming command of 2 AF in 2011. (He now serves as the AETC vice commander.) For his part, Col. Palmer initially received an officer performance report indicating he met standards, but he was soon informed 2 AF hadn't properly coordinated on this evaluation – even though it was signed by both Col. Axelbank and Maj. Gen. Patrick. Two months later, Col. Palmer received a referral OPR, with no reason given as to why it had been marked down. When he appealed his punishment to Maj. Gen. Patrick, the 2 AF commander rejected it, as did his boss, Gen. Rice.

The impact of these adverse actions on the former BMT squadron commanders was immediate. Although one was able to convince the AETC commander to rescind his LOA (which explains the decline in the total number of officers punished between 2012 and 2013), the rest saw their once promising careers put on hold. A couple had recently been selected for promotion to Colonel, but their line numbers were canceled once they received paperwork. Several of these officers filed complaints with the Air Force Inspector General, which took the unusual step of actually investigating their claims. (I would not be so lucky, as we'll see in Chapter 12.) Remarkably, in late 2014 SAF/IG reportedly found both Gen. Rice and Col. Turner had abused their authority by taking these adverse actions, and the Secretary of the Air Force wrote these officers to personally acknowledge they were wronged.

Meanwhile, the Air Force seems to have quietly held Col. Turner accountable for her actions. She left AETC to become the Air Mobility Command staff judge advocate at Scott AFB, Illinois, in 2013, and was subsequently named to the "Role of the

Commander" subcommittee of the Department of Defense's "Response Systems to Adult Sexual Assault Crimes Panel"[62] – an ironic appointment, given how she wrongfully punished AETC commanders during her previous assignment. When she was nominated for promotion to Brigadier General in October 2013, however, her past seems to have caught up with her: the Senate returned her nomination without confirmation in January 2014.[63] No explanation was provided for this rejection, but it was likely related to this staff judge advocate's role as enforcer during the Lackland sex scandal.

While it is encouraging to learn the Air Force investigated this senior-leader misconduct, and appears to have held at least one officer responsible for abusing her authority, the apparent fate of Col. Turner is an all-too-rare anomaly. Gen. Rice retired in late 2013, and so likely escaped any repercussions for his wrongful actions. The former BMT squadron commanders have yet to have their promotions reinstated, more than a year after they were exonerated. And the Air Force refuses to release the SAF/IG report of investigation into this matter, despite repeated Freedom of Information Act requests. (In response to my own FOIA request, I was informed the information I sought "pertains to an open investigation," and "could reasonably be expected to interfere with law enforcement proceedings"[64] – an odd assertion, considering how long ago the investigation supposedly concluded.) Rather than publicly acknowledge the abuse of authority by AETC leadership in response to the Lackland sex scandal, the Air Force has opted instead for a cover-up – and all but guaranteed that such senior-leader misconduct will continue to recur with impunity.

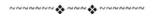

Maj. Gen. Woodward completed her report of investigation, entitled "Developing America's Airmen: A Review of Air Force Enlisted Training," on August 22, 2012. Her 38-person

---

[62] "Brigadier General (Select) Lisa Turner," Response Systems to Adult Sexual Assault Crimes Panel official site

[63] "PN929 – Col. Lisa L. Turner – Air Force," U.S. Congress official site

[64] Matthew R Bartlett, response to FOIA request #2016-01174-F, February 4, 2016

team conducted approximately 90 interviews at BMT, and made site visits to various AETC bases and Army basic combat training at Fort Jackson, South Carolina. They also administered a survey to over 18,000 personnel, and conducted focus groups with BMT trainees and with MTI spouses.[65] Altogether, the team produced 22 findings and 46 recommendations for action, grouped into six broad categories.

Under the heading of leadership, Maj. Gen. Woodward found training squadron commanders "created an environment where offenders operated undeterred and undetected," while the lack of other officers and over-reliance on MTI instructor supervisors "created a near single-point-of-failure for commanders' oversight." Moreover, most commanders were "unfamiliar with the unique aspects of BMT when they took command," and were perhaps not the highest-quality candidates available. Staffing these squadrons with inexperienced and under-qualified first sergeants exacerbated the problem, and MTIs often kept them in the dark about misconduct. Substantiated misconduct "was often dealt with using disciplinary tools less severe than warranted by the facts," and BMT "had no specific criteria or time standards for reporting allegations of sexual assault, sexual harassment, unprofessional relationships, maltreatment, and maltraining." Finally, BMT leadership failed to track disciplinary trends and deter future misconduct.[66]

The Woodward report also called for improved MTI selection and manning, as well better training and development for all BMT personnel. It found airmen were assigned to MTI duties without meeting established selection criteria, including appropriate rank and experience levels, while mental health screening did not adequately weed out unsuitable candidates. MTI manning was "insufficient to ensure an optimal training environment," and excessive MTI tour lengths "contribute to cultural and professional stagnation."[67] Furthermore, Maj. Gen. Woodward identified several training deficiencies at BMT. Leadership and instructors alike were "unable to recognize behavioral indicators of sexual assault, sexual harassment, unprofessional relationships, maltreatment, and maltraining," and trainees were not retaining important information on these topics.

---

[65] Woodward report, p. x-xii

[66] *Ibid.*, Chapter 2

[67] *Ibid.*, Chapter 3

MTIs with substantiated allegations of maltreatment or maltraining were not decertified, retrained, or administered behavioral modification to prevent future infractions. Finally, as I discussed in the previous chapter, "BMT culture seems to place greater value on instructor status and skills than on Air Force core values and NCO professionalism," so she recommended continued support for MTI development programs that "promote a culture of mutual respect and correctly balance both instructor proficiency and NCO professionalism."[68]

Reporting, detection, and climate constituted the next category of findings in the report. Maj. Gen. Woodward found allegations of unprofessional relationships and sexual assault were not always properly investigated, and barriers existed to trainees reporting such allegations. The report recommended installation of hotline phones in each dormitory, better tracking of comment box critiques, and increased presence of Sexual Assault and Response Coordinators and chaplains in BMT squadrons. It found ineffective detection and prevention measures enabled MTIs to isolate and exploit trainees, as did their inappropriate access to trainee personal information.[69] The report also noted the need for better policy and guidance. Recruits should be briefed on Air Force policies regarding sexual assault, sexual harassment, unprofessional relationships, maltreatment, or maltraining before they arrived at BMT, and AETC should develop a standardized survey to collect data pertaining to misconduct in the training environment.[70]

Second Air Force had already implemented several disciplinary policies that addressed Maj. Gen. Woodward's concerns. On August 8, Maj. Gen. Patrick withheld initial disposition authority under the Uniform Code of Military Justice for sexual assault cases, and required that all cases of sexual assault and unprofessional relationships be reported to 2 AF through command channels. "Additionally, commanders at all levels must immediately report initial allegations of unprofessional relationships or sexual assault to the servicing judge advocate's office and provide frequent updates thereafter."[71] The same day,

---

[68] *Ibid.*, Chapter 4

[69] *Ibid.*, Chapter 5

[70] *Ibid.*, Chapter 6

[71] Maj. Gen. Leonard Patrick, "Withholding Initial Disposition Authority under the Uniform Code of Military Justice in Sexual

he also withheld initial disposition authority and imposed mandatory reporting requirements for cases of verbal or physical maltreatment, maltraining, and hazing.[72] Two weeks later, he provided a list of "reportable offenses" that must be up-channeled via a formal "Misconduct Report" within 24 hours of allegation or observation: verbal/physical maltreatment, maltraining, hazing; unprofessional relationships; fraternization; all violations of Article 120 (rape, sexual assault, wrongful sexual contact) and Article 125 (sodomy), UCMJ; and attempts to commit these offenses.[73]

Last but not least, Maj. Gen. Woodward called for greater gender integration at BMT, which she felt was important "to foster mutual respect, provide strong role models of both genders, and prepare Airmen for the operational Air Force." The report recommended creating MTI teams of four instructors for every two trainee flights, with a minimum of one female instructor per team.[74]

"Recent misconduct at BMT tears the fabric that holds us together as an Air Force because it destroys our trust, faith, and confidence in each other," the report concluded. No institution wanted to eliminate sexual misconduct from its ranks more than the Air Force, as evidenced by the aggressive investigation that brought this misconduct to light, and the intense scrutiny applied to BMT over the preceding year. Although the team felt supervisors and commanders at every level were now fully engaged, and many positive changes had already been made, additional steps were "crucial to reinforcing our commitment to zero tolerance, with action that holds perpetrators accountable, and ensures that we address all of the factors that brought us to this point." Taken together, this comprehensive set of

Assault Cases and Under AETC Policy in Unprofessional Relationship and Fraternization Cases," August 8, 2012

[72] Maj. Gen. Patrick, "Withholding Initial Disposition Authority and Mandatory Reporting Requirements in Maltreatment, Maltraining, and Hazing, cases as Defined by Air Education and Training Command Policy," August 8, 2012

[73] Maj. Gen. Patrick, "Reporting of Maltreatment, Maltraining, Hazing, Unprofessional Relationships, and Sexual Offenses," August 20, 2012

[74] *Ibid.*, Chapter 7

recommendations "will help reform the culture at BMT and ensure safe and effective training for all of our Airmen."[75]

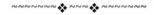

After meeting with members of Congress and other government officials the following month, General Rice commented on the status of these inquiries. "I would suspect that the United States Air Force has not conducted an investigation of this magnitude in many, many, many years. We have spent literally tens of thousands of hours in the investigative process to ensure that we do investigate every alleged incident of misconduct and we will continue to do that until we have run every lead down to its logical conclusion," he said. "I want to ensure that what we do is enduring and that a future commander of Air Education and Training Command isn't sitting in a place like this answering the same question."[76] He added, "The leaders I've met with in Washington have shared helpful input, which will help guide the Air Force as we develop the best means to address the problems identified during the investigations." He announced plans to release the Woodward report, as well as detailed actions to address the way ahead, after he briefed Air Force leadership in late October.[77]

In early November 2012, Gen. Rice provided a review of Maj. Gen. Woodward's commander-directed investigation to the Secretary of the Air Force. "Given the nature of the BMT environment, the opportunity for abuse of power must be understood and eliminated," Gen. Rice declared. He reiterated the AETC leadership commitment to thoroughly investigate all allegations of misconduct, care for the victims, hold perpetrators of misconduct accountable while protecting due process for those accused, and correct the underlying problems that led to the misconduct. Gen. Rice drew three overarching conclusions from the Woodward investigation: weaknesses had developed over time

---

[75] *Ibid.*, Chapter 8

[76] Kristin Davis, "Tough assignment awaits new training wing boss," Air Force Times, September 23, 2012

[77] Air Education and Training Command Public Affairs, "AETC commander addresses military training investigation report," AETC official website, September 21, 2012

in institutional safeguards meant to dissuade, deter, detect, and hold accountable individuals who engage in unprofessional conduct; "leadership failed to detect and prevent these weaknesses;" and "our MTIs did not sufficiently police themselves."[78]

Leadership stood out as the most important area to address, the AETC commander declared, since strong leadership "can overcome weaknesses in institutional safeguards and/or weaknesses in the MTI culture, while average or weak leadership "will struggle to successfully navigate through the unique challenges that exist in the BMT environment."[79] To correct this deficit, AETC added an additional 40 officer billets to BMT's manpower books, including Majors to direct operations in each squadron and Captains as flight commanders in each section, and selected high-potential officers to fill the BMT squadron commander positions opening up in 2013. The Woodward report also called for each BMT squadron to have a "diamond-wearing" first sergeant – that is, fully trained senior NCOs authorized to wear the distinctive lozenge on their rank insignia – with at least a year of experience. Leadership training was enhanced for BMT personnel, and new policies were implemented to ensure alleged misconduct was properly reported. Maj. Gen. Woodward recommended that MTIs accused of sexual assault, sexual harassment, or unprofessional relationships involving trainees or students immediately be removed from the training environment, and permanently eliminated from the career field if the allegations were substantiated. Maltreatment and maltraining would also result in immediate removal, but the MTI might be rehabilitated through remedial training and recertification.

AETC grouped together another dozen Woodward report recommendations under the heading "MTI Culture," through which they hoped to dissuade MTI misconduct. These initiatives began with MTI selection criteria, including a minimum grade of Staff Sergeant (E-5), no record of disciplinary action throughout their entire career, and assessments by the losing commanders and group superintendents. In addition to beefing up mental health screening, operational psychologists would be detailed to BMT to implement the psychological support model used in Air Force survival, evasion, resistance, and escape and

---

[78] AETC Commander's Report to SecAF, p. 3
[79] *Ibid.*, p. 3

parajumper/pararescueman training. MTI professional development efforts were also bolstered, with three new positions to support the BMT "Deliberate Development" program and continuation training requirements. But the biggest changes would be in the area of MTI manning. AETC committed to filling more than 500 authorized positions, enough for two MTIs per trainee flight, with a female MTI assigned to each four-person instructor team. The Air Force would improve the incentive program for MTI duty, and implement a non-volunteer selection process if too few qualified candidates signed up to meet these targets. The length of MTI tours would be shortened to a maximum of three years, and airmen must spend at least four years in their primary career field before returning to MTI duty, with no back-to-back special duty assignments.

The remaining institutional safeguards – to deter and detect MTI misconduct, and hold any perpetrators accountable – would also be strengthened. These included briefing new recruits both before and after they arrived at BMT on what constitutes sexual assault, sexual harassment, unprofessional relationships, maltreatment, and maltraining, and improving trainee reporting and critique monitoring. New wingman procedures instituted under Col. Palmer, which prohibited trainees from being alone outside the dorms, were institutionalized, and MTIs were denied access to trainees' private information. Other institutional safeguards took longer to implement. These included improving trainee access to sexual assault and response coordinators and chaplains, as well as reporting hotlines in the dormitories. Video surveillance, charge of quarters, and entry control procedures would also be improved, as would tracking and archiving MTI misconduct actions. Finally, behavioral skills specialists were called in to develop an indicator set to detect sexual misconduct, and investigative procedures and resources would be enhanced.

Gen. Rice committed to implementing all but one of the recommendations from the Woodward report – he balked only at shortening the length of the BMT course – and he promised additional improvements, including the establishment of a quarterly oversight council, implementation of metrics, and increased grade requirements. AETC would "increase the experience level of leaders by upgrading the squadron first sergeant positions from master sergeant to senior master sergeant and the squadron superintendent positions from senior master sergeant to chief master sergeant." Moreover, the command would also "increase the required grade level for MTI duty to technical sergeant" – higher even than the Woodward report recommendation – "which will bring more experience and maturity to the MTI corps."[80] AETC would select "high-potential officers" to take command of the BMT squadrons turning over in the summer 2013, and operations officer billets were restored to all seven BMT "street" squadrons – those that "push" trainee flights – to be filled immediately by officers on temporary duty assignments until permanent replacements could arrive.[81]

Other changes outlined in this report to the SecAF include a new 2 AF alleged misconduct reporting policy, which required all maltreatment, maltraining, hazing, unprofessional relationship, and sexual misconduct allegations be reported to the 2 AF commander. The 37th Training Wing further required that all MTI misconduct involving trainees be reported within 24 hours of discovery, and prohibited commanders from disposing of a case without first notifying the wing commander and consulting the servicing staff judge advocate.[82] "Sexual attraction, power, and money are three of the most corruptive elements of the human condition," the report concluded, "and two of these three are present in the BMT environment. If we do not take steps to address these corruptive elements persistently and positively, we will find ourselves in the same situation at some point down the road."[83]

On November 14, 2012, Gen. Rice and Maj. Gen. Woodward held a joint press conference at the Pentagon to announce the results of her investigation. "In simple terms, what happened is we had a breakdown of good order and discipline among a relatively few but not insignificant number of our instructors," Gen. Rice explained. "How this happened is attributable to weaknesses and gaps in the institutional safeguards that are designed to prevent this kind of behavior," he continued. "Why this happened is related to insufficient leadership oversight concerning preventing and detecting these gaps and weaknesses, and an inadequate level of self-policing by our instructors." When asked if MTIs closing ranks – choosing loyalty to each other over Air Force core values – explained what went wrong at Lackland, Gen. Rice demurred: "I'm reluctant to say that more than anything is the contributing factor."

[80] *Ibid.*, p. 4-7
[81] *Ibid.*, p. 28
[82] *Ibid.*, p. 35
[83] *Ibid.*, p. 47

He was nevertheless optimistic the report's recommendations would bring lasting improvements, and said he did not need new legislation to fix problems at BMT.[84]

AETC made steady progress towards implementing the recommendations from the Woodward report, and in January 2013 Gen. Rice declared half of the 46 recommendations had already been implemented.[85] By the following September, AETC leadership was able to express cautious optimism about their BMT transformation initiatives. The number of MTIs under investigation for serious misconduct had topped out six months earlier, and there had been no new sexual misconduct reports since the previous summer. However, some MTIs complained this progress had come at a high price for those tasked with turning civilians into airmen. An increasing number of airmen were being non-voluntarily selected for MTI duty, and many veteran instructors had seen their tours extended. They still worked long hours, and leave requests were routinely denied. Instructors faced stiff punishments for minor infractions, and were so concerned about staying out of trouble it was hard to get the job done.

Gen. Rice acknowledged, "We are working our military training instructors for longer hours versus shorter hours and having less coverage," suggesting this reduced the vulnerability of trainees to abuse. The other option would be to bring in a lot of new instructors at once, as AETC had done before the Lackland sex scandal. "We had some experience with that and quite frankly, it didn't work out very well," the AETC commander said. "We decided to take a more deliberate approach. That means it's going to take us some time to build up the force," as much as 18 to 22 months. "Right now, when you look at the numbers, this is the low point in terms of manning. We'll start to rapidly increase every month. We're on the way to some place better," he said.[86]

---

[84] Sig Christenson, "Lackland leaders cited in scandal," *San Antonio Express-News*, November 15, 2012

[85] Gary Martin, "Panel criticizes handling of Lackland abuse complaints," *San Antonio Express-News*, January 24, 2013

[86] Kristin Davis, "Sexual misconduct reports hit 0 at basic," *Air Force Times*, September 24, 2013

As he looked back on the scandal at the end of his career in 2013, Gen. Rice reflected on where MTI culture may have gone astray. "I don't think it was a cultural problem where we had a large percentage of training instructors who were either involved or even knowledgeable that this was going on," he said. "I do think it was a cultural problem from the perspective of not enough vigilance within the [MTI] cohort to aggressively police themselves." As the ones closest to the problem, MTIs "are likely going to see the signs of it before anyone else, and you can't just assume that things are proceeding as they should just by looking on the surface. This is the type of challenge that you have to look below the surface in order to see."[87]

Things looked much different from the perspective of the MTIs. For example, in 2014 an ex-instructor conducted an "ask me anything" session on Reddit, a popular social-networking site, about his experiences during the Lackland sex scandal. Posting under the username "Banuvan," he purported to have been at BMT since 2009, where he "pushed flights with 8 of the people who spent time in jail" while assigned to the 324 TRS and 326 TRS. His first-hand account offers a fascinating behind-the-scenes glimpse at an organization that lost its way. (I have independently confirmed the identity of this former MTI, who actually worked in my squadron before I was relieved of command.)

"Honestly it sickens me to see what happened and the abuse of power that some MTIs displayed," he wrote. "They were a total disgrace to every single member of the military," and those instructors "who did the absolutely horrible stuff needed to get punished." While he had never worked with the most notorious perpetrator, SSgt Walker, Banuvan sat through portions of the trial. "It was eye opening," he wrote, and the news accounts of his crimes seemed largely correct. "There were MTIs who broke rules and needed to be punished." That being said, he never had a clue about his eight colleagues who ended up in jail. "I would come to work and go home when I was able to (not very often). I didn't party or know how these guys even had the time to do these things." Some

---

[87] "Edward Rice, AF general who handled Lackland instructor scandals, retires," October 15, 2013

of the things he'd heard about those MTIs he knew personally he "just couldn't believe they had actually done."

Despite the media painting all MTIs as sexual predators, Banuvan felt most of his colleagues were good folks. "We have a job to do and we love what we do. The few (big picture it was very few folks) really messed it up for everybody." He felt the handling of the scandal "started out as a good thing," but then "leadership took it to the extreme. It became a witch hunt in which MTIs had no way to fight back." The area defense counsel and inspector general were of no help, Banuvan explained. "Because of the attention that was given to the issues the AF was forced to do something. Unfortunately they took it so far that a common saying here is 'if I leave with all the stripes I came here with then I did a good job.' Everything was being directed from the stars above."

Banuvan was present during the commander-directed investigation by Maj. Gen. Woodward, and read the report her team produced. "There are good suggestions and bad ones inside. Unfortunately more of the bad suggestions were implemented than the good ones." During the investigation, he watched a Chief Master Sergeant interview a trainee, and their conversation went like this:

> Chief: *Hey trainee, how are you today?*
> Trainee (comes to attention, gives a reporting statement like she was taught): *Everything is great sir.*
> (Chief tells the trainee to relax, because that wasn't necessary when talking to him.)
> Chief: *Are you sure you are doing OK trainee?*
> Trainee: *Yes chief, everything is great.*
> Chief: *Are you sure? You know you can talk to me.*
> Trainee: *Everything is great chief.*
> Chief: *Trainee, talk to me and tell me what's wrong.*
> Trainee: *Everything is great chief. Nothing is wrong.*
> Chief (looks at me standing there with a glare, when he saw my campaign hat in my hand): *If anything comes up, come talk to me.*

"This is how investigations went and are still happening with MTIs," he concluded. ("Chief: *Can you show me on the doll where the MTI touched you?*" another user posted in response.)

"To put it in perspective on how badly they were fishing for things to punish people for," this MTI continued, "I went through basic training in 2002 and got an email in 2012 [asking] if I wanted to report anything my MTI did while I was in BMT." He noted how MTIs were removed from training and investigated for anonymous trainee critiques without ever being told why. For example, one of his supervisors was in a "holding pattern" for eight months while he was under investigation. "He never knew what it was for. After the investigation was completed he was given orders to a new assignment. He still to this day doesn't know why he was investigated and this happened in 2012." In another case, a friend of his was talking to another instructor about his plans to get drunk that weekend, when some trainees went marching by and overheard his conversation. They reported him for being unprofessional and talking about his personal life in front of them, so he lost his hat and was sent back to his career field.

Moreover, not every MTI who faced court-martial was a criminal. Banuvan described the case of another friend of his who was convicted of having sex with tech school airmen. "Sounds horrible right? That's what the AF tells you. What they don't tell you is that he met these two women at a club off duty in civilian clothes. He had no prior knowledge of who they were or that they were in the AF. They had consensual sex between adults." During the trial, these students testified in his defense, yet he was sentenced to jail and discharged. "I was with him when his sentence came down. The prosecutors came over to him and apologized to him for having to pursue his case." This defendant's military career was cut short simply because he was an MTI.

The scandal "completely ruined BMT for quite a few folks and even hit into the personal lives of many people," including the author. "After all of this came out about my buddy there was a letter drafted among us single people as a joke. It was a slew of questions you had to ask everybody you met and had an interest in before you initiated a conversation with them," regarding their military service and training status. "It was hilarious while at the same time had enough truth behind it to make it scary and pathetic."

This MTI's own "oh shit" moment came when he was called in by OSI in early 2012 because they were investigating an MTI with whom he used to work. "The way questions were asked and they tried to direct the conversation and manipulate my thought process and answers scared the hell out of me." As he watched events unfold, Banuvan noted there was really no hard evidence in most cases, merely "he said/she said" testimony. This really brought into focus how much power trainees have. "It is at a point now where if a trainee says you did something then you did it and that's final."[88]

---

[88] "Banuvan," "I was an MTI from 2009-2014 amid the entire scandal. I pushed flights with 8 of the people who spent time in jail. AMA," *Reddit*, July 18, 2014 (https://www.reddit.com/r/AirForce/comments/2b1t38/i_was_a n_mti_from_20092014_amid_the_entire/)

Chapter 3: Red Dragon Rising

With the purge of Colonel Axelbank and Colonel Palmer in the late summer of 2012, Air Education and Training Command installed a new leadership team at Joint Base San Antonio-Lackland. Col. Mark Camerer quietly took the reigns of the 37th Training Wing in early September, in a change-of-command ceremony uncharacteristically closed to the media. A former airlift pilot, Camerer had recently navigated the 436th Airlift Wing at Dover AFB, Delaware, through turbulence in the wake of the 2011 mortuary affairs scandal. This "pro from Dover" was reportedly a protégé of General Darren McDew, a fast-rising mobility officer whom Pentagon insiders predicted might someday become the first African-American Chief of Staff of the Air Force. (I had actually worked with Col. Camerer a couple of years earlier, when I was stationed at Joint Base Elmendorf-Richardson, where he was the vice commander of the local 3rd Wing.)

In an interview a couple of weeks later, Camerer laid out his perspective on the Lackland sex scandal. "My overarching goal is to ensure I have the nation's trust that their sons and daughters are safe when they join the United States Air Force," he said. "I think I bring some experience to the job, a fairly diverse background, a fresh look at everything that transpired here before my arrival," he added. He immediately met with group and squadron leadership from across the wing, and conducted a commander's call with the Military Training Instructor corps on September 18. "We talked about where we're at. They are 100 percent dedicated to the job at hand," Col. Camerer said. "We share a common goal – they want to be trusted. Those who are here ... are outraged at the criminal – and it's criminal – misconduct that has occurred." Although the Woodward investigation wrapped up a month earlier, the wing commander said he was still forming an opinion as to what caused the scandal at BMT in the first place. "We are marching down every avenue that we think a perpetrator might have used to leverage their control," he noted. "What I would really like the focus to be on is that we ... want to create an environment where everybody realizes the importance of the core values. We want to create an environment where if someone is victimized," they feel comfortable coming forward – and should someone be able to perpetuate this crime, "we can catch them," he added. "We will absolutely restore our nation's trust in those airmen that are still left behind to deal with the aftermath of those who have committed criminal behavior," Col. Camerer vowed.[89]

Colonel Deborah Liddick assumed command of the 737th Training Group on September 21, receiving the unit guidon from Col. Camerer in a public ceremony during the weekly Basic Military Training graduation parade. While she was not the first woman ever to lead BMT – an organization then embroiled in a sex scandal affecting dozens of female trainees – Col. Liddick's appointment nevertheless drew attention to her gender. "Well, first of all I'm a United States officer, I am a colonel, I am a good commander that happens to be female," she boasted. Col. Camerer described his new subordinate as "the best-qualified officer that I think I could have made a recommendation for," noting she was "an experienced, seasoned commander who could deal with this situation." He claimed her gender made no difference: "She has the skills, the attributes, the capabilities to do the job. She has them or she doesn't. I think I've made the right choice. Time will tell."[90]

Col. Liddick certainly appeared to be qualified for her new position, at least on paper. She was a graduated group commander, having previously led the 56th Maintenance Group, an AETC unit at Luke Air Force Base, Arizona, the largest of its kind in the Air Force. After relinquishing command on July 10, 2012, she was reassigned to the AETC headquarters staff at JBSA-Randolph. Expecting this to be her last assignment, she reportedly had every intention of retiring from the Air Force, until she was suddenly plucked from obscurity to lead BMT.

It's not clear who ultimately picked Col. Liddick for this gig. Col. Camerer indicated he had a hand in the selection, but it's unlikely the recently installed 37 TRW commander made the final call. Camerer's boss, Maj. Gen. Leonard Patrick, was likely consulted as well, particularly since the Second Air Force commander was himself in charge of the 37 TRW in 2008-09. But it was the AETC commander, General Rice, who personally notified Col. Liddick she would be moving across town to JBSA-Lackland to lead the Air Force's largest training group.[91]

---

[89] Kristin Davis, "Tough assignment awaits new training wing boss," *Air Force Times*, September 23, 2012

[90] Sig Christenson, "Woman now heads AF training at Lackland," *San Antonio Express-News*, September 26, 2012

[91] Mike Joseph, "Liddick takes command of Air Force Basic Military Training," AETC official website, September 27, 2012

Col. Camerer's prediction – that time would tell if Col. Liddick was the right choice to lead BMT during this critical period – would sadly come true, and a lot sooner than anyone realized.

Col. Liddick didn't reach group command by accident. "I've known I wanted to be an Air Force officer for a long time," she said during a 2011 interview at Luke AFB, where she served as the 56 MXG commander. "I got my commission through the Reserve Officer Training Corps program, and even as a second lieutenant, I would tell people I am going to be an O-6 commander in maintenance one day. That was my goal." She gained confidence playing field hockey and lacrosse in high school, on teams that were undefeated New York state champions all four years. "By the time I reached college, I didn't even know how to react to losing. I had to learn what it felt like to lose a game," she bragged. "We had the drive, as a team, to keep winning and we set that as our goal every time," she recalled. "That intense winning attitude made us successful. When I look back on that – how successful we were – I know it was our teamwork." That same teamwork was the secret to her success in the Air Force as well, Col. Liddick claimed. "In maintenance, it's all about the team," she said. "The load crew, crew chiefs, avionics, ammo Airmen – it takes all of them to keep a jet flying, it's never about just one person. Each individual in the MXG has a role, a place, a mission to complete," she explained. "It really all boils down to working together to get the job done," said Liddick. "When you are part of a team, you have to bring you're [*sic*] "A' game every day. It becomes less about you, about the individual, and more about how you can help others – how you can make the team successful."[92]

Col. Liddick reiterated this sentiment a few years later in an interview with her college alumni magazine. "I always go back to my field hockey experience and my ROTC experience at Wilkes," she said. "It's a team effort. I learned the importance of teamwork. I cannot do this job – or any job – alone." Although she originally expected to attend the United States Air Force Academy, she couldn't secure an appointment to this elite institution, so she

---

[92] Capt. Carla Gleason, "Getting to know your Group CC: First things first," Luke AFB official website, September 9, 2011

settled instead for a small school in rural Pennsylvania. There she played field hockey for the "Lady Colonels," foreshadowing Col. Liddick's ultimate Air Force rank. Her colleagues remember her as focused, goal-oriented, determined, and committed. Not surprisingly, promotion to O-6 wasn't the extent of her career ambitions. "I went in as a second lieutenant and, because I believe in setting goals, I wanted to be a general." This was not the only unattainable objective she set for herself over the years – for example, this former athlete also struggled to achieve a perfect score on her Air Force fitness assessment – but she saw value in such impossibly high standards. "If you set goals, good folks will rise to that expectation," she explained."[93]

But not every member of Col. Liddick's team shared her intense winning attitude. One officer who worked for her at Luke claimed to have heard "horror stories" about her "gross misconduct" from some of her company-grade officers. "Completely inappropriate and morally bankrupt behavior from Col. Liddick," he commented on a Facebook page. (In an e-mail exchange, he later described her as "a bat shit crazy commander" and "a terrible person that has destroyed small areas of the Air Force wherever she went.") "Yeah she was my MXG CC right before I retrained," another former subordinate wrote. "Definitely an 'emperor without clothes' type atmosphere," he continued, where you "couldn't say anything contradicting or honest assessment of what's really going on without her making you public enemy #1." Her new subordinates at Lackland would soon share such sentiments.

Col. Liddick wasted no time making her mark on BMT. She issued an order on day one requiring all 737 TRG personnel "to report any and all incidents of maltreatment and maltraining" up the chain of command,[94] the beginning of a systematic process to identify and eliminate every malefactor in her command. Col. Liddick shared the "law and order" mentality of her boss, Col. Camerer, as well as Col. Adam Oler, 802d Mission Support Group

[93] Vicki Mayk, "Commanding Presence," *Wilkes Magazine*, Winter 2014, p. 7-11
[94] Col. Deborah A. Liddick, "Duty to Report," September 21, 2012

staff judge advocate, who oversaw the recently established Lackland "prosecution task force." These lawyers assessed there was a significant breakdown of good order and discipline at BMT between 2009 and the summer of 2012. They advocated enduring vigilance to curtail misconduct at the lower end of the spectrum, so as to prevent escalation of misbehavior and facilitate self-policing and leadership accountability.[95] Col. Camerer implemented a weekly staff meeting to review each and every incident of alleged misconduct, making it abundantly clear he expected group and squadron commanders to come down hard on any MTIs who got out of line.

Such a zero-tolerance approach – akin to the "broken windows" model of policing, which focuses on the importance of disorder in generating and sustaining more serious crime – effectively criminalized even the most trivial policy violations, such as the use of profanity or dropping trainee mail on the floor. "If you don't stop the small stuff, that's when it can grow into big stuff," Col. Liddick noted in a September 2013 interview.[96] However, this approach did not clearly distinguish between good people making minor mistakes, on the one hand, and bad people who will only go on to commit worse offenses, on the other. Very little discretion was left to commanders to exercise their judgment about the airmen they led.

At her first group commander's call, Col. Liddick established the tone of this new command climate. In front of an auditorium full of MTIs embroiled in the largest sex scandal in Air Force history, the transactional leader who replaced the popular Col. Palmer flatly declared she had no vision as to where BMT would be in a few years. She was not a strategic thinker, she confessed, but was instead focused on the near-term tasks of rooting out rogue MTIs and ensuring a safe training environment for new recruits. Many instructors in attendance came away with the impression that she viewed all of them with suspicion, and was just waiting for these potential perpetrators to slip up.

---

[95] Col. Donna Holcombe, 802 MSG/JA, "MTI/MTL/Instructor Misconduct Reporting & Investigations," misconduct training slides for commanders, operations officers, and first sergeants, April 6, 2013

[96] Karisa King, "Changing times at Lackland," *San Antonio Express-News*, September 15, 2013

They had reason to be worried: disciplinary data confirm MTIs were punished much more often – and much more severely – during the Camerer/Liddick era. While the total number of MTIs receiving nonjudicial punishment began climbing steadily after 2009, no more than a few such "Article 15s" resulted in a reduction of rank each year. That all changed in 2012, however, when this rate suddenly tripled; nine MTIs lost stripes that year, and another nine suffered the same fate in the first half of 2013. Among the alleged offenses was adultery and a sexual relationship with a recently graduate technical training student who had not yet reported to her first duty station; attempted nonphysical relationships with multiple students; and providing alcohol to a minor and assaulting a trainee by hitting the recruit with food, as well as pursuing relationships with multiple students. However, many of these cases did not involve sexual misconduct or trainee abuse. For example, an MTI lost a stripe in January 2013 for domestic abuse and disorderly conduct, and another was found guilty of a false official statement, wrongful appropriation, and dereliction of duty.

In fact, only one MTI punished in an Article 15 hearing during the first half of 2013 did not lose a stripe: a Staff Sergeant who had nonphysical but unprofessional relationships with three technical training students. Prior to 2012, on the other hand, commanders who sentenced MTIs to a reduction in rank were far more likely to suspend the bust. In 2011, for example, seven MTIs whose initial penalty included a loss of rank got a reprieve. They included a Technical Sergeant who made sexual comments to female trainees and started an unprofessional relationship with a former trainee via Facebook; a Staff Sergeant who stole money earmarked for trainee t-shirts and repeatedly lied about it; and a Technical Sergeant and Senior Airman who physically and verbally maltrained recruits.[97] With these new sheriffs in town, however, MTIs were far more likely to lose a stripe – or even go to prison – than they would have been for similar offenses in previous years.

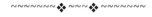

---

[97] "Kristin Davis, "Blue rope loses stripe for minor offenses," *Air Force Times*, June 17, 2013

Despite her lack of vision or strategic leadership, Col. Liddick soon set about systematically executing each of the 46 recommendations from Maj. Gen. Woodward's commander-directed investigation. Ten were already in place by early November, and 23 had been fully implemented by January 2013. In addition to the dozens of recommendations handed down in the Woodward report, AETC imposed several other manpower changes. These were meant to strengthen BMT leadership experience levels by upgrading line-squadron superintendents to Chief Master Sergeant; increasing the grade of first sergeant positions to Senior Master Sergeant; and setting Technical Sergeant as the minimum grade for MTI candidates. AETC also increased the overall number of MTI manpower authorizations, and added 55 student billets for newly arrived instructors-in-training so they would no longer count against overall MTI manning levels until fully qualified. While Maj. Gen. Woodward recommended the maximum MTI tour length be shortened to three years, AETC tacked on an additional six months in recognition of the lengthy MTI training timeline. Of course, until enough new MTIs could be trained to increase manning to an acceptable level, many of those already there saw their tour lengths involuntarily extended and leave requests rejected.

On top of all these changes, Col. Liddick introduced a significant organizational initiative of her own. Concerned that new MTIs weren't being indoctrinated the same way across the group, she consolidated all MTI initial qualification training into a single unit, the 323d Training Squadron. "I established a trainer squadron that everyone is assigned to, so that everyone is learning the same rules, learning the same tasks, in the same way," the group commander later explained. [98] Previously, MTI School graduates would report directly to their assigned line squadron, where more experienced MTIs would offer on-the-job instruction. Under this new arrangement, graduating MTI students are teamed up with trainers in the 323 TRS until they achieve "training qualified" status, and are only then assigned to their designated line squadron.

Unfortunately, these various manpower changes were not well thought out or implemented. For example, while great care was put into selecting the squadron commanders who reported for duty in 2013, and the new operations officers were of generally

---

[98] "Commanding Presence," p. 10-11

decent quality, much less attention was paid to identifying the right officers to serve as BMT flight commanders. Some of these Captains had previous leadership experience, or brought useful insights from their own prior enlisted background, and so proved highly capable at adjusting to the challenges of BMT. Sadly, this was not the norm, as many Air Force career field managers filled these new positions with whatever company-grade officers happened to be available – including many who had never before supervised or worked with enlisted personnel, or had previously been passed over for promotion. Worse, BMT had no plan to smoothly implement flight commanders into its operations. These inexperienced junior officers were assigned to sections without adequate training or even a job description. They were typically crammed into the same office as the enlisted instructor supervisors whose duties they were usurping, without a clear delineation in roles and responsibilities between these seemingly redundant positions.

Whatever merit adding officers to oversee enlisted training may have had in principle, its haphazard implementation set up both the flight commanders and instructor supervisors for failure. Col. Liddick initially mandated these junior officers would directly supervise all the MTIs in their sections, making the incumbent section chiefs even more irrelevant. On the other hand, many members of the BMT staff treated the flight commanders as if they were some sort of temporary experiment. As one officer explained to Col. Liddick, it's hard enough for a newly assigned flight commander to establish credibility in a position that's been around for a while; but when the position itself is new, establishing credibility becomes a monumental challenge. Col. Liddick seemed taken aback by this observation, suggesting she had not thought through the implications of this particular transformation initiative.

Bringing in Chief Master Sergeants to serve as senior enlisted leaders for each 60-person BMT line squadron was like stocking a small pond with big fish, and these E-9s – several of whom had already served as group superintendents or command chiefs at the wing level or higher – chafed under the limited authority and influence granted by Col. Liddick. Furthermore, even though these superintendent billets were still coded 8B000, and half of the Chiefs who reported for duty in 2013 had previously served as MTIs, none were authorized to wear campaign hats. For Col. Liddick, this reflected her emphasis on being a good noncommissioned officer over identifying as an MTI. However, this gave the impression to the demoralized instructor corps that BMT leadership did not consider MTIs good enough to serve as squadron superintendents, and the only way they could aspire to such a leadership position would be to return to their primary career fields. Finally, upgrading these E-8 authorizations eliminated positions to place Master Sergeants who earn promotion, not an insignificant dilemma considering the number of high-speed E-7s now performing MTI duties.

This problem, in turn, is a consequence of AETC's decision to increase the minimum grade for MTI candidates to Technical Sergeant. Instructor slots formerly filled by Staff Sergeants or even Senior Airmen are now increasingly going to senior NCOs, for whom line instructor duties often represent a step backward in terms of career progression. As with the Chiefs, the influx of Master Sergeants created a top-heavy manning profile that is difficult to manage, with too many exceptional performers chasing too few leadership opportunities (e.g. MTI instructor supervisors). This imbalance will likely have adverse effects on the promotion potential of many of these Master Sergeants down the road.

Consolidating MTI training into a single squadron created a different sort of imbalance. Although the 323 TRS is a line squadron like all the others, each of its instructors is an experienced, certified trainer, who was plucked from one of the other line squadrons to fill out its all-star roster. In practice, this means new arrivals begin their 42-month tours in the 737th Training Support Squadron, where they attend the MTI School and complete an apprenticeship in the 323 TRS; then they are reassigned to a line squadron, where they gain experience leading trainee flights on their own; and after about a year on the line, those who demonstrate leadership potential are again reassigned to the 323 TRS as trainers. Meanwhile, the 323 TRS is staffed exclusively by experienced MTIs, but suffers its own high turnover rate as trainers are typically rotated out after about a year to other duties, often in different squadrons, to prevent burnout. The adverse effects of this manpower churn were sadly predictable. MTIs are shuffled around to as many as four squadrons during their 3.5-year BMT tours, destroying on any sense of stability or unit identity for them and their families. Squadron leadership, on the other hand, is constantly scrambling to replace its higher performing MTIs, wreaking havoc on esprit de corps and continuity.

~~~~~~~ ❖ ~~~ ❖ ~~~~~~~

From the beginning, Col. Liddick made clear looked upon the MTI corps with suspicion, and she was determined to eliminate any instructors who stepped out of line. One of her first victims was MSgt Jeff Jordan, an instructor supervisor in the 321 TRS. This "Blue Rope" MTI was on his second tour at BMT in June 2012 when a female trainee accused SSgt Donald Davis, an instructor in his section, of unwanted sexual contact. MSgt Jordan spoke with the trainee's student leaders, who revealed she and her wingman were disruptive flight members. MSgt Jordan next sought guidance from the squadron superintendent, SMSgt James White, who asked the instructor supervisor to look into any student leader reports for references to disciplinary issues. SMSgt White also indicated he and the squadron commander, Lt. Col. John Duda, had already discussed the fate of these two trainees with Col. Palmer. (These leaders apparently suspected the trainees had falsely accused SSgt Davis, and they were reportedly considering whether to initiate discharge actions or merely recycle them, making them repeat earlier weeks of training.)

MSgt Jordan notified the trainees they might be recycled for poor performance, and also reached out to SSgt Davis, who had been removed from the training environment pending investigation, via text message to see if he had any "dirt" on his accusers – that is, documented derogatory information that would warrant their recycle. Other personnel he consulted, including the first sergeant and a few fellow MTIs, thought a lateral transfer to another squadron would be a better solution. When MSgt Jordan reported back to SMSgt White that there was insufficient justification to recycle either trainee, the superintendent directed him to arrange the transfer of one of the trainees "due to a conflict of interest per the squadron commander," and properly document her deficiencies.[99] On June 27, MSgt Jordan dutifully recorded this trainee's transfer to the 322 TRS in the Basic Training Management System database.[100]

---

[99] MSgt Jeffrey L. Jordan, "Response to NJP (Article 15 Consideration), dated 19 Nov 12," November 26, 2012
[100] Basic Training Record (Continuation Sheet) entry, June 27, 2012

Nearly five months later, this trainee and her wingman, A1C Aubrey Tournade, testified in an Article 32 evidentiary hearing in the case against their former MTI, SSgt Davis. The latter claimed MSgt Jordan reprimanded them for bad performance, removed them from their flight, and threatened to recycle them, while the alleged sexual assault victim testified SMSgt White gave her an ominous warning: "If I knew what was best for me, that I would keep my mouth shut about this whole incident," she said. An OSI agent submitted text messages retrieved from SSgt Davis' cell phone as evidence, including one from MSgt Jordan seeking "dirt" on these trainees. As a result of that testimony, prosecutors initially sought to tack on a charge of conspiracy against Davis, but they withdrew the request after his attorney asked for a delay in the case so he could question Jordan and White. An Air Force spokesman said officials had already launched an investigation into these two airmen, and "they either have or are in the process of being held accountable for their actions," he said.[101]

The following Monday, Col. Liddick made good on that threat against MSgt Jordan. She offered him punishment under Article 15, Uniform Code of Military Justice, for his handling of this situation. But the charges do not clearly specify what MSgt Jordan supposedly did wrong: "You, who knew of your duties at or near JBSA-Lackland, Texas, between on or about 1 June 2012 and on or about 30 June 2012," the group commander wrote, "were derelict in the performance of those duties in that you willfully failed to refrain from wrongfully endeavoring to recycle" two trainees in his squadron, "as it was your duty to do."[102] Parsing this convoluted accusation, it would seem Col. Liddick was proposing to punish this MTI for nothing more than attempting to hold back a couple of trainees, a routine administrative action at BMT. She didn't clarify what made this behavior "willful" or "wrongful," or accuse MSgt Jordan of violating any specific order, policy, or instruction, let alone committing a crime under the UCMJ. It is a mystery how these nonsensical allegations survived legal review before they were presented.

---

[101] Karisa King. "AF case against trainer is expanded," *San Antonio Express-News*, November 17, 2012

[102] AF Form 3070B, *Record of Nonjudicial Punishment Proceedings (MSgt thru CMSgt)*, served by Col. Liddick to MSgt Jordan, November 19, 2012

MSgt Jordan immediately contacted the local area defense counsel on November 19 to discuss options for challenging these charges. Under Article 15, the accused has the right to demand trial by court-martial in lieu of nonjudicial punishment by the commander. However, his newly assigned defense attorney advised against trying to fight the charges in court; at that point in the unfolding Lackland sex scandal, the prosecution task force had yet to lose a case against an MTI accused of misconduct, and there were 18 other defendants ahead of him awaiting possible court-martial. Bottom line, the overworked and understaffed ADC office would not be able to provide MSgt Jordan an adequate defense. He could have instead hired a private attorney to aid in his defense, but he was going through a divorce at the time, and fighting to retain custody of his children. Effectively out of options, MSgt Jordan elected to waive his right to court-martial and accept his nonjudicial punishment. He provided a written response to the allegations, acknowledging that some of the things he did and said during his inquiry "perhaps displayed poor judgment," considering the sensitivities surrounding the Davis investigation.[103]

Unfortunately, Col. Liddick had an agenda. She actually admitted to MSgt Jordan she planned to make an example of him so others would understand she was not to be challenged. Because this case didn't involve sexual misconduct, it offered the group commander a quick, clean kill. On December 5, she upheld her inexplicable charges and formally reprimanded MSgt Jordan. "As a Senior NCO in the United States Air Force," she wrote, "you are expected to serve as a role model for Airmen – someone whom they can emulate and trust to do the right thing. You should uphold the core values at all times. Your behavior failed to meet these standards when you endeavored to recycle Airmen without cause after one of them filed a complaint against a Military Training Instructor for unwanted sexual contact. Your actions were perceived as retaliatory toward these Airmen – this is unacceptable! Airmen expect to be able to trust Senior NCOs to be forthright and conduct themselves in accordance with the highest standards. You have tarnished this trust." For this supposed offense, he was immediately reduced in rank to Technical Sergeant, and ordered to forfeit almost $1,800 in pay.[104]

---

[103] MSgt Jordan, NJP response
[104] Col. Liddick, *Record of Nonjudicial Punishment Proceedings*, December 5, 2012

This was a shocking outcome. MSgt Jordan was severely punished for having "endeavored to recycle Airmen without cause," when in fact he was just doing his job. This instructor supervisor had more than sufficient cause to look into whether those trainees ought to be recycled, an inquiry he pursued with the explicit endorsement of his superiors. Moreover, he could not have "endeavored to recycle" these trainees on his own, as he had no authority to execute such an action at his level. Rather, he was merely gathering information for his commander and superintendent so they could make an informed decision. While his actions may have been "perceived as retaliatory" by these trainees, there is no evidence MSgt Jordan took or threatened to take any unfavorable personnel action against either of them for the complaint against SSgt Davis. Nevertheless, Col. Liddick chose to destroy the career of this instructor supervisor, while taking no apparent action against the squadron superintendent who orchestrated these actions and advised the trainees to keep quiet about it. When now-TSgt Jordan asked to appear before her to appeal his demotion, Col. Liddick scornfully reminded him she could just as easily have taken two stripes.

As it turned out, when the case against SSgt Davis finally went to trial in January 2013, he was acquitted of the sexual contact charges stemming from that trainee's allegations. In addition to a lack of physical evidence, three of her flight-mates testified the alleged victim was untruthful.[105] This result seemed to exonerate TSgt Jordan, whose "endeavors" to recycle this airman and her wingman seem to have been justified after all. Surely this constituted just the sort of "rare and unusual case where a question concerning the guilt of the member" had arisen, so he petitioned his chain of command to set aside his punishment.[106] The wing commander, Col. Camerer, did elect to consider this request, but denied it without further explanation in April 2013.[107]

Adding insult to injury, TSgt Jordan's squadron commander, Lt. Col. Duda, recommended the permanent removal of his MTI campaign hat and elimination from the career field. In a

---

[105] Karisa King. "AF instructor is sentenced to hard labor," *San Antonio Express-News*, January 31, 2013
[106] TSgt Jordan, "Non Judicial Punishment Supplemental Action Request," February 26, 2013
[107] Col. Mark D. Camerer, "Memorandum for Technical Sergeant Jeffrey L. Jordan," April 30, 2013

memo dated December 20, 2012, he claimed, "TSgt Jordan had an Article 15 preferred for indecent assault and obstruction of justice." Not only were these nowhere close to being the correct charges, TSgt Jordan's actual offense offered no basis for withdrawing his MTI status. According to the *Air Force Enlisted Classification Directory*, qualification for this special duty precludes any record of nonjudicial punishment reflecting a lack of character or behavioral/emotional control; based on sexual assault, sexual harassment, physical abuse or an unprofessional relationship; or for verbal maltreatment or financial irresponsibility.[108] Although none of these conditions applied in this case, the 737 TRG superintendent, CMSgt Williams, concurred with the recommendation,[109] and Col. Liddick permanently stripped TSgt Jordan of his hard-earned MTI status. This didn't, however, mean TSgt Jordan would be leaving BMT. Having lost a stripe, he now faced high-year-of-tenure restrictions that precluded his reassignment, and there were no jobs at Lackland in his specialty. So he remained in limbo for nearly two years as the 321 TRS "PT/Supply NCO," until his retirement in October 2014. Nevertheless, despite the humiliation he suffered at the hands of his group commander, this former "Blue Rope" remained an absolute professional until the very end.

Just before he retired, TSgt Jordan received character reference letters from two unexpected sources. One was A1C Tournade, who questioned why SMSgt White had never been held accountable for instructing MSgt Jordan to recycle or transfer her. "In my opinion, fair punishment was not distributed at the closing of the investigation. It left one individual with more punishment than necessary and another individual, more deserving of punishment, without any reprimand at all."[110] The other was from CMSgt Williams, Col. Liddick's former senior enlisted leader. He stated he was quite surprised when he heard his boss was considering demoting MSgt Jordan, and he told her he thought this was "a bit much." He now claims he questioned the allegations against TSgt Jordan, who "deserves to be a Master Sergeant."

---

[108] *Air Force Enlisted Classification Directory* (AFECD) Part II, April 30, 2014, p. 327-28
[109] Lt. Col. John F. Duda, "Permanent Withdrawal of MTI Status – TSgt Jeffrey L. Jordan," December 20, 2012
[110] A1C Aubrey Tournade, "Character Statement for TSgt Jeffrey Jordan," August 27, 2014

Despite the Chief's faith in the system throughout his 30-year career, "the system got this one wrong!"[111]

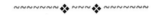

     Another senior NCO whose career Col. Liddick ruined was SMSgt "LG," who became Lt. Col. Duda's senior enlisted leader in October 2012. She earned her blue rope as a Master MTI during a previous BMT assignment, then went on to further distinguish herself as a squadron superintendent in her primary career field. At her previous base, she also served as executive officer to the wing commander, then-Colonel Robert LaBrutta, who would pin on a star and assume command of 502d Air Base Wing and Joint Base San Antonio in 2013. The 737 TRG superintendent, CMSgt Williams, personally recommended SMSgt "LG"'s return to BMT, where she replaced SMSgt White as the 321 TRS superintendent.
     Shortly after she arrived, this brand-new Senior Master Sergeant ran afoul of newly implemented policies at BMT. In November, an instructor supervisor informed SMSgt "LG" that he had corrected an MTI in his section for some infraction. Since this Master Sergeant had reportedly already taken care of the situation, the new superintendent took no further action.[112] Then in January 2013 as she was preparing to leave town to attend the Senior NCO Academy at Maxwell AFB, Alabama, SMSgt "LG" had another minor slip-up. A package containing records of individual counseling (AF Form 174) on a couple of MTIs had been routed to her for review before this disciplinary paperwork would be filed in their personnel information files, as required by 2 AF policy. She signed off on the routing slip, but forgot to hand the folder over to the squadron operations officer before departing on her trip.[113]
     Soon after SMSgt "LG" returned to Lackland, she received a letter of reprimand from the group commander. "Investigation has revealed," Col. Liddick wrote on March 20, 2013, that "you were derelict in your duties in that you failed to follow a 37 TRW/CC order, which requires reporting of all MTI misconduct occurring

---

[111] CMSgt (ret) Kenneth A. Williams, ""Character Statement for TSgt Jeffrey Jordan," July 27, 2014
[112] SMSgt "LG", "Response to Letter of Reprimand, dated 20 March 2013," March 25, 2013
[113] SMSgt "LG", LOR response

[*sic*] the presence of trainees within 24 hours of discovery." SMSgt "LG" allegedly received "multiple reports of such misconduct, but failed to forward them" to her squadron commander, and "the misconduct was not appropriately reported to Wing Leadership" as a result. "Whether the result of complete disorganization on your part, or a failure to understand the importance of the reporting requirement, your misconduct falls far below the standards and expectations of a Senior Noncommissioned Officer, and is a violation of the Uniform Code of Military Justice. Worse, it has caused me to seriously question [*sic*] judgment." Col. Liddick concluded by putting SMSgt "LG" on notice: "You must accept and carry out your duties and responsibilities in a manner commensurate with established standards for Senior NCOs in the United States Air Force. Nothing less will be accepted from someone of your grade and position in the 737th Training Group while I am in command."[114]

This reprimand was all kinds of wrong. First of all, Col. Liddick appears to have conflated unrelated incidents, lumping together an episode from November, which SMSgt "LG" chose not to report, with a separate gaffe involving already completed counseling in January. More importantly, the order Col. Liddick accused SMSgt "LG" of violating did not actually apply to her. Weeks after he assumed command, Col. Camerer issued this order, requiring all alleged misconduct by MTIs or other instructors in the presence of trainees be reported to the servicing legal office no later than 24 hours after discovery. "The misconduct will be reported by the squadron commander or his/her designee," the order continued, and notifications shall also include the group and wing commanders. [115] This policy only imposed reporting requirements on squadron commanders and their designated representatives – typically the squadron operations officers. Unless Lt. Col. Duda had so designated his superintendent, SMSgt "LG" was not even subject to the 37 TRW commander's order, contrary to Col. Liddick's claim.

The group commander had issued her own order requiring all 737 TRG personnel to report incidents of maltreatment and maltraining, with an important caveat: "You may address the issue

---

[114] Col. Liddick, "Letter of Reprimand (LOR)," March 20, 2013
[115] Col. Mark D. Camerer, "Order to Report Allegations of Military Training Instructor (MTI), Military Training Leader (MTL), and Instructor Misconduct," September 17, 2012

by reporting the incident to the individual," but "repetitive or more serious acts" must be reported to the individual's chain of command.[116] SMSgt "LG"'s handling of this incident appears to have complied with these criteria as well, so this group-level policy also imposed no duty to report the alleged misconduct further up the chain.

Neither the 37 TRW nor 737 TRG orders applied to SMSgt "LG"'s subsequent clerical error at all. The January incident involved records of counseling already completed, presumably long after the MTI misconduct had been reported to the wing. Moreover, when SMSgt Juan Vargas, 322 TRS first sergeant, investigated her alleged misconduct, he found it unsubstantiated. SMSgt "LG" had "no intent to hide or deceive the commander" when she accidently left the folder on her desk, where it was discovered a month later.[117] At worse, her action temporarily delayed the filing of this paperwork in the members' personnel folders, but neither AETC nor 2 AF PIF policies imposed a time limit for this. While these two incidents may reflect minor lapses in judgment or attention to detail, they did not rise to the level of punishable misconduct.

As harsh as SMSgt "LG"'s punishment was, it might have been much worse if her squadron commander had been left to his own devices. The day after Col. Liddick upheld the LOR, Lt. Col. Duda provided his senior enlisted leader written mid-term performance feedback. "Whether by omission or commission, failure to report had deleterious effect on squadron and discipline," he wrote, encouraging her to "learn and grow from the error." He suggested she use her "abilities to recover from [this] error," and "mentor as the great SNCO you have demonstrated yourself to be." He wished her the best of luck, noting the changing dynamics at BMT had provided a "school of hard knocks" lesson, but she would go on to do "wonderful work" in her career field. "What can we learn from this experience?" he asked rhetorically. "First, be mindful of those we lead...second, listen to those we follow and if they are wrong, try to advise a better way."[118]

---

[116] Col. Deborah A. Liddick, "Duty to Report," September 21, 2012
[117] SMSgt Juan D. Vargas Jr., "MR 321 TRS-2013-014," March 4, 2013
[118] Lt. Col. John Duda, AF Form 932, *Performance Feedback Worksheet (MSgt thru CMSgt)*, for SMSgt "LG", March 26, 2013

His reference to a return to her career field betrayed the squadron commander's true intentions. On March 29, 2013, the 321 TRS initiated action to remove SMSgt "LG"'s special experience identifier, stop her special duty assignment pay, and eliminate her as an MTI "for disciplinary reasons" that "permanently disqualify her from performing MTI duties."[119] Less than two weeks later, Lt. Col. Duda requested her return to her primary Air Force specialty code,[120] and even recommended SMSgt "LG" be denied the Air Force Good Conduct Medal based on her removal from MTI duty "for disciplinary reasons."[121] Not only had Lt. Col. Duda once again misinterpreted the AFECD requirements for MTI duty, he also overstepped his authority by attempting to permanently withdraw MTI status without the group commander's approval.

Thankfully, SMSgt "LG" had the strong support of Col. Liddick's acting senior enlisted advisor, SMSgt David Milne, who did what he could to mitigate her punishment. The group commander reinstated SMSgt "LG" as an MTI on April 18, but specified she "will not be performing training duties."[122] Instead, the Col. Liddick reassigned her to the 737 TRSS, where she led MTI Recruiting efforts until given another shot to prove herself as a superintendent that summer. She also ensured Lt. Col. Duda marked SMSgt "LG" down in only one category ("standards") on her annual enlisted performance report, and used her additional rater comments to praise her as an "Outstanding SNCO" who was "deserving of recent promotion."[123] When I assumed command of the 737 TRSS just weeks after this evaluation closed out, I would never have guessed how traumatic the last few months had been for my new superintendent – or how much worse it would get in the coming year.

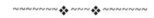

[119] AF IMT 2096, "Classification/On-the-Job Training Action," March 29, 2013
[120] AF IMT 2096, April 9, 2013
[121] Lt. Col. John F. Duda, Jr., "Denial of Air Force Good Conduct Medal," April 9, 2013
[122] AF IMT 2096, April 18, 2013
[123] AF Form 911, "Enlisted Performance Report (MSgt thru CMSgt)," signed by Col. Liddick on June 20, 2013

These obviously weren't the only airmen unfairly punished at Lackland during this period – not by a long shot. Leaving aside for the moment the dozens of cases the Air Force prosecuted at courts-martial, countless other members of the 737th Training Group suffered punishments at the hands of Col. Liddick and Col. Camerer all out of proportion to their supposed transgressions. Pursuing a "where there's smoke, there's fire" approach to justice, these senior leaders hammered subordinates over the most trivial matters. While a full accounting of these victims may never be known, below are several stories of overzealous persecutions by the so-called "Butcher of BMT" and her boss, "Career Crusher" Camerer. Names are withheld to protect the innocent, and what's left of their mangled careers.

One Master Sergeant came under investigation over allegations he maltreated trainees three years earlier by forcing them to eat vomit off their trays in the dining facility. His squadron commander issued him a letter of reprimand, and he spent the next five months on administrative duties at the nearby Defense Language Institute's English Language Center, a favored destination for MTIs under suspicion of misconduct, while his inquest dragged on. Despite interviewing over 400 trainees, investigators found only three who claimed to have witnessed this alleged incident, and they never actually spoke with the purported victims. When the allegation was eventually found unsubstantiated, the squadron commander reinstated the MTI and rescinded his LOR. Not satisfied with this outcome, however, Col. Liddick pulled the case up to her level and issued the MTI a letter of admonition, an administrative action slightly less severe than an LOR. She refused to award him an end-of-tour medal when he departed Lackland soon afterwards, and noted on his enlisted performance report that he didn't receive performance feedback due to his removal pending investigation. These prejudicial administrative actions will likely make his promotion to Senior Master Sergeant difficult, but he remains determined: "when I do make it I am definitely sending her signed stripes," he wrote me in a private message.

Another MTI got into trouble for allowing a trainee to help him with his homework. This instructor was enrolled in college when he happened to learn a trainee in his squadron had a master's degree in the very subject he was studying. The trainee seemed eager to offer his expertise, so the MTI soon asked him for assistance with a paper he was writing. This incident came to light only two years later, after the MTI had gone on to earn a blue rope and promotion to Master Sergeant. The investigation that followed turned up no evidence the trainee felt coerced or had actually written the paper, and his squadron commander saw no reason to do more than merely counsel this senior NCO. However, when he briefed his intentions at a 37 TRW status of discipline meeting, Col. Camerer was reportedly furious that this alleged unprofessional relationship wasn't receiving a harsher punishment. He pulled the case up to the wing and issued the MTI an LOR for this trivial offense, ensuring his elimination from this special duty. Ironically, this Master Sergeant was detailed to the Warhawk Fitness Center during the investigation, where he was running the local fitness assessment cell when Col. Camerer came in for a fateful semiannual assessment in January 2013 – more on that encounter below.

Then there was the Master Sergeant who was wrongfully punished for an off-duty incident when he was not at fault. He was hosting a party at his house where his supervisor, a fellow MTI, became drunk, so they refused to let her drive home. She became belligerent, prompting the host to call the police and to forcefully defend his wife when his boss began attacking her. Both the local police and district attorney agreed he responded appropriately under the circumstances, but his squadron commander, Lt. Col. Mike Arndt, thought otherwise. Not only did the 319 TRS commander punish the attacker, he also issued an LOR to this MTI, and Col. Liddick eliminated both of them for their involvement in this incident. This MTI spent his final months at Lackland working behind the scenes in the BMT Reception Center, and left with no MTI ribbon or end-of-tour medal, plus a mark-down on his enlisted performance report. While this particular story had a happy ending – these adverse actions were unexpectedly reversed over a year later – it was merely the exception that proves the rule about injustice during this era at BMT.

On the other hand, not all airmen who committed misconduct were severely punished. For example, when the 326th Training Squadron commander publically groped a member of the Lackland legal team, Col. Camerer only issued him a letter of admonition, and allowed him to finish out his command tour. And as we will see in the next chapter, Col. Camerer also failed to hold the first sergeant from that very same unit accountable for denouncing his new commander to the media. Clearly, the chain of command at Lackland could overlook misconduct when it suited them.

"Organizational change is pretty difficult anywhere," Col. Liddick confessed just before she retired in 2014, "and that's why I'm proud as I leave here: BMT is in a much better place."[124] This was a highly debatable claim. While many of the Woodward report recommendations were welcome and long overdue improvements, additional measures dreamed up by AETC and its subordinate commands actually made things worse. Whatever merits these BMT transformation initiatives may have had, the way Col. Camerer and Col. Liddick communicated, implemented, and enforced them left much to be desired. They compounded this problem by releasing a steady flow of locally generated policies affecting nearly all aspects of the training enterprise, creating a bewildering array of restrictions with no apparent rhyme or reason. For example, Col. Liddick objected to traditional MTI jargon, of "street" squadrons "pushing" flights, claiming this language was too "ghetto" – she insisted instructors instead say "line" and "lead," and never refer to trainees as kids or children. She also insisted each line squadron be functionally interchangeable, with very little latitude for innovation or distinct unit identity. Gen. Rice seemed to realize the plan they devised might not be 100 percent correct, but senior leaders at Lackland refused to make any course corrections, no matter what turbulence they encountered.

They not only rejected mounting evidence of discontent among the MTIs corps, they also disregarded their squadron commanders and senior enlisted leaders who warned of unintended consequences. Col. Camerer solicited advice from the BMT superintendent, CMSgt Williams, before his first commander's call with the MTIs in 2012, but he quickly stopped listening to counsel. Col. Liddick seemed to resent the senior enlisted leader she inherited from Col. Palmer, and refused to include CMSgt Williams in most decisions affecting the MTI corps. Noting his boss seemed to talk at her subordinates, rather than to them, the

---

[124] Mike Joseph, "Basic military training commander to conclude 25-year Air force career," *Lackland Talespinner*, June 6, 2014 (republished on AETC official website, "BMT commander retires, reflects on experience")

superintendent suggested Col. Liddick try to build a rapport with them, but she refused: "Chief, I'm intimidated by the MTIs," she responded. His exclusion only grew more complete; she apparently never once checked on her superintendent while he was recovering from surgery for nearly two months in 2013, and she refused to attend his retirement ceremony later that year.

Other senior NCOs had no better luck getting through to leadership. For example, when the BMT first sergeants complained to the new group superintendent, CMSgt Richard Sutherland, about how bad the MTIs were treated, he reportedly dismissed their claims and insisted the instructors were happy. Then again, this E-9 never seemed very sympathetic to the enlisted personnel under his care. For example, when the topic of special duty assignment pay came up at a group staff meeting in October 2013, CMSgt Sutherland confessed he didn't know why MTIs were receiving this extra money. Several squadron commanders immediately chimed in, jealously mocking their subordinates for spending bonuses on flashy new cars and other frivolities. This was a shameful, unprofessional spectacle: not only was a senior enlisted leader questioning whether his fellow noncommissioned officers deserved their compensation, he was doing so in front of a roomful of field-grade officers, each of whom are paid far more than their subordinates.

But it's not surprising that Sutherland, who never earned a campaign hat – and apparently didn't have the sense to keep his mouth shut on issues he knew nothing about – wouldn't be an effective advocate for the MTIs. As the 8B000 functional manager, he had a duty to advocate for effective inducements to attract and retain high-quality instructors. This shouldn't have been tough after the Woodward report endorsed improving the MTI incentive program, yet the Air Force actually considered lowering MTI special duty assignment pay the following year.[125] With friends like Sutherland, MTIs don't need enemies.

But the BMT superintendent wasn't their only "frenemy." The first sergeants next approached Col. Camerer, who apparently turned them away and reported their insubordination to Col. Liddick. Finally, they approached the 502d Air Base Wing command chief, CMSgt Alexander Perry, but he declined to get involved. On the other hand, when BMT squadron superintendents

---

[125] Stephen Losey, "Special pays may be reduced for MTIs," *Air Force Times*, May 9, 2014

took their concerns all the way to the AETC commander, General Rand, in May 2014, he advised them to be patient, and give him six weeks to improve the situation. This just so happened to be the timeline until Col. Liddick's retirement.

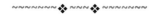

While organizational change can indeed be difficult, Col. Camerer and Col. Liddick failed to heed even the most basic principles associated with this endeavor. Nearly two decades earlier, the renowned organizational management guru John P. Kotter outlined a classic eight-stage process for leading organizational change: create a sense of urgency; build a guiding coalition; form strategic vision and initiatives; enlist a volunteer army; enable action by removing barriers; generate short-term wins; sustain acceleration; and institute change.[126] However, most major transformation efforts fail because organizations do not take a consistent, holistic approach to changing themselves, nor do they engage their workforces effectively. The Lackland sex scandal obviously provided the necessary sense of urgency to implement the BMT transformation initiatives, but the senior leaders in charge lacked strategic vision and the ability to clearly communicate it. They relied exclusively on their command authority to motivate squadron leadership, failing to recruit change agents within the ranks and making almost no effort to reach out to the MTIs on the "street." The only obstacles they removed were recalcitrant subordinates, never recognizing the way their own leadership styles hampered progress. To their credit, they did occasionally celebrate short-term wins and avoid premature declarations of victory, but this was mostly to placate Congress and the public rather than to gain buy-in from the airmen they led.

The truth is, they just didn't seem to care – and they had no incentives to act otherwise. When the Air Force brought Col. Camerer and Col. Liddick to Lackland to clean up the mess at BMT, they seem to have been offered a Faustian bargain: Do whatever it takes to prevent any further sexual assaults, and these fixers would be rewarded with unaccountable power. There was no need to fear legal sanction from the servicing 802 MSG staff judge advocate, as

---

[126] Kotter International, "The 8-Step Process for Leading Change," accessed October 6, 2015

Col. Oler and his "prosecution task force" seemed more interested in convictions than justice. And they would not face rebuke from their superiors, since the 2 AF commander, Maj. Gen. Patrick, was himself implicated in the Lackland sex scandal that began on his watch as 37 TRW commander. He provided top cover for their abuses, and effectively ensured any complaints or appeals brought no relief to their victims. In the end, these leaders adopted an attrition model of organizational change, eliminating or simply waiting out the "old hat" MTIs as their tours of duty came to an end, to be replaced by a new generation of instructors indoctrinated in the post-scandal paradigm. Time, it seemed, was on their side.

Col. Camerer often liked to claim he led by example. "I want the airmen under my command to be able to look at me and say that's what absolute professionalism looks like," he stated in an interview soon after coming to Lackland.[127] But his conduct was not always so exemplary. For example, when Gen. Rice traveled across town to visit BMT in April 2013, he conducted a commander's call with hundreds of MTIs in attendance, along with squadron, group, and wing leadership. Col. Liddick had to leave early to officiate a trainee graduation ceremony, leaving Col. Camerer holding the bag when things turned ugly. The trouble started after an MTI in the audience complained she was facing nonjudicial punishment and elimination, and lacked support while her husband was deployed. The wing commander rose to the defense of local leadership, unleashing a torrent of gripes and grievances from the disillusioned MTI corps. One after another, instructors voiced their opinions to Gen. Rice about their mistreatment, and the sense that no one was listening to them. True to form, the wing commander adamantly insisted this was all nonsense, and none of these things were happening. Gen. Rice, remained calm throughout this spirited feedback session, and in another forum later that day noted there was obviously a disconnect with the wing regarding his intent vis-à-vis the MTIs. Col. Camerer, on the other hand, was livid at the disrespect he'd been shown. He gathered together the entire BMT leadership

---

[127] Kristin Davis, "Tough assignment awaits new training wing boss," Air Force Times, September 23, 2012

cadre – commanders, superintendents, operations officers, first sergeants, even instructor supervisors – for an emergency meeting late that afternoon, and proceeded to blast them all for that morning's outburst.

This is not the only time MTIs saw this side of Col. Camerer's personality. Perhaps the most notorious examples of the wing commander berating his subordinates came during his semiannual fitness assessments. The Air Force considers it every airman's responsibility to maintain physical fitness standards, which include measures of body composition (abdominal circumference), muscular fitness (push-ups and sit-ups), and aerobic fitness (1.5 mile run, or a walk if on a waiver). Each component is scored based on the member's gender and age, and airmen must meet the minimum values for each component as well as achieve an overall composite score of at least 75 out of 100 possible points. The results of these assessments are reflected in every officer and enlisted performance report, and a failure can result in a referral evaluation or worse – as when Col. Tim Bush was relieved of command of the 319th Air Base Wing at Grand Forks AFB for failing the waist measurement.[128]

When Col. Camerer came in for his semiannual fitness assessment at the Warhawk Fitness Center on January 30, 2013, he reportedly struggled with the push-up component, and multiple bystanders witnessed him yell at a fitness assessment cell augmentee for not counting all his repetitions. Six months later, Col. Camerer opted to trek across town to Fort Sam Houston to take his fitness assessment on July 24. Rather than wear the required Air Force physical training uniform, he was observed by several witnesses dressed in MTI-style PT gear – black shorts and dark grey t-shirt – with "37 TRW Commander" printed across the back. As in January, the FAC augmentee who administered the muscular fitness components was an MTI under investigation. Col. Camerer's official push-up count dropped substantially during this assessment, but there is no indication he made a scene about it this time around. He compensated for this setback by improving his performance on other components, and so passed this PT test by a much wider margin.

The following week, Col. Camerer made a point of recognizing a couple of "battlefield airmen," technical training

---

[128] Jeff Schogol, "Colonel relieved of command for failing PT test," *Air Force Times*, March 20, 2013

instructors from the 37th Training Group, at the wing staff meeting for preparing him for his latest fitness assessment. He credited their early-morning workouts several times each week with helping him lose 14 pounds and improving his PT test results. Meanwhile, the fitness assessment cell manager, Willie Mastin, was removed and reassigned to a small gym on a remote part of the base, and the local staff judge advocate, Col. Oler, announced that a commander-directed investigation had been launched against the FAC for alleged procedural irregularities. He again briefed the wing staff in early December that the CDI had substantiated this allegation, and failing fitness assessments would be invalidated on a case-by-case basis. Twice during this period, on August 26 and again on December 3, Col. Camerer also made a point during staff meetings of warning his subordinate commanders of serious consequences if a commander, superintendent, or other squadron leader failed a fitness assessment – a not-so-subtle reminder of the fate his fellow wing commander (and personal friend) suffered at Grand Forks AFB.

Not surprisingly, it is widely rumored at Lackland that Col. Camerer actually failed those fitness assessments in 2013 – not once, but twice – but somehow managed to cover it up. There is no direct evidence of this allegation: his official scores for both PT tests were satisfactory, and no witnesses have so far been willing to go on the record claiming these results were falsified. And yet the innuendo persists, and not just among lower-ranking airmen at BMT; at least one group commander, a group superintendent, and multiple squadron commanders and senior enlisted members from across the wing are known to have repeated it amongst themselves as if it were a credible claim. This conspiracy theory has as much to do with the command climate Col. Camerer cultivated at Lackland as with any facts surrounding these particular incidents.

Let's begin with Col. Camerer's reported conduct during his PT tests. He publicly berated a FAC augmentee over how many push-ups he counted, even though his official score on this component was actually quite high. Is it possible the wing commander – who held the fate of this particular MTI in his hands – used his superior position to win the argument? One witness who was present said Col. Camerer "acted a complete ass about it" – and this apparently wasn't the first time, according to an airman who served as a physical training leader in Camerer's squadron nearly a decade earlier. It seems unethical that Col. Camerer was tested by personnel under his command, especially while they were subject to investigation. Another MTI involved in administering the January test, who was also then under investigation, later posted this opinion to a Facebook page: "This man was the last person to consider my fate and career. HYPOCRITE in all aspects of his being."

Perhaps Col. Camerer went to a different FAC for the second test to avoid such conflict of interest – but why then did he wear an unauthorized uniform with his duty title emblazoned across the back, if not to ensure favorable treatment from the FAC staff? And it seems odd that the number of push-ups he completed dropped so significantly between January and July, when other components improved thanks to the efforts of his personal trainers. Did these "battlefield airmen" fail to focus on his push-us? Or was Col. Camerer simply willing to accept the FAC augmentee's lower count without argument on this occasion, since he was confident his other component scores would put him over the top?

Col. Camerer's subsequent actions tended to reinforce suspicions about his fitness assessments. He bragged about enlisting his subordinates to get him in shape for the July test, which struck some of us as an abuse of authority. (Did these NCOs actually volunteer for this unusual duty?) Although he was not directly responsible for the CDI against the FAC,[129] which resulted in some scores being thrown out, it looked to skeptics like a cover-up, or at least an attempt to raise doubts about the administration of PT tests during this period. Is it a coincidence that the FAC manager – who happened to be present both times Col. Camerer tested – was exiled to an out-of-the-way fitness center even before the 802 MSG commander launched the CDI? Or could this have been an attempt to silence a potential witness? Even after Col. Liddick retired and Col. Camerer relinquished command of the wing, their former subordinates were still scared to speak out. When my wife, Caroline, attempted to meet with a witness to discuss what he saw, his squadron commander, Lt. Col. Dat Lam, reportedly ordered him not to talk to her. Meanwhile, the hapless FAC manager was quietly restored to his position only in late 2014, after Col. Camerer departed Lackland.

Perhaps there's nothing to these rumors. Sure, Col. Camerer behaved poorly when he abused a FAC augmentee, and he

---

[129] "Commander Directed Report of Investigation [...] Concerning Alleged Irregularities in Fitness Assessment Cell Procedures," October 7, 2013

wore the wrong PT uniform for a fitness assessment, but these don't rise to the level of serious misconduct. He may also have abused his authority by drafting subordinates as personal trainers and persecuting the FAC and its staff. But when you consider how many airmen Col. Camerer and Col. Liddick punished over the mere perception of impropriety, without compelling evidence of misconduct, it seems hypocritical to hold these senior leaders to a different standard. As I will explain in later chapters, Col. Camerer relieved me of command in part over an allegation that I merely created the appearance of unprofessional relationships and favoritism, based on the testimony of a handful of people in my squadron. On the other hand, there's a widespread perception that Col. Camerer covered up his fitness assessment failures, and many of his subsequent actions reinforced the appearance of impropriety. If unfounded rumors and innuendo were enough to destroy my career, how is it that Camerer is now a Brigadier General?

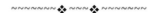

In July 2013, the RAND Corporation conducted an anonymous survey of around 240 MTIs to solicit feedback on their quality of life. Although the results were briefed to AETC and BMT leadership in October, they were not publicly revealed until the following year, when the *San Antonio Express-News* and *Air Force Times* each obtained copies of the findings. The MTI responses revealed a sharp distrust of group and wing leadership, and a widespread fear of trainees. "I am terrified I'm going to have my career ended by a trainee that drops a comment because I hurt his feelings or they just don't like me," one instructor wrote. A number of MTIs believed the rules had changed so dramatically, trainees now held more power than their instructors. "I'll give it to you in a nutshell: trainees run this place, MTI's are afraid constantly of getting in trouble over hurting a spoiled 18-year-olds' feelings, and no one is willing to change that," another instructor wrote. "Leadership does not back us up. At all," the instructor continued. "I feel as though [BMT] is overcorrecting and it's actually making the Air Force worse." MTIs also expressed concerns about the BMT commander, Col. Liddick. One said, "It is very apparent that she does not trust anyone who is an MTI and she continues to discredit the feedback given to her on decisions made."[130]

"By far the worst mistake I have ever made is becoming an MTI," another respondent admitted. "There is not an MTI who would stay here right now. When MTIs talk, they talk about when they are going to leave, not how much they like this place." Another instructor wrote, "I feel that MTIs are being treated like we are all criminals because of a few who made some very bad decisions. I feel that our wing leadership treats us as such." One instructor described a policy that if any MTIs were ever caught criticizing Col. Liddick's leadership, they would be taken to task. "If I remember correctly, we once removed a foreign dictator from power for something very similar to this," the MTI wrote. "Right now if you are a more seasoned instructor it feels as though you are under a spotlight and everything you do is looked at to ensure nothing wrong is being done. I understand that things need to be checked but not everybody did something wrong. Tell us what is going on in BMT. We never hear about the MTIs that do something good or bad, so we all still feel that everything we do is for nothing," another instructor said.

Many MTIs also expressed concern for the quality of airmen they were producing. "We are not setting these trainees up for the Air Force outside BMT. Instead, we are sheltering them and giving them unrealistic low expectations of what is waiting for them outside of these dormitories," one respondent wrote. "I really don't know how to say this, but training should be hard. The trainees should feel a sense of accomplishment. The poor product we are pushing out now has become the standard. I really hope I'm not around to see the next war," another MTI said. Part of the problem was the recent empowerment of new recruits. "We promote a critique system (which I am all for when there [is] a cause for it) but these trainees know all they have to do if they don't like you is fill out negative ones and you're in trouble. I've heard trainees talk about it. This is crazy," one MTI wrote. "I am finding that trainees are more commonly trying to look for a reason

[130] Sig Christenson, "In survey, Lackland drill instructors rip leaders, say they fear recruits," *San Antonio Express-News*, May 29, 2014

to report someone, and MTIs are scared to train because they feel they will be reported for something," another respondent wrote.[131]

These articles about the long-forgotten RAND survey created quite a stir when they were published in May 2014, but the journalists had barely scratched the surface of MTI frustration and fear. The survey's open-ended comments offered a revealing snapshot of instructor attitudes in July 2013, just a couple of weeks into my tour at BMT. Although we squadron commanders were briefed on the survey findings in October, I was only vaguely aware at the time of the deep animosity and anxiety the instructors had expressed. BMT leadership chalked up some of the more scandalous remarks – such as comparing the Liddick "regime" to that of Saddam Hussein – to a handful of disgruntled malcontents, veteran MTIs who were on their way out the door. However, this was not at all the case. Nearly two-thirds of respondents shared their thoughts on working conditions, leadership, and quality of life as an MTI, almost all of which was critical of the contemporary BMT environment. Far from just the bitter "old hats," this represented over 40 percent of training-qualified MTIs. Looking back, it is uncanny how accurately they captured the mood of the moment, after almost a year under the toxic leadership of Col. Liddick and Col. Camerer.

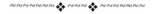

Not long after these articles came out, a former MTI going by the name "Banuvan" offered his own thoughts on the MTI survey during an "ask me anything" discussion on the Reddit social networking site. It was "completely ignored by leadership," he noted, "and they just went along the path that they thought was best without really discussing anything." Unfortunately, "it was up to Col. Liddick to determine how to do it," he added. "One thing people don't realize about BMT is that everything is viewed as an emergency here," he continued. "Every decision made is a knee jerk reaction. Nothing is thought out prior to implementing new rules and changes." As a result, "MTIs are, in a nutshell, glorified babysitters. Trainees shouldn't be scared of their MTIs," this instructor conceded, "but they should respect them at the very

[131] Kristin Davis, "Survey shows Lackland MTIs 'scared to train',"
Air Force Times, May 29, 2014

least. Col. Liddick imposed rules that completely undermine what an MTI is supposed to be teaching trainees."

For example, "It was common knowledge that yelling was a fundamental aspect of BMT." Many MTIs yelled for the shock value, or they were young and still learning the job, but Banuvan and others did so for instructional purposes. "If I yelled at a trainee to pin their hands to their side it wasn't because I liked yelling and wanted to exert my authority. It was because without looking I knew that there were others within the flight that also didn't [have] their hands pinned to their side. By yelling at one person it sent a mental reminder to everybody to pin their hands. This helped me by allowing me to say it once rather than 15 times." On one occasion, he was marching behind a flight of brand-new recruits during "zero" week shouting commands ("Get in step, swing your arms, cup your hands, etc."), but when they arrived at the squadron, his instructor supervisor pulled him aside. Col. Liddick had overheard him yelling, and she complained he did it too much and "needed to tone it down." Her perception "was completely made in ignorance of the basis for yelling and about myself as an instructor and my style of teaching." Right or wrong, the opinions of instructors didn't seem to matter. Col. Liddick deemed yelling unnecessary, so now you don't hear it around BMT anymore, "and it shows in the discipline of flights."

As a result of these changes, Banuvan noted, the quality of BMT graduates appeared to be going downhill. Recent graduates "expressed their disappointment at the 'toughness' of BMT." They didn't want a *Full Metal Jacket* type experience, "but they have complaints about everything from the ease of PT to the inconsistencies of instructors. It's disheartening." This wasn't just some "old hat" MTI complaining about "kids these days." however. "The generation currently coming into the military are very intelligent people overall," Banuvan explained. "They lack common sense and decision making skills though. Because of this it takes a different type of training." He attributed this to technological advances and the availability of information on the Internet. "Once I realized this I changed my training strategy completely." Modern trainees also "like to know the why," Banuvan continued. Although he hated this attitude – "The 'why' is because I told you so and gave you a lawful order," he thought to himself – he used it to his advantage. "I explained the 'why' to my student leaders so they understood the 'why' and it trickled down. This job has huge basis in psychology and sociology. It requires adaptability and being able to see where your flight needs help and focusing on that while reinforcing their strengths." While many MTIs were unwilling to change, "we have a mission to do. How we accomplish that mission has no bearing as long as you stay within the rules. The end result is what matters."

Banuvan acknowledged that MTI duty could be a career killer. "It is easier to get in trouble here," he noted, "as everything you do is under a microscope." Moreover, "You now have TSgts and MSgts doing the same job that SrA and SSgts should be doing," and Senior NCOs now have the same exact EPR bullets as more junior MTIs. "The people they are getting to come here are good people," he noted, who were probably great in their primary career fields, but "the majority of them have no desire to be here or to do this job." Airmen "who have been forced into this job don't have the mentality or personality that this job used to require. Not saying anything bad about the new folks. They had no choice in the matter. This position was volunteer only for a reason though."[132]

---

[132] "I was an MTI from 2009-2014 amid the entire scandal," July 18, 2014

Chapter 4: Prodigal Daughter

Among the transformation initiatives implemented at BMT, one the Air Force rarely talked about was the selection of "high-potential officers" as squadron commanders. General Rice, in coordination with our respective career field leadership, handpicked all six of us to come to Joint Base San Antonio-Lackland in 2013. Each of my colleagues was a graduated squadron commander, including one who held half a dozen commands prior to BMT. He had been promoted ahead of his peers to Lieutenant Colonel, and like me was selected to attend senior developmental education in residence. He and I had also earned Bronze Star medals during overseas deployments, and another commander and I received recognition for our joint service. All in all, this was a fairly talented bunch of officers, if I do say so myself, and we were each determined to make a difference at BMT.

Yet the Air Force never saw fit to publicly celebrate these airmen who answered our nation's call. They also missed the chance to publicize that two of us were San Antonio natives. I was of course born and raised there, the son of Air Force "brats" and grandson of World War II aviators. My counterpart, Lt. Col. Elisa "Liz" Valenzuela, was the daughter of a prominent community organizer, and had actually been assigned to BMT twice before: first as an enlisted trainee, then again as a young officer. Surely our stories would make for an attention-getting headline in the local paper: "Hometown Heroes to Reform Basic Training," or perhaps, "Prodigal Airmen Return to Lackland." I actually pitched this story idea to the wing public affairs officer, but she showed no interest.

Instead, our group and wing leadership relentlessly abused us. I was relieved of command on dubious grounds, as was another commander who lost his job a year later (more on that in Chapter 17). But none of us was so mercilessly mistreated as Lt. Col. Valenzuela. We often felt Col. Liddick resented the entire "Class of 2013," since she had no meaningful input into our selection, and most assuredly would have picked a more pliable and compliant bunch of officers. Her animosity against her fellow female commander, however, seemed motivated by altogether different factors. Liz often bitterly joked that, when she was hand-selected to return to BMT, she felt like a rock star ... but after how she was treated there, now she just felt like a rock.

With the repeal of the Department of Defense's "Don't Ask, Don't Tell" policy in 2011, the prohibition against gays, lesbians, and bisexuals serving openly in the military was finally lifted. I had always opposed this ban, which needlessly excluded otherwise competent and honorable service members simply for their expressed sexual preferences. I grew up with close relatives who were homosexual, and witnessed first-hand how my aunt served with distinction as an Air Force officer, all the while forced to compromise her integrity by hiding her sexual orientation. Long since declassified as a mental disorder, homosexuality was becoming increasingly accepted in American society, and it was only a matter of time before the military adjusted its policies accordingly.

The implementation of the "DADT" repeal went surprisingly well. Despite warnings that gays serving openly in the military would be disruptive to good order and discipline, or result in an exodus of personnel opposed to the change, the Armed Forces managed this transition relatively smoothly. Still, not all veteran service members embraced this new paradigm, and some even complained of reverse discrimination, as they now felt compelled to keep silent about their contrary views. This tension remained particularly acute until the Supreme Court declared the "Defense of Marriage Act" unconstitutional on June 26, 2013 – the day before I arrived at JBSA-Lackland – but it wasn't until January 2014 that the Department of Defense finally extended full military benefits to same-sex spouses.

One airman who did not seem fully reconciled to these changes was Col. Liddick. She reportedly expressed homophobic views to others on multiple occasions. For example, she questioned why a particular Chief Master Sergeant being considered for a BMT squadron superintendent position had no husband or children, and suggested Air Force personnel records ought to indicate sexual orientation to assist in such hiring decisions. (That Chief didn't end up getting the job.) Another instance was at a wing staff meeting, when Col. Liddick complained to Col. Camerer about the potential disruption of openly gay officers serving as squadron commanders. Then there was the operations officer from one of the BMT squadrons who Col. Liddick stratified second-to-last among her peers, probably suspecting she, too, was gay. When she discovered Col. Camerer had recommended this Major to serve as the executive officer to the commander of Air Force Recruiting Services, Col. Liddick asked him to recall the recommendation letter. It seemed clear this group commander considered homosexuality to be a disqualifying factor for leadership in her Air Force.

Ironically, many observers wondered whether Col. Liddick might herself be a closeted homosexual. More than one lesbian at Lackland expressed the opinion that my boss longed to play on their team, and her mannish demeanor earned her the nickname "Gary Busey" within the group. The way Col. Liddick ravenously stared at my wife only confirmed these suspicions for some observers. Although she was married, her husband's job with the U.S. Fish and Wildlife Service meant they had been living apart for several years. Such separations didn't seem to bother Col. Liddick much; as she admitted in a 2014 interview, she didn't find deployments difficult, since she could focus on the mission while her spouse back home "had to deal with paying the bills and shoveling the snow."[133] The few times Terry Liddick came down to San Antonio and joined his wife at military ceremonies or social events, their relationship did not seem particularly intimate. (For example, during my change-of-command ceremony, Mr. Liddick was overheard making fun of his wife as she repeatedly mangled the name of the outgoing commander's child during her remarks.) Some witnesses even questioned whether he, too, might secretly be gay. Could theirs have been a marriage of convenience to forestall any questions about Col. Liddick's sexuality during the "DADT" era? If so, her negative attitudes about gays in the military might have stemmed from a lifetime of her own spent living in the closet.

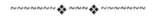

Such issues were of more than just passing concern to Lt. Col. Liz Valenzuela, who assumed command of the 326th Training Squadron in May 2013. She and her wife, Bunny, were both originally from San Antonio, where Liz enlisted in the Air Force in 1998. After earning her commission, she returned to BMT in 2002 as a squadron operations officer and executive officer for two 737 TRG commanders. Now she was back at Lackland, once again working for a woman. When they sat down for one of their first

---

[133] "Commanding Presence," p. 10

meetings, Col. Liddick emphasized the important role then-Major Valenzuela had to play as a female BMT squadron commander. Liz responded that the best mentor she ever had was actually a previous BMT commander, Col. Gina Grosso, who is now the three-star general in charge of Air Force manpower, personnel and services. Col. Grosso would take her company-grade officers out to lunch each quarter, and played an active role in advancing each of their careers. Col. Liddick was not impressed: "I don't do lunch, I don't mentor," she declared. "I do feedback!"

Major Valenzuela was already a graduated squadron commander, having led the 422d Supply Chain Management Squadron at Tinker AFB, Oklahoma, where she earned a "definitely promote" recommendation. As Liz relinquished that command in early May 2013, her leadership warmly embraced Bunny as her spouse. Not so at her next assignment. Liz rushed her family down to San Antonio so she could take charge of the 326 TRS, whose previous commander had quietly surrendered his post after being admonished by Col. Camerer. When Col. Liddick learned Liz planned to introduce Bunny as her spouse as she assumed command of the 326 TRS less than a week later, the group commander objected that this might imply official Air Force endorsement of same-sex marriage. ("DOMA" had not yet been overturned.) Col. Liddick insisted Liz clear her planned remarks with her before the ceremony, and she even called Liz's previous commander to chastise him for his past public support of her same-sex spouse. She also initially forbade Bunny from serving as a squadron Key Spouse.

This was only the beginning of Col. Liddick's blatant harassment of her only female squadron commander. When Liz first arrived at Lackland, Col. Liddick asked if she would be living in base housing like most other BMT squadron commanders. Liz explained she had already contracted to build a house off base, which was scheduled to be complete before her assumption of command. However, when Col. Liddick learned the Valenzuelas still hadn't moved into their house months later due to a construction delay, she was apoplectic, accusing Liz of having lied to her about purchasing a house. It's not clear why the group commander was so upset about them living off base, since they weren't even eligible to live in base housing until the Department of Defense extended benefits to same-sex spouses. Nevertheless, Col. Liddick questioned Liz's integrity in writing during her initial performance feedback: "Always tell me the truth...don't talk around the issue, i.e. housing issue with family."[134]

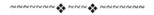

The abuse didn't end there. Lt. Col. Valenzuela, Bunny, and one of their children each had significant medical issues, which occasionally required the squadron commander to take time away from work. Col. Liddick would only begrudgingly grant leave, however, and seemed to resent Liz sending her operations officer, Maj. Gregg Potter, to cover meetings in her place. For instance, the group commander became angry when Liz skipped a routine weekly graduation ceremony to attend to her son's medical emergency, and yelled at her for missing a wing staff meeting due to her own medical appointment. Col. Liddick refused to approve leave for this squadron commander to accompany her son on his first day of school, even though Liz needed to explain her son's special medical needs to his teachers. Sure enough, the staff didn't know how to react when he presented with symptoms three days later, and her son ended up unnecessarily hospitalized. Even when the group commander did grant leave, she would micromanage the dates and demand detailed itineraries. She also went out of her way to prevent Liz from accompanying her trainees to an event off base on Thanksgiving Day. (I'll discuss this incident in more detail in the next chapter.)

Another example: Lt. Col. Valenzuela notified Col. Liddick via e-mail in late January 2014 that Bunny was having surgery on February 12, so she would be requesting leave on that day and possibly the next. Liz reminded her of Bunny's upcoming surgery at a group staff meeting on February 10, but Col. Liddick became angry, and later blasted Liz for blindsiding her in front of the other commanders. When Liz re-sent her the original e-mail, her boss persisted: "I had no idea you wanted the day off? These are the times you need to communicate with me."[135] Nevertheless, she reluctantly agreed to grant leave. However, on the morning of the

[134] Col. Liddick, AF Form 724, *Performance Feedback Worksheet (Lt thru Col)*, for Maj. Valenzuela, July 8, 2013
[135] E-mail exchange between Lt. Col. Valenzuela and Col. Liddick, "326 update," February 10, 2015

surgery, the group commander called Liz to chastise her for not showing up for work that morning.

Col. Liddick also went out of her way to ridicule Lt. Col. Valenzuela's squadron and her subordinates. After touring the 326 TRS recruit housing and training facility, Col. Liddick accused the commander of not taking pride in her unit, since there were water-stained tiles in one of the classrooms. Liz had to remind her they had a leaky roof and no money allocated to replace tiles. At a routine standardization and evaluation meeting, several BMT squadrons were found to have committed the same minor policy violation, but Col. Liddick singled out the 326 TRS, lecturing Maj. Potter and a flight commander for their squadron's failure of leadership. When one of her MTIs developed an innovative software program to account for trainee whereabouts completely on his own initiative, Lt. Col. Valenzuela and CMSgt Williams recommended him for an Air Force Achievement Medal, but Col. Liddick refused to recognize his accomplishment. The group commander even embarrassed the 326 TRS superintendent, CMSgt Reginald Murrell, for leaving work at 4 pm one day to celebrate his birthday, rather than staying behind for a pop-up visit by the Air Force Surgeon General. "Wow, birthday plans are more important than a visit from the AF Surgeon General, 2-star, and multiple O-6s!" she wrote to Lt. Col. Valenzuela in an e-mail.

Col. Liddick publicly humiliated Lt. Col. Valenzuela at a BMT commander's call on January 29, 2014, just before an Air Education and Training Command unit effectiveness inspection. When the group commander asked if there were any questions, the 326 TRS commander stood and reminded the audience that AETC inspectors had been writing up airmen at other bases for starching their Airman Battle Uniforms and walking around while talking on their cellphones, in violation of AFI 36-2903, *Dress and Personal Appearance of Air Force Personnel*. She felt this was "low-hanging fruit," simple mistakes to avoid getting a write-up. In response, Col. Liddick announced to the audience that she starched her ABUs, and asserted the starched uniform looks more professional. She assured her subordinates in the auditorium that they didn't have to worry about the policy, and if the inspectors said anything about this, she would "take the hit." In so doing, Col. Liddick undermined the authority not only of her squadron commander, but also the AETC inspectors charged to monitor this type of noncompliance. She also abused her authority by condoning a clear violation of Air Force policy, and unduly influencing others in her command to follow suit. Many people in the group seemed confused afterward, wondering what other rules they could ignore, and how Col. Liddick could punish people for violating policies when she was so dismissive of an Air Force instruction with which she didn't personally agree.

Given the toxic command climate Col. Liddick fostered, it should have come as no surprise when Lt. Col. Valenzuela's entire leadership team decided to retire from the Air Force within a year of their arrival at Lackland. Yet the group commander assumed Liz was somehow to blame. She accused the 326 TRS commander of having so many issues, even her first sergeant was retiring – when in fact, the "Shirt" had publicly cited group leadership as a reason for leaving the Air Force. About two weeks later, the deputy group commander, Lt. Col. Jim Upchurch, asked Maj. Potter if his retirement had anything to do with the squadron commander's leadership. On the contrary, both the operations officer and first sergeant asked Lt. Col. Valenzuela to officiate their retirement ceremonies, and Maj. Potter even explicitly requested that Col. Liddick not attend his shindig. The group commander insisted on showing up anyway, abusing her authority right up to the end of this officer's career. Col. Camerer later lectured his squadron commanders at a wing staff meeting about this incident, clearly siding with his toxic subordinate.

The 326 TRS commander often didn't see eye to eye with her boss on disciplinary issues. Soon after she arrived at BMT, Maj. Valenzuela inquired about a Technical Sergeant in her squadron who was issued nonjudicial punishment for what appeared to be a minor policy violation. Col. Liddick took a stripe, garnished her wages, removed her from the MTI corps, and ensured she was issued a referral enlisted performance report. Col. Liddick claimed SMSgt Milne, who was acting group superintendent at the time the punishment was administered, advised her this was the right thing to do. However, when Maj. Valenzuela followed up with this senior NCO to learn more about the case, he reportedly denied having suggested such a harsh punishment. Col. Liddick soon summoned the squadron commander to her office, where she questioned her loyalty and directed her to stand down, or else she would be "dealt with."

Around that same time, another Technical Sergeant in her squadron was accused of "hot boxing" trainees by making them engage in strenuous physical training inside the dormitory. Maj. Valenzuela wanted to remove this MTI for this flagrant violation of established policy, but Col. Liddick insisted they give him another chance. Less than six weeks later, he was again accused of maltraining when he had a flight do "speed drills," where they would run down from the dorm, form up outside, then race back upstairs to their beds on command. This was apparently repeated multiple times, until one of the trainees accidently caught his finger in a doorjamb, breaking his pinkie. When Liz again approached Col. Liddick regarding punishment, her boss berated her for the poor behavior of this instructor, apparently forgetting it was her idea to give him another chance. This time she was allowed to eliminate him from the MTI corps, but Col. Liddick allowed him to remain at BMT, working in the 319 TRS at the Basic Expeditionary Airman Skills Training site.

In late June 2013, Maj. Valenzuela was briefing her squadron on the sexual assault prevention and reporting program, when she mentioned the case of a former 326 TRS instructor who had appeared on the cover of the *Air Force Times* two weeks earlier. SSgt Dcoridrion Hicks had been a "Blue Rope" MTI before he lost his hat and a stripe in April 2013 for incidents dating from 2011. He was widely suspected of covering up the sexual misconduct of SSgt Luis Walker, although no charges were ever filed.[136] After the interview with Hicks was published, Col. Camerer made it known he didn't care what the public outside the fence was thinking, since the MTIs understood why he was punished. He directed his squadron commanders to conduct small meetings to talk about inappropriate sexual behavior and their duty to report. After Maj. Valenzuela briefed her squadron, SrA Hicks filed a complaint with the inspector general claiming she falsely alleged he "helped rape trainees with SSgt Walker." This was not true, as a subsequent investigation showed, yet Col. Liddick nevertheless formally counseled Maj. Valenzuela in August. She recommended this squadron commander "select topics that are appropriate and that do not effect [sic] any memeber [sic] of your organization or staff" – even though the whole point of the exercise was to discuss the subject of the *Air Force Times* article. This documented verbal counseling was meant to make Maj. Valenzuela more aware of her

---

136 "Blue rope loses stripe for minor offenses," June 17, 2013

comments, since "Perceptions sometime becomes someone [*sic*] reality."[137]

On the other hand, Col. Liddick objected to the administrative actions Lt. Col. Valenzuela took against another one of her subordinates for substantiated misconduct two years earlier. It was too late to offer nonjudicial punishment for his offense, so the 326 TRS commander issued him a letter of reprimand and opened an unfavorable information file, while his supervisor, CMSgt Murrell, referred his enlisted performance report. In an astoundingly hypocritical e-mail, Col. Liddick complained, "an LOR, UIF, and Referral EPR is not in-line with what we have done in the past to other MTIs (one time physical maltreatment) plus there is NO other allegations since 2011...I have a lot of BMT experience on these types of cases, and I think you are being too harsh."[138] The day after Christmas, the group commander summoned Lt. Col. Valenzuela to her office and threatened to report her behavior to Col. Camerer. She also told Liz she had better change her mind, since her own officer performance report was coming up – a blatant abuse of authority and attempt to exercise undue command influence.

Col. Liddick made good on her threats to poorly appraise Lt. Col. Valenzuela's performance. During her midterm performance feedback in January 2014, Liz was rated "above average" in only two out of six areas. Col. Liddick documented a laundry list of gripes about her hapless subordinate. For example, she questioned her about "high-fiving" graduating trainees as they completed the weekly Airman's Run. The squadron commander would stand at the finish line to encourage and motivate these graduating airmen, allowing them to slap her hands as they passed by. Col. Liddick suggested this was unprofessional and a violation of the BMT no-contact policy – a ludicrous claim, considering MTIs are expected to shake hands with these same airman at the weekly

---

[137] Col. Liddick, AF IMT 174, *Record of Individual Counseling*, for Maj. Valenzuela, August 9, 2013
[138] E-mail exchange between Col. Liddick and Lt. Col. Valenzuela, December 23, 2013

Coin Ceremony, just hours after the run.[139] "How would it look if I went around high-fiving people for a good job?" Col. Liddick persisted. Lt. Col. Valenzuela told her she actually got the idea from a previous 737 TRG commander she worked for, who would routinely congratulate each and every single trainee in this way at the BMT culmination ceremony.

Col. Liddick went on to question Lt. Col. Valenzuela's judgment ("You need to think through your decisions--you react too fast"), fairness ("perception is you take care of those who are close to you"), time management ("Watch your schedule, don't delegate too many meetings to your DO"), and communication ("You need to do a better job keeping me informed of what is going on in your sq"). When the topic turned to her next assignment, Liz indicated she had previously been vectored to serve as a deputy Mission Support Group commander or work at the Pentagon, but Col. Liddick dismissed these preferences. She suggesting her records weren't strong enough, and she should instead consider force management programs for early retirement. On the bright side, Col. Liddick thanked Liz for her support, "especially with spouse programs w/Bunny," but then ended on an ominous note: "I know you support the decisions we make...but there is no need to keep asking 'why'...you should understand the 'Whys' in BMT by now."[140]

In contrast to Col. Liddick's lukewarm evaluation of the 326 TRS commander, Lt. Col. Valenzuela's subordinates gave her command climate high marks. During a December 2013 assessment, 81 percent of her squadron reported favorable unit cohesion and pride, and the same number appeared pleased with their supervision. While only 66 percent reflected positive motivation and morale, they didn't blame their squadron commander: "The decline in morale, at least in my morale is not 326th leadership," one respondent wrote, "but the rules and regulations that must be imposed by our leadership because of what's coming down from the top."[141]

Col. Camerer publicly praised the results of the 326 TRS climate assessment as a benchmark for the wing, and suggested

---

[139] "Changing times at Lackland," September 15, 2013
[140] Col. Liddick, AF Form 724, *Performance Feedback Worksheet (Lt thru Col)* for Lt. Col. Valenzuela, January 28, 2014
[141] E-mail exchange between Lt. Col. Valenzuela and 502 ABW Equal Opportunity Office, "UCA Outbrief," April 4, 2014

Col. Liddick highlight them in Liz's annual officer performance report. When her OPR closed out in April 2014, however, the group commander had actually removed the reference to this favorable assessment from Lt. Col. Valenzuela's draft OPR. Both she and Col. Camerer (Liz's additional rater) damned her with faint praise in the final version: "On-target Sq commander," "Led squadron w/passion," "Analog leader committed to core values." Col. Liddick noted Liz "Diffused life staking incident" (whatever that means), and credited her with directing 60 inquiries of MTI alleged misconduct, but made no mention of her actually leading anything at BMT. Neither of her raters bothered to stratify Liz against her peers or push her for senior developmental education in residence, and their assignment recommendations – "will be ready for MSG Deputy next," "consider for Gp/CD next"[142] – were enough to stop her once promising career in its tracks. This was the last straw for Lt. Col. Valenzuela, who soon after filed complaints with the AETC inspector general and her Congressman.

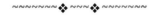

But these slights pale in comparison to how Col. Liddick mistreated one of Liz's subordinates she suspected of being gay. At Christmas 2013, this MTI reached out on Facebook to one of his former trainees, who was then a student at Keesler AFB, to see how he was doing at his follow-on technical training school. He later explained he was worried about this student, who reminded him of himself as a young airman, so he reached out to offer encouragement and mentorship. No matter the motive, such contact is prohibited by AETC policy, as it could degenerate into an unprofessional relationship between the instructor and pupil. Unlike previous cases that resulted in prosecution, however, the instructor and his former trainee were both male. Col. Liddick apparently thought this might be "grooming" behavior pursuant to sexual misconduct, and seemed determined to make an example of this instructor. When Lt. Col. Valenzuela indicated she intended to issue him a letter of reprimand, the group commander pulled the case to her level and administered nonjudicial punishment instead. During a subsequent meeting with this MTI, the group

---

[142] Col. Deborah Liddick and Col. Mark Camerer, AF Form 707, *Officer Performance Report (Lt thru Col)*, April 5, 2014

superintendent, CMSgt Sutherland, actually noted how strange it looked that a Technical Sergeant with no wife or girlfriend was reaching out to a young man, seemingly questioning his sexual orientation.

Surprisingly, Col. Liddick wanted to keep this disgraced instructor at BMT for the next six months to keep a close eye on him, so she allowed him to stay in the 326 TRS as the "PT/Supply NCO." She warned, however, that if anyone had a problem with him, even if it were unsubstantiated, she would "nail him and he is dead." Lt. Col. Valenzuela authorized him to wear distinctive gear when engaging in physical training, to distinguish him from the new recruits in their standard-issue Air Force PT uniforms. However, when Col. Liddick saw him wearing black MTI-style shorts and a squadron morale shirt during the weekly Airman's Run, she was not at all pleased. She pulled Liz aside later that morning and insisted this disgraced MTI wear regular PT gear "like an airman in our USAF, who needs to conduct himself like an NCO!" When Liz objected this would make him look like a trainee, Col. Liddick said that is precisely what she wanted.[143] The next day, Col. Liddick accused Lt. Col. Valenzuela of being disloyal for not supporting her punishment, and said she was rethinking leaving this NCO in her squadron since she might lie to protect him.

It is indeed ironic that Col. Liddick would jump to conclusions about other people's sexual orientation based on their marital status or lack of offspring, since she herself had no children and seemed perfectly content living alone with her dog. Moreover, the group commander was quick to suspect an MTI who expressed concern for a trainee of the same gender was a closet homosexual, when she herself was notorious for favoring female subordinates. She typically selected women as her executive officers and assistants, and when she visited trainee flights or worked out with them in the morning, she appeared to pay much more attention to the ladies. Now, this may simply have been out of concern over preventing their sexual victimization at BMT, or she may have felt an affinity for her sisters in arms who reminded her of her own struggle to make a name for herself in a male-dominated profession. But it is revealing that the only women she seemed to have no patience for were those she believed to be lesbian.

---

[143] E-mail exchange between Lt. Col. Valenzuela and Col. Liddick, March 21, 2014

Lt. Col. Valenzuela certainly had no intention of pushing a gay-rights agenda during her time in command, especially considering the animosity of her commander and others at BMT. Unfortunately, it was only a matter of time before she found herself in the middle of a controversy making national headlines. Three months into then-Major Valenzuela's command tour, the 326 TRS first sergeant, SMSgt Phillip Monk, went to the media with a sensational revelation: "I was relieved of my position because I don't agree with my commander's position on gay marriage." He claimed he was "essentially fired" for not validating her view that expressing opposition to same-sex marriage was discriminatory. He also accused his boss – labeled "an open lesbian" in a Fox News article published on August 14 – of calling a local Air Force chaplain a bigot for preaching homosexuality is a sin. "We've been told that if you publicly say that homosexuality is wrong, you are in violation of Air Force policy," he said. "Christians have to go into the closet," Monk continued. "We are being robbed of our dignity and respect. We can't be who we are."[144]

A 37 TRW spokeswoman immediately clarified that SMSgt Monk had not been punished. However, after SMSgt Monk participated in a Fox News television interview with the president of the Liberty Institute a couple of days later, Col. Camerer launched a commander-directed investigation into two allegations: that SMSgt Monk was improperly removed from his duties because of his personally held beliefs about homosexuality, and that he had made a false official statement to the press about being fired. He appointed Col. Richard Anderson, commandant of the Defense Language Institute's English Language Center, to quickly get to the bottom of this controversial case. His findings and conclusions, which Col. Camerer officially endorsed on September 27,[145] offer a revealing glimpse into the lengths these senior leaders would go to avoid controversy.

---

[144] Todd Starnes, "Airmen Punished for Objecting to Gay Marriage," *Fox News Radio*, August 14, 2013
[145] Col. Richard Anderson, *Commander Directed Report of Investigation Prepared by Col. Richard Anderson, Investigating Officer, Concerning Discrimination & False Official Statement*, September 16, 2013, p. 136

SMSgt Monk had served as a first sergeant at Lackland since 2011, and was scheduled to rotate back to his primary career field once he returned from deployment in May 2013. He was expected to move to the 59th Medical Group sometime that summer, with a report-no-later-than date of September 30. After briefly meeting his new commander, Maj. Valenzuela, Monk went on post-deployment leave, but when he returned to work in early June, he reportedly told a colleague he "did not agree with homosexuals and he was going to have issues in the squadron because the commander is a lesbian." Around that same time, Maj. Valenzuela was making plans for her upcoming promotion ceremony, and she remarked she did not want a particular chaplain to give her benediction based on his views on homosexuality. SMSgt Monk would later claim she called the chaplain a "bigot," and said she didn't know "what kind of people believe that type of crap," but Liz and another witness denied she said that.[146]

On July 13, an MTI conducting an "Airmen's Time" discussion with his 326 TRS trainees shared his views on homosexuality, which several trainees found discriminatory. Maj. Valenzuela initiated an alleged misconduct report on this incident as required by policy, which she routed through Col. Liddick to the staff judge advocate. The squadron commander intended only to verbally counsel this MTI for his relatively minor mistake, but the base legal office recommended she formally admonish him for verbal maltreatment. She opted to compromise by issuing her subordinate a written letter of counseling.[147] Such a difference of opinions – a squadron commander not wanting to make a big deal out of the situation, while the SJA insisted on harsher punishment – played out time and time again over such disciplinary actions at Lackland.

However, the first sergeant did not agree with this proposed course of action. When Maj. Valenzuela discussed the case with SMSgt Monk on July 26, he argued the MTI shouldn't be punished for merely exercising his right to free speech. In another conversation two weeks later, Monk again defended the MTIs right to voice his opinion on homosexuality to his trainees, and refused to concede those comments were discriminatory. Witnesses deny he ever expressed his religious beliefs during these meetings. By this point, SMSgt Monk's replacement had already arrived for duty,

---

[146] *Ibid.*, p. 7-8
[147] *Ibid.*, p. 8

so Col. Liddick recommended he start work immediately, without any turnover. Monk later claimed he had been forced to take leave and banned from the squadron, but the evidence doesn't support either assertion.[148]

Col. Anderson was unequivocal in his conclusions: SMSgt Monk was reassigned "to an expected and welcomed duty assignment on or near the expected date without prejudice, albeit amongst turbulence arising from a disagreement with his commander over a vetted, measured, lawful, and necessary corrective action taken against a subordinate in the squadron. No adverse actions were taken against [SMSgt Monk] because of his religious views. Indeed, no adverse actions were taken against him at all." He found the first allegation unsubstantiated.[149]

The investigating officer's analysis and findings regarding the second allegation are a bit more convoluted, however. Having established that SMSgt Monk's "statement to the press that he was removed because of his religious beliefs was false," Col. Anderson embarked on "an inquiry into whether [he] subjectively knew that his statements were false." Based on his training and experience as a first sergeant, SMSgt Monk "should have known that discriminatory remarks on the basis of sexual orientation are against Air Force policy," and that airmen cannot "say whatever they want, whenever they want, so long as they truly believe what they are saying." The investigating officer therefore found it unreasonable that SMSgt Monk did not stand by his commander's decision to counsel a subordinate, and also found it unreasonable for him to believe Maj. Valenzuela "directly or constructively took any adverse action again him based on his religious beliefs."

Nevertheless, Col. Anderson was not convinced SMSgt Monk knew his statement to be false when he made it. Despite assurances from two Chief Master Sergeants that he had not been fired, "it appears possible he still believed it." Moreover, since his free-speech objections "may have been rooted in his deeply held, but unspoken religious views," he likely thought his removal was based on his commander's opposition to those religiously-founded objections, even though he never shared this religious foundation with Maj. Valenzuela. Therefore, "no matter how unreasonable his belief that he was removed because of his religion was," SMSgt Monk "truly believed it," and he did not make these statements

---

[148] *Ibid.*, p. 8-10
[149] *Ibid.*, p. 23

with the intent to deceive – two elements that must be proven for punishment under Article 107 of the UCMJ, "Making False Official Statements."[150]

Next, Col. Anderson turned his attention to Article 134, a catch-all for "disorders and neglects to the prejudice of good order and discipline in the armed forces" and "conduct of a nature to bring discredit upon the armed forces." The investigating officer asserted that, while "there may have been some effect on morale in the 326 TRS and some turbulence across the Air Force" after SMSgt Monk repeatedly and falsely denounced his commander to major national news outlets, "his words did not have the required effect of interfering with or preventing the orderly accomplishment of the mission, or, presenting a clear danger to loyalty, discipline, mission, or morale of the troops." He also rejected the argument that this protected speech was prejudicial to good order and discipline. "There has been no evidence presented during this investigation to suggest that the 326 TRS or any of its personnel have been less effective in completing their mission," he noted, and "insufficient evidence exists to demonstrate a direct and palpable connection with military mission and environment" for these statements to be service discrediting. Finally, Col. Anderson applied a balancing test to weigh SMSgt Monk's freedom of speech against Air Force interests in preventing such statements to the press. He concluded the main impact on the Air Force was negative publicity, as "no significant mission, morale, or discipline impact could be shown."[151] He therefore found this allegation unsubstantiated as well.

In 2014, I reached out to Captain Michael Junge, a professor at the U.S. Naval War College who specializes in the study of inquiries used to relieve military officers, to get his opinion on Col. Anderson's report of investigation. "Honestly, I'm not even sure why there was an investigation" into the first allegation, he replied, but the investigating officer dealt with "correctly if a bit oddly." As for the second allegation, that "is the crux of the issue. [He] seems to think that legal maneuvering and wrangling the phrases and specifications makes it OK to unsubstantiate the allegation. However, the intent and spirit of both the false official statement and general article were violated. Caught up in all of this are the freedoms of speech and religion...but neither in reality is

---

[150] *Ibid.*, p. 26-27
[151] *Ibid.*, p. 27-28

part of the issue. They are being used by a simple minded and immature senior NCO to complain about how he was treated when he couldn't act professionally...when in reality nothing was done to him." Bottom line, CAPT Junge concluded, "I am at a loss for how someone could determine that his comments to the press are NOT prejudicial to good order and discipline. The investigating officer seems to accept ignorance as an excuse, and the level of ignorance from an E8 is something I'd accept from an E5 or E6 and expect in an E3...but not in an E8. Especially one who'd been otherwise advised by his peers." If CAPT Junge had been in command, he "would have detached for cause SMSGT Monk and ensured that he retired as soon as humanly possible by ensuring that he could not reenlist. And he'd never have had a command slot again. He was someone the [commanding officer] should have counted on for advice, and when that advice was rejected but still legal and ethical he needed to execute. And he couldn't do that."[152]

After acknowledging airmen cannot "say whatever they want, whenever they want, so long as they truly believe what they are saying," the investigating officer in this case absolved SMSgt Monk of responsibility for doing just that. It was as if he were channeling George Costanza, from the sitcom *Seinfeld*, when he offered this laughable legal advice: "Jerry, just remember. It's not a lie ... if you believe it."[153]

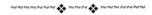

The Air Force did everything it could to quickly put this debacle behind them. In October, AETC issued a press release on the results the investigation of now-Lt. Col. Valenzuela and SMSgt Monk. "The weight of the evidence shows that religion was never discussed between the two," Col. Camerer stated. "In the end, this is a case about command authority, good order and discipline, and civil rights – not religious freedoms," he said. Yet the Air Force would not be taking any disciplinary actions as a result of the investigation, and even announced SMSgt Monk had been approved

<hr />

[152] E-mail response from CAPT Michael Junge, "Re: CDI analysis," June 25, 2014
[153] "The Beard," *Seinfeld*, Season 6, Episode 15, originally aired February 9, 1995

for a Meritorious Service Medal,[154] which he was awarded upon his retirement in February 2014. The Liberty Institute immediately spun this as an official exoneration of their client,[155] who had meanwhile become a fixture in certain right-wing political circles. Days after the CDI results were announced, SMSgt Monk participated in a panel discussion at the Family Research Council's annual Values Voter Summit,[156] and the FRC published a slick promotional video sharing his story in December.[157] (While he was not in uniform, this active-duty airman was clearly identified by his military rank in both appearances.) Monk returned to the Values Voter Summit two years later to be honored for standing up for religious freedom alongside the likes of Kim Davis, the Kentucky county clerk who was jailed over her refusal to issue marriage licenses to same-sex couples.[158] He also appeared in a campaign ad for presidential candidate Ted Cruz.[159]

Col. Camerer had a point when he said this case was about command authority, good order and discipline, and civil rights, rather than religious freedoms. But by taking no action against a senior noncommissioned officer who continued broadcasting ridiculous allegations about his openly gay boss long after they were proven false, the wing commander did real damage to the Air Force, his organization, and the professional reputation of Lt. Col. Valenzuela. This first sergeant made no effort to seek redress of his perceived grievance through the chain of command, the inspector general, or even his Congressional representatives before taking his case to the media. Even if SMSgt Monk initially believed he was

---

[154] Oriana Pawlyk, "AF: Religious intolerance claim unsubstantiated," October 11, 2013

[155] Liberty Institute, "U.S. Air Force Awards Senior Master Sergeant Phillip Monk Prestigious Decoration Despite Religious Discrimination Claim," February 18, 2014

[156] Tyler O'Neil, "US Christians at Values Voter Summit: Religious Discrimination in America Is Real, Increasing," October 14, 2013

[157] FRC Media Office, "Video: Senior Master Sgt. Philip Monk Discusses Military Religious Freedom Incident," Family Research Council, December 20, 2013

[158] Cheryl Wetzstein, "Planned Parenthood, gay marriage top topics at Values Voters Summit," *The Washington Times*, September 25, 2015

[159] Ted Cruz, "Stand for Religious Liberty," Ted Cruz 2016 official website, August 23, 2015

fired for his religious views, his version of events was long ago debunked; continuing to tout this nonsense years later is attributable either to willful ignorance or deliberate deception, not honest misunderstanding.

The conclusions Col. Anderson reached were ridiculous, but I suspect they are precisely what Col. Camerer wanted from his investigating officer: an excuse to do nothing to punish an insubordinate senior NCO espousing culturally conservative views – which he likely shares – while leaving Maj. Valenzuela twisting in the wind. This impression was reinforced in January 2014, when Col. Camerer admitted to Liz that he launched the CDI into the allegations against her even though he did not believe they were true, and he refused to release the report of investigation to her once she was exonerated. She had to submit a Freedom of Information Act request to learn the rest of the story.

Soon after her former first sergeant began spreading lies about her, Maj. Valenzuela started receiving death threats, and no longer felt safe travelling into town in her Air Force uniform. The vice wing commander recommended the 326 TRS commander change her official e-mail address to reduce the amount of hate mail, but Col. Liddick refused to authorize this, advising her subordinate to toughen up and "get a thicker skin." The group commander claimed she also got threats, so Maj. Valenzuela should just learn to deal with it. Perhaps it was poetic justice, then, when a conservative blog tarnished Col. Liddick's reputation as well, mistakenly assuming it was the BMT commander who was a lesbian.[160] Another blogger later compounded this mistake by suggesting Col. Liddick's supposed sexual orientation had something to do with her later mistreatment of me.[161]

On the bright side, Col. Liddick's harassment abated somewhat after Liz informed her she had sought outside counsel from the OutServe-Servicemembers Legal Defense Network, an advocacy group for the lesbian, gay, bisexual and transgender military community. She also mentioned she had been approached by major news outlets to tell her side of the story. It seems likely this timely support is all that prevented the group commander from targeting Liz for relief of command – not because of anything

---

[160] "Mustang" (pen name), "USAF Pursues Gay Agenda," *A Texas View* blog, October 7, 2013
[161] Dee, "Another Commander: Relieved of command," *TeaParty.org*, May 31, 2014

she'd done, but because of who she was. Unfortunately for me, Col. Liddick soon set her sights on a different squadron commander to fire.

Chapter 5: Beginning of the End

In early September 2013, the Basic Military Training Triennial Review committee met to discuss the future of BMT. Chaired by the Air Force director of force development, its membership includes the Chief Master Sergeant of the Air Force and Command Chief Master Sergeants from across the service. This committee meets at JBSA-Lackland at least every three years to provide oversight of the BMT program, reviewing Air Force requirements for graduate performance, military training, field training, and other items. Their two-day 2013 symposium took place in the 737 TRG conference room, and my squadron hosted a social at the BMT Reception Center at the end of the first day. Each of the group's squadron commanders, superintendents, and select other enlisted members were in attendance that evening, and Mr. Steele even ordered special BMT polo shirts for the occasion. I for one had a good time discussing my perspective on BMT with the other guests that evening.

The following Monday, September 9, the squadron commanders were again gathered in the 737 TRG conference room for our weekly staff meeting, when Col. Liddick informed us she had received worrisome feedback about the previous week's social event. All but one of the new Chief Master Sergeant squadron superintendents reportedly complained they had no authority at BMT, and some squadron commanders apparently expressed concerns about certain policies, including disposition authority for misconduct allegations. Col. Liddick proceeded to lecture us about trust and loyalty, and gave us all an ultimatum: "you're either with me or against me." She then went around the conference room table asking each of us to confirm we were with her – like a scene out of a gangster movie. I couldn't help but feel this was some sort of threat against those of us she judged to be not "on board" with her policies.

That same evening, I received a cryptic e-mail from Col. Liddick, asking me to come see her about an unspecified "favor." When I reported to her office first thing the next morning, she proceeded to make me an offer I couldn't refuse: Would I be willing to give her packing boxes for her upcoming do-it-yourself move? My boss had noticed my wife, Caroline, owned a lot of clothes, and she learned we had an inordinate number of wardrobe boxes from our recent move. She was planning to relocate the following summer, and she and her husband, Terry – who worked for the U.S.

Fish and Wildlife Service up in South Dakota – were trying to save money on moving expenses. I found this solicitation of a gift from my superior incredibly awkward, and had no idea why she was worrying about these boxes nine months in advance of her move. Then again, setting aside some of our wardrobe boxes seemed like a relatively small price to pay to curry favor with my boss.

Of course, we hadn't actually moved into our house yet, and it would be months before we finished unpacking all the boxes. So it came as a surprise when I received another e-mail from Colonel Liddick on Columbus Day, October 14, asking if she and Terry could swing by my house that afternoon to pick up the wardrobe boxes – and would I mind giving her our address? I demurred yet again, but it was only a matter of time before Col. Liddick's persistence would finally pay off. When her husband returned to town to celebrate Thanksgiving, my boss cornered me yet again about the boxes, which I finally surrendered as requested. But my compliance and generosity paid no dividends; less than a month later, Col. Liddick removed me from command, and set in motion the complete destruction of my career.

By most accounts, my first few months in command were successful. My airmen were getting our mission accomplished, morale seemed to be improving, and none of my subordinates had failed a fitness assessment or been arrested for driving under the influence. I had also launched several initiatives I hoped would bear fruit over time. For example, I directed the "Deliberate Development" team to expand their services beyond MTIs, providing in-house professional development to augment leadership skills to other populations. I helped develop an MTI career progression process, designed to systematically identify high-performing noncommissioned officers for career-enhancing positions. I coordinated with Behavioral Analysis Services and the Military Training Consult Service to improve mental health support to both trainees and MTIs. I was laying the groundwork to move much of my squadron into the new Recruit/Family Inprocessing and Information Center ("RFIIC"), which I requested be dedicated to CMSgt Gary Pfingston, a former MTI and MTI School commandant who went on to become Chief Master Sergeant of the Air Force. I was also preparing my squadron to assume responsibility for the 324 TRS transition flight the following summer, and to support the eventual establishment of a "capstone" program during the final week of basic training.

I instituted periodic squadron physical training to improve the fitness of my airmen and their sense of unit pride, and I also led the effort to select a squadron mascot. With the help of the TRSS Private Organization, we provided each member a tech t-shirt and hoodie bearing our new "Raptor" logo. Meanwhile, Caroline was planning several upcoming family-oriented events with the other spouses, including a BMT children's fall festival at the end of October and another holiday party for the kids in December. Since both Col. Liddick, and her deputy, Lt. Col. Jim Upchurch, had come to BMT without their spouses, Caroline quickly became the most visible "better half" in the group.

Yet there were signs of trouble on the horizon. My relationship with Col. Liddick was strained, exacerbated by a couple of minor disagreements over personnel issues in my squadron. She had also chastised me for hosting a party at my house, and for interfering with the work hours of MSgt Walls, who split her first-sergeant loyalties between the two of us. At the time, I chalked up our differences to personality conflict, a conclusion that seemed borne out by a couple of professional development seminars put on by my "Deliberate Development" team in late October and early November.

Mr. Kamel and SSgt Little had administered personality assessments to all the field-grade officers in the group, and sorted us into cohorts during these sessions according to our supposed temperaments. Of the six officers who had recently assumed command, four of us – Lt. Col. Valenzuela, Lt. Col. Lam, Lt. Col. Gallagher, and me – were classified as "rationals," who sometimes question authority not out of disloyalty, but so as to better understand the reason behind policy decisions. Col. Liddick and the rest of the commanders, on the other hand, were all "guardians," preoccupied with responsibility and duty. When Col. Liddick noticed the split, she observed this must be why she had so many problems with those of us in the "rationals" camp.

At the group staff meeting after the first seminar, my fellow commanders had nothing but praise for SSgt Little. Lt. Col. Gearhart claimed he was blown away by how "squared away" this noncommissioned officer was, and Lt. Col. Gallagher noted you don't often see Staff Sergeants able to present in front of an audience like that. Col. Liddick agreed, and declared she "could see him as a Chief Master Sergeant running the Air Force" some day.

She seemed significantly less enthusiastic about my spouse, however.

When we were on break during that first "DD" seminar, I happened to be discussing Caroline's personality type with the instructors (she's an extrovert, in case you haven't already guessed). Out of nowhere, Col. Liddick interjected that she didn't know what to do with my wife. I often got the impression my boss was jealous of Caroline – or maybe even a little covetous of my wife – and she seemed to resent us as the "popular kids" at BMT, as if this insecure leader were still in high school. At the time, this seemed like a random outburst, but it would soon become clear Col. Liddick wasn't the only airman my wife rubbed the wrong way.

Caroline's most strident critic was the MTI School commandant, MSgt Pickett. He initially struggled in his new job, and seemed to resent the fact that Caroline got along better with his subordinates than he did. He complained to whomever would listen that the commander's wife was interfering in the MTI School and undermining his authority as commandant. Worse, because Caroline naturally had my ear, he seemed to fear rumors of his incompetence would reach me, and negatively influence his upcoming enlisted performance report. He got no sympathy from my superintendent, however. SMSgt "LG" was quite familiar with my leadership style by this point, and she presumably defended my wife and me against these baseless accusations. But other members of my key leadership team turned out to be more receptive to such innuendo, as we would learn the hard way.

Word on the street was that MSgt Pickett was "circling the drain" as commandant, and his toxic leadership style had earned him various unflattering nicknames. Some called him "Little Napoleon," a petty tyrant who micromanaged his subordinates, while others knew him as "Spotlight," always eager to claim credit for the accomplishments of others. My wife naturally made me aware of such rumors when she heard them, but I always took them with a grain of salt. Nevertheless, I began to notice similar patterns during my own interaction with the commandant. For example, whenever I scheduled a "walkabout" in the MTI School, most of the instructors seemed to have been dispatched out of the office for one reason or another, leaving me to deal exclusively with their boss. On one occasion, when SMSgt "LG" and I happened to find some instructors available in the schoolhouse with whom to chat, MSgt Pickett hovered in the background, occasionally butting in to steer the conversation in his preferred direction.

As the 737 TRSS commander, I had a unique personnel challenge: mine was the only BMT squadron with students assigned, as opposed to basic trainees. These were mid-career airmen, mostly Technical Sergeants and Master Sergeants, who had come to Lackland to serve as MTIs, whether voluntarily or otherwise. Once they completed the MTI course, they were technically no longer students, but remained assigned to my squadron as they accomplished several months of on-the-job training at the 323 TRS. AETC imposed stringent rules restricting relationships with students and trainees, so I felt it important to address any misconceptions about who was a student and how we should treat them. After coordinating with Col. Liddick and the base legal office, I published a policy letter in October, clarifying it was appropriate for MTI students to attend official social functions, and that graduates of the MTI course were not subject to student restrictions.[162]

Although MSgt Pickett never commented on my proposed policy letter when I sent it out for coordination, he nevertheless seemed displeased about me extending an invitation for MTI students to attend unit events. As it turned out, this new policy came just in time. The week after it was published, a spouse from another squadron posted a message on a Facebook community page declaring MTI students weren't welcome at the upcoming BMT children's fall festival. Caroline quickly responded, quoting from my letter in her own post on the BMT Key Spouse page. This should have settled the matter, but she soon heard rumors that MSgt Pickett was falsely accusing her of writing this policy.

Our squadron offered to construct a box maze for kids to crawl through at the BMT children's fall festival on October 26. Caroline and I brought in hundreds of empty boxes from our recent move to support this effort, and she even offered to cook for anyone who helped set up and monitor this activity. In addition to our two Key Spouses and their significant others, several other volunteers – including SSgt Little, Mr. Kamel, a civilian from the processing flight, and even SMSgt Watkins from the 331 TRS – helped assemble an impressive labyrinth. Like us, several of these

---

[162] Lt. Col. Perry, "Professional Relationships with Military Training Instructor (MTI) Students," October 9, 2015

folks had no children of their own at this event, yet they selflessly volunteered their time on a Saturday for the sake of the unit. The first sergeant, MSgt Walls, and my operations officer, Capt. Sprouse, were no-shows as usual, but MSgt Pickett and his family did make an appearance just as we were putting the finishing touches on the maze. In retrospect, he seemed to be there less to participate in the festivities than to keep an eye on his subordinates, and perhaps see how many students showed up.

These MTI students formed their own opinions of the commandant. One class leader later complained MSgt Pickett was never around, and he "never came into our classes to add his knowledge or expertise, much less to check on his instructors to see how they were doing." She remembers him pulling her aside in the hallway to ask how things were going. "It almost felt as if he wanted me to dime someone out, or provide him some feedback about the school house of sorts, but I read right through his BS. I told him all was good and went on with my business." She said he reminded her of "one of those tyrant leaders who had the mentality of 'do as I say, not as I do.'" Another student said MSgt Pickett seemed a little suspicious, "like someone I would NEVER trust." She was having a difficult time finding her command voice early on, so she solicited tips on a Facebook page from current and former instructors. Later that day, "MSgt Pickett came in and 'counseled' the entire class on posting something on that page because it makes the schoolhouse look incompetent." It came as no surprise to her that MSgt Pickett would later "stoop so low" as to betray his commander, since he was one of the few instructors at the schoolhouse "who were in it for reasons other than molding airmen and new MTI's."

Tensions with MSgt Pickett soon came to a head. In late October, he repeatedly approached me requesting a feedback session, so I met with him late on Monday, October 28. Ominously, he insisted on bringing the first sergeant with him to act as a witness, claiming he feared retaliation. He began by revealing he knew he wasn't my first choice for commandant, saying CMSgt Williams had spilled the beans. He then proceeded to explain how he was scared of the "undue influence" exercised by the "Deliberate Development" contractor, Mr. Kamel, over the former BMT superintendent, and he also accused a handful of other senior "Blue

126

Ropes" – SMSgt Milne, the former MTI School commandant; SMSgt Watkins, the 331 TRS superintendent (and his rival for the commandant position); and another E-8 from the 324 TRS – of bad-mouthing Col. Liddick. MSgt Pickett further declared Mr. Kamel wasn't meeting the intent of his contract, and accused him of conspiring with my wife to subvert his authority. As evidence, he claimed that when Caroline cooked a "spaghetti dinner" for folks in our building the previous week, Mr. Kamel and SSgt Little spent three hours with her. He also suggested Caroline was planning an "exclusive" party for all her helpers at that weekend's BMT children's event.

I managed to hold my temper throughout this tirade, listening patiently to a delusional subordinate accuse my wife of conspiring against him and interfering with his job. When it was my turn to talk, I pointed out a few inconsistencies in his allegations. For example, his subordinates couldn't have possibly spent three hours at that luncheon with Caroline, since they were teaching class until noon that day, and my wife left just after 1 pm. Besides, I had already heard through the grapevine that MSgt Pickett had counseled SSgt Little for spending only two hours with Caroline, not three. I also told MSgt Pickett I heard he had accused Caroline of writing policy and interfering in the MTI School, but he denied having made such claims. Twice during the encounter, he became so emotional he had to step out of my office to regain his composure. At no point, however, did he accuse me directly of any misconduct, or implicate the squadron superintendent, SMSgt "LG," as part of a "Blue Rope" clique.

At the end of the meeting, I told MSgt Pickett that he'd given me plenty of things to think about, so I'd need some time to get back to him before proceeding. Afterwards, I asked MSgt Walls to stay behind so we could compare notes on what just happened. I expressed surprise that a senior noncommissioned officer would make such outlandish allegations, but she leapt to his defense, claiming "it took courage" for him to bring these issues to me.

When I arrived at work the next day, MSgt Walls mentioned MSgt Pickett had already met with Col. Liddick first thing that morning, and she was scheduled to sit down with the group commander shortly. I suspected they would be discussing the accusations MSgt Pickett made the previous afternoon, so I insisted on attending this meeting with my boss, her deputy, and the first sergeant. Col. Liddick acknowledged MSgt Pickett had come to her with his paranoid allegations, but she, too, defended him for the "courage" it took to raise these issues, echoing the first sergeant's sentiments. Col. Liddick appeared to accept each of the MTI School commandant's allegations as true, and blamed me exclusively for any conflict between us. She began by asking if I ever "hang out" with Mr. Kamel or SSgt Little. I reminded her of the party at my house the previous month, which we had previously discussed, and I also informed her of the dinner my wife cooked for SSgt Little's mother on October 12. She counseled me not to "hang out with them socially" in the future. While conceding my wife was "doing a good job," my boss suggested we avoid any further "house parties" and be careful about Caroline's communications within the squadron.

We next discussed the chain of command for the "Deliberate Development" team. I told Col. Liddick I found MSgt Pickett's recent behavior unprofessional, and I judged his leadership style to be too rigid and controlling. He seemed too emotionally invested to be objective, and he did not appear to have the trust or support of his subordinates. I suggested he might be in over his head trying to manage the MTI School, the "DD" team, and the MTI Recruiting functions he retained when he was selected for his current position. (Previous commandants had only been responsible for the schoolhouse, but his predecessor, CMSgt-select Milne, had overseen "DD" as well.) I recommended we consider spinning off "DD" from the MTI School again, and have this team work directly for my operations officer, Maj-select Sprouse, who I felt was ready for increased responsibility.

Col. Liddick rejected this proposal, and asserted we needed to get our money's worth from the "DD" contractor. When the new contract began in 2014, she declared, Mr. Kamel would work directly for MSgt Pickett. (In fact, the contractors work for the 737 TRG training director, Dr. Munro, under the new contract.) Finally, Col. Liddick issued me an ultimatum. She directed me to clearly lay out my expectations for MSgt Pickett, and give him 30 days to meet them. Although she acknowledged this wasn't a group-level problem, if we could not work out our differences, she threatened to realign the entire MTI School under the 737 TRG and have MSgt Pickett work directly to her.

In hindsight, this whole incident felt like a setup. MSgt Pickett was very insistent about meeting with me, yet he gave me no time to address his concerns before going to my boss. She already seemed quite familiar with the details of his allegations, however, suggesting she'd known about them for a while by the time I met with her. I suspect Col. Liddick may have encouraged MSgt Pickett meet with me to lodge his complaints, so as to protect himself from any adverse actions I might have been contemplating, since these would now look like reprisal. The irony is, I never had any intention of firing the MTI School commandant, and I wouldn't have dreamt of making down his EPR without offering him timely feedback and allowing him a chance to recover. Then again, my leadership style is a bit different than these two toxic leaders.

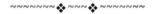

As instructed, I provided MSgt Pickett written performance feedback a few days later, on October 31. Although I marked the form as an initial feedback – since I had not previously provided written guidance as MTI School commandant – my comments reflected a sober assessment of his accomplishments over the past two months. I requested he use the chain of command, and give me a chance to solve problems before elevating them outside the squadron. He should also avoid micromanagement, and respect the role of the "DD" NCOIC to lead that team. I warned him never to stifle communications between his subordinates and squadron leadership, as that would only breed distrust. I advised him to provide positive feedback to good performers, and take care when counseling or reprimanding subordinates, as word tended to get around at BMT. I praised him for some of his initiatives at the schoolhouse, and encouraged him to nurture the "DD" team, which provided invaluable services to the MTI corps and BMT leadership.[163] I also informed him Col. Liddick had given me 30 days to address the most serious issues between us. He asked me point-blank whether his "firewall 5" EPR – the highest possible evaluation – would be at risk if he couldn't meet all my expectations by that deadline. I reassured him he had until the end of his annual evaluation cycle to correct every deficiency, but I expected see considerable improvement in the coming weeks.

After separately counseling Mr. Kamel to refrain from being so outspoken about MSgt Pickett's leadership style, I gathered the MTI School commandant and the three members of

---

[163] Lt. Col. Perry, AF Form 932, *Performance Feedback Worksheet (MSgt thru CMSgt)*, for MSgt Pickett, October 31, 2013

the "DD" team on Monday, November 4, to clarify their chain of command. I reaffirmed "DD" would remain under the oversight of the MTI School commandant, as before, but MSgt Chavez would remain in charge of day-to-day "DD" operations, so MSgt Pickett must work through the "DD" NCOIC on substantive issues. However, since MSgt Chavez was a Reservist assigned to a different squadron, he could not rate on his subordinate, SSgt Little. Therefore, I confirmed MSgt Pickett would be SSgt Little's rater, in close coordination with MSgt Chavez. I also clarified the role of the contractor, Mr. Kamel, as a subject-matter expert with no actual authority over the other members of the team. MSgt Pickett seemed relieved he would not be held responsible for "DD" operations, and he actually admitted to me he may have come on too strong earlier.

After so much drama, this bit of mentoring seemed to do the trick. I had no further run-ins with MSgt Pickett, and I was relatively satisfied with his improved performance over the next couple of months. Nevertheless, as subsequent events would demonstrate, the MTI School commandant and a few co-conspirators continued to plot my downfall behind the scenes.

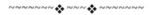

Col. Liddick called me back into her office a few weeks later, on November 18, to deliver some more bad news. "You're not going to like this," she began, before announcing she was transferring my superintendent, SMSgt "LG," to another squadron. She explained that the incumbent 319 TRS superintendent was departing BMT in January, and she needed a replacement as soon as possible. When I objected that her responsibilities as 737 TRSS were at least as demanding and significant as anything she might be asked to do in the 319 TRS, Col. Liddick noted that the 319 TRS superintendent position was an E-9 billet, while my squadron rated only an E-7. This didn't seem like a very good reason for the move, and I couldn't help but wonder if she was simply reassigning SMSgt "LG" to make my life more difficult. My suspicions deepened when I learned my superintendent wasn't the only eligible senior noncommissioned officer available to move. SMSgt Laroy Newhouse, who was then 320 TRS superintendent, had recently been selected for promotion to Chief, and was available to fill the 319 TRS position, but Col. Liddick chose instead to move him to the 37 TRW Inspector General staff. Similarly, SMSgt Watkins was sent to work for 37 TRW/IG around this time, rather than filling the soon-to-be vacant 319 TRS billet.

Thankfully, it would be several weeks before SMSgt "LG" departed the squadron, so we had time to find a replacement. A few days later, the new BMT superintendent, CMSgt Sutherland, came to my office with a suggestion: How about MSgt Chris Bell? He was the second-highest stratified E-7 in the group, after the notorious MSgt Pickett. However, having interviewed MSgt Bell for the MTI School commandant position a few months earlier, and interacting with him in his stan/eval capacity as we prepared for an upcoming compliance inspection, I wasn't sure how good a fit he would be as my senior enlisted leader. My reservations only increased when I spoke to his current squadron commander, who was not impressed with his performance as an instructor supervisor, and indicated he had previously been fired from a superintendent position in a different squadron. On the other hand, no one could argue with his expertise regarding BMT. Selected as "Blue Rope of the Year" in 2000, he'd been an MTI for an astonishing 16 years straight – so long, in fact, that he'd forfeited his primary Air Force Specialty Code. He had also served in several leadership positions in various extracurricular organizations.

CMSgt Sutherland also mentioned MSgt Pickett, the MTI School commandant, and MSgt Daniel Dupont, an MTI from the 331 TRS whom I had also interviewed for that position, while SMSgt "LG" suggested I think about MSgt Chavez, the "Deliberate Development" NCOIC, for the role of superintendent. Needless to say, MSgt Pickett was not a viable option as my senior enlisted leader, while CMSgt Sutherland objected that MSgt Chavez was a Reservist, and he worried MSgt Dupont had arrived too recently at BMT to serve effectively in this position. I had no qualms with either of these gentlemen serving as my superintendent, and I also recognized that when Senior Master Sergeant results were released in March, we'd likely have some new names to consider for this position.

Not surprisingly, Col. Liddick once again rejected my suggestions. The day before Thanksgiving, she came to my office to inform me she was installing her own favored candidate in a key leadership position in my squadron. When I sat down with MSgt Bell to welcome him to the squadron the following week, I took a different tack than I had with MSgt Pickett. I admitted up front that I had heard some not-so-flattering things about him, including that he'd previously been fired as superintendent in a different squadron. (He seemed surprised by this, suggesting either that my information was faulty, or his commander at the time hadn't been entirely honest with him.) However, I continued, I wouldn't hold any of that against him in his new position. I intended to evaluate him solely on his performance as my superintendent, with a clean slate. He seemed to appreciate my candor, and we got along well during the short time I remained in command. And for the record, when promotion results were released a few months later, the new 737 TRSS superintendent's name was on the list.

On the bright side, it was about this time I realized I had a role to play in reestablishing the "Blue Rope" program. AETC published a guidance memorandum in June 2013 outlining MTI training and development standards, but I remained unaware of the existence of this document until November. It designates the 737 TRSS commander as responsible for both the Master Instructor and Master MTI programs at BMT, including appointing program managers, reviewing and endorsing candidate applications, assigning professional projects, and certifying completion of all program requirements.[164] I immediately designated the two senior-most "Blue Ropes," SMSgt "LG" and SMSgt Barron, as the Master MTI program managers, and named MSgt Dupont and TSgt Akeem Parks, an MTI School instructor, to lead the Master Instructor program. When I back-briefed Dr. Munro of my actions, she seemed pleased I was taking such an interest in pushing forward with these programs. The first "Blue Rope" competition under the new standards took place the following month.

Thanksgiving is an important time of year in the 737 TRSS. My squadron organizes "Operation Home Cooking," which has been matching BMT trainees with local families for nearly four decades. Jim Steele and members of the training support flight manage this enormous undertaking, signing up and vetting thousands of volunteers, who come on base to the BMT Reception Center on Thanksgiving Day to claim a pair of lucky trainees (they are never

---

[164] AETC Guidance Memorandum 36-03, *Military Training Instructor Training and Development*, June 11, 2013

without a wingman). All are returned safely by the end of the evening, usually without incident.

Trainees in their final week at BMT are issued town passes for the day, so they may spend Thanksgiving with any family members who have come to see them graduate. On the other hand, most first-week trainees gather for a holiday meal in one of the BMT dining facilities. But several flights of these new recruits are offered a special treat. Since 2007, Cypress Grille, a restaurant in nearby Boerne, Texas, has been opening its doors to a couple of flights – approximately 100 basic trainees – for a gourmet meal. Not to be outdone, the Harley-Davidson dealership in Boerne soon began hosting four BMT flights for a catered Thanksgiving meal, complete with games and free phone calls home.

Traditionally, the 737 TRSS commander would accompany the trainees to Cypress Grille, along with their squadron commander and their respective families, while a handful of MTIs would chaperone the trainees at Javelina Harley-Davidson. In 2013, however, one of my fellow squadron commanders, Lt. Col. Liz Valenzuela, was a "hog driver" who wanted to join the festivities. As a San Antonio native previously assigned to BMT, Liz was familiar with our Thanksgiving tradition, and she wanted to escort her trainees to the Harley dealership. When Mr. Steele learned of her interest, he offered to let her participate. He made sure the trainee flights bound for Javelina were drawn from Liz's squadron, the 326 TRS.

But Lt. Col. Valenzuela wasn't the only motorcycle-riding officer assigned to BMT that year. The deputy group commander, Lt. Col. Upchurch, also owned a Harley, so Liz recommended he join her on this holiday ride. However, Col. Liddick had other ideas. About a week before Thanksgiving, she announced Liz would not be going to Javelina after all, and Lt. Col. Upchurch would accompany the trainees instead. When Liz mentioned this to me the next day, I immediately resolved to get to the bottom of it. Mr. Steele told me Col. Liddick had personally instructed him to drop Lt. Col. Valenzuela in favor of her deputy, so I went straight to Lt. Col. Upchurch to straighten out the situation. He offered a number of excuses why Liz should be left behind. He noted this was his last BMT Thanksgiving before he retired, while Liz had another year in command. I suggested they could both go, but he insisted Liz should really be home with her family. (His stayed up in Idaho throughout his Lackland tour.) I countered that her family was expecting her to be at the Harley-Davidson dealership that day. But what about the MTIs who wouldn't get to come along, he asked? They should be home with their families, I replied.

Miraculously, I actually got my way on this issue. Col. Liddick relented, and allowed both Lt. Col. Upchurch and Lt. Col. Valenzuela to ride to Boerne that day. (Liz's family followed along on one of the buses.) Meanwhile, Lt. Col. Paul Burger, his wife, Laura, and his parents joined Caroline and me on the trip out to Cypress Grille. As our buses pulled into town, local police vehicles escorted us down Main Street, which was lined by cheering citizens showing their support for the troops. Even the mayor showed up to thank the trainees for their service. We had a wonderful time with the trainees, most of whom were away from home for the holidays for their first time. Nevertheless, although Col. Liddick never spoke to me about this issue, I have no doubt she didn't appreciate me standing up for Lt. Col. Valenzuela. Such an act of defiance can't have gone unnoticed.

The day before Thanksgiving, Col. Liddick once again confronted me about the wardrobe moving boxes she felt I had promised her. Caroline and I had brought in many of our boxes at the BMT children's fall festival the previous month, and we intended to use them again for the same purpose in 2014, so we were storing them at the 737 TRSS warehouse on base. (We expected to retrieve these sturdy containers for our next move, after my command tour was complete in 2015.) Earlier that morning, Col. Liddick had informed me she was hiring MSgt Bell over my objections, so when she cornered me about the boxes later that day, I felt I had no choice but to comply. I directed her to the warehouse where she could find the moving supplies, hoping my generosity might actually be appreciated, and perhaps win me favor with my difficult supervisor.

Of course, that's precisely why soliciting or accepting gifts from a subordinate is a violation of federal law. So is offering a gift to a superior – but then again, I never offered, as e-mails between Col. Liddick and I make clear. The final written exchange in this series began later that day, when my boss confirmed she had taken 17 wardrobe boxes, and asked me to deliver the associated hanger bars. I dropped those off in her office the day after Thanksgiving … and made sure to save all the incriminating e-mails for a rainy day.

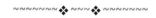

Whatever brownie points I may have accrued for surrendering those wardrobe boxes to Col. Liddick didn't last long. Less than a week later, we were again at odds over a personnel issue in my squadron. Just before Thanksgiving, I had received the results of an end-of-course survey from an MTI School class that recently graduated. When asked if their instructors had established a positive learning environment, one anonymous respondent replied affirmatively, but added a comment about a couple of incidents he or she found "borderline unprofessional," including being "scolded" by the squadron superintendent, SMSgt "LG."

I was already quite familiar with this episode, which occurred back in October. SMSgt "LG" had overheard some MTI students in the restroom complaining about having to participate in mandatory squadron "wingman day" activities. She wasn't sure which students made the comments, so she decided to mentor the entire class on professional behavior. When she told me what she planned to do, I wholeheartedly supported her initiative, and she later back-briefed me on how she handled it. I received the end-of-course critique the following month, and discussed it with the MTI School commandant, MSgt Pickett, who concurred SMSgt "LG" had handled the situation appropriately.

I gave this incident no more thought until I received an e-mail from Col. Liddick on December 4. She indicated a member of the group staff had flagged this critique as evidence of potential "maltreatment" by SMSgt "LG." Col. Liddick asked me to determine if this incident warranted initiating an alleged misconduct report, a special 2 AF investigatory procedure implemented in the wake of the Lackland sex scandal. I assured my boss I was well aware of this situation, and SMSgt "LG" had behaved professionally. Col. Liddick was apparently not convinced, since she then accused SMSgt "LG" of "yelling" and giving the MTI students a "butt chewing," even though the end-of-course survey comment made no such implication. In fact, it did not indicate any kind of maltreatment or other activity covered under instructor misconduct policies.

Without further ado, Col. Liddick launched an inquiry into this incident the following day. She apparently informed the wing commander, Col. Camerer, of the alleged misconduct, and appointed a member of her staff to interview the entire MTI School class. As I expected, none of them claimed SMSgt "LG" yelled, used profanity, or otherwise abused them, although a few didn't

135

appreciate her scolding the entire class for the comments of a few. The following Monday, December 9, Col. Liddick notified me the investigating officer had cleared my superintendent of misconduct. However, I only learned a formal AMR had been generated for this incident the following month, when it appeared on a consolidated misconduct report tracker.

Although Col. Liddick had previously assured me she was supportive of my superintendent, I was starting to get the impression she didn't like SMSgt "LG" very much. For example, when we learned the Department of Defense's "Response Systems Panel" was coming to Lackland in December to discuss the role of commanders in preventing and responding to sexual assault, Col. Liddick indicated that the commanders of four particular squadrons would participate, along with the superintendents of the remaining squadrons. However, the e-mail invitation that followed included representatives from every squadron except the 737 TRSS, so I asked the meeting organizer to invite SMSgt "LG" as well. When this didn't happen, I asked Col. Liddick if there was some reason my squadron was being excluded. She told me it was because neither SMSgt "LG" nor I had much experience handling sexual assault cases. I found this explanation curious, as our squadron then had a pending case of trainee-on-trainee sexual assault; one of our MTIs had been acquitted at court martial of rape several months earlier; and another former MTI had just been released from confinement after a conviction for unprofessional relationships with trainees. But this wouldn't be the last time Col. Liddick would lie to me.

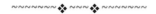

December is the season for holiday parties, and Caroline and I had plenty of shindigs to attend at the end of 2013. My wife had been out of town receiving medical treatment at the Mayo Clinic after Thanksgiving, and returned just in time for the 37 TRW holiday party on December 7. Her hair had recently fallen out due to chemotherapy, so the wives of several other squadron commanders wore scarves or hats to show solidarity with my terminally ill spouse. Col. Liddick seemed to avoid us at this gathering all evening, but Col. Camerer made a point of talking to Caroline. He graciously told her he and his wife, Julie, pray for Caroline by name every night. He also thanked her for coming to BMT graduation parades and other events every week, and for helping make me a great commander. (Caroline insists he actually thanked her for making me "the best commander we have," a compliment impossible to reconcile with his subsequent persecution of me just a few weeks later.)

The next day, we gathered at the BMT Reception Center for the 737 TRG children's holiday party. Each squadron set up various games and other activities, while my wife and one of our Key Spouses operated chocolate fountains for the kids. Besides a visit from Santa Claus, the highlights of the afternoon was a reading of *'Twas the Night Before Christmas* by our very own "Grinch," Col. Liddick, who seemed quite uncomfortable with so many kids around.

A week later, my squadron held its own holiday party at a local hotel resort. As there was no assigned seating, Caroline and I found a place at a table near the center of the room, where we were soon joined by SMSgt "LG" and her husband; the unit chaplain and his wife; and Mrs. Milne and her daughter. Mr. Kamel and SSgt Little, who were both good friends with the Milnes, took the last two empty seats across the table. My operations officer, Maj. Sprouse, arrived late, after most of the seats were taken, and so sat at a different table, while my first sergeant, MSgt Walls, had just returned to town and so did not attend. Col. Camerer and his command chief, and Col. Liddick and her husband, all stopped by for a few minutes early in the evening, but none of them stayed for dinner.

An MTI School instructor, TSgt Brian Fisher, served as master of ceremonies, and he was joined by SSgt Hite in entertaining the crowd throughout the evening. At one point SSgt Hite called me up on stage for an interview, asking me awkward, leading questions to see what kind of response he could get out of me. For example, he asked, "Is there anyone in the squadron you hate?" Thinking this a joke, I denied hating anyone in my unit, but made no promises about anyone else in the group building, which my unit shared with Col. Liddick's staff. The festivities also included a "best dressed" contest among the ladies, where Caroline made quite an impression decked out in her festive blue bob wig. (Although I find my wife irresistible, I was secretly thankful she finished as runner-up, as it might have appeared inappropriate for the commander's wife to beat out my subordinates and their spouses.) Towards the end of the evening, there was a contest to create and decorate a Christmas tree at each table, using any materials available. Our table chose to decorate Mrs. Milne's seven-year-old daughter, but that wasn't the oddest aspect of this game: for some reason, MSgt Pickett chose to abandon his table to join our group for this event, presumably either to insinuate himself with his commander or to keep an eye on his subordinate, SSgt Little.

After the party, several members of my squadron invited Caroline and me to join them in the hotel bar. I saw no harm in this, as it would allow me to keep an eye on things as our unit event wound down. Not surprisingly, TSgt Fisher, SSgt Hite, and their wives were there, along with another MTI – the president of the TRSS Private Organization, which sponsored the party – and her husband. SMSgt "LG" also dropped in with her husband, as well as the inseparable Mr. Kamel and SSgt Little. The evening ended without incident, and everyone made it home safe.

The following week, Caroline and I attended one last holiday party, for the 320th Training Squadron. But we weren't there as guests; rather, we and a few other folks volunteered to babysit the unit's children upstairs in the BMT Reception Center.

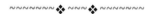

The primary source of income for the TRSS Private Organization, my squadron's booster club, was periodic five-kilometer "fun runs" held on base around the BMT campus. A retired Army officer, Ray Kenny, started this tradition more than two decades earlier, when he was assigned to the Defense Language Institute Foreign Language Center at Lackland AFB. In addition to marketing and course management, he and his wife, Carole, would provide t-shirts and race bibs for participants, plus trophies for the winners, through her firm, "Carrie & Company." Over the years, these 5K runs came to be associated with BMT, and my squadron eventually assumed responsibility for organizing these races, with most proceeds going to the TRSS Private Organization and various charities.

I was introduced to the Kennys at a BMT 5K event held soon after I assumed command. Mr. Kenny followed up with an office call in early August, to which I invited my subject-matter experts, Jim Steele and Laurie Pozorski. I soon discovered my staff was concerned about some of Carrie & Company's business practices, and they often found the Kennys unresponsive to BMT requirements. In late 2012, in fact, they attempted to switch vendors, but Mr. Kenny convinced my predecessor, Lt. Col.

Granstrom, to maintain the arrangement I inherited. In my conversations with Mr. Kenny, however, he always made it clear that he looked to me, as 737 TRSS commander, to have the final word regarding the program.

After careful consideration, I decided it was not in the government's interest to continue relying exclusively on a single vendor for all race support. There had never been a contract in place for the services provided by Carrie & Company, so I proposed that we hire a different vendor for the upcoming race in January so we could determine if we were getting the best value for our money. When Ms. Pozorski informed Mrs. Kenny of this proposed change on December 10, Mr. Kenny insisted on meeting with me the following day. During that meeting, he made numerous allegations impugning the integrity of my staff, while reiterating that he respected the chain of command and my role as commander. He asked me to get back with him later that week or early the next week to discuss the issue further. He later dropped off a sealed package marked "EYES ONLY Lt. Col. Perry," containing a 37-page report outlining his position in this matter.

That weekend, we conducted another 5K race. As usual, the Kennys were there providing logistical support, and helping Col. Liddick and me hand out trophies (I once again took home a prize in my age category). The following Monday, December 16, I sent an e-mail to Col. Liddick indicating my squadron would be making a few changes to how we managed the 5K runs in 2014. In response, she simply wrote, "pls come see me before we may [*sic*] the change official."[165]

As requested, I met with my boss soon afterwards, right outside her office. During our short conversation, she accused me of "threatening the livelihood of a small business" – Carrie & Company – and she claimed the vendor we had selected for the next race – Basic Video Productions, the company responsible for producing weekly BMT graduation videos – was involved in a "scam" with BMT. Finally, she inexplicably asserted only she had the authority to make changes to the program, since it was her signature on the request seeking approval for the races. This was the first time she had ever spoken to me about the 5K runs, or indicated she exercised any authority over the races.

---

[165] E-mail exchange with Col. Liddick, "5K way-ahead," December 16, 2013

Col. Liddick was referring to an electronic staff summary sheet I submitted to her for coordination back in August, seeking approval from base leadership for BMT 5K runs in calendar year 2014. The eSSS clearly stated that the 737 TRSS scheduling section (Ms. Pozorski's shop) hosts and is responsible for all run operations, and proceeds go to the TRSS Private Organization or other designated charities. It did not specify which, if any, vendor we would utilize to support the races. Col. Liddick coordinated on this eSSS indicating her concurrence on September 9 – but it was my signature, not hers, at the bottom of the form.[166]

When I met with Mr. Kenny again the next day, I informed him we would not, in fact, be switching vendors for the race in January as we had previously indicated. However, I did not share with him any details of my conversation with my boss, or indicate to him that she claimed to be in charge of the program. Mr. Kenny repeated his allegations about members of my staff, which I found to be unprofessional and inappropriate coming from a vendor seeking to do business with the government. He also insisted he had not shared his concerns with anyone but me and Lt. Col. Granstrom. This was clearly not true, as he had evidently spoken to Col. Liddick about this issue at the event that weekend. I expressed my disappointment that a vendor who had faithfully supported BMT for over two decades would so adamantly oppose our suggested changes, and I suggested to him it had been a mistake to lie to me and betray my trust in this way when we have no contractual obligation to his company. Our heated confrontation ended with me asking him to leave my office; he apparently proceeded directly from there to my boss's office down the hall.

Col. Liddick called a meeting that Friday, December 20, to discuss the way ahead for the BMT 5K races. Ironically, she proposed that we conduct future BMT 5Ks "in house," with little or no reliance on outside vendors. Mr. Steele, Ms. Pozorski, and I quickly developed a plan, which I shared with Col. Liddick and the other stakeholders via e-mail on December 24. Had we implemented her guidance as directed, we would have been able to cut trainee entrance fees nearly in half, while still raising just as much money for the TRSS Private Organization and charity.[167] But

---

[166] Electronic staff summary sheet for 2014 5K runs, August 30, 2013

[167] E-mail to Col. Liddick, "BMT 5K vector," December 24, 2013

this exercise was apparently just for show: Col. Liddick made no change to the races, which remained in the hands of Carrie & Company for the next nine months, until her successor finally pulled the plug.

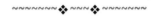

In the wake of the Lackland sex scandal, Air Education and Training Command implemented more stringent policies regarding personnel information files. The AETC commander issued a policy letter in October 2012 directing that "units must establish PIFs to document general misconduct, substandard performance and other derogatory information on all permanent party officer and enlisted members assigned to AETC." It also established the policy that "PIFs should transfer with the individual during intracommand reassignments."[168] The Second Air Force commander issued a separate policy letter in November 2012 directing 2 AF units to establish internal procedures to "ensure that PIFs, and all contents, transfer with the military instructor upon all transfers of position within AETC. All contents within the PIF must remain in the PIF upon change of supervisors."[169]

Air Force policy memoranda such as these expire after no more than year, so both AETC and 2 AF later republished their PIF policies in more permanent formats. In September 2013, 2 AF issued a guidance memorandum requiring all training wings institute and maintain internal policies for PIF review, but the new policy did not include any reference to retention of PIF contents, or specify how long derogatory information remains in a PIF.[170] AETC reiterated in December 2013 that units must "establish and maintain" PIFs for derogatory information, and specified circumstances when commanders and supervisors must review the PIF, but also made no reference to how long derogatory

---

[168] Gen. Rice, "Personnel Information Files (PIF) Policy," October 6, 2012

[169] Maj. Gen. Patrick, "Policy Regarding Review of Personnel Information Files (PIFs),"
November 8, 2012

[170] 2 AF Guidance Memorandum 36-01, *Standards of Conduct and Training*, September 17, 2013

information remains in a PIF, or who has the authority to remove such information from a PIF.[171]

Meanwhile, we continued to operate at Lackland as if the original policy memos were still in effect, relying on our chain of command to interpret policies issued by higher headquarters. For example, in late September Col. Liddick clarified that unsubstantiated alleged misconduct reports should not be placed in PIFs, and authorized commanders to remove any that had previously been filed. Around the same time, we were informed during a 2AF "BMT 101" training course that squadron commanders have the authority to add or remove items from PIFs, as "the pendulum is slowly swinging back." (It turns out these instructions came straight out of the new 2 AF guidance memorandum, but we were not made aware of the existence of this document until early January 2014.) In another meeting in late October or early November, Col. Liddick explicitly authorized her commanders to remove derogatory information from PIFs so long as the paperwork did not concern misconduct addressed by an AMR (for example, a letter of counseling for simply being late to work), and the issue had already been addressed in the member's performance report. Based on her guidance, several squadron commanders later removed documents from PIFs, including Lt. Col. Gallagher, Lt. Col. Lam, and Lt. Col. Valenzuela.

On December 20, 2013, it was my turn. It had always bothered me that my squadron superintendent, SMSgt "LG," had a letter of reprimand in her file issued by Col. Liddick the previous March, for nothing more than a minor administrative oversight. While I could do nothing to correct this particular injustice, I could at least remove this document from her PIF in accordance with Col. Liddick's instructions, as the LOR wasn't the result of an AMR, and it had already been reflected by a mark-down on her previous enlisted performance report before I assumed command. Moreover, SMSgt "LG" had performed superbly in my squadron, and I knew she was held in high regard by the previous BMT superintendent, CMSgt Williams. The current group chief, CMSgt Sutherland, also expressed his support to me for keeping SMSgt "LG" at BMT long enough to put the mark-down behind her and make her competitive for promotion. Even Col. Liddick once told me she felt SMSgt "LG" had fully recovered from her earlier

---

[171] AETCI 36-2909, *Recruiting, Education, and Training Standards of Conduct*, December 2, 2013

setback. Considering all this, I saw no reason not to remove the LOR before she transferred to another unit.

On her final day in the 737 TRSS, I removed my superintendent's LOR from her PIF. I asked the unit program coordinator, Cynthia Coleman, to update the contents log, and I locked the LOR in a drawer in my office for safekeeping. (I felt it best not to actually destroy this document just yet, in case Col. Liddick reversed herself.) Four days later, Col. Liddick called me into her office and asked what happened to SMSgt "LG"'s PIF. I confirmed I had removed the LOR but still had it in my office. When she asked why I had done this, I reminded her about how she had previously authorized us to remove non-AMR materials from PIFs. She angrily denied having given such guidance.

After the meeting, I e-mailed my fellow BMT squadron commanders to confirm my recollection of our boss's PIF policy, which several of them did. But that Friday, Col. Liddick sent an e-mail reminding them about the (expired) AETC and 2 AF policy letters, with the following bottom line: "pls do not remove anything from the PIF!" She didn't copy me on the e-mail, however, as she'd already removed me from command the previous day.

One of the aspects of command I most enjoyed was the opportunity it offered my wife and me to be magnanimous. As the senior-ranking officer in the unit, I felt a responsibility to care for my subordinates and their families – and thankfully we had the resources to do so. Caroline and I picked out the floor plan for our house with the intention of hosting frequent get-togethers for my squadron. We began buying baby gifts long before the TRSS Private Organization offered to reimburse us, and my wife never asked for compensation for her home-cooked meals for the unit. Such generosity simply felt like the right thing to do for an officer in my position.

Whenever a special event came to town, we were in the habit of buying extra tickets to share with others. For example, I bought four tickets to a friendly match between the U.S. women's national soccer team and Australia at the Alamodome, intending to give the second pair away. First dibs went to my father, who is a rabid soccer fanatic and used to coach me in high school, but he already had seats. When I learned my Key Spouse, SMSgt "LG"'s husband, was a soccer coach, I offered the tickets to him – but he, too, already had plans to go. In the end, we took the wife and daughter of one of my fellow squadron commanders, Lt. Col. Arndt, with us to the game.

Similarly, when we heard the Moscow Ballet would be performing their "Great Russian Nutcracker" later that year downtown at the Majestic Theatre, we again purchased extra tickets. Caroline and I like to attend "The Nutcracker" each holiday season, and we'd enjoyed seeing this particular ballet company the previous year in Baltimore, Maryland. What I was really looking forward to, however, was returning to the Majestic, a magnificent National Historic Landmark built in 1929. I initially offered the extra tickets to my friends on Facebook in early November, but there were no takers. Later that month, Caroline and I were in a holiday party planning meeting with my superintendent and a couple of TRSS Private Organization officers, when the conversation turned to door prizes. Out of the blue, SMSgt "LG" mentioned she thought tickets to a show at the Majestic would make a great door prize, as this was somewhere she'd always wanted to go.

Since SMSgt "LG" would soon be transferring to a different squadron, Caroline and I decided our tickets would be a fitting going-away gift for her and her husband for all their service to the squadron. They accepted our offer, and accompanied us to the show on Monday, December 23 – three days after my now-former superintendent formally left the squadron and ceased being my subordinate. We had a wonderful time that evening, and never imagined this innocuous social engagement would later be used against us.

Our last opportunity to socialize with my subordinates came on Christmas Day, on what turned out to be my last full day in command. We were across town at my aunt's house finishing up our holiday meal when Caroline noticed a troubling Facebook post by MSgt Chavez. He shared a picture of a half-eaten sandwich, a soda, and a book, with the caption, "Feeling defeated." When Caroline messaged him, he indicated he was alone for the holiday, but might go see his grandmother later that evening. My wife invited him to stop by our house on his way, and he accepted. We rushed home, Caroline whipped up her famous green chile chicken enchiladas, and we watched "Rudolph the Red Nosed Reindeer" together while enjoying the holiday spirit.

But this holiday spirit didn't last long. The next day, Col. Liddick removed me from command.

~~~~~~~~ ❖ ~~~ ❖ ~~~~~~~~

Six months later, I bid a belated and bittersweet farewell to the squadron I once led. This e-mail I sent to my former subordinates succinctly sums up my feelings about my short tenure at the helm of the 737 TRSS:

Raptors, it's been far too long since I last spoke to most of you – the no-contact order which prevented us from reaching out to each other during this difficult period was lifted just three weeks ago. It saddens me that I was not able to bid you a proper farewell as your squadron commander. I am honored to have had the opportunity to lead the 737th Training Support Squadron, and to work with such a remarkable group of absolute professionals. In our short time together, we skillfully accomplished our critical mission, providing superior operations support, personnel processing, medical response, and instructor development to Basic Military Training. Our diverse and talented team selflessly supported the foundational development of tens of thousands of world-class Warrior Airmen. I will forever be proud of what we accomplished during my tour in the TRSS.

Most of all, I feel like we left the TRSS better than we found it. Last summer, I took command of a squadron where many sections felt neglected or ignored, so my wonderful wife, Caroline, and I focused on improving unit cohesion and esprit de corps. I'd like to think my frequent "walkabouts" in each of your work centers, Caroline's home-cooked catered luncheons, periodic squadron PT, even the selection of our awesome squadron mascot brought us closer to this goal. We paid particular attention to our large civilian workforce, which suffered disproportionately due to sequestration and the government shutdown, and coordinated closely with the TRSS Private Organization to serve the needs of all its members. And we undeniably improved the family support network, establishing an exceptional Key Spouse program which was recognized last year by Gen. Rand and earned one of our spouses a wing-level annual award.

145

Unfortunately, I won't be able to finish what we started. I have been held accountable for allegedly violating an administrative policy, saying things that were perceived to undermine command authority, and giving some folks the impression that I favored certain subordinates over others. As a squadron commander, I was naturally held to a very high standard, and regrettably I lost the confidence of our chain of command. I am deeply disappointed to have made the mistakes I did, and fallen so short of my superiors' expectations during my time in the TRSS. But let me reassure you – there is no truth to any rumors you may have heard that I engaged in more serious misconduct. The wing commander himself declared that I didn't do anything illegal, immoral, or anything like that, and the Air Force Times published an article on the subject over the weekend which has already gone viral (http://www.airforcetimes.com/article/20140531/NEWS/3 05310038/). My integrity remains intact, and my conscience is clear.

I truly enjoyed my time in command of the TRSS, and I have no regrets about the direction my leadership team and I were taking the squadron. I am proud of how well you fared during the AETC compliance inspection, and I'm certain you are tackling other challenges – including the RFIIC move and absorbing the 324 TRS transition flight – head on. And I know you will welcome your new commander as warmly as Caroline and I were received. I sincerely appreciate the support of those of you who stood by us throughout this ordeal. We wish y'all luck with whatever comes next ... the TRSS may be unseen, but you're always on target![172]

---

[172] E-mail to members of the 737 TRSS, "Unseen, on target," June 2, 2014

Chapter 6: Waiting for the Other Shoe

The day after Christmas 2013, I received an unexpected phone call from the deputy group commander, Lt. Col. Upchurch. He told me Col. Liddick wanted to meet with me at noon, and she also wanted to see my operations officer, Maj. Rob Sprouse. I had given Rob the day off to spend time with his family, but Lt. Col. Upchurch insisted we call him in to work.

I headed down the hall to Col. Liddick's office at the appointed hour, and she got right down to business. She handed me a copy of a restraining order, which directed me to "refrain from contact with any and all military, civilian, and contracted members of the 737th Training Support Squadron." Additionally, I was to "reframe [sic] from contacting" my former squadron superintendent, SMSgt "LG," "form [sic] the 319th Training Squadron." Col. Liddick said I was the subject of an ongoing commander-directed investigation, and she ordered me "not to discuss any case under investigation" with any member of the 737th Training Group.[173]

I was flabbergasted. What investigation? Who ordered it? What were the allegations? With a straight face, Col. Liddick claimed it was her boss, Col. Camerer, who initiated the CDI, but she didn't know what the allegations were, exactly. Incredulous, I asked if I had been relieved of command. No, I was just temporarily removed, she responded. Maj. Sprouse would run the squadron while the investigation ran its course, and I would be relocated elsewhere on base until this was all resolved. Although it was fine for me to speak to other squadron commanders, she also advised me not to talk to her former superintendent, CMSgt (ret.) Williams. Before she dismissed me, Col. Liddick suggested I get in touch with the area defense counsel for legal representation.

The group commander then turned me over to my new "wingman," Lt. Col. Upchurch, who monitored me as I collected my laptop and other belongings from my office. We convoyed in our personal vehicles over to Medina Annex, a separate part of the base several miles away from BMT, where I was set up in a small, windowless office in the 342d Training Squadron. This would be my new home for the next three months.

---

[173] Col. Deborah Liddick, "No Contact Order," December 26, 2013

The next morning, I again met with Col. Liddick. I told her about a rumor I'd heard, that MSgt Pickett was insisting my no-contact order also applied to my wife, and his subordinates had a "duty to report" any attempted contact by either of us. She denied having issued such an order regarding my wife, or even discussing my situation with anyone but Maj. Sprouse. She also reiterated she didn't know what the allegations were – or rather, that she hadn't read them.

Later that day, Col. Liddick called the other squadron commanders into her office to announce I had been removed from command and was under investigation. When one of them asked her what the allegations were, she once again claimed not to know. (I'm told Lt. Col. Chad Gallagher laughed out loud at this ridiculous assertion, probably figuring there's no way Col. Liddick would remove one of her commanders without at least knowing why. He was apparently later counseled for this outburst.)

Lt. Col. John Gondol reportedly asked Col. Liddick to clarify her policy on removing documents from personnel information files, probably suspecting this was one of the reasons behind my removal. Col. Liddick stated no one was to remove anything from a PIF, and again insisted she had never given us permission to do so. At this point, Lt. Col. Liz Valenzuela reminded her of a particular case where the group commander had, in fact, authorized her to remove paperwork on someone in her squadron. (I later learned Col. Camerer tacked on a PIF-related allegation to my ongoing CDI that very same day.)

That evening, two of my colleagues, Lt. Col. Valenzuela and Lt. Col. Dat Lam, and their wives came over to our house to console Caroline and me. Both commanders were sympathetic to my plight, as each had been a frequent target of Col. Liddick's abuse. Caroline suggested the only thing that would save me is if enough of the commanders banded together and took their concerns up the chain of command. Col. Camerer was obviously part of the problem, and his boss, Major General Patrick, was stationed at Keesler AFB in Mississippi. That left General Rand, commander of Air Education and Training Command, whose headquarters was across town at JBSA-Randolph. If only he knew how toxic the leadership environment was at Lackland, he'd be sure to intervene. Or so we reassured ourselves that evening.

I can say with confidence that each and every one of the BMT squadron commanders considered Col. Liddick the worst commander they had ever worked for. (Each of them had said as much to either my wife or me.) But that didn't mean they all had the courage to take a stand. As much as they might sympathize with me during the investigation, and quietly support me behind the scenes, most of them were unwilling to say or do anything that might endanger their own careers or risk their retirement pension. This is why toxic leaders so often get away with abusing their subordinates: no good deed goes unpunished.

Over the next few months, I continued meeting with my fellow squadron commanders during our regularly scheduled weekly breakfast at the base golf course – they were unwilling to extend an invitation to Maj. Sprouse while I was under investigation, much to Col. Liddick's chagrin. Inevitably, however, as the CDI dragged on, my relationships with most of my former colleagues became increasingly strained. The Gallaghers invited Caroline and me to their New Year's Eve party, and we watched the Super Bowl with the Lams, but before long the invitations stopped coming. Worse, Caroline was ostracized by some of the other spouses, who had so recently pledged their undying friendship. Loretta Gallagher and Jen Arndt were the first to go, "unfriending" my wife on Facebook and spreading rumors about her to the other spouses. When Caroline extended an invitation to lunch with the wives, Jen responded she had "no free time for the foreseeable future" almost three weeks before the event. Two by two, almost all of these couples distanced themselves from the pariahs they once called friends.

Still, Caroline persevered in representing herself as a dutiful commander's wife. She attended a going-away luncheon for an MTI School instructor, where she was warmly greeted by most of my subordinates (with the notable exception of Maj. Sprouse and MSgt Pickett). Although we naturally weren't invited to the 37 TRW annual awards banquet, Caroline reached out afterward to members of my squadron to congratulate them on winning. Having first cleared it with the 737 TRG protocol officer, Nancy Conley, my wife made an appearance at a weekly BMT graduation parade as she so often did – but Col. Liddick's reaction suggested it would be better if she stayed away until my CDI wrapped up. Ms. Conley also included Caroline on an e-mail requesting assistance encouraging spouses to attend a town hall meeting with the wives of the wing's senior leaders, but there wasn't much my wife could do, as the 737

TRSS Key Spouse program had quickly collapsed in her short absence. Nevertheless, my first sergeant, MSgt Walls, inexplicably reached out to Caroline to see if she wanted to continue presenting gift baskets to new mothers in the squadron, until she apparently thought better of it. We suspected at the time – and the report of investigation later confirmed – that my first sergeant was one of the principal witnesses against me, so this offer seemed a bit insincere.

Caroline even accepted an invitation to lunch with Julie Camerer, the wing commander's better half, in January. Julie seemed surprised to hear folks were concerned about Col. Liddick's leadership, as Debbie always seemed so "well put together," and her husband felt she had "all her ducks in a row." When she hosted a brunch for BMT squadron commanders' spouses the following month, my wife made sure to attend. As the ladies discussed ways to improve morale in their respective units, Caroline offered a cautionary tale: "Be very careful about what you do, because it can be misconstrued and made into something ugly." She gave the example of taking soup to an airman recovering from surgery, which was later used against me as evidence of favoritism. "That's not why he's in trouble," Julie was overheard saying under her breath to Lesia Fisher, the vice wing commander's wife. "You don't get in trouble just for that."

Obtaining a lawyer turned out to be more difficult than I anticipated. When I went by the local Lackland area defense counsel, they informed me they couldn't represent me. As a squadron commander, I had pursued disciplinary action against several subordinates, who turned to the local ADC for help. Since I might return to duty and do it again, it would be a conflict of interest for them to take my case. I would have to request an ADC from a different base. As it turned out, Lt. Col. Valenzuela had previously been in a similar situation, when Col. Camerer launched a CDI against her over a frivolous allegation. She beat the rap with the help of an attorney stationed at Altus AFB, Oklahoma, who was now quite familiar with the senior leaders persecuting me. I reached out to this Captain to represent me as well.

Obtaining the allegations against me proved harder still. Day after day I sat alone in that windowless office, having no clear idea of what I'd been accused. Not that I didn't have my suspicions.

Clearly my former superintendent, SMSgt "LG," was involved somehow – why else would I have been specifically ordered not to contact her? I also guessed removing paperwork from her personnel information file had something to do with it, since Col. Liddick had brought up the PIF policy when she notified the other squadron commanders about my removal. Then there was that time the MTI School commandant, MSgt Pickett, complained about me – but we had settled that issue months earlier, right?

After more than a week had passed with no word about my fate, I went ahead and e-mailed Col. Camerer directly. I explained that no one had contacted me regarding the CDI or notified me of the allegations they were examining, and respectfully requested he put me in touch with the investigating officer so I could clear up any misunderstandings. Col. Camerer replied that I should be patient, but I soon received word through my ADC that my wing commander didn't at all appreciate me reaching out to him.

A few days later, I had another chance to communicate with Col. Camerer in person. His nomination for promotion to Brigadier General was announced that week, so he threw a party for himself that Friday at the Gateway Club, across the street from the wing headquarters. (Ironically, that was the same day Col. Camerer's son graduated from BMT, his accomplishment now overshadowed by his father's unexpected – and some would say undeserved – good fortune.) Everyone who was anyone was there: general officers and wing commanders from across the base; 37th Training Wing group and squadron leadership; even the officer I had since learned was leading my investigation, Lt. Col. Matthew McConnell, deputy commander of one the wing's technical training groups.

Caroline and I joined the throngs of well-wishers at the club that day, awkwardly exchanging pleasantries with my colleagues. When we finally inched our way to the head of the receiving line, all Brig. Gen. (sel.) Camerer had to say to me was "hang in there." Those were the last words the wing commander would speak to me until he issued me a letter of reprimand two months later. Somehow he lost confidence in my ability to lead my squadron without ever bothering to talk to me or hear my side of the story.

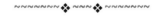

Finally, on January 13, 2014 – nearly three weeks after the CDI began – Lt. Col. McConnell sent me a list of the allegations he was investigating, as well as several pages of questions he wanted me to answer. I didn't realize it at the time, but the investigating officer had already interviewed at least 18 witnesses by this point, so he had a very good idea of the nature and scope of the evidence in my case. Yet his questioning gave no hint of some of the more scandalous accusations made against me, and I was offered no opportunity to defend myself against baseless rumors and easily refuted claims.

Altogether, there were five official allegations against me:

1. Between on or about 6 September 2013 and on or about 16 December 2013, Lieutenant Colonel Craig Perry, 737 TRSS, JBSA-Lackland, Texas, undermined the command authority of Colonel Deborah J. Liddick, 737 TRG/CC when he made comments in staff meetings regarding her involvement in the official functions of the 737 TRSS in violation of Article 92 and/or 134, Uniform Code of Military Justice.

2. Between on or about 6 September 2013 and on or about 16 December 2013, Lieutenant Colonel Craig Perry, 737 TRSS, JBSA-Lackland, Texas, undermine the command authority of Colonel Deborah J. Liddick, 737 TRG/CC when he made statements to Mr. Raymond C Kenny, Jr., about an official 737 TRG function in violation of Article 92 and/or 134, Uniform Code of Military Justice.

3. Between on or about 6 September 2013 and on or about 14 December 2013, Lieutenant Colonel Craig Perry, 737 TRSS, JBSA-Lackland, Texas, engaged in unprofessional relationships with enlisted personnel in his organization and/or interacted with select personnel in his unit on terms of military equality in violation of AFI 1-1, paragraph 2.2 and AFI 36-2909, paragraph 2.2 and Article 92 and/or 134, Uniform Code of Military Justice.

4. Between on or about 6 September 2013 and on or about 16 December 2013, Lieutenant Colonel Craig Perry, 737 TRSS, JBSA-Lackland, Texas, make [sic] comments and/or engage [sic] in actions that demonstrated lack of support for the 37th Training Wing's current initiatives with regard to basic military training in violation of Article 134, Uniform Code of Military Justice.

5. On or about 24 December 2013, Lieutenant Colonel Craig Perry, 737 TRSS, JBSA-Lackland, Texas, directed the destruction of the Personnel Information File (PIF) on [SMSgt "LG"] in violation of AETC/CC's Personnel Information File (PIF) Policy, dated 16 October 2012 and 2 AF/CC's Policy Regarding Review of Personnel Information Files (PIFs), dated 8 November 2012.[174]

I was apparently under investigation for failing to obey lawful general orders or regulations (Article 92), or engaging in conduct that constituted "a disorder or neglect to the prejudice of good order and discipline in the armed forces, or of a nature to bring discredit upon the armed forces" (Article 134). Also, I was facing charges of pursuing relationships with subordinates that "detract from the authority of superiors or result in, or reasonably create the appearance of, favoritism, misuse of office or position, or the abandonment of organizational goals for personal interests,"[175] even going so far as to fraternize with certain enlisted members, a crime under the UCMJ. Finally, I stood accused of violating policy letters written over a year earlier.

The accompanying list of 50 questions offered a little more insight into the nature of these allegations. For example, I was asked to confirm if I made comments to members of my squadron "that were intended to or could be reasonably interpreted as undermining the command authority of Col. Liddick or anyone else" in my chain of command, such as:

"I thought I was the commander, not her," as it pertained to Col. Liddick making decisions affecting personnel in or the activities of the 737 TRSS

"Col. Liddick is too involved in squadron matters"

---

[174] Allegations against Lt. Col. Perry, January 13, 2014
[175] Air Force Instruction 36-2909, *Professional and Unprofessional Relationships*, May 1, 1999

153

I was *"unconcerned with going against Col. Liddick's wishes"* because I was retirement eligible or because I already had 19 years of service

"I will wait her out"

"She will be gone in 6 months and I will still be here for a year and a half"

Mr. Kenny *"hitched his wagon to the wrong star"*

I was also asked about comments I allegedly made that were "intended to or could be reasonably interpreted as demonstrating a lack of support of initiatives with regard to BMT":

> *"Officers do not belong in BMT"*
>
> *"MTIs are not allowed to be MTIs anymore and they aren't allowed to do their job"*
>
> *"A Director of Operations is not necessary in the 737 TRSS"*
>
> I *"don't know what to do with a Director of Operations"*

I was even asked to answer for comments allegedly made by others, including *"Col. Liddick lacks self-confidence in her leadership, so she always hires Maintenance people who she knows and can control,"* and *"Here at BMT, we don't need the officers and Chiefs, all we need is MTIs and getting back to basics."* It was not at all clear, however, how any of these alleged statements served to undermine the group commander's authority.

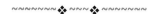

At last, here was my long-awaited opportunity to explain my side of the story. I immediately drafted responses to each of the investigating officer's questions, but my ADC advised me not to take the bait so quickly. Instead, she suggested I address just the official allegations, and leave any more detailed answers for the in-person interview. Three days later I sent Lt. Col. McConnell a seven-page rebuttal.

I reported to the 37 TRG headquarters building for my interview with the investigating officer one week later, on January 22. After some initial small talk, we retreated to the group conference room and dialed up my ADC on the speakerphone so she could advise me during my interrogation. Lt. Col. McConnell pretty much stuck to the script he'd provided me the previous week, with perhaps a dozen additional questions based on my initial written response. At the time, I felt confident I had cleared up any misunderstandings about my conduct, and this ordeal would soon be over.

Before I could leave, however, the investigating officer had to hand me off to someone in my chain of command – a standard precaution to keep distraught suspects from harming themselves or others. While I waited for my designated "wingman," Lt. Col. Upchurch, to arrive, I noticed SSgt Tommy Little outside the investigating officer's office. I guessed he was there to sign his official witness statement for my CDI. When I returned to my office-in-exile that afternoon, I sent Lt. Col. McConnell a copy of the answers I had previously accomplished. The following day, he provided me a consolidated summary of my interview, and I returned to his office to sign my official statement on January 24. (I later learned his final report of investigation closed out on this same date, suggesting my testimony had little impact on the investigating officer's conclusions.)

I assumed it wouldn't be much longer before this whole issue was resolved, and I could get back to work. As it turned out, however, it took more than six weeks for me to learn which allegations against me had been substantiated. At the time, I suspected this delay was because Col. Liddick wasn't happy with the preliminary CDI findings, which I imagined confirmed I hadn't actually done anything wrong. After the acquittal of TSgt Gayden, she reportedly expressed frustration that a "rapist" in my squadron had gone free as a result of an "OJ Simpson" defense, but this time she would make sure the charges stuck. My suspicions were reinforced when I learned Lt. Col. McConnell had made several appointments on Col. Liddick's calendar during the course of the investigation, and he was observed meeting with the 737 TRG commander on multiple occasions. Unless these two were carrying on an unprofessional relationship of their own, it seems likely Col. Liddick was meeting with the investigating officer to discuss my case, potentially exercising undue command influence. Nevertheless, Lt. Col. McConnell's report of investigation indicated he met with this witness only once, and he purportedly made no changes to the report during the subsequent six weeks.

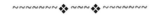

In the meantime, I sat alone in my windowless office, day after day, with no assigned duties. I was still barred from contacting anyone in my squadron, or discussing any case under investigation with personnel assigned to BMT. In practice, this meant avoiding my usual haunts, such as the BMT shoppette or various lunch spots around Lackland, but at least I had plenty of time to train for an upcoming Austin half-marathon on the hills of Medina Annex.

When Col. Liddick scheduled a BMT commander's call for January 29, ahead of an AETC inspection the following month, I was faced with a dilemma. Should I attend this mandatory function, and risk running into some of my off-limits subordinates? Or should I stay away, and potentially face additional charges for failure to go to an appointed place of duty? I didn't put it past my group commander to set a trap like this for me, and it would do me good to be around people again, so I decided to show up that morning accompanied by a chaperone, Lt. Col. Valenzuela, who volunteered to run interference with any of my subordinates who tried to speak with me. While this seemingly satisfied the terms of my no-contact order, my group leadership didn't approve. When Col. Liddick spotted me in the lobby at the BMT Reception Center, she sent her deputy to confront me. Lt. Col. Upchurch proceeded to yell at me in front of the crowd, before kicking me out of the event.

The AETC Inspector General team soon rolled into Lackland, setting up shop in some unused offices in the very same building where I had been exiled at Medina Annex. My squadron fared well in the unit effectiveness inspection, and two elements – the MTI School and the instructor corps – earned excellent ratings. As part of their inspection, the IG team assembled representative panels of BMT personnel to discuss unit climate. When I heard a rumor that Maj. Potter, the 326 TRS operations officer, had denounced Col. Liddick in one of these meetings for the toxic leadership environment she created, I was inspired to speak out as well. Just before the inspection wrapped up, I made my way upstairs to meet with the AETC/IG, Col. Christopher Richardson, on February 7. While he obviously couldn't comment on the merits of my numerous grievances with Col. Liddick, I got the impression he, too, didn't like her very much, and he encouraged me to file a formal complaint. And so, two weeks later, I submitted more than a dozen allegations of reprisal, abuse of authority, unprofessional relationships, harassment of subordinates, and legal and policy violations involving my chain of command. (How this and other IG complaints were mishandled is the subject of Chapter 12.)

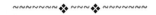

After more than 10 weeks in limbo, I was finally summoned to report to the wing commander on Monday, March 10. I feared this delay did not bode well for me. I was hopeful the CDI hadn't substantiated any of the allegations against me, but I worried Col. Liddick or Col. Camerer may have encouraged the investigating officer to modify his findings. It took quite a while for the Lackland legal office to complete its eight-page review of my CDI, a reflection, perhaps, of the investigation's poor quality. On the other hand, I was cautiously optimistic Col. Camerer had come to his senses after his selection for promotion, and would think twice before firing a squadron commander for anything short of serious misconduct or gross incompetence. After all, it was rumored that several current and retired general officers had weighed in on my behalf, both directly with Col. Camerer and with his superiors at AETC and the Pentagon, urging moderation in my case. (I had even reached out to the JBSA commander, Brig. Gen. Robert LaBrutta, to intervene on behalf of SMSgt "LG," his former subordinate, but he declined to get involved.) Would any of this make a difference?

I wore my service dress uniform that day, in keeping with military tradition when facing possible disciplinary action, and observed another Air Force tradition by sporting cheesy facial hair in celebration of "Mustache March." My wife, Caroline, came along for moral support. Lt. Col. Upchurch arrived soon after we did, but my commander, Col. Liddick, apparently couldn't be bothered to witness my reckoning. After several minutes I was ushered into Col. Camerer's office, joined by Lt. Col. Upchurch and Col. Oler, the Lackland staff judge advocate. I proceeded directly to the wing commander's desk, formally reported as ordered, and stood there at attention as Col. Camerer read aloud from my letter of reprimand:

> *A Commander Directed Investigation substantiated three serious allegations against you. First, between September and December 2013, you wrongfully made statements undermining the command authority of the 737th Training Group Commander. These statements caused members of*

your unit to question your conduct, to the prejudice of good order and discipline within your squadron. Second, during that same period, you engaged in conduct with subordinate personnel that created the appearance of unprofessional relationships and favoritism. This behavior had a tangible, direct, negative impact on members of your unit by creating an impression of partiality, which negatively affected good order and discipline inside your unit. Lastly, in December 2013, in contravention of established policy that you are aware of, you wrongfully removed a Letter of Reprimand from a Personnel Information File; the wrongfulness of this action at the time was reflected by your decision to maintain the removed document in your locked desk.

You are hereby reprimanded! As a field grade officer, and more importantly as a squadron commander, you must maintain an exemplary standard of professional behavior. Instead, your conduct has brought great discredit to yourself and to the United States Air Force. Undermining command authority, creating the appearance of favoritism, and callously violating established policy constitutes unacceptable behavior by someone of your rank and position. I find your actions reflect an appalling failure to appreciate what is expected of you as an officer and commander. Note that I am considering placing this Letter of Reprimand in an Unfavorable Information File. Additionally, let me by crystal clear -- any further misconduct by you will place you in jeopardy of much more serious action.[176]

I was utterly flabbergasted by what I was hearing. How could the CDI have substantiated such baseless allegations? After acknowledging the LOR with my signature, I was dismissed, with only three duty days to submit any matters I wished to be considered concerning this correspondence.

---

[176] Col. Mark Camerer, "Letter of Reprimand (LOR)," March 10, 2014 (emphasis in original)

Chapter 7: Undermining Authority

When Colonel Camerer reprimanded me for misconduct, he didn't offer much detail about what I had supposedly done wrong. The wing commander concluded I wrongfully made statements about my boss, Col. Liddick, but it wasn't clear what these were or how they undermined her authority. He accused me of behaving inappropriately towards certain subordinates, without indicating how or with whom. And he suggested my retention of a document in my desk proved I had a guilty conscience about something. Such nebulous charges would be pretty tough to fight without access to the evidence against me.

Thankfully, by some miracle my attorney obtained a copy of the 48-page report of investigation from the JBSA-Lackland legal office, just a couple of days after I received my reprimand. The first time I read through it, I was sickened to discover some of the things that had been said about me. On further inspection, however, I began to put this testimony into perspective. Although the witness names were redacted, it was easy enough to decipher who had accused me, and of what. It turns out only a handful of my subordinates actually denounced me, along with Col. Liddick and a couple of other members of the group staff. In fact, of the 20 witnesses interviewed, fewer than half had anything negative to say about me. But that was more than enough for Col. Camerer, who had a reputation for requiring only two witnesses to substantiate misconduct, no matter how many other airmen attested to the subject's innocence.

Moreover, it was immediately obvious this commander-directed investigation hadn't been very thorough. For example, although I was accused of making statements undermining my boss's authority during staff meetings, Lt. Col. McConnell failed to interview all of the personnel who routinely attended such weekly gatherings, including half of my flight chiefs and the managers of various unit programs. I later learned some witnesses urged the investigating officer to talk to specific personnel who could offer relevant testimony, but he didn't bother to contact them. On the other hand, one of my former subordinates told me he received a call regarding the CDI, but when this potential witness denied I ever said anything bad about my boss, the investigating officer never followed up to schedule an interview.

Witness selection was just one of several flaws with this CDI. Almost none of the testimony against me was corroborated by more than one witness, while much of it was clearly hearsay. Most of the claims lacked any specificity in terms of time or location, making it difficult to discern the chain of events described. Moreover, Lt. Col. McConnell actually offered compelling arguments in my favor for a couple of the substantiated allegations, then inexplicably reversed himself to find against me. Over eight months later, in response to a Freedom of Information Act request, I received additional documents related to the CDI, including over 100 pages of witness statements and other evidence. These records provided invaluable context for the testimony, revealing critical details the investigating officer left out of his report. Unfortunately, I didn't have access to this information when I initially appealed my punishment, but I've included it where appropriate throughout the discussion that follows.

Included in this trove of evidence were the original complaints that prompted my CDI. The first was from my operations officer, Maj. Rob Sprouse, who submitted a laundry list of gripes and innuendo on December 19, 2013. The second complainant was Mr. Ray Kenny, the t-shirt vendor who signed his statement that same day. Ironically, Lt. Col. McConnell used less than half of my DO's testimony, and he found the vendor's allegation unsubstantiated. Yet these dubious claims were enough to convince my chain of command to remove me from command and systematically destroy my career

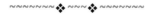

The first allegation the CDI substantiated was that I "undermined the command authority" of Col. Liddick when I "made comments in staff meetings regarding her involvement in the official functions" of the 737th Training Support Squadron. Altogether, the investigating officer cited testimony from five members of my squadron claiming I made such statements, although none of them clearly stated where or when they allegedly heard these comments. Lt. Col. McConnell didn't ask me about all of them, so I was unable to address several of these alleged remarks in my testimony. But I did not recall making any of the statements he asked me about, and my squadron superintendent, SMSgt "LG," also denied hearing me make any of the comments attributed to me. In fact, not a single witness corroborated any of my alleged statements regarding my boss:

1. Col. Liddick "is too involved in 737 TRSS business." My operations officer, Maj. Sprouse, claimed I said this, but SMSgt "LG" denied I made any "outright negative comments regarding [Col. Liddick's] involvement" in the squadron. She testified that we "had discussions about processes and whether or not it was the best way to get things done." My superintendent "could sometimes sense frustration, but there were no negative comments."

2. "I thought I was the commander." The squadron unit program coordinator, Ms. Coleman, claimed I made statements to this effect at staff meetings, expressing frustration with Col. Liddick. SMSgt "LG" testified she never heard me make comments such as this, and no other witnesses corroborated this or any other allegation.

3. My squadron first sergeant, MSgt Walls, suggested I frequently inserted "slick" comments into conversations regarding Col. Liddick's involvement in the squadron, and it was "pretty clear" to her that I did not care for Col. Liddick. However, no examples of such comments were provided, and I was not informed of this claim during the CDI.

4. "I have 19 years in, I don't care if I get promoted, and I have already bought a house in San Antonio." The Military Training Instructor School commandant, MSgt Pickett, testified I made such a statement, implying I was unconcerned with defying Col. Liddick.

5. MSgt Pickett also stated he heard some senior enlisted members in the group "publicly disparage" Col. Liddick and say things such as, "she lacks confidence in her leadership abilities and that's why she hires maintenance people whom she has known and can control." While he denied ever hearing anyone say this in front of me, he claimed to have heard me "paraphrase a similar remark." Upon learning that the new group superintendent was also from the maintenance career field, I allegedly said, "go figure." I was not asked about this specific comment, but I did testify that during "Deliberate Development" seminars,

"there were frank and honest discussions about differing personality styles." Someone could have said that "Col. Liddick lacks self-confidence in her leadership," but in that context I "would view it as interpreting personality styles versus disrespect. It is important to understand differing personality styles, as those differing styles can lead to tension over policy." SSgt Tommy Little, a "DD" instructor, also mentioned that while I "had never said anything negative about personnel," Col. Liddick "has made comments about clashing with the squadron commanders because of the differing personality types."

6. "You are my Shirt, not Col. Liddick's." MSgt Walls also stated I had an issue with her being first sergeant for both my squadron and the group staff. She claimed to have heard me say, "I guess you are her (Col. Liddick's) Shirt," after Col. Liddick pulled her out of a squadron-level meeting to attend to group issues. She also testified I told her to report to me whenever Col. Liddick asked her to do something.

7. "I'll ride her out." The chief of the training support flight, Mr. Steele, testified, "there was a known conflict" between Col. Liddick and me "about where TRSS personnel should sit in the building." Following a meeting where Col. Liddick overruled my "desire to have [SMSgt "LG"] in her own office instead of sharing an office with [Maj. Sprouse]," I supposedly stated, "I'll just ride her out." Col. Liddick testified I disagreed with her direction that "she wanted each squadron's DO to be collocated with the squadron Superintendent" in the same office, and MSgt Walls also stated I had issues with Col. Liddick "moving people's workspaces around the building." However, no one else corroborated my alleged statement.

8. "There is someone in the group building I hate." MSgt Pickett testified there was a "get to know the commander" skit during the squadron holiday party. The master of ceremonies, SSgt Joshua Hite, asked me if there was anyone in the squadron I hated, and I apparently responded, "in the squadron, no, how about the group building." The MC said "ok," and I allegedly responded

162

there was someone in the building I hated. MSgt Pickett assumed I was referring to Col. Liddick. I testified I could not remember saying that, but if so I was simply playing along with a joke.

9. "We all have our nemesis." Maj. Sprouse alleged I made this comment, which he guessed was referring to Col. Liddick. [177]

For some reason, Lt. Col. McConnell also included testimony in this section regarding the hiring of MSgt Pickett, and my subsequent clashes with the MTI School commandant. SMSgt "LG" noted I had my "#1 choice for MTIS Commandant," but when I took that name forward, Col. Liddick told me "that person would not be an option." She claimed I seemed disappointed I could not have my top pick, but I elected to hire my second choice, MSgt Pickett. When asked about me questioning Col. Liddick's involvement in the squadron, SSgt Little also referred to this hiring action. He said I told the "Deliberate Development" section and other MTI School personnel that I "was leaning towards" hiring SMSgt Howard Watkins, 331 TRS superintendent, to be the commandant. He indicated I preferred SMSgt Watkins "because he has a degree in psychology and much BMT experience," but I "spoke highly of all three candidates." He also explained that my "tone was matter-of-fact and not complaining."[178]

Elsewhere in the report of investigation, the investigating officer included testimony suggesting my hiring preferences demonstrated lack of support for 37th Training Wing priorities. Col. Liddick testified I "had only been in command for 2 months" when I recommended SMSgt Watkins be hired as the MTI School commandant, and I "strongly argued against [MSgt Pickett]." However, she noted, I "could provide no examples of [SMSgt Watkins] supporting [her] initiatives to transform BMT." MSgt Pickett, on the other hand, "was stratified as the #1 MSgt in BMT,

---

[177] Lt. Col. Matthew McConnell, *Commander Directed Report of Investigation Prepared by Lt. Col. Matthew McConnell, Investigating Officer, Concerning Degradation of Command Authority, Unprofessional Relationships, Failure to Maintain Military Good Order and Discipline, and Violation of AETC and 2 AF Policies*, January 24, 2014, p. 8-10, 31
[178] *Ibid.*, p. 9

and he was to be placed in the #1 MSgt position in BMT." Mr. Steele told a similar story: "[SMSgt Watkins] was said to not support [Col. Liddick's] BMT transformation initiatives. Furthermore, [Col. Liddick] asked Lt Col Perry why [she] would not hire [her] #1 MSgt into the #1 MSgt job. Lt Col Perry then agreed with [her] point." For good measure, Col. Liddick also noted we disagreed over who should replace SMSgt "LG" as 737 TRSS superintendent, so she made the decision for me, placing MSgt Bell, "the #2 MSgt," in this position. [179] (For the record, the superintendent is the senior enlisted position in the squadron, and so higher in the unit hierarchy than a mere flight chief such as the MTI School commandant.)

Similarly, Lt. Col. McConnell cited testimony from Col. Liddick about my strained relationship with MSgt Pickett. She stated she gave me "60-90 days to straighten out this relationship," or else she would "move the MTIS Commandant and School and have them report directly to her." MSgt Pickett testified I told him "he had 30 days to fix issues in MTIS," and when asked what would happen after that, I allegedly said I "would relook at MTIS and Deliberate Development (DD)." I testified I gave the commandant feedback as instructed, telling him he had until the end of the annual reporting cycle to meet all expectations but I wanted to see improvement within 30 days.[180]

By citing such testimony under this allegation, the investigating officer seems to imply I disregarded the group commander's intent by not informing MSgt Pickett he might be moved if we couldn't get along. On the other hand, he took no notice of the discrepancy in our timelines, or the fact that Col. Liddick gave me less than 60 days before removing me from command. Considering I had seemingly straightened out my relationship with MSgt Pickett well within the 30-day deadline she imposed, I suspect Col. Liddick testified she had given me longer so as to avoid any embarrassing questions about how well things had been going.

Whatever I may have thought of Col. Liddick, there was no evidence I took any actions to undermine her, and she clearly got her way in every instance. In response to this allegation, I offered the following statement: "I have not made comments to anyone in the 737 TRSS which were intended to or could be reasonably

---

[179] *Ibid.*, p. 31
[180] *Ibid.*, p. 8-10

interpreted as undermining the command authority of Col. Liddick. I respect the chain of command and the role of the group commander to direct the activities of subordinate squadrons. I have done my best to adjust to the changing demands of command in the 737 TRSS, as well as exercising command authority over the 737 TRG and 37 TRW staffs, during such a turbulent period in BMT history. If I have occasionally expressed confusion over appropriate roles and responsibilities, I certainly meant no disrespect to Col. Liddick or any other senior leader.

"It is important to put any comments which may have been attributed to me into the proper context," I continued. "Truth be told, many members of my squadron and the group have become disgruntled over the last year and a half, and have expressed frustration to me with various policies and their fear of reprisals if they speak out. I have reassured them that together, we would work to make BMT a better place during my tenure as squadron commander. I also emphasized that I was not so concerned for my own career that I wouldn't stand up for their interests. At no point, however, did I encourage or tolerate disrespect for authority or noncompliance with BMT policies, and I have always made every effort to understand, advocate, and implement Col. Liddick's policies."[181]

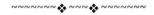

How to reconcile these multiple, uncorroborated statements with my memory of making none of them? Lt. Col. McConnell concluded that, whether I was "cognizant of it or not," the "variety of statements and the number of witnesses who reported them" suggest that I "likely made statements expressing frustration with [Col. Liddick's] involvement in squadron matters" and/or my "dislike for her." Despite my denials, the investigating officer concluded the "preponderance of the evidence" suggests I "made comments such as those mentioned."

Well, so what if I did? Lt. Col. McConnell conceded that, "as individual statements, they do not rise to the level of undermining [Col. Liddick's] command authority nor being prejudicial to good order and discipline." However, "the totality of the statements and the wide audience they were made to rose to an unacceptable level

---

[181] CDI witness statements, p. 111

and resulted in [Col. Liddick's] authority being undermined." Moreover, Lt. Col. McConnell asserted my statements were causing members of my squadron to question my conduct, "which is prejudicial to good order and discipline." However, he cited no testimony from my subordinates supporting this claim, nor any other evidence good order and discipline were somehow compromised. He also didn't clarify what he meant by "wide audience," since none of my alleged statements was corroborated – even those I supposedly said in public forums.

On the bright side, Lt. Col. McConnell acknowledged I "may have been expressing frustration rather than deliberately trying to undermine Col. Liddick's authority." He speculated that it was likely I was "not fond of Col. Liddick either personally or professionally due to her leadership style," and the fact she had overruled some of my decisions and recommendations. Furthermore, as the deputy commander of a different training group, the investigating officer sympathized that commanding a support squadron "is by nature a potentially frustrating position."

And yet, Lt. Col. McConnell still had his doubts: "I think a reasonable person could argue otherwise, and that the statements while rude and inappropriate, did not constitute undermining [Col. Liddick's] authority. I also think that these statements cannot be definitively determined to rising to the level of undermining her authority. Whether or not the statements rise to such a level to conclude the allegation is substantiated or unsubstantiated, the issue is the relative severity of the comments, which in this case they are not that severe. It also should be noted that these comments did not produce any tangible reported results in the form of the breakdown of the change [*sic*] of command or [Col. Liddick's] guidance being disregarded." I couldn't agree more with this analysis!

Nevertheless, the investigating officer inexplicably rejected his own "reasonable person" argument, concluding I "did undermine the command authority of 737 TRG/CC by making comments regarding her involvement in the official functions of the 737 TRSS in violation of Article 92 and/or 134, Uniform Code of Military Justice." While I "likely made the comments out of frustration, and the comments appear to have had no actual or reported impact on the functioning of the chain of command, they nonetheless had the effect of undermining her authority and were prejudicial to good order and discipline."[182]

Lt. Col. McConnell reiterated this nonsensical argument in his final recommendations as well. "While Lt Col Perry did make comments that a reasonable person could regard as undermining [Col. Liddick's] authority, he likely did so out of frustration as opposed to actually trying to undermine her authority. Additionally, while his actions did prejudice good order and discipline, in actuality his words had no effect on the actual function of the chain of command or accomplishment of the mission. Lt Col Perry should be counseled that making statements that expose his frustration with or dislike of [Col. Liddick] give the appearance that he is undermining [Col. Liddick]. He needs to stop making statements like the ones mentioned and better control his emotions and moderate his comments."[183] If only a reasonable person had been writing this report, perhaps the investigating officer would have reached different conclusions.

The second CDI allegation again involved my supposed undermining of Col. Liddick's command authority, this time by making comments to a civilian vendor, Mr. Ray Kenny, about "an official 737 TRG function." The function was a series of five-kilometer races at BMT organized by the TRSS Private Organization, my squadron's booster club, and managed by the 737 TRSS scheduling section. "Carrie & Company," a small mom-and-pop business, provided t-shirts, bibs, and trophies in exchange for a portion of the race registration fees. As Lt. Col. McConnell correctly pointed out, because these races were fundraisers sponsored by the TRSS Private Organization, neither Col. Liddick nor I actually had authority to make decisions about how they would be conducted. For the purposes of the CDI, however, the investigating officer felt "this distinction is immaterial" because both of us "were under the same misconception." The real issue is whether Col. Liddick gave me an order not to make any changes to the races.

At no point did it occur to me I might be overstepping my authority by making such decisions, in coordination with my staff

---

[182] McConnell report, p. 11-12
[183] *Ibid.*, p. 45

and TRSS Private Organization leadership in my unit. While Mr. Steele testified he emphasized to me "the fact that the 5K runs are TRG runs, not TRSS runs," it was clear in my mind these were squadron functions. I'm not sure how, when, or why the runs became the responsibility of the 737 TRSS, but following the July 2013 "Beach Run" (which my predecessor officiated), Col. Liddick told me I "had the next one." Moreover, when I submitted an electronic staff summary sheet for approval of the 2014 race calendar, clearly stating the 737 TRSS scheduling section hosts and is responsible for all run operations, Col. Liddick signed off indicating her concurrence.

As I discussed in an earlier chapter, things went downhill after my staff notified Carrie & Company, on December 10, 2013, that we would be using a different vendor in an upcoming race. Mr. Kenny complained to Col. Liddick at that weekend's race, and when I sent Col. Liddick a note the following Monday, December 16, regarding our plan, she responded, "pls come see me before we may [sic] the change official." This e-mail exchange, and our subsequent conversation outside her office that same day, are the only times we ever discussed authority over the 5K races. I met with Mr. Kenny again the next day, and informed him we would not be switching vendors for the race in January after all. He repeated his allegations about members of my staff, and insisted he wanted to work things out at our level. Despite his assurances, however, it was obvious he had gone to Col. Liddick the previous weekend. I told him it had been a mistake to lie to me and betray my trust in this way, when we have no contractual obligation to his company. I then asked him to leave my office.

Mr. Kenny proceeded directly to Col. Liddick's office, and he filed a formal complaint against me later that week, on December 19. (He later offered substantially the same testimony during the CDI.) Mr. Kenny claimed I was making decisions about BMT 5K races, "whereas Col. Liddick had told him that she had informed [me] she had decision-making authority over the races." He later testified that during our conversation, I indicated I "would be making decisions regarding vendor services for BMT 5K races, not Col. Liddick," and he also alleged that I made statements to the effect that Mr. Kenny "hitched his wagon to the wrong star, because [Col. Liddick] is gone in 6 months and I'm here for another year and a half."[184]

---

[184] *Ibid.*, p. 13-14

In his analysis, Lt. Col. McConnell separated my alleged statements into two different categories: those that were "rude and inappropriate in the conduct of professional business," and those that "could have potentially undermined Col. Liddick's command authority." Although there was no way to definitively determine who said what, the investigating officer concluded "the preponderance of the evidence" shows that I "probably did make rude and inappropriate statements." Although I remembered saying none of this, "as evident from Allegation 1 to the preponderance of the evidence suggests a pattern" – in other words, Lt. Col. McConnell was calling my credibility into question, based on his erroneous findings from a completely separate allegation. He also suspected that, "if the subject of who had the authority to make decision [sic] came up," I clearly expressed my opinion that I had such authority, and I "most likely did make such statements."

"However," Lt. Col. McConnell continued, "I do not believe such statements undermine [Col. Liddick's] authority. As rude as it is, it is a fact that Lt Col Perry is scheduled to remain in command of the 737 TRSS for a year past [Col. Liddick's] scheduled departure from the 737 TRG. Thus, whatever real or perceived influence Lt Col Perry may have over the 5K races, it will extend beyond [Col. Liddick's]." He also noted that her e-mail response did "not constitute an order or even clear guidance that [Col. Liddick] had decision making authority over the races, vendor services, etc." In fact, the investigating officer felt her response made it sound like I did have decision-making authority over the races, but that she wanted to be consulted. "I am not questioning the truthfulness of [Col. Liddick's] testimony," he clarified, "I simply don't think she provided clear guidance."

As for Mr. Kenny, the investigating officer felt it worth noting that he was "the only person that has anything to gain personally from how the races are conducted and who would be making the decision regarding which vendor was selected," as the proceeds from the races went to the TRSS Private Organization and charity. "While I am sure the respective commanders appreciate having revenue for the PO and supporting charity," Lt. Col. McConnell concluded, "in the grand scheme of things it does not impact mission execution." Mr. Kenny and his company, on the other hand, "make a profit on these races, and changing vendors or scaling back the races would impact his profit." Although the investigating officer had no evidence that anyone provided false or misleading testimony, Mr. Kenny was aware that I favored using another vendor and Col. Liddick favored continuing to use his company. "This has to be considered in evaluating the facts related to this allegation."

In the end, Lt. Col. McConnell concluded I did not undermine the command authority of Col. Liddick: "If he made statements as alleged asserting that he had authority over the BMT 5K races, he did not do so in violation of a clear, lawful order not to do so. As such, his conduct could not be prejudicial to good order and discipline in the armed forces or was of a nature to bring discredit upon the armed forces."[185] Although he found this allegation unsubstantiated, he nevertheless recommended I be counseled: "While Lt Col Perry did not undermine [Col. Liddick's] authority with regards to the statements he made to Mr. Kenny about the BMT 5K races, he likely made comments that were rude or inappropriate and were both unnecessary and unprofessional. Lt Col Perry should again be counseled that he needs to better control his emotions and moderate his comments."[186]

These first two allegations – one substantiated, the other not – offer revealing insights into Lt. Col. McConnell's approach to this CDI. The investigating officer correctly noted Mr. Kenny's conflict of interest, but he didn't apply similar skepticism to other witnesses who may have felt they stood to benefit by testifying a certain way. Consider the principal complainant, Maj. Sprouse, who was placed in charge of the squadron during my absence, and ultimately replaced me in command. Similarly, MSgt Pickett expressed concern to me over his "firewall 5" enlisted performance report, suggesting he, too, may have had motive to replace me as his rater.

Lt. Col. McConnell claimed not to question my reliability with respect to my alleged statements, yet he discounted my testimony regarding both allegations. In the first case, he suggested I might not be cognizant of making statements expressing frustration or dislike, and by the second allegation he'd apparently concluded my denials were part of a pattern. Yet the

---

[185] *Ibid.*, p. 16-17
[186] *Ibid.*, p. 45

investigating officer never applied similar logic to statements by my boss. When Col. Liddick testified she gave me clear instructions via e-mail that I was not to make any changes to the BMT 5K runs, the investigating officer refused to question the truthfulness of her obviously untrue testimony.   As we'll see with subsequent allegations, Lt. Col. McConnell's deference to Col. Liddick suggests a pattern of a completely different sort.

The investigating officer's bias was particularly evident in his suppression of my testimony regarding the BMT 5K runs. In my initial response, I wrote that, during our short conversation outside her office, Col. Liddick accused me of "threatening the livelihood of a small business," and she claimed the vendor we had selected for the next race was involved in a "scam" with BMT. She also "inexplicably asserted that it was her signature on the eSSS seeking approval for the races, so only she had the authority to make changes to the program."[187] Lt. Col. McConnell took no notice of these comments, which seemed to indicate Col. Liddick was playing favorites among the vendors, and betrayed a certain cluelessness in reference to her role in the program.

Almost as an afterthought, the investigating officer noted that Col. Liddick met with me and members of my staff (including the TRSS Private Organization president) on December 20 to discuss the way ahead for future BMT 5K races.[188] What he failed to mention was that, just four days after she accused me of "threatening the livelihood of a small business," Col. Liddick now suggested we conduct future BMT 5Ks "in house," with minimal reliance on outside vendors like Carrie & Company.[189] Had Col. Liddick actually implemented this proposal, we might have saved race participants – nearly all of whom are basic trainees – roughly $14,000 per race. But she had no intention of following through. In hindsight, it seems she was trying to distance herself from her previous outburst regarding Carrie & Company, and appear disinterested in the fate of this (or any other) vendor. This charade may have been meant to protect her against any backlash from the commander-directed investigation she knew would soon be coming. (As it turns out, my wife, Caroline, happened to run into Mr. Kenny at a local restaurant over a year later, and she struck up a conversation with him about my case. He told her he had been

---

[187] CDI witness statements, p. 112
[188] McConnell report, p. 13
[189] CDI witness statements, p. 113

pressured to file a complaint, he was directed to rewrite it several times, and he was assured I would be relieved of command as a result.)

This isn't the only relevant testimony Lt. Col. McConnell left out of his report. Regarding the selection of an MTI School commandant, the deputy group commander, Lt. Col. Upchurch, noted SMSgt Watkins "came out on top when the board for Commandant was conducted in the TRSS," but he falsely claimed I then recommended MSgt Daniel Dupont, who "came out 2nd, but [he] lacked experience." According to Lt. Col. Upchurch, when the group commander chose to hire MSgt Pickett instead, I "hated that choice and that [she] made it."[190]

The investigating officer also did not include some revealing testimony from Col. Liddick. She asserted I seemed to be "influenced by other people" in hiring an MTI School commandant, suggesting the senior enlisted leaders I consulted were not qualified to weigh in on the candidates under consideration. In her account of my conflict with MSgt Pickett, she misremembered her instructions and confused the sequence of events. She testified she did not know if MSgt Pickett was aware of her "60-90 day timeline," but she claimed MSgt Pickett came to see her after a meeting with me and the first sergeant "which did not go well" – a reference to our confrontation on October 28, 2013. Col. Liddick asked for a meeting with MSgt Walls the next morning to find out what happened the previous afternoon, but I "inserted" myself into this meeting on October 29.[191] The problem with this account is that Col. Liddick didn't issue her 30-day ultimatum until that morning, so I couldn't have made MSgt Pickett aware of it the previous afternoon.

MSgt Pickett's recollections of that October 28 encounter are also illustrative. He testified he sought out this meeting to discuss "what [he] regarded as unprofessional behavior" between me and members of the "Deliberate Development" team. During this meeting, I allegedly "laughed several times about points being raised," and MSgt Pickett "got emotional and left." When he returned to continue the meeting, I allegedly "became defensive about the points [he] was raising." He also confirmed he met with Col. Liddick following our meeting.[192] In fact, MSgt Pickett didn't

---

190 *Ibid.*, p. 74-75
191 *Ibid.*, p. 92-93
192 *Ibid.*, p. 65-66

accuse me of anything that afternoon, but rather complained of the influence the "DD" contractor, Mr. Kamel, was exerting over my wife and a handful of senior "Blue Ropes." The allegations he made were ludicrous, but I promised I would look into his concerns and get back to him shortly. He didn't give me that opportunity, and also didn't bother to touch base with the BMT superintendent, CMSgt Sutherland, before going straight to the group commander. Given her reaction the next morning, I am confident Col. Liddick already knew all about his allegations, and she may have even put him up to demanding that meeting with me.

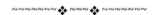

In the end, I was found to have violated "Article 92 and/or 134" of the UCMJ, even though Article 92 – failure to obey order or regulation – clearly doesn't apply, while Article 134 is merely a catch-all "general article." But if my alleged comments about my boss were so bad, why wasn't I charged with something more serious? No mention was made of Article 89, disrespect toward superior commissioned officer; or Article 117, provoking speeches or gestures; or even Article 133, conduct unbecoming an officer and a gentleman. Of note, the investigating officer specifically asked each witness if I ever disparaged Col. Liddick or anyone else in the chain of command, and not a single person claimed I did. Nevertheless, I believe my subordinates convinced Col. Liddick I was bad-mouthing her and actively undermining her authority, and this was her principal motivation for seeking my relief of command. The additional allegations I'll discuss in the next two chapters were merely icing on the cake.

Unfortunately, the conclusion I violated Article 134 by prejudicing good order and discipline simply does not hold up to scrutiny – especially when compared to the findings of another commander-directed investigation Col. Camerer ordered just six months earlier. As I discussed in a previous chapter, SMSgt Phillip Monk falsely accused his squadron commander of firing him for his religious beliefs, and he repeatedly denounced her as a lesbian in the national media. Yet the investigating officer in that case concluded SMSgt Monk did not violate Article 134, and my wing commander concurred. This is ludicrous. CAPT Michale Junge, a professor at the U.S. Naval War College and noted authority on such investigations, later offered me his comparative analysis of our two cases: "if you see to make the point that the O6 you had issues with was inconsistent in understanding the law and regulations, then I think you have an argument." Given the recent results of the Monk case in the same wing, "there is clearly more at issue in the command," he concluded.[193]

---

[193] E-mail response from CAPT Michael Junge to Lt. Col. Craig Perry, "Re: CDI analysis," June 25, 2014

Chapter 8: Deliberate Development

Of the five allegations lodged against me during my commander-directed investigation, two of them concerned my supposed lack of support for various Basic Military Training transformation initiatives. I was accused of advocating a "back to basics" approach, with no need for officers or Chief Master Sergeants. Instead, I was reportedly enamored with Military Training Instructors, and valued elite "Blue Ropes" above all others. According to this narrative, the center of my attention was the "Deliberate Development" team, whose bidding I supposedly did as squadron commander. Although "DD" was itself one of the transformation initiatives General Rice endorsed, several subordinates and superiors seemed convinced I was somehow dragging BMT back to the bad old days.

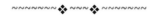

The third allegation from the commander-directed investigation seemed the most serious: that I engaged in unprofessional relationships with enlisted personnel in my squadron, and interacted with select personnel "on terms of military equality" – in other words, fraternization, a crime under the Uniform Code of Military Justice. The CDI report identified three subordinates whom I allegedly favored: SMSgt "LG," my squadron superintendent; Hassan Kamel, a government contractor assigned to the "Deliberate Development" team at the MTI School; and SSgt Tommy Little, an enlisted "DD" instructor. In his report, the investigating officer, Lt. Col. McConnell, noted there was "so much testimony provided alleging an unprofessional relationship, favoritism, or the perception thereof" between me and these three subordinates, he had to use a different format to summarize it all.[194] What he failed to mention was that he found only five members of my 100-person squadron who claimed to share such perceptions, along with Col. Liddick and her leadership team. He also gave no indication of the volume of dubious testimony he left out of his report.

Although the accusation of an unprofessional relationship with SMSgt "LG" came as a surprise, allegations concerning Mr.

---

[194] McConnell report, p. 18

Kamel and SSgt Little were old news by the time the CDI began, as I had been counseled months earlier about this perception. Several witnesses cited the fact that all three of these subordinates attended the going-away party Caroline and I threw for the outgoing MTI School commandant, SMSgt Milne, before he departed for Korea. After my operations officer, Maj. Sprouse, falsely complained about not being invited, Col. Liddick advised me not to throw any more parties at my house. Then there was that dinner Caroline and I hosted for SSgt Little's mother when she flew into town to visit her son. Col. Liddick lectured me about this incident as well – but in their subsequent CDI testimony, both she and her deputy embellished their accounts. The group commander said she counseled me "on how meeting with subordinates at a bar or at [my] house can create the perception of unprofessional relationships or favoritism." According to statements not cited in the report, both Col. Liddick and Lt. Col. Upchurch claimed I admitted to bumping into someone at a bar, "but only one time." (For good measure, my boss noted she "does not know if Lt Col Perry routinely meets with personnel at bars.")[195] I honestly have no idea where they got this idea, or whom they think I met at a bar, as I never said any such thing. Col. Liddick merely instructed me not to "hang out socially" with Mr. Kamel or SSgt Little, nothing more. Whatever she told me, however, this counseling had its desired effect: in his report of investigation, Lt. Col. McConnell observed, "no other incidents of this behavior were noted" after Col. Liddick talked to me on October 29, 2013.

This isn't the only example of Lt. Col. McConnell leaving out relevant testimony in his report. For instance, some witnesses took issue with the fact that the "DD" contractor and noncommissioned officer sat at the same table as Caroline and me at official social events. MSgt Walls complained she wasn't seated at our table at the MTI Association honors banquet,[196] neglecting to mention the event organizers assigned seating – and Caroline and I went out of our way to make room for her at our table. Maj. Sprouse testified he expected to sit with us at the squadron holiday party,[197] but SMSgt "LG" flatly contradicted this claim. "Though there was no assigned seating at the Holiday Party," she wrote in an official statement several months later, "the Director of

---

[195] CDI witness statements, p. 74 and p. 92
[196] *Ibid.*, p. 61
[197] *Ibid.*, p. 50 and p. 134

Operations asked the party committee to ensure he did not sit near the Commander. His spouse did not care for the Commander's spouse. I am positive he and his spouse sat themselves where they did on purpose."[198] If this account is true, Maj. Sprouse's formal complaint and subsequent CDI testimony constitute false official statements.

Maj. Sprouse further testified I stayed after the holiday party and "closed the bar down,"[199] while Mr. Steele claimed to have seen pictures on Facebook of "the head table guests" and me at a bar after the party.[200] Neither witness alleged anything improper happened there that night – in fact, neither was present to observe these goings-on for themselves. Nevertheless, according to his testimony, my operations officer later mentioned to me "the inappropriateness of staying that late at the party" where my subordinates were drinking, and I supposedly made a comment at the next commander's call, that "some people have a problem with me spending time with/having a good time with my people."[201] I have no recollection of saying this, and once again the investigating officer chose not to include this inflammatory testimony in his official report.

These weren't the only social situations witnesses objected to. Maj. Sprouse testified there was a close relationship between me and Mr. Kamel, whom he claimed was friends with my wife and "uses her to get things accomplished." MSgt Walls stated she believed I "hang out" out with Mr. Kamel and SSgt Little, and we "go to dinners together." She also indicated she had seen pictures of the two of them with me in civilian clothes off duty, while MSgt Pickett stated "there are said to be several Facebook pictures" of me and the subordinates I allegedly favored, where we were "clearly off duty and in a social setting." Yet no one produced any of these alleged photographs as evidence, or corroborated the claim I had dinner with anyone in the squadron apart from the incidents documented above. MSgt Walls even mentioned that MSgt Chavez came to our house on Christmas, suggesting this was somehow inappropriate.[202] The irony is, had the first sergeant been doing

---

[198] SMSgt "LG", rebuttal to LOC issued by Col. Vincent Fisher, April 28, 2014
[199] McConnell report, p. 18
[200] *Ibid.*, p. 21
[201] CDI witness statements, p. 50
[202] McConnell report, p. 18-20

her job properly, and actually concerning herself with the morale of personnel in our unit, this airman might have reached out to her instead.

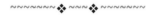

Several witnesses also seemed to think I favored the "Deliberate Development" contractor professionally. Maj. Sprouse testified Mr. Kamel could "circumvent" him and come straight to my superintendent or me, while Mr. Steele indicated I favored those two subordinates above others. The MTI School commandant, MSgt Pickett, stated there was "blatant favoritism" by me towards Mr. Kamel and SSgt Little, and he felt "he has no say" in what they do. When MSgt Pickett "would attempt to hold them accountable on certain things," Mr. Kamel allegedly went right to me "so as to undermine" the commandant. He further claimed to have heard we had "secret meetings," and noted, "Lt Col Perry has said that he has ways to collect data on the MTIS issues and that his wife hears things." Finally, MSgt Pickett felt that Mr. Kamel "is consistently out of bounds and that Lt Col Perry shelters him."[203] Curiously, the example MSgt Pickett offered to support this claim actually occurred after I was removed from command, when I was in no position to shelter anyone. "At the onset of this investigation," he testified, "a no contact order was issued to Lt Col Perry, barring any communication with squadron members. When learning of this, [Mr. Kamel] exclaimed, 'Not even the fucking president can tell me who I can have contact with.'"[204]

MSgt Pickett also testified I favored the "DD" instructor. After he gave SSgt Little official feedback, and "mentioned avoiding any perception of favoritism," the commandant was told he was not going to be SSgt Little's supervisor. He claimed my superintendent, SMSgt "LG," "avoids talking to [SSgt Little] in hopes that she can avoid reprisal," and she asked someone "to get an answer from [SSgt Little] as to whether or not he was re-enlisting because she knew it would cause her a problem with the commander." The unit program coordinator, Ms. Coleman, confirmed I directed her to

---

[203] *Ibid.*, p. 18-22
[204] CDI witness statements, p. 66

delay changing SSgt Little's rater to the MTI School commandant,[205] but no one corroborated the rest of MSgt Pickett's testimony.

Even if what these witnesses claimed were true, does it indicate that I engaged in unprofessional relationships with these two subordinates? Throughout the CDI, the investigating officer treated Mr. Kamel as if he were just another enlisted member, rather than a government contractor to whom different standards of conduct apply. Moreover, Lt. Col. McConnell failed to acknowledge the contractor worked directly for me, and was not one of MSgt Pickett's subordinates. I consulted with him from time to time on "Deliberate Development" initiatives, valuing the deep insight into the organization and its personnel he had gained during seven years at BMT. Lt. Col. McConnell also completely disregarded the operational "DD" chain of command, which ran through MSgt Chavez. The investigating officer did concede there was "a serious misunderstanding or disagreement over how the DD section functions within MTIS, who has operational, administrative, and tactical control (OPCON, ADCON, TACON), and their chain of command," but this was merely an afterthought in his final report, rather than weighed as evidence exonerating me. Furthermore, he failed to acknowledge that most of these issues had already been dealt with months earlier, when Col. Liddick counseled me not to "hang out" with these particular subordinates and threatened to remove the MTI School from my squadron if I did not placate MSgt Pickett. Finally, the investigating officer failed to show that anyone actually benefitted from my supposed favoritism. As both Mr. Kamel and I testified during the CDI, when I had the opportunity to offer a spot promotion to SSgt Little in July, I declined because he had not completed a Community College of the Air Force degree.

For his part, SSgt Little acknowledged a perception that I favored "Deliberate Development," but he argued that all BMT commanders gave this same impression. The reality, he testified, was that commanders interact with "DD" differently because "they operate at a different level of organizational development" – at the strategic rather than operational or tactical level. As such, the communication can be interpreted as showing favoritism. "For example, a MSgt may wonder why a SSgt from DD is solicited for and giving organizational development advice to a squadron commander, instead of the MSgt's advice on the matter being solicited." Mr. Kamel concurred, stating if I showed favoritism

---

[205] McConnell report, 19-20

towards their section, "so do many of the other senior leaders in the 737 TRG," including Col. Liddick. "Deliberate Development serves everyone in BMT from the line instructor to the commander, and many commanders have utilized DD. It is normal for DD to work with commanders and their spouses or anyone else in an environment that they are most comfortable. This may include going to a meal with them or visiting their home.[206]

Ironically, if anyone at BMT was perceived to favor SSgt Little, it was Col. Liddick. As I discussed in a previous chapter, she selected him to represent BMT to the media on multiple occasions, and routinely scheduled him to brief distinguished visitors on the "DD" program. The group commander also often referred to this E-5 as her "wingman," and suggested she "could see him as a Chief Master Sergeant running the Air Force." She even asked SSgt Little to preview one of her commander's call presentations and coach her on her delivery – a role she usually entrusted to the more experienced "DD" contractor, Mr. Kamel.

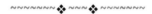

Air Force instructions state, "relationships are unprofessional, whether pursued and conducted on or off-duty, when they detract from the superior-to-subordinate authority, or reasonably create the appearance of favoritism, misuse of an office or position, or the abandonment of organizational goals for personal interests." According to Lt. Col. McConnell, the compilation of testimony against me was overwhelming: "Lt Col Perry may not have intended to have an unprofessional relationship or show favoritism, and his actions may not have resulted in any real benefits of favoritism. But both his subordinates and 737 TRG leadership believe that there is favoritism or the perception of favoritism being shown by Lt Col Perry" toward Mr. Kamel and SSgt Little – as well as toward SMSgt "LG," as I will discuss in the next chapter.

"The impacts of this perception are tangible," the investigating officer continued, since MSgt Pickett believed "his subordinates can circumvent the chain of command to get their way, and that he cannot hold [Mr. Kamel] accountable to do his job." If anyone was circumventing the chain of command to get

---

[206] *Ibid.,* p. 20-21

their way, however, it was the MTI School commandant, who went over my head to Col. Liddick with his complaints. In any case, MSgt Pickett wasn't accountable for Mr. Kamel, who was contractually obligated to report directly to me, and the commandant had only administrative responsibility for "Deliberate Development." Moreover, any concerns he or any other witness had about these subordinates circumventing the chain of command had been definitively laid to rest two months earlier. By the time they testified, this issue should have been water under the bridge.

"It is worth noting," Lt. Col. McConnell graciously conceded, "that following counseling Lt Col Perry for having a party at his house and a dinner at his house to which only certain squadron personnel were invited, no other incidents of this behavior were noted." He also concurred with me that MSgt Chavez "being invited and briefly visiting his house on Christmas can be viewed as helping a squadron member in need." Furthermore, "since the counseling sessions, the only incident of Lt Col Perry socializing with personnel under his command" was when Caroline and I took my former superintendent – who was then no longer assigned to my squadron – and her husband to see "The Nutcracker." Again, water under the bridge. "As mentioned above, other than [Mr. Kamel] and [SSgt Little] sitting at the head table at the Christmas party, it appears that there have been no more overt social situations that contribute to the perception of favoritism."[207]

But perceptions are reality in today's Air Force. Even though these subordinates came to my house on only two occasions several months earlier, and even though I obeyed my boss's direction not to host any more parties or "hang out" with them socially, I was judged to be actively carrying on unprofessional relationships with these personnel. This despite the fact that neither of them benefitted in any way from my supposed favoritism, and any questions about the contractor circumventing the chain of command had been laid to rest long before this investigation began. Whatever the merits of this allegation may have been back in October 2013, there was no longer any basis to conclude I was doing anything wrong. I was fully in compliance with my commander's guidance, and was meeting the letter and intent of Air Force instructions, yet I was nonetheless found guilty. This was strike two.

---

[207] *Ibid.*, p. 28-29

While the investigating officer found the fourth CDI allegation – that I "made comments and/or engaged in actions that demonstrated lack of support for the 37th Training Wing's current initiatives with regard to basic military training" – to be unsubstantiated, Lt. Col. McConnell still used elements of this charge against me. He examined three sets of accusations that he suggested, "could be viewed as demonstrating a lack of support" by me for 37 TRW initiatives. First, I was alleged to have made statements that I did not support officers in BMT, or an operations officer in my squadron; second, I was accused of failing to investigate alleged misconduct by my superintendent, SMSgt "LG," disregarding established procedures; and third, a group of "Blue Rope" MTIs were allegedly influencing me and/or working to undermine Col. Liddick and initiatives to transform BMT.

Before the CDI began, Maj. Sprouse provided a sworn statement alleging I had, among other things, given the impression that I was not supportive of recent initiatives to put officers and Chief Master Sergeants in BMT. He later testified I advocated for a "back to basics" approach, which he interpreted as "meaning that BMT is an enlisted program and does not require officer oversight. It is about enlisted heritage and enlisted traditions." He accused me of condoning the sentiment that "we don't need officers in BMT," and my actions were "dragging BMT back to where it had been before the sex scandal." Other witnesses offered similar testimony. The deputy group commander, Lt. Col. Upchurch, stated that I "was undermining [Col Liddick's] vision, guidance, and directives for how BMT needs to operate," and cited an e-mail in which it seemed as though I was "trying to take 737 TRG initiatives and turn them into 737 TRSS initiatives." (He did not produce this alleged e-mail for the CDI.) Mr. Steele went further: "it was rumored that Lt Col Perry held a 'back to basics' meeting with all squadron MTIs, in which they discussed BMT going back the way it was before the transformation. One of the topics was having MTIs go back to running BMT, rather than officers." [208] However, none of these accusations were corroborated, and I honestly have no idea what any of these witnesses were talking about.

---

[208] McConnell report, p. 30-32

MSgt Pickett was even more specific. He indicated that under my leadership (and that of my superintendent), "it was felt as though BMT was taking a step backwards, to the way that it was before the transformation initiatives." He claimed I "seemed to want to go back to the way some things were, before the changes." For example, I supposedly "wanted to decentralize the MTIS practical portion of the training. Rather than have all MTIS students push flights at the 323 TRS, the MTI training squadron, [I] would rather farm out MTIS students to various [line squadrons], as had been done in the past. BMT moved to all new MTIs training in the 323 TRS to ensure one standard of training." That actually sounds like a really good idea, as I explained in an earlier chapter, and the 323 TRS commander, Lt. Col. Chad Gallagher, did discuss this eventuality with me and others on multiple occasions. While we appreciated the need to establish a single standard of qualification training, we also saw the disruption this consolidated "trainer squadron" was having on MTI manning and morale across BMT. I was far from alone in questioning the long-term sustainability of this model – but I knew better than to propose dismantling Col. Liddick's most momentous initiative. This was an issue best deferred to the next BMT commander, by which point the adverse impacts would be more obvious.

Additionally, MSgt Pickett testified, "Lt Col Perry would rather MTIs not receive their campaign hats until they have pushed their first flights, whereas currently they receive them when they graduate MTIS, when they are awarded the MTI Special Duty Identifier and Air Force Specialty Code."[209] This is another flat-out lie, and MSgt Pickett knew it. It was actually Col. Liddick who directed me to look into whether we ought to stop awarding hats at graduation, so I queried several BMT squadron superintendents and civilian staff who served as MTIs back in the day about this proposal. Reaction was mixed, with the civilians mostly recommending we reinstitute the old approach, and the Chief Master Sergeants generally counseling we keep things the way they were. In the end, I saw no compelling reason to change, so Col. Liddick dropped the issue. I was actually on the record as advocating against both of the positions the MTI School commandant ascribed to me, yet Lt. Col. McConnell didn't bother asking me about them. Nevertheless, the investigating officer included this uncorroborated testimony in his report.

---

[209] *Ibid.*, p. 30-31

Witness testimony regarding the role of my operations officer is particularly baffling. MSgt Walls claimed I treated Maj. Sprouse "as the #4 person in the chain of command, not #2," and that I had stated the superintendent was my #2. "Overall, Lt Col Perry does not care for the Director of Operations (DO) position," MSgt Walls complained. "He did not share things with [Maj. Sprouse] or [her], essentially he communicated only with [SMSgt "LG"]." The unit program coordinator, Ms. Coleman, also stated, "Lt Col Perry has mentioned that he doesn't think the squadron needed a DO, and that he is not sure what his role is. If [she] cannot get in touch with Lt Col Perry she will go to [SMSgt "LG"] first, then the First Sergeant and then to [Maj. Sprouse], which is her opinion on the unofficial chain of command." Even the new squadron superintendent, MSgt Bell, stated that, while I had not expressed an opinion about having officers in BMT, it seemed to him that Maj. Sprouse "had no role in decision making in the squadron," and he was "unsure why [he] was left out of the loop." [210] (The investigating officer attributed a similar sentiment to Lt. Col. Upchurch, although the deputy group commander had merely relayed that Maj. Sprouse "feels pushed to the side and taken out of the loop by Lt Col Perry.")[211]

As a former operations officer myself, I can't understand why anyone would accuse me of not knowing what to do with a DO. I testified I was "proud to be part of such a high-powered leadership team featuring CMSgt superintendents, SMSgt first sergeants, and DOs and flight commanders in every squadron."[212] I speculated that, when I mentioned to Col. Liddick that "DD did not belong in MTIS and maybe they should work for the DO and that the DO had enough 'band-width' to supervise DD," this could have been interpreted as Maj. Sprouse being underutilized.[213]

For her part, SMSgt "LG" stated she "has always viewed Maj. Sprouse as #2 in the squadron," and she "was surprised to learn that others did not see the chain of command that way," and "shocked when she learned that some in the squadron saw her as #2." She said she and Maj. Sprouse "tried to split up duties."[214] (They did, after all, share an office.) She elaborated further several

[210] *Ibid.*, p. 30-32
[211] CDI witness statements, p, 75
[212] *Ibid.*, p. 115
[213] *Ibid.*, p. 128
[214] McConnell report, p. 22

months later: "I never viewed myself in a position above the Director of Operations or the First Sergeant. An example of this is when I first arrived in the Training Support Squadron there was no routing or tracking of correspondence that needed to go to the Commander for signature. Many times squadron personnel would just take a piece of paper to the UPC and ask her to have the Commander sign it. I instituted a squadron routing slip and ensured that the Director of Operations and the First Sergeant were included on the routing. The Director of Operations was above me on the routing and if he was inadvertently left off, I would always counsel the individual who prepared the routing slip on the proper chain of command. Several times the Director of Operations thanked me for doing so."[215]

I found these allegations simply baffling. As I testified to Lt. Col. McConnell, I never made comments or engaged in activities that demonstrated a lack of support for 37 TRW initiatives with regard to BMT. Specifically, I didn't make any of the statements attributed to me in the CDI: "officers do not belong in BMT," "MTIs are not allowed to be MTIs anymore and they aren't allowed to do their job," "a DO is not necessary in the 737 TRSS," or that I didn't know what to do with an operations officer. I also had not heard the comment, "Here at BMT, we don't need the officers and Chiefs, all we need is MTIs and getting back to basics." On the contrary, I had been one of the strongest proponents in the group for the speedy and effective implementation of recommendations from Maj. Gen. Woodward's 2012 CDI. I felt we had definitely turned a corner, and BMT was quickly getting back on track.

One witness who came to my defense was Mr. Kamel, who believed I did not take issue with the BMT transformation initiatives. "Rather he only questions whether or not BMT is doing things the right way. He often plays devil's advocate in this process. Once a decision is made, he is on board." He added, "Lt Col Perry feels that we can't hold MTIs hostage for past mistakes, and that BMT must heal and move on from the past."[216]

Nevertheless, Lt. Col. McConnell somehow found the witnesses who reported I made statements that I did not support officers in BMT or a DO in my squadron to be "credible in this regard." He felt I "either did not utilize or underutilized [Maj. Sprouse] to the point it was a distraction in the squadron," and my

---

[215] Rebuttal to LOC issued by Col. Fisher
[216] McConnell report, p. 31

"opposition to Col. Liddick's guidance that the DO and Superintendent work together in an office furthered the distraction." Without providing any actual evidence to back up these claims, he concluded, "Lt Col Perry's comments and actions lend credence to the general perception that he does not support the addition of officers to BMT in general." Nevertheless, the investigating officer stated, "I do not think Lt Col Perry's conduct rises to the level of a lack of support for BMT initiatives, and I certainly do not think that his behavior was prejudicial to good order and discipline." Rather, "With regards to officers in BMT, his conduct constitutes poor leadership on his part by not effectively utilizing his personnel ([Maj. Sprouse]), and it was not prejudicial to good order and discipline. If he had told the members of his squadron to ignore [Maj. Sprouse] or submitted an Authorization Change Request to have the DO position deleted, that would have been a different matter."[217]

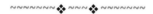

The final element of this CDI allegation was that a group of "Blue Rope" Master MTIs was allegedly influencing me and working to undermine Col. Liddick and initiatives to transform BMT. Ironically, it was a fellow "Blue Rope" – the MTI School commandant, MSgt Pickett – who first made this allegation. During our meeting on October 28, 2013, he suggested to me that the "Deliberate Development" contractor, Mr. Kamel, was exerting undue influence on my wife and several "Blue Rope" senior NCOs, including the former group superintendent, CMSgt Williams; the former MTI School commandant, then-SMSgt Milne; the former 331 TRS superintendent, SMSgt Watkins; and a former 324 TRS instructor supervisor. He repeated this claim during the CDI, testifying that there "seem to be remnants of the old 'Blue Rope Society'," and that I chose to surround myself with "these people." (Of note, all the MTIs he referenced had departed BMT by the time the CDI began.) MSgt Pickett also accused me of seeming "to be in the weeds with the Blue Rope program," apparently forgetting that 2 AF Guidance Memorandum 36-03 gave the 737 TRSS commander responsibility for overseeing the Master Instructor and Master MTI ("Blue Rope") programs.

---

[217] *Ibid.*, p. 34-35

Maj. Sprouse testified he "feels that Lt Col Perry seems to have a certain reverence for the MTI hat and blue rope culture." He believed I "was brought into a group of 'old hats' who were used to doing things the old way, meaning before the transformation of BMT began." Among those in that small group were the same MTIs MSgt Pickett complained about, with whom I "shared the 'Back to Basics' mentality as the way to do business in BMT." He further stated he felt "the chain of command in the 737 TRSS had more to do with having an MTI hat or a blue rope and less to do with rank. In other words, 'the hat hierarchy' trumped rank." MSgt Walls echoed this accusation, stating, "Lt Col Perry seems to favor MTIs, specifically Blue Ropes over others."[218]

None of these witnesses provided a shred of evidence to support their claims, which were particularly nonsensical; after all, "Blue Ropes" were acknowledged as the top 10 percent of the MTI corps, and nearly every MTI in my squadron – including the senior enlisted leader (SMSgt "LG") and one of my flight chiefs (MSgt Pickett) – wore a blue rope on their campaign hats. Moreover, the mission of our squadron was to support BMT operations and produce new instructors, so who better than experienced MTIs to turn to as subject-matter experts? Finally, apart from Maj. Sprouse and MSgt Walls, Lt. Col. McConnell didn't bother to interview anyone in my squadron who wasn't a current or former MTI, so he had no basis to evaluate the claim I favored MTIs over others. Had the investigating officer simply glanced at our squadron awards display on the hallway leading to my office, he would have seen that the 737 TRSS Senior NCO of the Year was MSgt Art Ayala – a personnelist, not an MTI.

Nevertheless, members of the group staff took this allegation even further. Lt. Col. Upchurch cited an e-mail I sent to him and Col. Liddick, saying "the TRG needs to better leverage the Blue Ropes." This was my "manifesto" on restoring trust, which the deputy group commander believed "was not meant as an act of defiance," but my thoughts on "how the TRG may more effectively get from point A to point B with the various policy initiatives in place." Nevertheless, he blamed SMSgt "LG" for trying to influence me "in the old ways of how BMT used to be run in order to move power within BMT to the Blue Ropes" – as if I were being initiated into a cult. He further claimed my superintendent "has been in BMT quite a while and is part of the old 'Blue Rope society'," a

---

[218] *Ibid.*, p. 30-31

particularly ironic accusation given she and Lt. Col. Upchurch arrived at BMT around the same time in late 2012. The 737 TRG superintendent, CMSgt Sutherland, also believed a "Blue Rope Society" probably existed, that SMSgt "LG" was part of it, and she "may be feeding information to Lt Col Perry." In his opinion, "there is definitely a 'Blue Rope' clique," and he offered up the same list of names as MSgt Pickett and Maj. Sprouse.[219]

CMSgt Sutherland further testified, "Anyone Lt Col Perry identifies as 'top-notch' is a part of that clique." To prove his point, the BMT superintendent provided a puzzling example. He noted, when we were hiring a new 737 TRSS superintendent, I suggested two candidates to replace SMSgt "LG". One (MSgt Chavez) was a Reservist, and the other (MSgt Dupont) was an MTI relatively new to BMT, "so Col. Liddick was not willing to approve that hire." I objected to the candidate CMSgt Sutherland suggested, MSgt Bell, but Col. Liddick hired him anyway since he was stratified as "the #2 MSgt in the group." What the group superintendent neglected to mention was that it was he who originally suggested I consider MSgt Dupont for this position, or that this "brand new" MTI had not (yet) earned a blue rope. The "#2 MSgt" who Col. Liddick favored, on the other hand, had been an MTI for 16 years straight, and was named "Blue Rope of the Year" in 2000. But it's not terribly surprising CMSgt Sutherland seemed so confused, since the 8B000 functional manager is not himself an MTI – let alone a "Blue Rope" – and had only been at BMT about three months when he offered his uninformed opinion.

So was there a "Blue Rope" clique at BMT? And was I initiated into their mysterious rites? Lt. Col. McConnell conceded he "was unable to definitively confirm that this clique exists or that Lt Col Perry is part of it." But based upon what he believed to be the credible testimony of these witnesses, he suspected a clique did exist, although the "extent to which it may have been able to influence Lt Col Perry is unable to be determined." The investigating officer concluded, "I strongly suspect that Lt Col Perry has taken bad advice from some of the senior MTIs mentioned above, but absent any evidence, I am not inclined to use that to substantiate the allegation." This is a revealing concession: "absent any evidence," the investigating officer was "not inclined" to use his mere suspicion to substantiate an allegation ... but that didn't stop him from citing this testimony without offering me or any other

---

[219] *Ibid.*, p. 32-35

188

rebuttal witnesses a chance to respond. He never specified what advice these MTIs supposedly gave me, or how it may have undermined Col. Liddick and initiatives to transform BMT. This is typical of the quality of analysis throughout the CDI, and further evidence of bias against the accused.

Secret meetings. "Back-to-Basics" strategy sessions. "Blue Rope" cliques. The conspiratorial tone of the testimony cited in this report of investigation would be laughable, had it not directly contributed to my relief of command. But as I've already shown, what Lt. Col. McConnell left out of his report is even more alarming. A careful analysis of this material raises serious questions about the credibility and motivations of these witnesses.

Let's begin at the beginning, with the formal complaint Maj. Sprouse filed a week before I was removed from command. He noted how "a select group of squadron members" was invited to a surprise party at my house, but my operations officer "never received a written invitation," he wrote, "and to my knowledge, the 1st Sgt didn't receive one either." My operations officer did acknowledge I offered a "verbal invitation," however, but apparently that wasn't good enough: "It seemed clear to me that the lack of a written invitation and last minute notification was intended to exclude me and prevent my attendance." Maj. Sprouse repeated this ridiculous accusation during the CDI, testifying I "casually mentioned" the party to him "in passing" the day before it took place, which he took to mean I "didn't really want [him] to attend."[220] Apparently my personal outreach wasn't good enough; Maj. Sprouse was waiting for an engraved invitation.

Maj. Sprouse also seemed preoccupied with the prerogatives of rank. He complained about a commander's call in September, when I called SMSgt Milne to the stage to bid farewell to the squadron. He had served as "Commander of Airmen" at that morning's BMT graduation parade, and I apparently commented on what a great job he'd done. According to Maj. Sprouse, I said, "for any officers in the audience who don't know how to march, that's how you do it!" (This was clearly a reference to the dozens of officers sitting in attendance at the parade that morning, but Maj.

---

[220] CDI witness statements, p. 50 and p. 134

Sprouse assumed I was referring only to him: "Lt Col Perry is keenly aware that I am his only other officer in the squadron.) SMSgt Milne then began to deliver his parting words, which Maj. Sprouse remembered as, "Here at BMT, we don't need the officers and chiefs, all we need is MTIs and getting back to basics!" My operations officer claimed I did not address this statement, but frankly I don't recall these words ever being said – and neither did any of the other witnesses who were present, according to their subsequent testimony. Nevertheless, Lt. Col. McConnell cited this completely uncorroborated statement in his report.

At the next commander's call, I announced quarterly award winners, and mentioned we didn't have any company-grade officers to compete in that category. Then-Capt. Sprouse confronted me back stage, informing me this was the second time I made public remarks to "belittle" him and his position, and stating: "in my 20 years of service I have never been so publicly denigrated as I was that day."[221] What Maj. Sprouse failed to mention in his formal complaint was that I immediately apologized to him, then explained to the entire squadron how my operations officer was no longer considered a CGO since his selection for promotion to Major. Both MSgt Walls and SMSgt "LG" recalled this incident, and how I corrected myself in front of everyone; neither thought I purposely meant to belittle this officer.[222] In fact, not a single witness felt I had ever disparaged Maj. Sprouse, but the investigating officer took no notice.

As noted above, several witnesses claimed I left Maj. Sprouse out of the loop. Col. Liddick went further, testifying she "believed there to be tension" between Maj. Sprouse and me, and my operations officer "seemed to be pushed into a corner." However, neither Maj. Sprouse nor any of his supporters could cite a single example of me shoving him aside or cutting him out of squadron decision-making, and several witnesses seemed to think we actually had a good relationship. That's what I thought, too, until I read what he said about me behind my back.

Another member of my key leadership team whom I allegedly marginalized was MSgt Walls. Col. Liddick noted she was handpicked to be a first sergeant at BMT, and she had an excellent record from her previous base. CMSgt Sutherland concurred, calling her "solid, a go-getter" who "advised Lt Col Perry on

---

[221] *Ibid.*, p. 134
[222] *Ibid.*, p. 60 and p. 102

matters, but he did not listen to [her]." Lt. Col. Upchurch similarly testified that I "should have used [her] talents and advice better."[223] Again, none of these witnesses offered any evidence to support their conclusions.

Lt. Col. McConnell completely ignored most the witness testimony related to my wife, Caroline, and her role in the squadron. (This was almost certainly by design, as Col. Camerer was rumored to be worried that targeting my terminally ill spouse would be a public relations nightmare.) Ms. Coleman stated she "seems to be around the squadron a lot, for hours at a time," and "is very hands on and involved in the squadron." She also stated my wife was on Facebook, "requesting all the MTIs as friends and bad mouthing TRG leadership." Maj. Sprouse mentioned my wife "was around the squadron a great deal and heavily involved in squadron matters. She would be in the building for hours at a time. Once she got to know people around the squadron, her presence and involvement became divisive." When he asked her once how she was doing, Caroline allegedly replied, "I'd be a lot better if we could get rid of this asshole commandant." MSgt Pickett also indicated the commander's wife "spends extensive time around the squadron, so much to the point that it became a distraction to the DD and MTIS staff." He claimed he brought this concern to SMSgt "LG," but she allegedly "advised him to not push back on it." When I was removed from command, Caroline "was said to have posted something to the effect of, 'Tyrant leadership is out to crucify good people'," which MSgt Pickett assumed was a reference to BMT. Several witnesses also noted Caroline and Mr. Kamel seemed to be friends, and the contractor would use her to get things done. According to MSgt Walls, the MTI School commandant believed if he told Mr. Kamel to do something he didn't want to do, the contractor would tell my wife, she would relay it to me, and Mr. Kamel would get his way.[224]

Reading through these witness statements, I also learned that some folks took issue with the policy letter I published regarding MTI students. Ms. Coleman testified my problems with MSgt Pickett began when I authorized graduates of the MTI School undergoing qualification training "to attend functions and socialize with permanent party," rather than treating them as students until they completed on-the-job training and reported to their line

---

[223] *Ibid.*, p. 75, p. 94, and p. 97
[224] *Ibid.*, p. 50, p. 57, p. 62, and p. 67

squadrons. MSgt Pickett falsely claimed this policy letter was routed on my wife's behalf, "relating to MTIS students having lunch with TRSS staff, cooked by [Mrs. Perry]. It was common knowledge that the letter was driven by [Mrs. Perry]." When he told Ms. Coleman about the letter, she supposedly said that, "because it was not yet signed, it was not yet a valid policy letter." The very next day, MSgt Pickett continued, my wife "was in the office ranting" about how the MTI School commandant said she was distracting to staff members. Following that incident, MSgt Pickett "made a point to seek out [Maj. Sprouse] and talk to [him] about the issue. During this conversation, Lt Col Perry was making faces in the window and making the situation very uncomfortable." Ms. Coleman also claimed Caroline "went on Facebook and stated that [MSgt Pickett] said Lt Col Perry's policy is wrong," and also claimed that the commandant was "bad mouthing" her.[225]

Sadly, it seems a few of my subordinates didn't much care for my wife. She was very engaged in the squadron, going out of her way to help me improve morale and unit cohesion. Caroline truly cares about people, and her selfless devotion to their welfare inspired the loyalty and affection of airmen across the organization. But she also rubbed some folks the wrong way. For example, MSgt Pickett seemed threatened by her, since the MTI School instructors appeared to trust Caroline more than him. He was widely considered an insecure leader struggling in his new role as commandant, and he perceived my wife as undermining his authority. MSgt Walls, on the other hand, seemed jealous of Caroline. People came to my wife with their problems, rather than entrust them to the squadron first sergeant. She testified how, when SSgt Little was in the hospital, she was not even aware of it, but my wife knew about it and informed me as well.[226] Maj. Sprouse's wife reportedly didn't like Caroline, either, which may explain my operations officer's antipathy. Ms. Coleman initially seemed to get along well with my wife, but when push came to shove she sided with her friends, MSgt Walls and MSgt Pickett.

Regardless of their motivations, however, these witnesses against my wife simply did not provide credible testimony. She never called my subordinates names or went on rants in the office, and she certainly didn't bad-mouth MSgt Pickett and BMT leadership on Facebook. (She did once post something about

---

[225] *Ibid.*, p. 57 and p. 67
[226] *Ibid.*, p. 62

"tyrant leadership," but this had nothing to do with Lackland; rather, it was a reference to a completely unrelated issue regarding a previous employer.) MSgt Pickett, in particular, was prone to making unsubstantiated allegations about my wife and me. For example, when Caroline catered a home-cooked lunch for people in the headquarters building, the commandant accused Mr. Kamel and SSgt Little of hanging out with her for three hours,[227] when in fact they weren't there for more than an hour or so. And the accusation that I stood outside an office and made faces at this subordinate is truly bizarre. It's really no wonder Lt. Col. McConnell chose to ignore this testimony, which only served to raise doubts about the integrity and judgment of his key witnesses.

It seems obvious in retrospect that these allegations against me had little to do with how I conducted myself, and everything to do with the fears and paranoia of Col. Liddick and her coterie of sycophants. There was nothing unprofessional about my relationships with Mr. Kamel or SSgt Little – and there was nothing reasonable about the misperceptions of my accusers. Ditto my association with "Blue Ropes" and other MTIs, in an environment where you can't swing a dead cat without knocking off a campaign hat. As an officer, I had no problem with my commissioned colleagues coming to Lackland, but I also recognized we couldn't solve the myriad problems with enlisted accession training all on our own. To claim I did not support the transformation of BMT is to completely ignore everything I said and did while in command.

Nevertheless, Lt. Col. McConnell recommended I be held "administratively accountable" for having an unprofessional relationship and "creating a perception of favoritism" towards Mr. Kamel and SSgt Little. On the other hand, he conceded, "It is worth noting that since he was originally counseled by Col. Liddick about the perception [I] was creating by socializing with selected squadron members, that behavior has stopped" regarding these two subordinates. Leaving aside the impossibility of me creating a perception in someone else's mind, the investigating officer acknowledged I had already resolved the issue months before I was removed from command.

---

[227] *Ibid.*, p. 90

Lt. Col. McConnell also again recommended I be counseled for an allegation he found unsubstantiated. "While Lt Col Perry's actions and conduct did not rise to the level of showing a lack of support for the wing's initiatives to transform BMT or prejudice good order and discipline," he wrote, "they did give the appearance of doing so. Lt Col Perry should be counseled that his conduct regarding the addition of officers to BMT, as well as his failure to include his DO in the chain of command and his failure to support the DO's role in the squadron is having a negative impact on his squadron." In addition, "Lt Col Perry's perceived association with former 'Blue Ropes' or supporting their desire to regain their power is damaging his credibility."[228] Never mind that none of the words or deeds attributed to me were true, and the so-called "clique" of Master MTIs was no more than an urban legend. Considering that Lt. Col. McConnell never offered me an opportunity to address this particular accusation, his concern about damage to my credibility seems cruelly ironic.

---

[228] McConnell report, p. 45

Chapter 9: Fraternization

In the previous chapter, I discussed how my commander-directed investigation found I had shown favoritism towards members of the "Deliberate Development" team in my squadron. Such accusations were not wholly unexpected, given how the group commander, Colonel Liddick, had previously counseled my on this subject. On the other hand, the allegation of an unprofessional relationship and fraternization with my superintendent, SMSgt "LG," came as a shock. She was the senior-most enlisted member in the squadron, and outranked all my military subordinates apart from my operations officer. Her position was to serve as a trusted advisor to the commander, particularly on matters affecting the enlisted force. Along with the first sergeant and operations officer, the superintendent was a key member of my leadership team, and the two of us were often expected to represent the squadron at official events such as base promotion ceremonies and BMT graduation events.

Yet several of my subordinates testified there was something improper about our relationship. Maj. Sprouse stated there was "a distinct level of closeness" between SMSgt "LG" and me. Although he "did not infer a sexual relationship," he did perceive a "level of attraction." MSgt Walls also indicated, "she does not feel anything sexual is taking place, although there are flirtatious behaviors exchanged," and we "frequently exchange looks." Maj. Pickett described us as "awkwardly close," and indicated we "share looks with each other and that it's obvious to many in the squadron." Mr. Steele testified there was a "perception of familiarity" between us, fostered by "[c]ertain looks such as 'googly' eyes" that we allegedly gave each other." Finally, Ms. Coleman stated we had a "personal relationship, and that "most of the unit" felt the same way. "It is clear that Lt Col Perry and [SMSgt "LG"] are friends and that it is beyond a normal working relationship," she testified.

Such insinuations are shameful and offensive. With all due respect to my former superintendent – who is undoubtedly a lovely and talented woman – I was not at all attracted to her. Although she bore some superficial similarities to my wife, Caroline, inasmuch as both are petite Hispanic females, no one in the squadron had any doubts as to my affections for my better half. Not to put too fine a point on it: Caroline is absolutely gorgeous, brilliant, and renowned at Lackland for her elegance and charm.

Everyone knew I was crazy about her, and that she felt the same way about me. Besides, both she and the superintendent's husband (a Key Spouse) spent so much time in the squadron, they surely would have noticed – or been tipped off by others – if the two of us appeared inappropriately intimate. And if Caroline had any suspicion of impropriety, there would have been hell to pay: "If his superintendent had a lazy eye, and I caught her looking at my husband cross-eyed," she used to joke, "I would have taken both of her eyes out with an ice-cream scooper."

Nevertheless, members of the group staff claimed to share this perception. CMSgt Sutherland testified he believed "there is definitely favoritism occurring in the TRSS, specifically favoritism and a possible unprofessional relationship" with SMSgt "LG." Lt. Col. Upchurch noted he believed "there is a close friendship between the Perry and ["LG"] families." Even Col. Liddick stated the relationship between me and my superintendent "appeared cozier than she would like to see it." She claimed that she moved SMSgt "LG" out of my squadron "in part because of the cozy relationship, as well as not following through on tasks." [229] However, Col. Liddick never informed either of us she felt this way, and she offered me a completely different reason for the transfer when she announced it in November. In fact, no one ever hinted to SMSgt "LG" or me that they perceived our relationship as too close or in any way inappropriate.

I had obviously misread Col. Liddick's attitude towards SMSgt "LG." Months earlier, my boss explained to me how she had defended my superintendent when her previous squadron commander attempted to eliminate her from the MTI corps over trivial allegations. In retrospect, it appears Col. Liddick was merely defending her prerogatives against an overzealous subordinate commander, rather than expressing support for this embattled senior enlisted leader. Nevertheless, although Col. Liddick issued her a letter of reprimand, she seemed supportive of SMSgt "LG" rehabilitation after that incident. So I was surprised when Col. Liddick announced she was moving my superintendent to the 319th Training Squadron, then refused to include her in a DoD subcommittee meeting on sexual assault. In hindsight, it's obvious alarm bells should have been going off for me, but I truly had no idea anyone other than MSgt Pickett had an issue with SMSgt "LG," or misperceived our relationship as anything but professional. In

---

[229] McConnell report, p. 18-21

truth, I don't think they really believed this, at least not yet. It was only after I was removed from command, during the heat of the investigation, that these witnesses coalesced around this false new narrative.

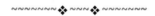

Several witnesses testified my superintendent and I socialized together off-duty. Maj. Sprouse stated, we "spent extensive amounts of time with one another, and socialized at lunch on at least two occasions." (He failed to mention I did the same with him.) MSgt Walls also stated I spent "extensive amounts of time" with SMSgt "LG," and my wife and I "frequently take SMSgt "LG" to lunch." She added, "Their families spend off duty time together," and she claimed to have seen pictures of me and my superintendent "off duty in civilian clothes." Moreover, my first sergeant suggested I seemed "to know much about SMSgt "LG"'s family but not that much about anyone else's." Ms. Coleman accused our families of dining together, and that we "often dine together and have intimate relationships with one another." MSgt Pickett even claimed that SMSgt "LG" confessed to him that she and I had dinner together, although she didn't corroborate this statement – since it never happened.

On the other hand, my superintendent testified she "was unaware that there existed a perception of friendship" between us, and she "was not friends" with me. I noted it had only recently come to my attention that someone perceived our relationship as unprofessional. "As my superintendent, she (along with my operations officer and first sergeant) naturally spent more time with me than other members of the squadron. However, we have not formed a personal relationship on terms of military equality – in fact, I never call [her] by her first name, and she has always shown me the utmost respect and deference to me and other officers and SNCOs."[230]

Apart from utterly unobjectionable claims of working lunches, none of the testimony regarding my superintendent and me was corroborated. Both SMSgt "LG" and I denied we ever had dinner or spent off-duty time together, outside of official functions such as the squadron holiday party. Furthermore, absolutely no

---

[230] *Ibid.*, p. 18-24

independent evidence was produced – such as those notorious pictures – to substantiate these claims. Moreover, SMSgt "LG"'s husband was a squadron Key Spouse, and routinely participated in BMT and unit events, so it is not unreasonable that my wife and I would know more about their family than others in the squadron. In short, there was absolutely no substance to these allegations.

The commander-directed investigation uncovered only two instances of unofficial social interaction between my superintendent and me. The first was when Caroline and I hosted the surprise party for the outgoing MTI School commandant in late September 2013. However, as Lt. Col. McConnell acknowledged, after Col. Liddick counseled me for having subordinates over to my house, "no other incidents of this behavior were noted." The other instance he identified of me "socializing with personnel under [my] command" was when my wife and I invited SMSgt "LG" and her husband to a performance of "The Nutcracker" ballet just before Christmas. Curiously, although at least three witnesses cited this incident, and SMSgt "LG" acknowledged going to the event,[231] Lt. Col. McConnell did not solicit any testimony from me about this during the CDI. If he had, I would have clarified the circumstances around the invitation, and pointed out that SMSgt "LG" had already transferred to the 319 TRS, and so was no longer under my command at that time.

Not only were my superintendent and I allegedly too familiar with one another, several witnesses also seemed to think I favored her professionally. Maj. Sprouse stated he felt as though he was viewed as "in the way," and that I would take the advice of SMSgt "LG" over his own. Further, he complained of being "pushed away or toward the back." If we disagreed on issues, I allegedly always sided with SMSgt "LG" and would "trivialize" Maj. Sprouse's position. As we saw in the previous chapter, several witnesses felt that I placed my superintendent above my operations officer in an "unofficial chain of command."

Col. Liddick claimed there was also tension between me and the first sergeant, MSgt Walls. We were not "clicking" the way we should, and I instead seemed to rely on SMSgt "LG." MSgt Walls complained I preferred my senior enlisted leader over other squadron personnel. She testified, the superintendent "knows that she has Lt Col Perry's ear, and she takes advantage of that. Lt Col Perry's guidance seemed to always come from [SMSgt "LG"]." Ms.

---

[231] *Ibid.*, p. 19-23, p. 37

Coleman echoed this sentiment: "She is always 'right there' with him. Lt Col Perry will not make a move without SMSgt "LG"'s blessing."[232]   What these subordinates seemed to forget was that the superintendent was their superior by virtue of both rank and position, and none of them cited any specific examples to support their claims. Lt. Col. McConnell nevertheless concluded that both Maj. Sprouse and MSgt Walls "feel excluded or that they lack inclusion in squadron matters, impacting their ability to do their jobs."[233]

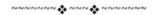

As with previous allegations, the investigating officer, Lt. Col. McConnell, left out a lot of important testimony from his report. A careful analysis of the witness statements and other evidence appended to the report of investigation actually reveals Air Force officers colluding amongst themselves and undermining their own credibility, while also exposing the investigating officer as either biased or incompetent. Had I been granted access to this evidence in a timely manner, I could have made a much more compelling case to my chain of command that this CDI was a sham. Instead, they chose to accept the investigating officer's faulty conclusions based on incomplete and misleading evidence.

In his original complaint against me, Maj. Sprouse comes across as an immature and petty junior officer who was jealous of the closeness he perceived between his commander and the senior enlisted leader. "In my opinion," my operations officer wrote, "this closeness has impaired my position and authority." He stated I had "developed a friendship with [SMSgt "LG"]" and "spent several hours each day talking with [her] in his office," an easily disproved claim. "They routinely travel to events together, and I have seen [her] make adjustments to his service dress uniform in my office that required [her] to put [her] hands inside his service dress jacket while he was wearing it," he added.[234]

Maj. Sprouse elaborated on this rather prurient insinuation in his subsequent testimony: "Lt Col Perry asked [SMSgt "LG"] to apply accoutrements to his service dress jacket, as

---

[232] *Ibid.*, p. 18-21
[233] *Ibid.*, p. 28
[234] CDI witness statements, p. 135

it had just come back [from] the dry cleaners. On one other occasion, Lt Col Perry was putting on his service dress jacket, and [SMSgt "LG"] was helping him to adjust something on it. However instead of him taking it off, [she] reached [her] hands inside the jacket while he was wearing it, which seemed inappropriate to [him] at the time." I can't help but wonder, would Maj. Sprouse have mentioned this incident if my superintendent had been a man? My senior enlisted leader and I were presumably on our way to a wing promotion ceremony, where we would appear onstage together representing the squadron, so it's really no surprise this "Blue Rope" MTI would want me to look my best. Clearly, neither of us thought anything of making minor adjustments to my outerwear in front of witnesses. As for carpooling to an official event, that's an exceedingly common occurrence among commanders and superintendents; none other than Col. Liddick and CMSgt Sutherland habitually traveled together in her staff car.

My operations officer went on to suggest it was entirely my idea for these two key leaders to have separate offices, "because [SMSgt "LG"] wanted her own" – a transparently disingenuous claim. He also noted an occasion when his officemate was having trouble opening the office door. After I came to her rescue, she allegedly grabbed my arm and exclaimed, "You're my hero!" It's not clear why he was standing around watching this scene unfold, rather than helping out a fellow airman in need, and I suspect she would have praised him or anyone else who bothered to assist. In any case, Maj. Sprouse concluded, "it was the strangest relationship he had seen in a command structure" in his 20 years of service.

In his report, Lt. Col. McConnell alluded to an incident where Maj. Sprouse claimed to have witnessed my superintendent and I "eyeing" each other. But he left out the rest of this rather revealing story. Following an Airman's Run one Thursday morning, my operations officer recalled seeing the two of us sitting together my office. SMSgt "LG" "was sprawled out on the couch with leg on the couch and [her] other foot on the floor," while I "was slouched in a separate chair directly across" from her. This onlooker testified it was clear we were both "eyeing" one another.[235] But the story doesn't end there. In her testimony, Col. Liddick recounted the same alleged incident:

---

[235] *Ibid.,* p. 49

On one occasion, [Maj. Sprouse] went to Lt Col Perry's office one morning before an Airmen's Run. [SMSgt "LG"] was in his office chatting, and both stood up abruptly when [Maj. Sprouse] walked in. Lt Col Perry said something to the effect of "We were just talking." When [Maj. Sprouse] asked to talk to Lt Col Perry, he asked if [SMSgt "LG"] could stay.[236]

There are several things troubling about this testimony. First, Col. Liddick obviously wasn't a witness to this scene, so her account is hearsay, presumably based on a prior conversation between her and my operations officer. Second, the group commander offers additional details not in Maj. Sprouse's version of events, suggesting either she made them up or he had changed his story. Third, the nature of these embellishments insinuates my superintendent and I realized we were doing something inappropriate, even though we were reportedly sitting in plain view with my office door open during regular business hours. The suggestion that we "stood up abruptly" makes no sense in this context – and depending on what Maj. Sprouse had come to talk about, it may have been perfectly reasonable for me to ask if the senior enlisted advisor should stay. Unfortunately, I have no recollection of this innocuous and entirely unremarkable incident, which says a lot more our accusers than it does about those they accused.

The testimony surrounding SMSgt "LG"'s transfer to the 319 TRS is also revealing. Lt. Col. McConnell cited Col. Liddick's claim that she "was moved out of the TRSS in part because of the cozy relationship, as well as not following through on tasks," without further elaboration, ignoring the obvious questions this statement raised. Let's begin with my superintendent's task management. CMSgt Sutherland testified, "[SMSgt "LG"] does not get things done" or follow up on issues. He "does not have faith in [her]" and "does not trust [her]," and he was "very careful about what [he] says around [her]." He mentioned an incident when he asked SMSgt "LG" to resolve an issue with trainee in-processing, but after "2-3 weeks of [him] trying to get results and follow up with [her], the problem was not fixed." On another occasion, SMSgt "LG" brought a plan to him for conducting "Blue Rope" evaluations. "[She] wanted to go back to the old way that it was conducted, which is against AETC policy," he added. Lt. Col. Upchurch testified

---

[236] *Ibid.*, p. 94

that, because of SMSgt "LG"'s "lack of performance in [her] role as superintendent, information did not flow freely from the TRSS and [she] did not meet TRG suspenses or complete TRG tasks satisfactorily." For good measure, Col. Liddick mentioned SMSgt "LG" "had failed as the 321 TRS superintendent before [she] was moved to the 737 TRSS."[237]

So if SMSgt "LG" was so bad at her job, flopping as superintendent in both the 321 TRS and 737 TRSS in less than a year, why on earth did Col. Liddick reassign her to serve as senior enlisted leader in yet another BMT squadron? No one on the group leadership team ever mentioned anything to me about my superintendent not meeting deadlines or completing tasks to their satisfaction, and that certainly wasn't the excuse Col. Liddick gave me when she announced her move to the 319 TRS. And of course at no point did my boss ever suggest my relationship with SMSgt "LG" appeared "cozier" than she would like to see it. So why was she reassigned? According to Lt. Col. Upchurch, "it was time for [SMSgt "LG"] to leave the TRSS when [she] did, as it was [her] normal rotation."

This bombshell revelation, buried on page 75 of the 287-page investigation file, has damning implications for Col. Liddick. It suggests either she deceived me about why she was transferring my superintendent to another squadron, or else she later made a false official statement to Lt. Col. McConnell about her motives for this move. If the group commander truly thought my relationship with SMSgt "LG" appeared unprofessional back in November, she had an obligation to counsel me immediately, as she had just weeks earlier regarding her perception about other subordinates in my squadron. To allow us to remain blissfully unaware of this perception, while leaving my superintendent in place another month, suggests my boss may have been setting me up for failure. Col. Liddick also should have informed me she thought my senior enlisted leader was falling down on the job, so I could mentor her to correct these deficiencies, and not simply make her someone else's problem with a lateral transfer. On the other hand, if Col. Liddick was telling the truth in November – an explanation seemingly corroborated by Lt. Col. Upchurch – then she made up the story about the "cozy" relationship after the fact. Either way, this was a clear-cut case of leadership malpractice.

---

[237] *Ibid.*, p. 75, p. 94, and p. 97

Lt. Col. McConnell not only left out testimony that undermined the credibility of his key witnesses, he also neglected to include several remarks exonerating me, and even misrepresented certain favorable comments. For example, the investigating officer cited a statement by MSgt Bell that he had a conversation with MSgt Walls on the perception of favoritism that existed in the 737 TRSS, but it's clear from the rest of his testimony that MSgt Bell didn't share this perception: "the relationship with [SMSgt "LG"] was a typical one for a new Commander and Superintendent," he said, and "nothing seemed out of the ordinary." He indicated I had talked to SMSgt "LG" for a significant amount of time regarding personnel moves, but I also spoke at length with other members of my leadership team on the same subject. Another example: Lt. Col. McConnell cited testimony from MSgt Chavez about "a perception of social lunches with certain personnel," but neglected to mention that this senior NCO said he did not see me "favoring any personnel over anyone else in the squadron," and every event he attended "has seemed like normal Commander socializing."[238]

The investigating officer also suppressed evidence favorable to me. For example, my superintendent described MSgt Walls as "a good person" who "sometimes seems tired and run down," but she was "still adjusting to BMT and still trying to figure out Lt Col Perry." MSgt Walls seemed to agree, acknowledging she "did not get off on the right foot" with me: "This was Lt Col Perry's first command," she testified, and I had already established a relationship with SMSgt "LG" before the first sergeant arrived in the squadron. Nevertheless, she claimed the superintendent and I "would discuss First Sergeant-type matters together" without her, never indicating what these might be. Yet another example: when discussing "The Nutcracker" incident, Lt. Col. Upchurch acknowledged that, "as a one-time occurrence during the holidays, it would possibly be acceptable, but such outings as the norm would not be acceptable."[239] The investigating officer made no effort to highlight such exculpatory evidence.

---

[238] *Ibid.*, p. 71-72 and p. 77
[239] *Ibid.*, p. 60, p. 74, and p. 105

As part of the CDI's fourth allegation – that I failed to support 37th Training Wing initiatives – I was accused of ignoring the established alleged misconduct report process. According to Lt. Col. McConnell, Maj. Sprouse provided a sworn statement that I had given him the impression I was "dismissive" of the AMR process.[240] However, in his subsequent testimony, Maj. Sprouse contradicted this claim, affirming I had "never made any negative statements about the AMR process."[241]

But that wasn't the real issue. This was about whether I had properly handled a comment by an MTI student in an end-of-course survey in October, which claimed SMSgt "LG," had "scolded" the class for behavior she considered unprofessional. As I discussed in a previous chapter, my superintendent informed me of the incident when it happened, and I wholeheartedly approved of the way she addressed it. However, when the critique made it to Col. Liddick in early December, she asked me to determine if this should be investigated as maltreatment under the AMR process. I assured the group commander I was already well aware of the circumstances surrounding this incident, and no maltreatment occurred. Col. Liddick persisted, accusing SMSgt "LG" of "yelling" at the students and giving them a "butt chewing," even though the anonymous MTI student never alleged anything of the sort.

In her CDI testimony, Col. Liddick again falsely claimed the critique had accused SMSgt "LG" of "yelling at MTIS students," and that I had simply "dismissed it," as I "was sure [SMSgt "LG"] was 100% professional." She also claimed Maj. Sprouse later made her aware that I had told SMSgt "LG," I "got it off her back."[242] In his original complaint, Maj. Sprouse alleged I was leaving for the day on December 5, 2013, when I stopped by SMSgt "LG"'s desk in the office they shared. I allegedly told her she "shouldn't worry about the complaint issue," as I had sent Col. Liddick a message that should have "gotten it off your back." I supposedly added, "it's just silliness," before departing.[243] Col. Liddick testified Maj. Sprouse "subsequently sent her an email detailing the conversation," and it was at that time she "brought the issue up to the TRG level and initiated the AMR for maltreatment, which came back unsubstantiated." However, this account doesn't quite add up. Col.

[240] McConnell report, p. 30
[241] CDI witness statements, p. 50
[242] McConnell report, p. 31
[243] CDI witness statements, p. 94-95 and p. 134

Liddick had already informed me she was going to appoint someone to look into this matter before I left work that day, so she couldn't have made this decision after this alleged conversation took place.

Lt. Col. McConnell concluded, "in not investigating thoroughly the possible AMR involving [SMSgt "LG"], Lt Col Perry failed to follow established policy. It certainly was not prejudicial to good order and discipline," however. It's not like I ignored AMRs altogether, encouraged personnel not to report, or impeded the investigation into SMSgt "LG"'s alleged misconduct. Rather, in his opinion, it was my alleged favoritism towards SMSgt "LG" that "resulted in [Col. Liddick] being pushed aside" and supposedly prompted my "disregard" of her AMR.[244] According to Lt. Col. Upchurch, I did not press forward with an AMR for my superintendent "belittling" students (an allegation no student ever made) because of my "favoritism toward SMSgt "LG."" CMSgt Sutherland also insisted my "lack of judgment regarding the AMR" was caused by favoritism.[245]

Although the critique didn't actually accuse SMSgt "LG" of yelling or anything else that could be considered maltreatment, and subsequent investigation confirmed this fact, Lt. Col. McConnell nevertheless concluded I "failed to appropriately handle the End of Course comment regarding yelling at MTIS students." He then proceeded to chastise me for my supposed error:

> He knew or should have known the proper procedures for handling a potential Alleged Misconduct Report, and that upon receiving such a comment, he was not supposed conduct an inquiry, not to evaluate the veracity of the complaint and dismiss it. It is likely, as noted by [Lt. Col. Upchurch] and [CMSgt Sutherland], that his perceived favoritism towards [SMSgt "LG"] clouded his judgment on the matter. I find this incident compelling, despite the fact that I agree that it probably had something to do with favoritism versus a general lack of support for the AMR process. As a squadron commander, Lt Col Perry needed to enforce the 2 AF/CC policies, not dismiss or circumvent them. This was not an act of omission; Col. Liddick gave him

---

[244] McConnell report, p. 35
[245] *Ibid.,* p. 20-21

the opportunity to properly deal with the situation and he essentially declined.[246]

This conclusion couldn't be more mistaken. Lt. Col. McConnell failed to cite my testimony in this matter, and it doesn't appear he bothered to even read the end-of-course survey critique that started it all. Had he done so, he would have realized Col. Liddick made this whole thing up. I immediately corrected my boss when she falsely accused SMSgt "LG" of "yelling" in our e-mail correspondence, yet she persisted in launching an AMR anyway. She knew subsequent investigation confirmed the students were merely scolded, not yelled at, yet she nevertheless cited this incident as an example of me not supporting the AMR process. Her lackeys, Lt. Col. Upchurch and CMSgt Sutherland, went even further, accusing me of favoritism for not needlessly persecuting my superintendent. These witnesses were either willfully ignorant of the facts, or intentionally trying to discredit SMSgt "LG" with false allegations of misconduct.

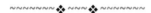

The final allegation against me was something of an afterthought, added once the CDI was already underway. I was officially accused of having "directed the destruction" of SMSgt "LG"'s personnel information file, in violation of an AETC and 2 AF policy memoranda from October and November 2012, respectively. Despite the fact that no element of this allegation was true – neither this PIF nor any of its contents were destroyed, and the specified policies were no longer in effect – the investigating officer, Lt. Col. McConnell, somehow convinced himself of my culpability.

At issue was the letter signed by the 2 AF commander, which stated, "All contents within the PIF must remain in the PIF upon change of supervisors."[247] I allegedly violated this when I removed a letter of reprimand from SMSgt "LG"'s PIF on December 20, 2013, the day she transferred to the 319 TRS. However, such policy letters are meant to be temporary, and in any case this

---

[246] McConnell report, p. 34

[247] Maj. Gen. Leonard Patrick, 2 AF/CC, "Policy Regarding Review of Personnel Information Files (PIFs)," November 8, 2012

particular policy had been superseded by 2 AF Guidance Memorandum 36-01, *Standards of Conduct and Training*, published September 17, 2013, which no longer prohibited removal of documents from PIFs. Moreover, Col. Liddick explicitly authorized her squadron commanders, in late October or early November, to remove derogatory information from PIFs, so long as this paperwork did not concern misconduct stemming from an AMR, and had already been considered in an enlisted performance report during the applicable reporting period. Two of my colleagues – Lt. Col. Chad Gallagher and Lt. Col. Rick Gerahart – confirmed this guidance in their CDI testimony, and at least four commanders reportedly acknowledged removing documents from PIFs.[248]

When Col. Liddick called me into her office on December 24 to ask me about SMSgt "LG"'s PIF, she denied having granted such authorization, and she did so again later that week when informing the other squadron commanders I was under investigation. During the CDI, however, Col. Liddick changed her story, testifying she "gave direction that if a commander wished to remove something derogatory from a member's PIF to bring it to [her] for review, and [she] would make the decision on whether to remove the item." The group superintendent, CMSgt Sutherland, claimed he remembered Col. Liddick saying she would be the one to make the decision to remove derogatory paperwork in PIFs, but her deputy, Lt. Col. Upchurch, denied there was any 737 TRG PIF policy.

The biggest concern these witnesses expressed was not that I violated some higher-headquarters policy, but that I had shown poor judgment in not asking Col. Liddick's permission first. She objected that I didn't come to her with this request, and that I pulled the LOR "without her knowledge or consent." CMSgt Sutherland noted that it was Col. Liddick who had issued the LOR to SMSgt "LG," so it was "common sense that no one would remove a derogatory piece of paperwork that someone of higher rank issued." Lt. Col. McConnell posed a hypothetical situation to the two other squadron commanders he interviewed about whether they thought they had the discretion to remove derogatory information from a PIF that was issued by someone above him in the chain of command. Both indicated there was no official guidance that covered that type of situation, but neither would remove paperwork in a situation like that without at least talking

---

[248] McConnell report, p. 37-38 and p. 42

to whomever issued it. Lt. Col. Upchurch stated he could possibly entertain a squadron commander removing derogatory paperwork from a PIF if he or she issued that paperwork, but only if approved at higher levels. He also revealed that it was he who discovered the LOR was missing, when he was gathering information for the AMR Col. Liddick initiated earlier that month against SMSgt "LG." Like that previous incident, Lt. Col. Upchurch stated he believed I removed this disciplinary paperwork due to my "favoritism toward SMSgt "LG.""

My unit program coordinator, Ms. Coleman, offered some particularly provocative testimony. She stated SMSgt "LG" had asked me "on several occasions" to remove her LOR, and she also requested I erase the record of this document from her PIF contents log. She further claimed to have witnessed me shred the LOR, apparently in front of SMSgt "LG."[249] But this was not true: I actually placed this document in a desk drawer in my office, a fact which the investigating officer acknowledged. When SMSgt "LG" denied knowing how the LOR was removed, Lt. Col. McConnell suggested SMSgt "LG" should be investigated "for suspicion of providing a false office [sic] statement."[250] On the other hand, he did not accuse Ms. Coleman of lying about witnessing me shred the LOR, or question the credibility of other testimony she provided.

Lt. Col. McConnell also did not "question the truthfulness" of Col. Liddick concerning her guidance regarding the removal of items from PIFs. "I simply do not think she realized there was confusion among her squadron commanders," he concluded, even though none of the commanders he interviewed seemed at all confused about her guidance. In the investigating officer's opinion, my actions did violate the 2 AF policy letter, although it contained a "clear gap" in guidance and was unenforceable under Article 92, UCMJ. Lt. Col. McConnell further noted one could also argue I violated Col. Liddick's guidance by removing an LOR on the grounds it was "AMR-related," since SMSgt "LG'"s paperwork "pertained to her failing to inform her squadron commander of multiple reports of MTI misconduct." However, in this case I "would then be guilty of not adhering to guidance Col. Liddick had no authority to give and that she does not remember giving."

On the other hand, Lt. Col. McConnell explicitly questioned my judgment: "I think Lt Col Perry made a bad decision regarding

---

249 *Ibid.*, p. 37-39
250 *Ibid.*, p. 46

removing the LOR from [SMSgt "LG"'s] PIF." First of all, he felt that the LOR in question was "AMR related," even though no AMR was initiated against SMSgt "LG" in that matter, and the LOR she received was not the result of an AMR investigation. The investigating officer also thought removing the LOR "showed either a lack of judgment or a lack of experience." I should have known that since Col. Liddick issued the LOR, it would have been appropriate to consult her before removing it. "But you cannot teach judgment or experience, and it is not surprising to me that as a first-time squadron commander Lt Col Perry did not possess the needed judgment or experience in such a matter." Lt. Col. McConnell thought I was "by and large" being truthful, but that I knew I was "taking a risk in removing the LOR from [SMSgt "LG"'s] PIF." He argued, "If he thought he was following guidance by removing a non-AMR-related LOR from her PIF after the applicable EPR reporting period, he could have done so any time after he took command instead of waiting until the day [SMSgt "LG"] out-processed the squadron. And he would not have retained it in his desk instead of destroying it."[251]

This brings us to what Lt. Col. McConnell thought was the "most egregious part" of my removal of the LOR: how it "relates to the favoritism" I showed or was "perceived to have shown" to my superintendent. "He either does not realize that he shows favoritism or creates the perception of showing favoritism towards [SMSgt "LG"], or he chooses to not know or not to care that this real or perceived favoritism exists," he concluded. "In removing this LOR he created the manifestation of the perceived favoritism that many of his subordinates and his commander testified to. But that does not equate to violating AETC/CC or 2 AF/CC PIF policies."

This was a remarkable inference for the investigating officer to draw, as only one witness, Lt. Col. Upchurch, testified that he believed I removed the LOR out of favoritism. Other than Ms. Coleman and (allegedly) SMSgt "LG," no other members of my squadron were even aware of this incident before I was removed from command, so it cannot reasonably have contributed to an appearance of favoritism. Moreover, to imply I chose not to know

---

[251] *Ibid.*, p. 42-43

or care about a perception of favoritism suggests that I ignored clear evidence such a perception existed. But not a single witness testified that they ever told anyone – not me, not my superintendent, not our spouses, not even each other – that they perceived our relationship as unprofessional. Was I expected to read their minds?

In the end, Lt. Col. McConnell concluded I did violate the 2 AF policy letter – but that I could not be held accountable under Article 92 for failure to obey an order or regulation. Moreover, with the subsequent publication of AETC and 2 AF guidance on the same subject, he concluded it seems they likely these policy letters "should have been voided or superseded and those publications do not contain a specific prohibition against removing derogatory information from a PIF." (In fact, such policy letters automatically expire after one year, according to Air Force Instruction 33-360.) Finally, he acknowledged I removed the LOR from the PIF "seemingly under the guidance of Col. Liddick." Having laid out a line of reasoning clearly exonerating me of this charge, the investigating officer's final sentence in this section is a jarring non sequitur: "I conclude this allegation is SUBSTANTIATED."

Did you catch that bewildering leap of logic? Lt. Col. McConnell acknowledged the policy I allegedly violated had expired and been replaced, and Col. Liddick gave her squadron commanders different guidance on this subject. Yet he nevertheless concluded that I alone had done something wrong. By his incomprehensible reasoning, the other squadron commanders who removed documents from PIFs under Col. Liddick's guidance also violated the policy. And if, as the investigating officer noted, Col. Liddick had no authority to give such guidance, then she too should have been held accountable. But the CDI wasn't an exercise in accountability; it was about manufacturing excuses to relieve me of command.

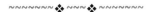

The legal test for fraternization between an officer and an enlisted member includes several factors, including "whether the conduct has compromised the chain of command, resulted in the appearance of partiality, or otherwise undermined good order, discipline, authority, or morale." The "acts and circumstances must be such as to lead a reasonable person experienced in the problems of military leadership to conclude that the good order and discipline of the armed forces has been prejudiced by their tendency to compromise the respect of enlisted persons for the professionalism, integrity, and obligations of an officer." Lt. Col. McConnell concluded not only that my relationship with SMSgt "LG" was unprofessional, but also that I had committed fraternization with my senior enlisted leader.

He claimed there was "strong evidence" that my "close association and social interaction (at official and non-official functions)" with my superintendent met the criteria for this offense, and numerous "reasonable" persons concluded good order and discipline had been disrupted.[252]

There are several problems with this conclusion. First, the evidence is far from overwhelming: most witness statements were not corroborated, and several of those that were suggest collusion rather than confirmation. Take, for example, the fact that multiple witnesses made a point of denying a perception of a sexual relationship between my superintendent and me, then turned around and accused us of engaging in seemingly intimate behavior. Yet not only did both of us adamantly deny any inappropriate conduct towards each other, our spouses – who were routinely in and around the squadron, and presumably would have noted any funny business – have vouched for our professional behavior. Another example: both MSgt Walls and Ms. Coleman were quoted saying almost exactly the same thing about how I favored my superintendent over all others. Was this coincidence, or paraphrasing by the investigating officer? Or is this an indication these witnesses (who happen to be personal friends) collaborated on their testimony? The testimony surrounding SMSgt "LG" and me dining together has a similarly rehearsed feel to it, since there is no evidence we shared even one evening meal outside of official functions.

Second, the investigating officer presented scant evidence that a perception of unprofessional relationships or favoritism compromised the chain of command, or undermined good order and discipline or morale. Among the "tangible" impacts of this perception was that MSgt Walls and Maj. Sprouse "feel excluded or that they lack inclusion in squadron matters, impacting their ability to do their jobs." However, in addition to our weekly staff meeting, the operations officer, first sergeant, and superintendent met regularly with me several mornings each week to discuss squadron

---

[252] *Ibid.*, p. 28-29

business. Furthermore, complaints that I valued the advice of my superintendent are absurd: she was my senior enlisted leader, a "Blue Rope" MTI with an impeccable record – at least until she ran afoul of Col. Liddick in early 2013. Neither of these subordinates offered even a single example of me siding with SMSgt "LG" over them.

Third, Lt. Col. McConnell asserted that the numerous witnesses who concluded good order and discipline was disrupted were "reasonable." I have already addressed the likelihood of collusion among these subordinates, several of whom had an incentive to embellish their testimony. Maj. Sprouse stood to benefit directly from my removal, and MSgt Walls and MSgt Pickett may have feared for their "firewall 5" enlisted performance reports. When they learned how receptive their additional rater, Col. Liddick, was to complaints about me, my days were numbered. Even if each and every one of these witnesses was telling the truth, what impact did my perceived behavior have on the squadron? Lt. Col. McConnell conceded that my actions "may not have resulted in any real benefits of favoritism," and none of the witnesses cited a single instance of unfair treatment. Rather, their testimony comes across as petty and biased, and it's hard to see how the relationship between me and my supposedly "favored" subordinates undermined good order and discipline, or affected the morale of any "reasonable" persons.

The investigating officer's analysis was flawed in several other ways. He presented multiple allegations against me without including any testimony from the accused, offering a one-sided, biased portrayal of my purported actions. Furthermore, he found only five people in my squadron who claimed to believe I was showing favoritism. This hardly suggests a widespread perception, especially considering the evidence of collusion among these witnesses and Col. Liddick, and the number of my subordinates who later provided character reference letters on my behalf (more on that in the next chapter). Moreover, Lt. Col. McConnell seemed oblivious to the fact that several of the alleged examples of favoritism were not known to these witnesses before I was removed from command, and so couldn't have contributed to their perception until after the fact.

Finally, perhaps the most inexplicable oversight by Lt. Col. McConnell involved Col. Liddick's testimony about my relationship with my superintendent. She claimed she transferred SMSgt "LG" out of the squadron "in part because of the cozy relationship."

However, it doesn't appear the investigating officer bothered to ask Col. Liddick whether she informed me this was the reason for the move, or counseled me or my superintendent for the appearance she accused us of creating. He also failed to note that most of the alleged incidents of favoritism occurred in the month following Col. Liddick's announcement of this move, on November 18, and so might been prevented had she properly mentored me. Col. Liddick's testimony, in fact, reveals an appalling failure of leadership, and casts doubt on the integrity of the entire investigation. I actually believe the allegation of unprofessional relationships with my senior enlisted leader was a complete fabrication, concocted after the fact to support my boss's witch-hunt.

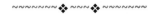

Col. Liddick's admission that she did not trust me or my superintendent is among the most alarming testimony offered during the CDI. Although the investigation was not yet complete when she made this statement, it was clear my commander had already made up her mind about me. While Col. Liddick never informed me she felt this way, her actions documented throughout the report of investigation clearly demonstrate her mistrust. It's not clear what we did to lose her trust, but considering how many times the CDI caught her in a lie, the source of mistrust seems to lie with the superior officer.

For example, Col. Liddick accused me of failing to initiate an AMR against SMSgt "LG," even though no misconduct was actually alleged, and she had already found the incident unsubstantiated before my CDI even began. She nevertheless cited this as evidence that I did not support the AMR process and other 37 TRW initiatives. Although the investigating officer found the overall allegation unsubstantiated, he agreed with Lt. Col. Upchurch and CMSgt Sutherland that my favoritism towards SMSgt "LG" clouded my judgment. A second example of Col. Liddick's mistrust was her allegation that I removed disciplinary paperwork from my superintendent's PIF. Again, she did not cite this as an example of favoritism by me, but Lt. Col. Upchurch did – and the investigating officer agreed.

And yet, elsewhere in the report of investigation, Lt. Col. McConnell concluded that my actions "may not have resulted in any real benefits of favoritism." If, as CMSgt Sutherland claimed, "It was common knowledge around the TRG that SMSgt "LG" had derogatory paperwork," [253] it's not clear how removing this paperwork from her PIF somehow manifested favoritism – or why other squadron commanders who also removed derogatory information from their subordinates' PIFs were not held to the same standard. Like the AMR allegation, this seems rather to be a manifestation of Col. Liddick's mistrust of the 737 TRSS leadership team.

The investigating officer thought the most "egregious" part of my removal of the LOR from SMSgt "LG"'s PIF was "as it relates to the favoritism" I was alleged to have shown to my superintendent, concluding I was either clueless or indifferent. Yet he presented no evidence I was ever aware this relationship was perceived as unprofessional, and he certainly did not build a case that I callously chose not to know or care. He didn't ask any of the witnesses if they informed me, my superintendent, or our spouses of their concerns, so it's not clear how we were expected to figure out that others were misperceiving (or worse, misrepresenting) my actions. Alarmingly, Lt. Col. McConnell actually documented evidence of duplicity by my commander towards her subordinates, suggesting Col. Liddick was plotting my downfall for months before she engineered my ouster. The compilation of testimony, in fact, reveals not fraternization and favoritism, but rather conspiracy and corruption.

Lt. Col. McConnell concluded, "Lt Col Perry has a fundamental misunderstanding of the definition of unprofessional relationship and the creation of perceptions of favoritism, and the impact his actions are having on the good order and discipline in the 737 TRSS and 737 TRG."[254] On the contrary, it was actually the investigating officer who was confused. Nothing about my behavior "reasonably" created the appearance of favoritism or detracted from my authority, and there was no evidence whatsoever I misused my position or abandoned organizational goals for personal interests. Air Force Instruction 36-2909, *Professional and Unprofessional Relationships*, notes that sharing off-duty interests on a frequent or recurring basis can be, or can reasonably be perceived to be, unprofessional:

---

[253] *Ibid.*, p. 39
[254] McConnell report, p. 28-29

While an occasional round of golf, game of racquetball or similar activity between a supervisor and a subordinate could remain professional, daily or weekly activities could result at a minimum in the perception of an unprofessional relationship. Similarly, while it might be appropriate for a first sergeant to play golf with a different group of officers from his or her organization each weekend, in order to get to know them better, playing with the same officers every weekend might be, or reasonably be perceived to be, unprofessional.

Considering I interacted with SMSgt "LG" outside of work and official social events only two times – at a surprise going-away party and the ballet – it was not reasonable to perceive our relationship as unprofessional based on this evidence. AFI 36-2909 also recommends actions in response to unprofessional relationships: "Experience has shown that counseling is often an effective first step in curtailing unprofessional relationships." Whenever it is apparent lesser administrative action may not be effective, an "order to terminate a relationship, or the offensive portion of a relationship, can and should be given."[255] Col. Liddick and Col. Camerer chose neither of these options, instead arbitrarily opting to remove me from command.

At the end of his report, Lt. Col. McConnell made a series of recommendations regarding my actions and conduct. He suggested I should be counseled about my "failure to initiate AMR reporting and investigation requirements," as well as the perception that I "did so as a function of favoritism" or my unprofessional relationship with my former superintendent. He continued,

While Lt Col Perry technically violated the 2 AF/CC policy on PIFs, that policy cannot impose compliance requirements. In addition, Lt Col Perry removed the LOR from [SMSgt "LG"'s] PIF under the guidance of [Col. Liddick]. If the policy was required to be adhered to, she had no authority to give such guidance. However, Lt Col Perry should be counseled that he demonstrated poor decision making and a lack of judgment in removing the LOR from [SMSgt "LG"'s] PIF, fostering the perception of favoritism by him towards [SMSgt "LG"].

---

[255] Air Force Instruction 36-2909, *Professional and Unprofessional Relationships,"* May 1, 1999

There's no "technically" about it: this 2 AF policy was no longer in effect at the time of this incident, and Lt. Col. McConnell went on to recommend that AETC, 2 AF, or 37 TRW "should issue clear guidance that there are no circumstances under which anyone can remove derogatory information from a PIF, if that is what is intended." This is precisely what Col. Camerer did in February 2014, before my CDI was even complete, confirming the higher-headquarters policy in place when I removed the LOR was not clear on this point.

In fact, Lt. Col. McConnell recommended I be counseled for each and every allegation, even those he found unsubstantiated. However, with only one exception, this was the most serious corrective action he recommended – not admonition, reprimand, and certainly not relief of command. In fact, it's clear the investigating officer expected me to return to the helm of the 737 TRSS. "Lt Col Perry needs to commit himself to correcting the perception of favoritism with both the members of command and 737 TRG leadership, and regain the trust of his subordinates and commander," he suggested. [256] Elsewhere in the report, he concluded the relationship between MSgt Pickett and me was "unrepairable,"[257] but he had no recommendation to address our working relationship. On the other hand, the departure of SMSgt "LG" from the 737 TRSS "should help some to correct the perception of favoritism."[258] If only Col. Camerer had heeded the advice of his investigating officer, I would soon have returned to command.

---

[256] *Ibid.*, p. 45
[257] *Ibid.*, p. 46
[258] *Ibid.*, p. 29

Chapter 10: Relief of Command

As we've seen over the last few chapters, the commander-directed investigation against me was a complete farce, a show trial meant to validate a preordained decision. The officer Col. Camerer selected to conduct the inquiry, Lt. Col. McConnell, was competing directly with me for stratification from our senior rater, as we were both in the primary zone for promotion to Colonel that year, an obvious conflict of interest. This investigating officer interviewed only enough personnel to support the allegations against me, and steered clear of those who might contradict the official narrative. He cherry-picked the most damning testimony, ignoring or misrepresenting any statements that might exonerate me or undermine the credibility of his key witnesses. He declared three allegations substantiated, but failed to present a compelling case I had done anything wrong. Several times he argued convincingly against his own conclusions, and his most damning finding – that I fraternized with my superintendent – didn't stand up to legal review. In the end, he made no insinuation I should be relieved of command, and the flimsy results of this sham investigation offered no basis to fire me or ruin my distinguished military career.

In an undated memorandum attached to the report, Col. Camerer noted his concurrence with the findings and conclusions of the investigating officer. However, the wing commander was under no obligation to follow Lt. Col. McConnell's recommendations when he reprimanded me on March 10, 2014. He claimed the CDI substantiated "three serious allegations" against me, yet he framed them differently than the investigating officer had. Col. Camerer reprimanded me for "wrongfully" making statements that caused members of my unit to question my conduct, and I also "wrongfully" removed an LOR from a PIF, "in contravention of established policy" of which I was aware. He asserted the "wrongfulness of this action at the time" was reflected by my "decision to maintain the removed document" in my locked desk, a conclusion different than that reached by the investigating officer. Most surprisingly, Col. Camerer alleged only that I "engaged in conduct with subordinate personnel that created the appearance of unprofessional relationships and favoritism" – not that I actually carried on such relationships or fraternized with anyone."[259]

I was initially given three days to submit a rebuttal for Col. Camerer to consider before making a decision about whether to uphold this reprimand, or perhaps downgrade or even rescind it. My area defense counsel not only obtained a copy of the CDI report of investigation, she also successfully petitioned for additional time to provide a response. I was ultimately afforded a full week to draft my refutation, as well as assemble as many character reference letters as possible – given that I was still barred by a no-contact order from communicating with any of my subordinates.

The redacted report of investigation was very useful in shaping my arguments. I was able to decipher who most of the complainants and witnesses were, which helped me put their testimony in context. I was also able to use many elements of the investigating officer's analysis and conclusions to make a case against his findings. I provided a first draft to my ADC on March 14, and she suggested some changes in how I handled the favoritism part of the response, which we discussed over the phone that weekend while Caroline and I were visiting the Houston Livestock Show and Rodeo. By Sunday, my seven-page response was complete.

I tried to strike a contrite tone in my rebuttal, knowing my fate was in Col. Camerer's hands. "I am ashamed to have brought such discredit upon myself and my squadron through my inappropriate words and deeds," I wrote to the wing commander. "I am sincerely sorry for the mistakes I have made in my short time as commander of the 737 TRSS, and I am distressed that I may not be afforded the opportunity to make amends. Please take this response into consideration when making your decision on the appropriate disposition of this case."

I addressed the most serious allegation first: "I am mortified that so many members of my squadron believe I have shown favoritism towards certain subordinates, and that my group leadership shared this sentiment as well. I have never intentionally

---

[259] Col. Mark Camerer, "Letter of Reprimand (LOR)," March 10, 2014

engaged in behavior which I considered unprofessional with any personnel under my command, and I had no idea the extent to which my actions had created the appearance of favoritism. I am truly sorry for my actions, and am thankful they have not resulted in any real benefits of favoritism for the affected members."

I noted "no one in my squadron or group leadership ever hinted to me they saw my relationship with my former superintendent as anything but professional and proper," and at no point did Col. Liddick share her concerns that our relationship was "cozier" than she liked. During my regular meetings with my key staff, I never sensed Maj. Sprouse or MSgt Walls felt excluded or were unable to do their jobs, and I was "saddened to discover they may have felt this way, and that they never brought any concerns to my attention." On the contrary, "the biggest complaint I heard from my DO and superintendent was that they were required to share an office, which hampered their ability to discuss sensitive issues or counsel squadron members." Maj. Sprouse "was also frustrated that the 737 TRG Training Director, Dr. Munro, treated him as an action officer for various BMT 'restoring the trust' initiatives, which took him away from his squadron duties," so consequently "I relied more heavily on SMSgt "LG," the next-most senior-ranking member of the squadron."

In my response, I tried to place my relationship with my superintendent in the proper context. Col. Liddick had advised me to "listen to my Chief" during my initial performance feedback, by which I assumed she meant my superintendent – and this was precisely the model I followed as a squadron commander and throughout my Air Force career. "Our professional roles require us to spend a great deal of time working together, and we've also both attended a number of official social functions." Furthermore, because her husband was a squadron Key Spouse, "Caroline and I got to know them and their family a little bit better than the other key leaders in my squadron, who attended extracurricular events infrequently if at all."

Another reason I didn't anticipate an allegation of favoritism towards SMSgt "LG" is the fact that I had "made every effort to cultivate similarly close professional relationships with the other members of my leadership team." I invited Maj. Sprouse and MSgt Walls to the party at my house, extended dinner invitations to each flight chief and the unit program coordinator, and treated Maj. Sprouse and Ms. Coleman to lunch. Caroline brought in homemade meals for each and every member of my leadership team, and we provided MSgt Walls and MSgt Ward welcome baskets when they arrived in the squadron. Bottom line, "I attempted to build a personal relationship with all my squadron leaders, and I feel that I would have developed the same level of closeness with Maj. Sprouse and MSgt Walls if they had been responsive to my efforts." Regarding my relationship with Mr. Kamel and SSgt Little, "I immediately corrected my behavior after it was brought to my attention" in late October 2013, and Lt. Col. McConnell noted no other incidents of alleged favoritism towards them since that time.

According to AFI 36-2909, "Experience has shown that counseling is often an effective first step in curtailing unprofessional relationships." Lt. Col. McConnell noted how I corrected my behavior in response to Col. Liddick's counseling, but "I was not made aware of the perception regarding my relationship with SMSgt "LG," for I would certainly have addressed this as well." AFI 36-2909 also advises, "Action should normally be the least severe necessary to terminate the unprofessional aspects of the relationship." With the departure of SMSgt "LG" and Mr. Kamel from the 737 TRSS, "there is no further risk of me creating the appearance of favoritism."

"The truth is," I continued, "I have never played favorites among my subordinates." One of my top priorities as commander was to promote unit cohesion and esprit de corps, and strengthen the family support network, so "Caroline and I tried to be very visible and accessible in all squadron work centers." We brought home-cooked food to every single flight, routinely reached out to anyone who was sick or celebrating the birth of a new baby, and welcomed each new MTI class by introducing them to their Key Spouses. "This program was such a success, Col. Liddick chose us to brief Gen Rand and his wife when they visited BMT."

Next, I addressed the allegation I made statements undermining Col. Liddick's command authority. "I sincerely regret saying anything which was interpreted as critical of my chain of command," I wrote, noting my confusion over the division of responsibility between the support squadron and group staff. I was relieved Lt. Col. McConnel noted that these comments "did not produce any tangible results, such as a breakdown of the chain of command or Col. Liddick's guidance being disregarded," but "I should have been much more careful in expressing myself to my subordinates."

Finally, I addressed "the most puzzling of the substantiated allegations": that I removed an LOR from SMSgt "LG"'s PIF "in contravention of established policy of which I was aware." Despite conflicting guidance on this issue, "I still deeply regret my actions." I acknowledged it was foolish to remove an LOR Col. Liddick issued without consulting her first, but "it never occurred to me my action was wrong, since I knew it to be consistent with Col. Liddick's guidance." She testified she authorized us to remove derogatory information from PIFs under certain conditions, and several BMT commanders, including myself, executed her guidance as we understood it. "Most disturbing was the appearance of favoritism I created by removing derogatory information from this particular PIF," I conceded, "considering the perception that existed of an unprofessional relationship between me and my former superintendent. Had I realized how widespread this perception was, I would never have acted so rashly. I have learned from this mistake and I am sorry that my decisions have lessened me in your esteem," I wrote the wing commander.

I ended this pathetic appeal with a recitation of my resume, noting "I did not get to this point in my military career by failing to live up to the expectations of my superiors." I was honored by my selection for squadron command, "all the more so when I realized the effort that went into assembling the current BMT leadership team": I "would hate to let you or any of them down." I respectfully requested Col. Camerer withdraw the LOR, or at least consider downgrading it to a letter of counseling or admonition. Whatever disciplinary action he ultimately took, I asked him to "please restore me to command of the 737 TRSS as soon as possible. I am confident I can continue to be effective in this position, and will correct the perception of favoritism and regain the trust of my subordinates and commander in my decision making and judgment."[260]

I managed to gather over a dozen character reference letters during that week in March, which I hoped would provide a more balanced perspective on my time in command than the

---

[260] Lt. Col. Craig Perry, "Response to Letter of Reprimand (LOR)," March 17, 2014

biased testimony of the handful of witnesses interviewed during the CDI. I was able to convince three of my fellow squadron commanders – Lt. Col. Dat Lam, Lt. Col. Liz Valenzuela, and Lt. Col. John Gondol – to write recommendations. Caroline reached out to several of my subordinates, including MSgt Danny Spaide, SSgt Melinda Hayes, SSgt Veronica Jackson, and Mr. Hassan Kamel, all of whom wrote letters of support. We also received responses from the former BMT superintendent, CMSgt Ken Williams, and the former MTI School commandant, CMSgt David Milne, as well as his wife, Pam, and SMSgt "LG"'s husband, a squadron Key Spouse. Finally, Caroline wrote a letter of her own, taking responsibility for her part in my circumstances. (My ADC also received letters from two other subordinates I allegedly favored, SMSgt "LG" and SSgt Tommy Little, but she opted not to share these with me or include them in the package.)

My fellow squadron commanders offered strong endorsements of me, all the more remarkable given the BMT command climate in those days. "Lt Col Perry is an exceptional human being," Lt. Col. Lam wrote. "I do not believe it is my place to judge him as a leader; however, I do think that I know him well enough to speak to his constitution and personal values." Lt. Col. Valenzuela called me "a great officer who has been hand selected at a very high level to come to BMT. He is an asset to our team and has been a great friend to us all," she wrote, and "one of the most professional and distinguished officers I have met." Lt. Col. Gondol was even more unequivocal: "As a BMT squadron commander, Lt Col Perry has an awesome responsibility training America's Airmen. Throughout the performance of his duties and during our personal interactions, he has constantly displayed the highest level of professionalism befitting an officer of the United States Air Force. Furthermore, he is a mentor and role model to other squadron commanders, as well as consistently in line with the vision and policy of senior leadership." He concluded, "Lt Col Perry is an exceptional squadron commander, role model and friend. He is deserving of continued trust as a commander, officer and Airman."

Lt. Col. Lam saw no evidence I had undermined our boss's authority. "I can attest that Lt Col Perry has always been a strong supporter of Col. Liddick within the Squadron Commander's circle and with all subordinates. In fact, he is usually the voice of reason as we Squadron Commanders navigate policy and guidance to ensure we provide support to our Group leadership." He concluded, "I have never witnessed him acting insubordinate or speaking negatively about Col. Liddick." Lt. Col. Valenzuela was similarly adamant: "I have not witnessed him speaking out against Col. Liddick, in fact he has been one of her strongest supporters." She offered a specific example, when Col. Liddick had received the results of the RAND MTI survey in October 2013. "She had a commander's call where she was very jovial about the whole thing and I was very surprised. Lt Col Perry kept telling us, that she took the comments to heart and she is being very positive and wants to change how the MTI's view her. He was always trying to present the group more specifically Col. Liddick in a positive light."

These squadron commanders also defended me against charges of unprofessional relationships. "In listening to Lt Col Perry's words and observing his actions with his personnel, I have always found him above reproach," Lt. Col. Gondol wrote. My superintendent and I sat next to him in weekly group staff meetings, and my "words, conduct and bearing are always professional and appropriate for a relationship between a senior officer and his senior enlisted advisor." The one time he witnessed me interact with SMSgt "LG" in a personal manner was during the group BMT children's fall festival, "when Mrs. Perry's medical condition caused her to become unconscious. Throughout the incident, it was clear that the interaction between SMSgt "LG" and Lt Col Perry was nothing more than a concerned airman helping another. Throughout the last 8 months I have known him, Lt Col Perry has comported himself in a manner consistent with other commanders I have known and observed." [261]

The other commanders agreed. "Craig epitomizes the term good wingman," Lt. Col. Valenzuela wrote. "I cannot imagine Craig having an unprofessional relationship with anyone." She noted Col. Liddick made it clear she should always have someone by her side as she did business in and around the squadron. "Many times, I have taken my superintendent with me when I make my rounds in the squadron or the first sergeant. I have had many working meals with my superintendent to discuss a myriad of issues. This is a common practice amongst the squadron leaders," as is commanders riding with their superintendents to weekly BMT graduation ceremonies. Moreover, "He is the first person who calls when anything goes wrong," such as when Caroline noted an

---

[261] Lt. Col. John Gondol, "Character Statement for Lt. Col. Craig Perry," March 14, 2014

"obvious cry for help" by MSgt Chavez on Christmas Day. "That was 100% the right thing to do. It is not a matter of favoritism it is a matter of human compassion. Given the same circumstances, I would have done the same." Lt. Col. Lam agreed. "He cares for his people, does everything within his authority to set all his people up for success. He does what all of us as leaders would do or wants to do when taking care of those that are entrusted to us," he wrote. "He is a person of high moral integrity and truly does embody our Air Force core values."

Lt. Col. Lam also addressed the final allegation. "In regards to the PIF policy, I believe there may be a miscommunication in interpreting the guidance." He recounted how Lt. Col. Gondol had asked Col. Liddick, "If not AMR related and the disciplinary action was already accounted for in an annual performance report, could we as commanders pull the disciplinary action from the PIF?" He noted the discussion went on for quite some time, "with all of us understanding that we were authorized to remove items from the PIFs as long as it was not related to an AMR and that it had already been used in an EPR or OPR."[262] For Lt. Col. Valenzuela, "The last allegation is the one I find beyond absurd." She guilelessly speculated, "If Col. Liddick had interviewed for the CDI, she would have told the IO that she told all the commanders to include Craig that it was okay to remove the documentation from the PIF." She recalled the guidance Col. Liddick gave the squadron commanders, and cited a specific example when the group commander allowed her to remove an LOR for a Technical Sergeant in her squadron. "This was a standing policy in our group." When Col. Liddick called the commanders into her office to announce my removal from command, and told them they should not pull anything else out of the PIFs, Lt. Col. Valenzuela "reminded her that when she told us it was okay to remove stuff, I removed [the Sergeant's LOR] and shredded it." Col. Liddick then asked the other commanders to write memoranda for record "to cover any items that were removed during that time frame." Lt. Col. Valenzuela concluded, "I was very surprised that Col. Liddick was not asked about her policy change. She can clear this up for Craig."[263]

---

262 Lt. Col. Dat Lam, letter to Brig. Gen. (sel.) Camerer, March 11, 2014

263 Lt. Col. Elisa Valenzuela, letter to Brig. Gen. (sel.) Camerer, undated

In addition to this trio of officers, I also obtained character reference letters from a couple of Chief Master Sergeants: the recently retired BMT superintendent, and the former MTI School commandant. CMSgt Williams was Col. Liddick's senior enlisted leader until he retired in October 2013 after a 30-year career. He noted how I was "hand-selected to command the 737th Training Support Squadron (TRSS) amidst the largest human capital management and sexual assault scandal in Air Force history," a tumultuous period when AETC "revamped the selection priority" and "chose only the highest qualified officers." During our interactions at group and wing-level meetings, he found me "to be very introspective and interested in gaining a broader perspective and understanding of his squadron, the group and the wing," with a "keen focus on key strategic and organizational priorities" that was "congruent with carrying out the wing's and group's stated direction."

Chief Williams had unique insight regarding my squadron superintendent. "In light of the increasing challenges in the scandal-ridden BMT environment, SMSgt ["LG"] was handpicked as part of the solution. I personally conducted a telephone conversation with SMSgt ["LG"] to explain the challenges and expectations of leaders within the evolving BMT construct." Because previous superintendents had insulated their squadron commanders from issues reaching their level, "My direction to the squadron superintendents was they remain in lockstep with their commanders." After reviewing her "record of sustained demonstrated performance from her previous assignment in BMT" and her subsequent growth within her Air Force Specialty Code, Chief Williams recommended she and her family return to BMT.

Contrary to the findings of my CDI – or the testimony of his successor – Chief Williams was impressed by my superintendent and me. "Lt Col Perry and Sgt ["LG"] aligned to form a professional leadership team from my observation. They adequately provided updates pertaining to his squadron during meetings. Sgt ["LG"] was very visible and by my accounts provided appropriate senior enlisted leadership to more junior members and sage counsel to Col Perry. Her character is above reproach. Furthermore, I personally observed other superintendents align with their newly selected commanders in the same manner."

Chief Williams also dismissed the notion I undermined Col. Liddck's authority. "The commanders agreed in principle with policies, though they visibly and vocally offered alternatives to how the policies would be implemented. I found the new leaders, especially Lt Col Perry, offered refreshing perspectives (none of which appeared disloyal) as basic training was undergoing much-needed cultural changes." He noted, "independent and intuitive thought would seem to lead to creative solutions in an insular environment as BMT was, and logically not default to disloyalty."

Chief Williams concluded, "[Lt. Col. Perry] was "selected to command by a trusted process. For 19 years, he consistently demonstrated he more than deserved to lead in the Air Force and more recently, within BMT...even with its wide range of emerging expectations. This aspiring leader was a valued asset to our Air Force when he was hired. I assert he is still a valued asset."[264]

CMSgt Milne also offered a letter of support. "My experience with Lt Col Perry was nothing short of exceptional," he wrote. "I found him to be very professional, helpful, and caring to me and the members that I supervised. He was very engaged in the school house operations at a time that was very difficult for most MTIs. BMT was coming out of its 'season' of sexual assault cases and morale had been low. Lt Col Perry visited our NCOs on an almost daily basis and expressed concern for his people."

When then-SMSgt Milne received orders to Korea for an unaccompanied tour, "Col. Perry and his wife, Caroline, immediately took interest in my family and have continued to support them during my absence. I cannot express to you how important that is. Lt Col Perry and his wife, Caroline, went above and beyond and for that, I am grateful for this great leader." He objected to the allegation that throwing a "going away" party for him and his family constituted unprofessional conduct. "This gathering was Lt Col Perry and his wife reaching out to my family while I was gone and thank me for a job well done," he wrote. "The party was a surprise and was not intended to be exclusive," as the attendees "were people that my wife invited because the party was for 'closer' friends." Based upon AFI 36-2909, "no inappropriate or unprofessional conduct was going on."

Chief Milne concluded with a personal appeal to Col. Camerer. "Sir, Lt Col Perry is one of the best officers I've ever

---

[264] CMSgt (ret) Kenneth Williams, "Character Statement for Lt. Col. Craig M. Perry," March 12, 2014

worked for. You know me well enough to know that I would not write a character reference statement about someone I didn't believe in or felt they deserved the punishment. Lt Col Perry is a man of character who embodies the Air Force Core Values. Please reconsider Lt Col Perry's punishment. The Air Force would be losing a great officer."[265]

Because I was subject to a no-contact order, I was unable to reach out directly to any of my subordinates for support. However, Caroline enlisted several of them to write character reference letters on my behalf. The most senior respondent was MSgt Spaide, the "Blue Rope" MTI in charge of the BMT Reception Center. While he did not know the specifics about my case, he could attest to his personal experience: "I've seen him show every single person that directly works with me, the same attention as anyone else. Most commanders are too 'busy' to make their way to each shop every single week, especially in a unit where most of his people work in geographically separated areas on Lackland, but he makes a point to go to all of his areas at least once a week. Lt Col Perry is a people person; he does things to make his subordinates morale as high as possible. He and his wife took it upon themselves to bring our entire section a home cooked lunch. He seemed to just want to sit and talk in order to get to know us better. He also took the time when one of my co-workers had a medical condition that was life changing and personally sent her flowers, in hopes to make the day a little less devastating for her and her family. That simple gesture made her day a little better. In my personal opinion, I believe he is a good and fair commander."[266]

Caroline also obtained a letter from MSgt Spaide's co-worker, SSgt Hayes. Due to medical limitations associated with her pregnancy, she had been detailed to the BMT Reception Center when she suffered a devastating miscarriage. "Lt Col Perry and his wife Caroline Perry reached out to our family offering support and the support of the squadron and sent a very thoughtful

[265] CMSgt David Milne, "Character Statement – Lt. Col. Craig Perry," March 13, 2014
[266] MSgt Danny Spaide, "Character Statement – Lt. Col. Craig Perry," March 14, 2014

arrangement of flowers." She continued, "I can only tell you from my personal experience that the loss of a child is something that haunts you, however knowing I had time to recover and the support of my leadership was very refreshing and helped in the healing process. I am grateful to have had that type of leadership present during such an emotional time in my life and career." SSgt Hayes also noted how "Mrs. Perry bringing food to our section specifically because our squadron is so spread out to support the many behind the scenes operations that help BMT run smoothly." During her limited time assigned to the 737th TRSS, "I have only seen positive things from Lt Col and Mrs. Perry relating to maintaining a high moral for the squadron. I do not know the reasons surrounding his removal however I can attest that any time they are present they make and effort to speak to everyone and ensure a positive environment exists in the squadron."[267]

Another of my subordinates who volunteered an endorsement had actually worked with me years earlier, when I was the Director of Operations at the 381st Intelligence Squadron at Elmendorf AFB, Alaska. SSgt Jackson was now assigned to Lackland, where she had worked in the 737 TRSS Processing Section and Personnel Systems Management Office and served as the TRSS Private Organization Treasurer. She declared, "all my interactions with Lt Col Perry were professional and not once did I ever witness any favoritism or an unprofessional relationship with any member in the squadron!"

SSgt Jackson dispelled the myth that I favored MTIs over others. "Lt Col Perry was the type of Commander this squadron needed because morale was very low when he arrived. In this squadron, being a personnelist sometimes felt like we were undervalued by the MTIs. It was not until Lt Col Perry took command that he showed us we were just as important as the MTIs were."

SSgt Jackson felt, "It was nice to have a commander that actually took the time out of his busy schedule to stop by our work centers to talk to people and see if we needed anything. Lt Col Perry and his wife took the time to care for every Airman, officer, civilian and family member in the squadron." She specifically recalled a luncheon Caroline catered for her flight. "I remember that day specifically because Lt Col Perry not only sent an e-mail to

---

[267] SSgt Melinda Hayes, "Receipt of Condolence Flowers – Lt. Col. Craig Perry," undated

the section superintendent to notify people, but he also walked around the entire section to make sure everyone was aware of the luncheon before it started. He wanted to make sure no one was left out. Lt Col Perry and his wife always tried to make time to participate in gatherings for awarding citizenship, birthdays, as well as formal and off-duty education graduations."

SSgt Jackson also offered behind-the-scenes insights regarding the squadron booster club. "Lt Col Perry made himself available to listen to our ideas and to talk about upcoming events, issues or concerns. He always allowed us to make the decisions and never once did he tell us we had to pay a certain group or person. Mrs. Perry took the initiative to come up with a plan for the children's Halloween and Christmas Parties. She requested to have a meeting with us and gave us her ideas. She asked us if we wanted to be a part of it and if we wanted to help out with paying for some of the items, however, if we decided we did not want to assist she and Lt Col Perry did not mind paying for the event. They both took time to plan, put together, and work these events for the TRSS members and their families. I have never seen a Commander working a children's holiday party, especially one that does not have children of their own. In my book, this speaks volumes on the type of leader Lt Col Perry is, he leads by example."

She concluded, "Out of my 10 years of being in the military I have not seen a commander so engaged and active in his squadron. Lt Col Perry sincerely cares about the people under his command and it is evident in his actions. From my experience, my last few Commanders rarely came by our work centers and their spouses were never involved. It was a breath of fresh air to have Lt Col Perry take command of the 737 TRSS. I have the utmost respect for Lt Col Perry and I hope that every Commander I have from here on out has the same leadership style."[268]

The last subordinate who provided Caroline a reference letter was Mr. Kamel, the contractor I allegedly favored. Although he had already testified during the CDI, this was an opportunity for this "Deliberate Development" consultant to provide a more measured assessment of me as a leader. Since 2005, Mr. Kamel had been charged with "developing a leadership development program, primarily to develop MTIs, Junior and Senior Officers and Enlisted personnel leadership skills through developing their self-

---

[268] SSgt Veronica Jackson, "Character letter for Lt. Col. Perry," March 13, 2014

awareness, self-management and ultimately, their relationship management of their peers, subordinates and supervisors." He had worked with lots of squadron commanders during that time, "but Lt Col Perry was one of the most professionally involved commanders. As soon as he assumed command and familiarized himself with the squadron's needs, he asked us in Deliberate Development Program to assist him in developing the necessary leadership skills at all levels within the TRSS," including among the Independent Duty Medical Technicians. "The TRSS Commander's vision was to create a highly customized 'mini-NCO Academy' that is imbedded and in touch with the daily challenges each team faces, to help coach them into how to best manage their stressful jobs; an effort that would lead to a highly resilient corps and their supporting units." He also noted how Caroline "was very interested in seeing how the program could benefit the MTI spouses by improving their work/home life balance. She had sought my council on multiple occasions and wanted to found a developmental program to better the MTIs' home life. That effort was duly noted by the MTIs and very much appreciated by their spouses."

Mr. Kamel acknowledged, "Lt Col Perry's involvement and reliance on Deliberate Development and our staff of two military personnel and one civilian contractor (myself) perhaps led to a misperception of favoritism." However, "none of us in DD have ever received any favors or special treatment from Lt Col Perry. If there were multiple meetings with him, that was due to the fact that he appreciated that we were the subject matter experts and would refer to us for suggestions and to inform him of the way ahead for Deliberate Development, a program in his charge." (He also noted, "I did get to meet with the Commander's wife more than with him.") He recalled how he once approached me when SSgt Little was thinking about separating from the Air Force, "and that if he did the organization I am working for may be interested in hiring SSgt Little. Lt Col Perry was very clear in cautioning me about the possibility of conflict of interest. That incident clearly illustrated to me how his integrity was beyond reproach."

Based on his extensive interactions with MTIs and other personnel in the squadron, Mr. Hassan attested I was regarded as "the best thing that happened to the TRSS in a long time!" He noted, "It wasn't long before it became very clear that Lt Col Perry had the perfect balance between vision, compassion for his people, firmness, foresight and leadership skills unrivalled by many officers, senior enlisted leaders and civilian executives whom I had worked with in my 14 year career as an executive coach and organization development consultant. I can attest to his outstanding leadership, professionalism and dedication to the Air Force; the development and growth of the people under his command and the welfare of their families. I would be privileged to work with Lt Col Perry any day. He is one that truly exhibits the art and science of leadership in all of his actions."[269]

The last set of character reference letters came from squadron spouses. My superintendent's husband was a medically retired Air Force veteran who had himself once been a "Blue Rope" MTI, and had now returned to BMT with his wife, SMSgt "LG." In their previous assignment, he had been a board member for the base enlisted spouses network, and along with Mrs. Melanie Hite, he served as a 737 TRSS Key Spouse under Caroline's mentorship. "Through these experiences and positions I am more than versed on professional and unprofessional relationships," he wrote. He continued, "my interactions with Lt Col Perry have been nothing but professional," including unit activities such as the summer picnic and children's parties, or when I welcomed incoming MTI School classes and introduced the Key Spouses. Although he had participated in similar events during their last assignment, now that his wife was squadron superintendent, he "was even more wary of any portraying the wrong perception."

This Key Spouse felt he and Mrs. Hite had "been treated with respect and gratitude for serving the families of his squadron. Lt Col Perry seemed to really care for not only his officers and airmen but also their families and proved this by volunteering his off duty time to set up and run events such as the 737th Training Group children's Halloween party and Christmas party even though he does not have any children of his own. While this may seem standard operations, not all of the squadron commanders assisted or attended these events. This is just one example of the type of actions that Lt Col Perry and his wife did to make every family member feel appreciated." He concluded, "At no point did I feel like

[269] Hassan Kamel, "Letter of Support for Lt. Col. Perry," March 11, 2014

I was receiving any benefits or favors from serving in this role for Lt Col Perry but I did see him strive to make all members of the 737th Training Support Squadron family feel important and part of the team."

SMSgt "LG"'s husband offered a unique perspective on my leadership, having served for several different commanders both in military and civilian roles. He wrote, "I do not have anything but the utmost respect and admiration for Lt Col Perry. His professionalism and leadership style is one that I have experienced before and was normally found in the best commanders I have worked for. Lt Col Perry is a leader that leads by example and given my past experiences I know that this is not always the case with every commander or leader. In my opinion I would say that Lt Col Perry is a leader that cares for and has a positive impact on his organization." In conclusion, "the Air Force needs more like him and this is coming from a veteran who is 100 percent disabled and still loves his Air Force with all his heart."[270]

Another spouse who answered the call was Mrs. Pam Milne, whose husband had departed on a remote assignment the previous year. "Caroline went out of her way to meet me as my husband was deploying to Korea for a year," she wrote. "I've been a military spouse for over 24 years and as a commanders wife she went above and beyond checking on myself and my daughter. She didn't have to do this with my husband leaving and no longer being in the squadron." The Perrys "made sure to invite me to the MTIA banquet and also the holiday squadron party. I've never had a commanders wife show such concern and reach out to me. They have been a breath of fresh air at BMT."

As for that notorious surprise going-away party, "It was so nice to see a commander and his wife take such good care of their squadron and make sure that they and their families are doing ok. If I had thought for one moment this would've come back on them and get them in trouble I would've never let them host this party for us." Mrs. Milne wanted to keep the guest list "on the smaller side" since Caroline "was generous to host it in their home and was planning to cook dinner. We in no way intended to leave anyone out. I invited people that I knew personally, and probably half the people were family and non military friends. I in no way thought she was showing favoritism, she's a genuinely caring person." She

---

[270] "Character Reference Letter for Lt. Col. Perry," March 11, 2014

concluded, "I wish there were more commanders out there that truly cared for their people."[271]

Last but not least, Caroline wrote a letter of her own to Brigadier General-select Camerer. "First and foremost," she wrote, "I would like [to] thank you for the opportunity to consider additional information before you make a final decision concerning my husband's career." Caroline proceeded to take responsibility for her part in my circumstances. "I haven't been a military wife long, and when we found out he was going to be a commander in BMT, we were both very excited. I truly believe my husband's success is my success. I immediately became willing to do whatever was necessary to support my husband in his new role. I may have become overzealous," she acknowledged. My wife noted how she had "attended every single spouse's event, training course, conference, town-hall meeting, and luncheons with leadership," and the spouses of senior Air Force leaders such as Gen. Rice and Gen. Rand consistently told her that "as a squadron commander's wife, you're in a unique position to help your husband and make a difference in his Airmen's lives." If Caroline gave the impression of favoritism or special preference, "it was not my intention as I gave every single person in the squadron the same opportunities. However, as it has become apparent that some people believe the contrary, I am truly sorry. I wish someone had told me. I wish I had a group level mentor. I am asking for the opportunity to learn from my mistakes, take corrective actions, and that my husband not be punished for my inadequacies."

Since there was no Key Spouse program when we arrived, Caroline decided to develop one from scratch. "During this endeavor, I encouraged my husband, who is a natural introvert, to get to know each and every squadron member, visit anyone who was sick or hospitalized, host events for each of his flights, have face time with his key leadership via lunches and dinner invitations, and to generally take the extra step to take care of our Airmen." Not only was our program highlighted in a brief to Gen. Rand in November 2013, but one of our own won Key Spouse of the Year for the wing. Unfortunately, "some of these things have been misunderstood, distorted and misconstrued by a very small fraction of the population." Things like "taking soup to a sick airman, having a going away party for our outgoing MTIS commandant, and sitting with key leadership at a holiday party are

---

[271] Pam Milne, "To whom it may concern," March 11, 2014

items being used against him as evidence of unprofessional relationships via the perception of favoritism."

Caroline assured the wing commander, "I know my husband better than anyone else in the world, and I can attest to the fact that he has no favorites, nor did he do anything intentional to allow for that perception. However, I now realize that my ideas and actions, without further explanation, could have led for a person to believe I had favorites, which then could have been attributed to my husband. In the end, it appears to be a series of misunderstandings with just a few people which, placed into context, are easily explained. But I can assure you, this is not a widespread sentiment throughout the squadron. I wish we has the opportunity to place all of the instances used against us in context, because I am certain it would absolutely change your assessment of the situation. I am not suggesting we did nothing to open ourselves to the misinterpretation of our actions, but I am adamant that with additional information, the potential for misunderstanding becomes clear."

My wife respectfully requested that the 37 TRW commander "counsel and mentor my husband, allow him to return to command, and successfully complete what he began. He has worked his entire life for this. It is within your discretion to allow this to be a lesson, a learning opportunity. He needs mentoring." She noted the moment Col. Liddick told me not to host any more parties at the house, "he immediately heeded her direction, but no one ever said anything else about any issue or perception." Given my "lifetime of achievements," she concluded, "I don't believe that it's worth essentially destroying his career" over "inaccurate perception and some misunderstandings." She pleaded with him to "use your years of experience, wisdom, and understanding to discern the difference between a mistake and a character flaw."[272]

On Thursday, March 27, 2014, I was summoned again to Col. Camerer's office to learn my fate. I was cautiously optimistic, as I believed my response had effectively rebutted every allegation against me, while the character reference letters I submitted

---

[272] Caroline Perry, letter to Brig. Gen. (sel.) Camerer, March 14, 2014

painted a picture wholly at odds with the flawed CDI findings. Moreover, I thought it entirely possible Col. Camerer had issued the LOR merely to appease Col. Liddick, and make an example of me to keep the other BMT squadron commanders in line. Now that he had been selected for promotion to the general officer ranks, I figured, he no longer needed to prove how tough he was on minor misconduct, and he might even want to show leniency in my case by downgrading the LOR to a letter of admonition or letter of counseling, or even withdrawing it altogether. Surely Brig. Gen. (sel.) Camerer realized firing a highly regarded squadron commander over such trivial allegations would not go over well?

Alas, I overestimated the judgment and savvy of this senior leader.

Caroline again accompanied me to the wing headquarters, and Lt. Col. Upchurch met us there as before. Remarkably, my commander and supervisor, Col. Liddick, once again didn't bother showing up to bear witness to the fate she helped engineer for her subordinate, a damning testament to her utter failure as a leader. I was ushered into the wing commander's office and offered a seat, an uncharacteristically kind gesture considering what came next. Without further explanation, Col. Camerer declared he was upholding the LOR, and relieving me of command of the 737 TRSS. I was directed to report back the next day for further guidance.

I was devastated. Throughout my career in the Air Force, I always trusted my chain of command to do the right thing. Such faith in the system is imperative for military organizations, where the orders of the officers appointed over you can have life or death consequences. I had my share of bad bosses and incompetent commanders over the years, but I always believed their superiors would ensure they didn't get away with anything too ridiculous. And so I assumed that, even if Col. Liddick didn't like me, and even if Col. Camerer was inclined to give her the benefit of the doubt, their higher-ups would recognize the folly of relieving me of command before he pulled the trigger. Surely he would have sought top-cover for this decision from his boss, the Second Air Force commander, Maj. Gen. Patrick, and it seems likely the AETC commander, Gen. Rand, would have been made aware beforehand. Yet he was allowed to proceed, disregarding common sense and the sworn statements of far more witnesses in my favor than his bogus CDI was able to muster against me.

The next morning, I shaved off my facial hair I had so carefully cultivated during "Mustache March" as a sort of protest against my fate. I had been betrayed by the Air Force I loved – and my betrayal was far from over. I reported as directed to Col. Camerer, who indicated I would now be detailed to the 937th Training Group at Fort Sam Houston until a new assignment could be found for me. When I inquired whether my no-contact order remained in effect, the wing commander seemed unaware I was ever under such restrictions, but he promised to look into it for me. (Not surprisingly, I never heard back from him on this matter.)

Later that day, Col. Camerer called a meeting of all his subordinate group and squadron commanders to announce my relief of command. One of them recorded the session, which revealed far more about the wing commander than it did regarding what I might have done to deserve my fate. In fact, Col. Camerer refused to explain his decision in any detail. "Generically, you can say something along the lines of, I lost faith or confidence in his ability to command the squadron," he told them. Even more vaguely, he added, "I tell you, think back on some of the things that I drew red lines on. Right? So you've got a track across a red line," leaving the audience to guess which colored mark he meant with this awkward aviation analogy. Even less helpfully, he added, "So, during his tenure here in his command, certain things happened that came to my attention, and I looked at those and decided there was enough credence to them, and they were serious enough that continuing in command was not warranted."

Rather than explain himself, Col. Camerer patronizingly appealed to his audience's sense of loyalty and trust. "You guys I think know me pretty well," he assured his subordinates. "My hope is that over the course of the last 18 or so months, you have an impression of me that I'm a balanced and reasonable person. I wouldn't take an action like taking someone out of command unless I had a good reason." Moreover, "I wouldn't relieve somebody unless I thought they couldn't continue to be effective." So if they heard any hear rumors, they should ask themselves: "Does that really sound like something Colonel Camerer would relieve someone of command for?"

The wing commander was dismissive of any media interest. "I don't expect a bit of press coverage out of this. Anyway, no press coverage is going to be initiated by the 37th Training Wing." After all, I hadn't done anything criminal. "He's not going to court martial, he's not going to jail or anything like that, he's just not going to be in the squadron. So, you're not going to see his name come up on the blotter or anything like that." Col. Camerer reiterated, "he's not going to jail at this time. He hasn't done anything illegal, immoral, or anything like that, he just isn't the guy to command that squadron right now." But just in case, he warned his subordinate commanders not to trust anything they might read in the paper. "I just caution you, as you have seen, you don't always get the full story. We've all seen instances of that, and how many stories have been out there in the press, and we can come back and say, yeah, about 10 percent true. Right?"

He was also dismissive of people writing character reference letters on my behalf. "I've gotten responses of support," he stammered, "and so when you read the letter, it's obvious that they don't have the entire story." He continued, "I know that there are some around the wing, especially in his unit, that are writing letters of support, 'I know exactly what this is about,' and then that's not what it's about." This message seemed directed at the three authors sitting there in the audience.

Col. Camerer pledged, "We'll look for another job" for me, "probably local. There are several things he can go do." In the meantime, he appealed to my fellow commanders to look out for me. "He's still a Lieutenant Colonel in the United States Air Force. He's still a great human being. OK? And you are still collectively, commanders, you're still collectively, you know, that pool of people … it's OK to be friends with him. I hope you don't turn your back on him. He and his wife will need your support as much as anybody." He concluded, "The Perrys are still nice people. They'll need people to wrap their arms around them and take care of them, and it's OK to be part of that network."[273]

Lt. Col. McConnell, the investigating officer from my CDI, was also in the room that day. According to another officer who was present, he seemed shocked as my relief of command was announced, and refused to make eye contact with the BMT commanders throughout the meeting. Col. Camerer had used his report of investigation to justify relieving me of command, even though Lt. Col. McConnell never recommended such a drastic step. (He later confessed to a colleague that he never imagined his report would be used to fire me.) And the wing commander's appeals for my colleagues to embrace me came off as disingenuous, given that

---

[273] Transcript of comments by Col. Mark Camerer to 37 TRW group and squadron commanders regarding relief of Lt. Col. Perry, March 28, 2014

he wouldn't even tell them what I had supposedly done wrong. If this was meant to intimidate them, it worked.

That Saturday, I went back to my old office in the 737 TRSS to collect my belongings. As I was removing mementos from the walls, Lt. Col. Upchurch came into the office and demanded I turn over my government laptop and Blackberry cell phone. I hadn't brought them with me, assuming I would have the weekend to download my documents and e-mails. Lt. Col. Upchurch was adamant: I must surrender these items immediately. Frustrated at this latest indignity, I made him follow me out to my house to collect the devices. When I arrived and told Caroline who was waiting outside, she stormed to the curb to give him a piece of her mind. She stood beside his driver's-side window waiting for him to acknowledge her presence. "I have a question for you," she finally said, motioning for him to roll the window down. "You're his wingman, right?" she asked rhetorically. "Did you know what decision had been made? Did you know they were going to fire him?" "No," he answered cautiously. "You're a liar," Caroline responded. "You should be ashamed of yourself."

Chapter 11: Collateral Damage

Simply relieving me of command was apparently not enough to satisfy my superiors. Instead, Colonel Camerer and Col. Liddick did everything in their considerable power to destroy my career, and even force me to retire from the Air Force. My wing commander established an unfavorable information file at the Air Force Personnel Center, and also placed the letter of reprimand in my officer selection record for my upcoming Colonel promotion board. When I submitted my preferences for senior developmental education, Col. Camerer made his intentions perfectly clear: "I removed Lt. Col. Perry from Sq/CC, issued a LOR & established a UIF. A referral OPR & a request to permanently remove him from SDE Select list is in coordination," he wrote to AFPC. "Do not select for SDE...if selected, consider AWC first," he recommended,[274] suggesting he also didn't think much of Air War College, the Air Force's flagship graduate-level program. (I was officially barred from any further in-residence developmental education on May 12, 2014,[275] although I wasn't notified until eight months later.) And of course, my officer performance report was referred, indicating I did not meet standards and had received an LOR.

Col. Liddick called me to her office to receive my referral OPR on April 9. In her "rater overall assessment" block of the form, she offered only a single bullet evaluating my job performance: "Updated Group's metrics and analog leadership program; program presented at RETOC [Recruit, Education & Training Oversight Council] quarterly--snr ldrs informed." The next two lines explained that I had received an LOR for "undermining command authority, creating appearance of unprofessional relationship and favoritism with subordinate personnel, and wrongfully removing a LOR from a subordinate's PIF." She left the remaining three lines blank, indicating she had nothing further to say about my six months in command. On the back side of the form, Col. Liddick indicated I did not meet standards in four areas: job knowledge, leadership skills, professional qualities, and judgment and decisions.[276]

---

[274] Col. Camerer, *SDE Preference Web-Based 3849*, April 18, 2014
[275] Lt. Gen. Samuel Cox, HQ AF/A1, "Removal of Senior Developmental Education (SDE) Select Status," May 12, 2014
[276] Col. Liddick, AF Form 707, *Officer Performance Report (Lt thru Col)*, April 9, 2014

I was given three duty days to submit rebuttal comments to my additional rater, Col. Camerer, which I did on April 14. I reiterated my actions did not warrant an LOR, and noted that issuing me this paperwork was clearly unfair, both in the type of standard applied and in the severity of the penalty imposed. I had been singled out for punishment, as other squadron commanders admitted to the same behavior for which only I was held accountable. Also, the harsh penalty Col. Camerer imposed far exceeded the recommendations of the investigating officer, as well as punishments handed down in other recent cases in the 37 TRW, including those of SMSgt Monk and the former commander of the 326th Training Squadron. Finally, Col. Camerer's comments to his subordinate commanders on March 28 regarding my character references – "it's obvious they don't have the entire story" – suggested he did not fully consider all the evidence available before making his decision.

I also noted how the commander-directed investigation revealed a disturbing pattern of behavior on the part of Col. Liddick, which I believe adversely affected my evaluation. She initially denied having authorized her squadron commanders to remove derogatory information from personnel information files, then testified she had in fact authorized us to do so under certain circumstances. I would not have acted as I did had Col. Liddick not provided this guidance, so if I was held accountable for wrongfully removing a document, then Col. Liddick should also be held accountable for authorizing such behavior. More troubling was Col. Liddick's testimony regarding why she removed my superintendent, SMSgt "LG," from my squadron. At no time did Col. Liddick inform me that this relationship "appeared cozier than she would like to see it," nor of any other reason for the move other than to fill a manning shortfall in another unit. If she felt I was engaged in an unprofessional relationship, she had an obligation to counsel me so that I could correct my behavior. Instead, she obscured her reasons for moving my superintendent, allowing this situation to fester for more than a month during which almost all the alleged incidents of favoritism occurred. Apart from the verbal counseling for hosting events at my house and socializing with certain subordinates, the CDI documented no other incidents of mentorship by Col. Liddick, and the only performance feedback I received during this rating period took place a mere three weeks after I assumed command. Among her initial expectations was that I should listen to my "Chief" on enlisted issues, by which I presumed she meant my squadron superintendent, yet my efforts to follow her advice by cultivating a close working relationship with my senior enlisted leader were later misperceived as favoritism.

I took particular offense to Col. Liddick indicating I did not meet standards in the "job knowledge" performance factor. None of the substantiated allegations suggest that I lacked the knowledge required to perform duties effectively, or questioned whether I strove to improve knowledge or apply knowledge to handle non-routine situations. In fact, the opposite was true, and Col. Liddick made no effort to capture my many accomplishments during my short time in command of the 737th Training Support Squadron. Her appraisal was clearly unreasonable, and did not accurately reflect my performance during the rating period.

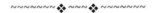

On April 15, I received some unexpected news: I was being reassigned to Barksdale AFB, Louisiana, where I must report for duty no later than May 31. I immediately contacted the intelligence officer assignment team at Air Force Personnel Center to find out why I was being moved, considering the variety of positions I was qualified to fill in San Antonio – home of the Air Force Intelligence, Surveillance and Reconnaissance Agency (since re-designated 25th Air Force); Air Force Cyber Command (24th Air Force); and a National Security Agency site. Besides, Col. Camerer publicly pledged to look for a local job for me, right? Well, according to the AFPC detailer, it was my chain of command that requested my reassignment, with the concurrence of Air Force ISR community leadership.

The following day, Col. Liddick summoned me back to her office to sign the final referral OPR. I was not surprised to find Col. Camerer had disregarded my rebuttal, but I didn't anticipate the turn the conversation took after we finished this paperwork. Col. Liddick brought up the assignment notification I received the day before, but she made no mention of which base I was going to, or the job I would be doing there. Instead, her only feedback concerned retirement options. Col. Liddick noted I had "seven days to make a decision," and if I had any questions, "there's probably a lot of people and sources" I could talk to "about different decisions and what it means ... whether you accept or not accept, retirement eligible and active duty service commitment, and all of that."[277]

These were the last words Col. Liddick ever spoke to me, and they were incredibly revealing. Col. Camerer had requested that I be relocated out of the local area, giving me just six weeks to outprocess and move my family to another state. He and Col. Liddick both knew San Antonio was my hometown, where my wife and I had recently built a house we couldn't afford to sell, and where Caroline was receiving advanced medical treatment for multiple life-threatening conditions. It suddenly seemed obvious this entire exercise – the CDI, the LOR, the referral OPR, and a short-notice assignment to an out-of-the-way base – was designed to force me out of the Air Force. Arbitrary and capricious don't even begin to describe such abuses of authority.

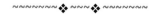

It was bad enough that my chain of command wrongfully relieved me of command and ruined my career. But these toxic leaders also went after each of the subordinates they accused me of favoring. By the time the dust settled, my former superintendent, SMSgt "LG," had been eliminated from the MTI corps; the "Deliberate Development" instructor, SSgt Little, was harassed and reassigned to a dead-end job in another squadron; and the "DD" consultant, Mr. Kamel lost his BMT gig to an unqualified contractor.

The first to go was Mr. Kamel. The Joint Base San Antonio contracting office issued a request for proposal for the "MTI Deliberate Development" contract on December 31, 2013. The incumbent, Otto Kroeger Associates, had held this contract since 2005, with Mr. Kamel as their only on-site representative. This year, the contract had been rewritten to include additional positions and responsibilities, and to have the contract employees report to the BMT training director, Dr. Munro, rather than to the 737 TRSS commander. According to the new performance work statement, the qualifications, education, and experience required for the "Behavioral Development Specialist" position – Mr. Kamel's job – included a minimum of two years experience with administering and interpreting Myers-Briggs Type Indicator

---

[277] Transcript of conversation between Col. Liddick and Lt. Col. Perry, April 16, 2015

results, as well as that the candidate be certified in MBTI and Emotional Quotient Inventory tools.[278]

On February 26, 2014, this contract was awarded to a new company, Hyperion Biotechnology, for proposing the lowest price technically acceptable offer.[279] However, the offeror did not clearly meet the minimum requirements of the solicitation. Specifically, the employee offered for the "Behavioral Development Specialist" position, Ms. Bekah Cleckler, did not have the required qualifications, education, and experience, as she was not certified in EQ-i tools at the time the contract was awarded. According to Multi-Health Services, Ms. Cleckler received her certification only in March 2014, after Hyperion Biotechnology won the contract. Furthermore, her job performance after the contract was awarded suggests she may not have been currently certified in MBTI tools or had a minimum of two years experience with administering and interpreting MBTI results. For example, she reportedly made classic typecasting comments to the "DD" staff, which could discourage people from self-validating a certain personality type. Also, the instruction she provided new MTIs did not adequately cover each of the four MBTI dichotomies, which has ethical implications.

Although it was the 502d Air Base Wing that approved this proposal, it seems likely their contracting office would have first checked with the 737th Training Group to confirm the Hyperion Biotechnology bid met minimum technical acceptability standards. If so, Col. Liddick may have directed or influenced this improper selection to get rid of Mr. Kamel. The group commander made her allegations against me while this bidding process was underway, and removed me from command in part over allegations of an unprofessional relationship and favoritism towards this OKA employee. On January 7, 2014, she testified she was "mindful" of Mr. Kamel because she believed he had "an agenda about doing his job as a Contractor." She also noted she had been informed he "was very upset with the no contact order between Lt Col Perry and members of the squadron."[280]

---

[278] FAR 52.212-2(f)(2) , technical acceptability subfactor 2
[279] Anastacio Ramos, 502 CONS/JBKABD, "Unsuccessful Offeror Notice, Request for Proposal (RFP) FA3047-14-R-0007, MTI Deliberate Development," February 26, 2014
[280] CDI witness statements, p. 94

Was Col. Liddick willing to jeopardize the professional development of the MTI corps to settle a score with a contract employee she didn't like? Despite his seven years of exceptional service to BMT, Mr. Kamel's company was not selected for this task, and the award went instead to an inexperienced vendor that didn't meet the minimum standards. I filed a complaint with the 502 ABW inspector general about this and another BMT contracting irregularity on June 3, 2014. I have no idea what ever became of this complaint, as I'm not entitled to receive a response since the alleged wrongs don't directly affect me, but it does not appear any corrective actions have been taken. Nevertheless, I felt it important to bring this latest potential ethical lapse on the part of the BMT commander to someone's attention.

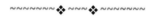

SSgt Little also experienced fallout from his alleged association with me. Along with Mr. Kamel, this "DD" instructor was called to testify during my CDI on January 7, 2014. When he returned to the MTI School, he claims his supervisor, MSgt Pickett, called him into his small private office and began quizzing him about his testimony. MSgt Pickett apparently wanted to know what his subordinate told the investigating officer, even though he knew they were not supposed to discuss these matters. (MSgt Pickett had already testified against me, twice.) While he was talking, MSgt Pickett reportedly proceeded to change his clothes in front of SSgt Little, undressing down to his underwear. SSgt Little later relayed to his co-workers that this behavior made him very uncomfortable. It was widely known MSgt Pickett was one of the principal complainants against me, and that he was alleging that I was engaged in an unprofessional relationship with SSgt Little, so this noncommissioned officer naturally interpreted undressing in front of him as a "power play" designed to intimidate him.

This isn't the first time MSgt Pickett had been noted changing clothes in his office. Rather than simply using the bathroom around the corner, he would post one of his MTI School instructors to stand guard outside his office. One passerby later observed, despite this sentry's efforts to hide MSgt Pickett's actions, "I could still see him through the blinds in states of half dress." It's entirely possible this MTI actually witnessed the events described by SSgt Little without realizing what was transpiring.

Someone who heard about this incident reported it anonymously to the Second Air Force Sexual Assault and Response Coordinator hotline around January 22 as a potential incident of sexual harassment. The following Monday, January 27, a 2 AF SARC hotline representative called SSgt Little to discuss options for counseling services, but no one ever followed up with him to investigate MSgt Pickett's misconduct. They did, however, notify 37 TRW leadership of the anonymous complaint, and forwarded it to the 737 TRG for action. Col. Liddick had an obligation to ensure this complaint of potential sexual harassment was thoroughly investigated, as required by AFI 36-2707, *Equal Opportunity Program*. However, there is no indication she consulted with the staff judge advocate or notified any member of 737 TRSS leadership, and she certainly didn't contact SSgt Little to confirm the allegation – even after I notified the Air Education and Training Command inspector general about this situation. Col. Liddick did, however, give the alleged perpetrator, MSgt Pickett, a heads-up, reinforcing the appearance of favoritism towards him.

Instead of properly investigating the complaint, Col. Liddick apparently resolved to remove SSgt Little from my squadron. During a group manning meeting around February 10, the group superintendent, CMSgt Sutherland, announced Col. Liddick was moving the "DD" instructor to a different job in another squadron, effective immediately. This proposed move appears to have been reprisal for the anonymous SARC hotline complaint, and was probably intended to protect MSgt Pickett and discourage SSgt Little from speaking out about his mistreatment. Cooler heads prevailed, however, as it was quickly realized there was no one available who was qualified to replace this talented "DD" instructor.

MSgt Pickett apparently also engaged in reprisal against SSgt Little. When Col. Camerer issued me an LOR on March 10, SSgt Little wrote a character reference letter on my behalf, which he forwarded to my area defense counsel. MSgt Pickett seemed troubled that SSgt Little was standing up for their disgraced squadron commander, and warned him that he was not to contact my wife or me due to the no-contact order that remained in effect. Soon afterward, SSgt Little coordinated with his team chief, MSgt Chavez, to report for work late so he could contact the education office and military personnel section regarding reenlistment options. When he came into the office later that day, MSgt Pickett confronted him, claiming he was not authorized to be absent and

245

accusing him of lying about his whereabouts. That Friday, MSgt Pickett issued SSgt Little an LOR for this trivial offense, explaining he was "trying to get his attention." Later that day, MSgt Pickett made a point of telling his subordinate, "I just wanted to let you know that, the other day when I was asking you about the character reference letter, I wasn't trying to tell you not to write it," or words to that effect. This seems to be the real reason MSgt Pickett issued the LOR: it was reprisal for making a protected communication to his chain of command on my behalf.

Because the area defense counsel office was closed that afternoon, SSgt Little went to see the first sergeant, MSgt Walls, to ask her for help in fighting the LOR. He described to her the incident of potential sexual harassment from a couple of months earlier, when MSgt Pickett undressed in front of him. MSgt Walls agreed to intervene, and subsequently convinced MSgt Pickett to withdraw the LOR – but she apparently took no further action to investigate or follow up on MSgt Pickett's earlier misconduct.

It was shortly after this that CMSgt Sutherland approached SSgt Little about moving to the 324th Training Squadron. He told him that the 324 TRS superintendent had personally requested him to direct that squadron's "Body/Mind/Spirit" program for recruits removed from training. However, when this "Blue Rope" MTI reported to that unit on April 14, it soon became clear they had no plan for him. Instead, he exclusively performed administrative "charge of quarter" duty, mostly at night, for the next several months. This was clearly unfair treatment, and a gross mis-utilization of an airman whom Col. Liddick used to routinely task to provide interviews to the press and brief distinguished visitors, and once described as someone she could see "as a Chief Master Sergeant running the Air Force."

The mistreatment of my squadron superintendent began before I even arrived at BMT, and went downhill from there. After Col. Liddick issued SMSgt "LG" an LOR in March 2013 over a minor administrative issue, she transferred the 321 TRS superintendent to the 737 TRSS to run the MTI recruiting section. A few months later, Col. Liddick again elevated her to superintendent status in her new squadron, just before I took command. My boss later explained to me she felt SMSgt "LG" had redeemed herself during that transition period, and deserved a second chance to serve as a senior enlisted leader. At the time, it seemed to me the group commander was looking out for a fellow female airman, but Col. Liddick's subsequent actions belied her kind words. In November, she announced she was transferring SMSgt "LG" to yet another squadron, and a couple of weeks later, she falsely accused my superintendent of "yelling" at MTI students.

Both issues would figure prominently in my CDI, which found I had fraternized with SMSgt "LG," and I was later reprimanded for creating the appearance of an unprofessional relationship with my former senior enlisted leader. But I wasn't the only one punished as a result of this investigation. Soon after I was relieved of command, the vice wing commander, Col. Vincent Fisher, issued SMSgt "LG" another LOR, claiming an investigation (presumably my CDI) revealed she engaged in conduct with me "that contributed directly to the appearance of an unprofessional relationship and favoritism." He also accused her of lying about the circumstances surrounding my removal of that earlier LOR from her personnel information file. Col. Fisher noted that "this is the second time in less than 17 months that [her] actions have compelled senior leaders to call [her] judgment into question," a reference to the LOR Col. Liddick issued her the previous year.

How did Col. Fisher get himself mixed up in this sordid affair? Such unfavorable personnel actions are usually administered by supervisors, squadron commanders, or someone else in the direct chain of command. Since the group commander issued SMSgt "LG" her previous paperwork, however, it's not surprising Col. Liddick avoided getting her hands dirty this time around. Col. Camerer would have been the next obvious choice to dole out this punishment, considering it was presumably the investigation he directed against me that was cited in the LOR. But the wing commander also washed his hands of this issue, delegating this dirty work to his deputy, an affable senior leader who was generally well liked around the base. This move may also have precluded SMSgt "LG" from later filing a redress of grievance under Article 138, Uniform Code of Military Justice, which only applies to wrongs committed by a commander.

Left holding the bag, Col. Fisher did as he was told and recklessly made allegations about which he had no direct knowledge. He accused her of lying without bothering to inquire into whether SMSgt "LG" had provided a false official statement, and she was easily able to produce evidence she had done no such thing. Apparently without coordinating with his boss, Col. Fisher rescinded the LOR, and replaced it with a letter of counseling on April 24 for the remaining allegation.[281]

The vice wing commander claimed my former superintendent's alleged behavior "directly impacted" members of the 737 TRSS, "which negatively affected good order and discipline inside [the] unit." But this is simply not true. Lt. Col. McConnell presented no evidence that SMSgt "LG" contributed to the appearance of an unprofessional relationship or favoritism, or that her behavior adversely affected members of the squadron. He cited only four specific examples of behavior on my part as evidence of an unprofessional relationship with my superintendent, for which she was in no way responsible. She had nothing to do with my removal of an LOR from her PIF, or my decision not to pursue an AMR for "scolding" MTI students. Accepting an invitation to a going-away party for the outgoing MTI School commandant cannot reasonably be construed as contributing directly to the appearance of an unprofessional relationship and favoritism, and attending a holiday performance of "The Nutcracker" when she was no longer assigned to the unit did not impact members of my squadron. My CDI simply offered no basis for taking this arbitrary and capricious administrative action.

In a response to her LOC dated April 28, SMSgt "LG" deftly countered the charges against her. She noted how, before she returned to BMT in 2012, she served as a squadron superintendent and executive officer to the 72d Air Base Wing commander, Brig. Gen. LaBrutta (who had since assumed command of the local 502 ABW and Joint Base San Antonio), at Tinker AFB, OK. "These positions required me to attend meetings as well as interact with Commanders and other Senior Leaders on a regular basis," she wrote, and her interaction with me as 737 TRSS commander "is very comparable to those I have had with other commanders when serving as a superintendent." Furthermore, as an Executive Officer she "interacted daily with the Wing and Vice Wing Commander. With this experience I feel that I understand what a working relationship entails." She noted her relationship with me "was based on mission requirements and was on a professional level." She found the allegation of favoritism "shocking" as she worked

---

[281] Col. Vincent Fisher, 37 TRW/CV, "Letter of Counseling (LOC)," April 24, 2014. *The previous paperwork was issued less than 14 months earlier.*

248

directly for me, which required her to have "continual official communication" with me.

SMSgt "LG" denied she had ever taken advantage of her position for personal gain, "and furthermore I never viewed myself in a position above the Director of Operations or the First Sergeant." She provided Col. Fisher a specific example of how she ensured all correspondence being routed to me for signature first went through MSgt Walls and Maj. Sprouse. She noted, "The Director of Operations was above me on the routing and if he was inadvertently left off, I would always counsel the individual who prepared the routing slip on the proper chain of command. Several times the Director of Operations thanked me for doing so."

My superintendent was unequivocal about her feelings for me: "I am not attracted to Lt Col Perry in any way whatsoever. I have never looked at him in a way other than professional. I have never thought of him in any other way than my supervisor." In her 21-year Air Force career, she was taught, "a good supervisor should know their subordinates and their families. Through different functions Lt Col Perry and his wife eventually met all five of my kids and they both knew my husband due to his role as a key spouse in the squadron." She noted the "abundance of Commanders and Superintendents in the Air Force who maintain decent working relationships which include daily interaction and knowledge of each other's families, and mine was no different." While her family "has never shared any meal with Lt Col Perry's family," SMSgt "LG" confessed to having lunch with Caroline and me once after a weekly BMT graduation parade, and on another occasion she and I shared a midday meal so brief she "wouldn't even consider this a 'working lunch' as we only had time to pick it up and come back." Again, "throughout my Air Force career there have been times when I have done this with co-workers, supervisors or my commander. I never even fathomed that this event would be taken out of context."

My former senior enlisted leader was "an extremely busy and dedicated wife, mother, and student with a full time job," with no patience for insinuations of impropriety with her squadron commander: "the allegations and perception of an unprofessional relationship with this man are, quite frankly, offensive," she declared. As the squadron superintendent, SMSgt "LG" thought it was important to attend the going-away party for CMSgt Milne, whom she'd known for over 10 years. She recalled speaking to both Maj. Sprouse and MSgt Walls earlier in the week about going to the party, but both indicated they didn't think they'd go. Months later, at the squadron holiday party, the superintendent and her husband sat at the commander's table rather than with some other group "because I did not want any of the flights to think I favored one over another." Maj. Sprouse, on the other hand, apparently went out of his way not to sit at my table. According to SMSgt "LG," he "asked the party committee to ensure he did not sit near the Commander. His spouse did not care for the Commander's spouse." Flatly contradicting Maj. Sprouse's sworn testimony during my CDI, SMSgt "LG" declared she was "positive he and his spouse sat themselves where they did on purpose."[282]

Nevertheless, Col. Fisher upheld the LOC on May 21, and her chain of command wasted no time using this administrative action as an excuse to remove SMSgt "LG" from the BMT environment. That very same day, her brand-new squadron commander, Lt. Col. Marcia Quigley, formally recommended her permanent removal from the MTI corps for failing to meet retention criteria for the 8B000 special duty identifier specified in the *Air Force Enlisted Classification Directory* – specifically, no record of administrative action "based on sexual assault, sexual harassment, physical abuse or an unprofessional relationship." Although this LOC only alleged she contributed to the appearance of an unprofessional relationship, and it did not involve trainees or students, this was enough for Col. Liddick. The MTI elimination package sailed through coordination, and by May 28 the BMT commander had stripped SMSgt "LG" of her AETC instructor badge and denied her an oak-leaf cluster for her MTI ribbon "for disciplinary reasons." In a curious twist, Lt. Col. Quigley's signatures on the AF IMT 2096, *Classification/On-the-Job Training Action*, are both dated "22042014" – April 22 – several weeks before she assumed command of the 319 TRS.[283] While this may simply be a clerical error, it could also indicate this paperwork was actually drafted by her predecessor, Lt. Col. Mike Arndt, in response to the LOR Col. Fisher originally issued. The BMT chain of command was apparently just waiting for an opportunity to get rid of this exceptional senior NCO.

[282] SMSgt "LG", "Response to Letter of Counseling (LOC), dated 24 April 2014," April 28, 2014
[283] MTI Elimination Package for SMSgt "LG," May 29, 2014

Ironically, it's not entirely clear what role, if any, these particular relationships played in my relief of command. Despite the investigating officer's assertion that I engaged in unprofessional relationships and committed fraternization, Col. Camerer didn't include either of these allegations in the LOR he issued me, claiming only that I "created the appearance of an unprofessional relationship and favoritism" with unspecified members of my squadron. Furthermore, when AETC later issued a statement to the press explaining why I was fired, they made no mention whatsoever of my relationships with the "DD" contractor and instructor. It is likely the Lackland staff judge advocate advised the wing commander against making this allegation, based on the flimsy evidence presented in the CDI report, and subsequent AETC statements seem to support this conclusion as well, as we will see in a later chapter.

So whatever happened to my star-crossed subordinates? After over eight years of dedicated service to BMT, Mr. Kamel was forced to relocate back to the East Coast, as his company had no other positions in the San Antonio area. SSgt Little actually found himself back in the 737 TRSS less than six weeks after his transfer, when the 324 TRS deactivated and its CQ function was folded into the support squadron. He departed BMT for his next assignment later that year, thankfully receiving a favorable enlisted performance report and end-of-tour medal. After she was eliminated from the MTI corps, SMSgt "LG" was reassigned to another unit at JBSA-Lackland, once again serving as a squadron superintendent despite her recent trials and tribulations. She was naturally disillusioned by the way she and her husband were treated by the Air Force they both served with such distinction.

The witnesses against me, on the other hand, were generally rewarded for their duplicity. Maj. Sprouse was formally designated 737 TRSS commander after I was relieved, until the officer Col. Liddick handpicked for the job – a fellow maintenance officer, Lt. Col. Jill Murphy – assumed command on June 2. MSgt Walls was selected for promotion to Senior Master Sergeant in March– but then again, so was MSgt Bell, the new 737 TRSS superintendent, while MSgt Chavez was promoted within the Air Force Reserves later that year. Although the "#1 MSgt in BMT," MSgt Pickett, had to wait until 2015 to make this cut, Col. Liddick found other ways to reward her favored subordinate. She named him the 737 TRG nominee for the prestigious Lance P. Sijan leadership award, despite the fact that the board assembled to select the winner had picked someone else. She also authorized him to leave BMT soon after she retired, well before his scheduled date of departure for his next assignment at Dyess AFB, Texas. In the meantime he was detailed across town to the JBSA-Randolph firehouse, where he was allowed to reorient himself to his primary career field at a location much closer to his home. Needless to say, such accommodations are not the norm at BMT, and suggest a much "cozier" relationship than was appropriate between the group commander and a flight chief in one of her squadrons.

Efforts by my chain of command to force me to retire or relocate, however, were less successful. When Col. Camerer requested I be moved out of the local area, he hadn't counted on the Exceptional Family Member Program assignment deferment process. Because of Caroline's various medical conditions, she was automatically enrolled in this program, and any reassignment was contingent on the gaining base offering her adequate medical treatment options. My wife had never before played the "health card" to gain sympathy or special treatment, and in fact we'd downplayed her medical needs during our previous military move to San Antonio. But it seemed unlikely she would be able to get the care she needed at Barksdale AFB or in the local Shreveport, Louisiana, area, which meant that if I accepted the assignment, there was a good chance it would later be canceled for this reason. I could also request an EFMP deferment, which could allow me to stay in San Antonio another year to support Caroline's ongoing treatment program. But there were no guarantees either of these options would work, and I might be made to move regardless of my wife's medical needs. After discussing my options with Caroline, I decided to accept the assignment and roll the dice on the deferment process. I wasn't ready to retire, and I was determined to stay and fight for my Air Force career.

It just so happened that Caroline's primary care manager at the Lackland military treatment facility had previously been assigned to Barksdale AFB, so he knew first-hand she wouldn't be able to get the care she needed at that location. The local EFMP special needs coordinator also indicated she supported a deferment to ensure Caroline's continuity of care. So on May 19, I submitted my EFMP deferment application to Col. Camerer. In it, I explained how Caroline had recently been diagnosed with several medical conditions, and my presence was essential in establishing and participating in her medical regimen there in San Antonio. After I detailing a laundry list of conditions requiring specialized care, I noted she was unable to drive herself to appointments at that time due to frequent blackouts, seizures, and side effects of medications. Her treatment program was at a critical juncture, and my continued presence was absolutely essential. Moreover, I did not believe that adequate services were available within my projected assignment locale to treat her multiple life-threatening conditions.

Meanwhile, my report-no-later-than date to Barksdale AFB was fast approaching. Until the deferment was approved, or my family member relocation clearance was denied through normal EFMP channels, I was still on the hook to move to Louisiana by the end of the month. When I tried to coordinate a RNLTD extension through my assignment team at Air Force Personnel Center, they refused. The EFMP special needs coordinator also submitted a formal request for a 60-day extension, but this too was denied without explanation. Caroline sent Col. Camerer a heart-wrenching plea for consideration, reminding him he once told her that he and his wife often prayed for her health.

However, as Col. Camerer noted in his response to my wife, it was actually my gaining commander at Air Force Global Strike Command who disapproved the request. My wing commander thanked Caroline for contacting him and giving him a chance to engage on our behalf – a brazenly hypocritical stance, as it was his idea to move me in the first place, knowing full well how sick my wife was. He pledged to call his counterpart at Barksdale that day to make sure he was aware of Caroline's issues, and he wished her "the best as you work your way through this transition."[284] We later learned that someone at Lackland had accessed Caroline's medical records during this period without proper access, perhaps hoping to find out whether she was really sick.

Thankfully, my gaining commander quickly agreed to a 15-day extension, which turned out to be more than enough time to complete the EFMP deferment processing. I was notified on June 3 that my assignment had officially been canceled, and a new job was found for me at JBSA-Lackland the following week. It was quite a relief to know we wouldn't have to move so soon, and we looked

---

[284] E-mail exchange between Caroline Perry and Col. Camerer, "RNLTD Extension," May 20-21, 2014

forward to spending at least another 12 months in my hometown. Little did we know, it would be our last year in San Antonio.

Chapter 12: Complaints Resolution

My quixotic relationship with the Air Force inspector general complaints resolution process began in early 2014, while I was waiting in limbo to learn the outcome of my commander-directed investigation. As I mentioned in an earlier chapter, I met with the Air Education and Training Command inspector general, Col. Richardson, when he was at JBSA-Lackland for a unit effectiveness inspection. After I explained my predicament, he suggested I file a complaint, which I did on February 18 – only the latest in a series of BMT squadron commanders to make formal allegations against our chain of command.

I began by accusing Col. Liddick of engaging in reprisal, after she threatened her squadron commanders for our protected communications with members of the BMT Triennial Review committee the previous September. (This was the notorious "you're either with me or against me" incident I described in Chapter 5.) I then suggested she had abused her authority by issuing me a no-contact order and arbitrarily and capriciously removing me from command of the 737th Training Support Squadron nearly two months earlier, then delaying my return to command after what I (incorrectly) assumed was a favorable outcome to the CDI. I claimed she knew, or should have reasonably known, that all five allegations against me were false, as we had discussed several of them previously, and she had never provided me written counseling or performance feedback before removing me from command and launching a formal investigation.

I went on to suggest Col. Liddick had usurped my command authority by arbitrarily reassigning my squadron superintendent, placing personnel in key leadership positions within my unit despite my opposition, and dictating the seating arrangement for personnel in my squadron. She had also pursued unprofessional relationships with members of my squadron, including MSgt Pickett, MSgt Walls, and even SSgt Little. I accused her of violating federal law (5 C.F.R. §2635.302) by pressuring me to give her wardrobe boxes, as well as disregarding Air Force Instruction 36-2903 by encouraging her subordinates to starch their Airman Battle Uniforms and directing officers to wear optional uniform items (BMT-specific physical training gear) for which they had to pay out of pocket.

Col. Liddick also harassed her subordinates, I alleged. She improperly marked down the enlisted performance report of a

255

former executive officer, and arbitrarily targeted several of her squadron commanders, including Lt. Col. Valenzuela. She also repeatedly harassed my former superintendent, SMSgt "LG," including reprimanding her the previous year, accusing her of "yelling" at MTI students, preventing her from participating in a sexual assault response panel, and arbitrarily reassigning her to a different squadron.

Col. Liddick wasn't the only senior leader I called out in my complaint. I also believed the wing commander, Col. Camerer, had abused his authority by not addressing the negative BMT command climate. He was well aware of the effects of Col. Liddick's toxic leadership style within the group, but he had taken no apparent action to correct her abuses. He was present when MTIs expressed their frustration with the command climate to General Rice the previous year. He received the results from the July 2013 RAND Corporation survey, in which MTIs expressed skepticism that their concerns would be acted on by leadership. When BMT first sergeants voiced their concerns to him over the command climate, he reported their perceived insubordination to group leadership. Finally, he admitted he launched the CDI against Lt. Col. Valenzuela regarding her first sergeant, SMSgt Monk, even though he did not believe the allegations to be true.

For good measure, I accused Col. Camerer of mishandling my CDI. At that point, he had already wasted over $25,000 in Air Force resources by allowing my removal from command with no assigned duties, and pulling the investigating officer from his job for an entire month to conduct the CDI. I believed this lengthy CDI negatively impacted unit morale, giving the impression I had been judged guilty without due process, and jeopardized my squadron's readiness for the AETC inspection. More troubling, I alleged Col. Camerer allowed Col. Liddick, one of the principal witnesses against me, to interfere with the CDI by coordinating too closely with the investigating officer. I believed she was not satisfied with the preliminary results of the investigation, and was probably slow-rolling the report until she could determine a way to permanently relieve me of command regardless of the CDI findings. Finally, it seemed Col. Camerer may have held up the closure of the CDI until after the AETC inspection was complete, further delaying my (hoped-for) return to command.[285]

---

[285] Complaint to AETC/IGQ, February 18, 2014

The following week, I submitted another allegation: that Col. Liddick failed to investigate an allegation of sexual harassment by MSgt Pickett, and that she may have engaged in reprisal against SSgt Little to cover up the misconduct. The AETC Complaints Resolution Division was unable to accept my third-party reprisal complaint on SSgt Little's behalf, and they ignored my earlier allegations against Col. Camerer, who had recently been confirmed by the Senate for promotion to Brigadier General, so was no longer subject to their authority. They did, however, add the rest of the allegation to my previous complaint.

That same day, the chief of the AETC complaints resolution division provided a final response to my complaint. His office dismissed my reprisal allegation, claiming I provided "no evidence of a valid protected communication" with the BMT Triennial Review committee, nor identified any "unfavorable personnel action" as a result. "The CDI and the temporary removal, in and of themselves, do not constitute UPAs," they concluded. On the other hand, they determined that my remaining allegations "would be better addressed in command channels," so they referred my case to the Second Air Force commander for further action.[286]

Thus began a convoluted tale of cover-up and abuse of authority involving Major General Leonard "Len" Patrick, who was then the 2 AF boss at Keesler Air Force Base, Mississippi. This former commander of the 37th Training Wing and Joint Base San Antonio had somehow flown under the radar during the Lackland sex scandal, and would soon return to JBSA as the AETC vice commander. In the meantime, he had the power to hold my group and wing commanders accountable for their actions, and help get my career back on track. An airman can dream, right?

I hadn't heard anything more about my complaint by the time I was relieved of command a month later, so I contacted the 2 AF staff judge advocate office as instructed on March 31. I reached out to Col. Brynn Morgan, who provided 2 AF newcomer orientation training at Lackland six months earlier. I had accompanied her on a tour of the BMT Reception Center and 331 TRS dorm during that visit, so I hoped she might recall meeting me.

---

[286] AETC/IGQ final response, February 27, 2014

She responded two days later, indicating 2 AF had received the complaint and it was currently under investigation. [287]   I subsequently learned the informal inquiry into my complaint didn't even begin until March 31[288] – suggesting 2 AF had just been sitting on it all that time, until my request for a status update spurred Maj. Gen. Patrick to action.

He appointed Col. Randy Hummel, a Reservist assigned to the 2 AF staff judge advocate office, as the investigating officer. Col. Hummel first contacted me on April 2, and we exchanged e-mails and phone calls over the next couple of days. I provided him all the details surrounding the wardrobe box allegation, including the incriminating e-mails from Col. Liddick documenting how she repeatedly asked for, and confirmed receipt of, this so-called gift. He also requested a copy of the 737 TRG operating instruction that authorized the wear of "MTI/Staff PT uniforms" to "provide distinct identification of instructors during daily BMT PT sessions."[289] Finally, I shared with him everything I knew about the anonymous sexual harassment complaint Col. Liddick failed to investigate, and I encouraged him to interview Lt. Col. Valenzuela, Lt. Col. Lam, and the recently retired CMSgt Williams.

Weeks passed without any word on the progress of this informal inquiry, and by May 16, my e-mails to Col. Hummel began coming back undeliverable. I again reached out to Col. Morgan, but she didn't respond, either. Finally, after another attempt on June 4, she informed me a "resolution letter" had been mailed to my home address on May 28 via certified mail. Where was this letter? She claimed the U.S. Postal Service attempted delivery on Saturday, May 31, but apparently no one was home. She suggested I go to my local post office to see if they would let me sign for it there. However, they had no record of this correspondence, and when I again contacted the 2 AF staff judge advocate on June 9, our e-mail exchange took an unexpected turn. "As I am now aware that you are represented by legal counsel," she replied, "I can no longer

---

[287] E-mail response from Col. Brynn Morgan, 2 AF/JA, "RE: AETC/IG complaint disposition," April 2, 2014
[288] Col. Randy Hummel, 2 AF/JA, "Informal Inquiry into IG Complaint, Lt. Col. Craig Perry," April 30, 2014
[289] 737 TRG Operating Instruction 36-2905, *BMT Physical Training (PT) Program*, September 21, 2011

correspond with you. I will contact your attorney, Ms. Melanie Cogburn at the Haddad Law Firm."[290]

As I will explain in Chapter 14, my wife had taken matters into her own hands, filing a civil lawsuit against Deborah Liddick over the wardrobe boxes in late May. A high-school classmate of mine, Ms. Cogburn, was representing her in this case, but she wasn't my personal attorney. When I informd her of this, Col. Morgan agreed to send the resolution letter to my area defense counsel instead, who scanned and e-mailed me a copy a few days later.

The long-awaited resolution letter was a bit of a disappointment. Dated May 22, it alerted me to the disposition of 14 separate allegations from my original AETC IG complaint. Maj. Gen. Patrick declared his inquiry had substantiated only a single claim: that the 737 TRG commander violated AFI 36-2903 by wearing starched ABUs and/or endorsing their wear by subordinates. Coercing a gift of used wardrobe boxes from a subordinate? Unsubstantiated. Failing to properly investigate an alleged sexual harassment complaint? Unsubstantiated. Abuse of authority, unprofessional relationships, harassing subordinates? All unsubstantiated.

Not surprisingly, my claims that Col. Liddick knowingly made false allegations against me related to undermining her authority, unprofessional relationships, and destroying material in a personnel information file were also found unsubstantiated; after all, my CDI had validated each of these allegations several months earlier. On the other hand, the resolution letter made no mention of the two CDI allegations of which I was cleared: that I undermined Col. Liddick's authority by making statements to an outside vendor about an official 737 TRG function, and that I demonstrated a lack of support for 37 TRW initiatives with regard to BMT. Were these false allegations? Maj. Gen. Patrick didn't say. In fact, the 2 AF commander gave no hint as to the rationale for any part of this finding, noting only that it was "found to be legally sufficient" before he personally reviewed and approved it. "Appropriate action will be taken against the individual who displayed the inappropriate behavior," he assured me. [291]

---

[290] E-mail exchange with Col. Morgan, ""RE: AETC/IG complaint disposition," June 9, 2014
[291] Maj. Gen. Leonard Patrick, 2 AF/CC, resolution letter, May 22, 2014

Considering Col. Liddick received a Legion of Merit medal upon her retirement from the Air Force on June 9, this assurance didn't amount to much.

In retrospect, the timing of my boss's retirement casts a suspicious light on the delay in my receipt of this resolution letter. If Maj. Gen. Patrick signed it on May 22, why didn't Col. Morgan purportedly send it to me until the 28th? My wife and I were home all day on the 31st, so why didn't our postal carrier deliver the letter or leave a notice of missed delivery? Why didn't our post office have any record of this certified letter? And why didn't Col. Morgan provide me a tracking number? Perhaps she simply didn't care if I was notified or not. Or perhaps she was delaying on purpose, so I wouldn't learn the results of this inquiry until after Col. Liddick could no longer be held accountable.

As for taking "appropriate action" against the individual responsible for the lone substantiated allegation, it may have already been too late. My colleague, Lt. Col. Valenzuela, filed her own IG complaint about the ABU starching incident on March 21, and she corroborated this and other allegations for Col. Hummel in early April. In response to her complaint, she recalls AETC/IG informing her that Col. Liddick had been talked to about this issue, well before Maj. Gen. Patrick signed the resolution letter substantiating the same allegation. If this timeline is correct, the informal 2 AF inquiry into my complaint did no more than validate an already-proven claim. In other words, it substantiated nothing at all, calling this entire exercise even further into question.

The week after I received the 2 AF resolution letter, I filed a couple of Congressional complaints, with Representative Pete Gallego and Senator John Cornyn, regarding my unfair treatment and abuses by my chain of command. Both members of Congress submitted inquiries into my case to the Department of the Air Force on my behalf later that month, and both received indistinguishable replies from Col. John Larson, chief of the Congressional inquiry division, later that summer.

On July 23, the Air Force Office of Legislative Liaison informed Rep. Pete Gallego how I was removed, investigated, and found to have committed offenses prompting my relief of command. They also recounted how my complaint to AETC/IG was handled:

After a thorough CDI, only two trivial technical issues were substantiated; that the 37 [sic] Training Group Commander starched her utility uniform and allowed subordinates to do so, and that she asked for and accepted moving boxes from the Perrys. 37 TRW/CC verbally counseled the 737 TRG/CC about the potential perception that could have been created regarding the moving boxes. No further action was deemed necessary.

The author concluded, "The allegations brought against Lt. Col. Perry and the 737 TRG/CC were thoroughly investigated and reviewed at multiple levels. The reviews determined the investigations and follow-on actions were appropriate."[292]

In less than 100 words, SAF/LL contradicted almost everything I thought I knew about the disposition of my allegations against my former boss. Col. Hummel emphasized he was only conducting an "informal inquiry" into my complaint, and Maj. Gen. Patrick also referred to this in his resolution letter only as an "inquiry," not a more formal commander-directed investigation. And this inquiry was certainly not thorough: only a handful of witnesses were interviewed, and none of us were asked to sign sworn statements affirming the truth of our testimony. The allegation that Col. Liddick violated federal law by coercing a gift from me was hardly a "trivial technical issue," and in any case the resolution letter clearly indicated, in capital letters, that this claim was "UNSUBSTANTIATED." Nevertheless, it was a pleasant surprise to learn Col. Liddick had in fact been chastised "about the potential perception that could have been created" by her unethical actions, even if there's no record of Col. Camerer instructing her to return our ill-gotten property. Finally, SAF/LL suggested the allegations that got me fired "were thoroughly investigated and reviewed at multiple levels," implying Lt. Col. McConnell's CDI hadn't been the last word on my case.

Senator Cornyn received an identical response on August 7,[293] again disputing the results of the informal inquiry into my IG

---

[292] Col. John Larson, response to inquiry by Representative Pete Gallego, July 23, 2014

[293] Col. Larson, response to inquiry by Senator John Cornyn, August 7, 2014

complaint. Either the Air Force was lying to these members of Congress, or Maj. Gen. Patrick had lied to me.

Not satisfied with this response, Rep. Gallego followed up with a second query regarding my case. In a letter dated September 9, the new chief of the Congressional inquiry and travel division, Col. Matthew Yetishefsky, acknowledged the 2 AF commander provided me the results of the "inspector general investigation" into my allegations against the 737 TRG commander on May 22. If I was not satisfied with that determination, the author continued, I should have requested further review from the very same general officer who made the original determination. However, I would have to provide "additional or new information not otherwise available during the inquiry," and the deadline for appeal had already passed. The Air Force made no effort to answer the Congressman's questions or resolve the apparent contradictions between the 2 AF resolution letter and the response to Rep. Gallego's initial inquiry. "We trust this information is helpful," Col. Yetishefsky signed off, having been no help whatsoever.[294]

Rep. Gallego followed up with a personal letter to me a few days later. He noted Caroline and I were in his prayers due to her serious medical condition, and thanked me for the initiative my wife and I took "to improve the lives of Airmen and their families through activities such as the Key Spouse Program." However, "these supportive efforts being unrelated to the favoritism issues raised by Air Force leaders," and considering I had "not yet fully exercised all avenues of appeal or additional review that are available to me," I must fully exhaust all available remedies before he could "ask the Air Force a third time if they followed all appropriate processes with respect to disciplinary actions" taken against me. "Please know your case has been reviewed by multiple levels within the Air Force – including up to a four-star command," he assured me. "In my experience," wrote this first-term Congressman, "a congressional inquiry makes any federal department – and particularly the military services – do a thorough review to ensure that they did not make an error."[295]

---

[294] Col. Matthew Yetishefsky, further reply to inquiry by Rep. Pete Gallego, September 9, 2014
[295] Rep. Pete Gallego, constituent casework follow-up letter, September 12, 2014

Pete Gallego had swallowed these lame Air Force excuses without question. After he lost his reelection bid that November, I hoped I might have better luck with his successor.

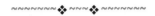

Intending to get to the bottom of the discrepancy regarding the 2 AF informal inquiry, I filed a request under the Freedom of Information Act later that month for a copy of Col. Hummell's report of investigation and other documents. On September 22, I received a response from Brig. Gen. Patrick Higby, commander of the 81st Training Wing at Keesler AFB, which indicated the local FOIA office had reviewed 58 pages of records, of which 49 were deemed "fully deniable" in accordance with several FOIA exemptions: 5 U.S.C. § 552(b)(5), concerning pre-decisional records, including those covered by attorney work-product privilege; exemption (b)(6), personal privacy; and exemption (b)(7)(C), records compiled for law enforcement purposes.[296]

Only nine pages were determined to be "partially releasable," including a heavily redacted copy of the 2 AF resolution letter and the evidence I myself provided Col. Hummell. In fact, only two of these pages contained any information I didn't already have. The first was a memorandum from Col. Hummell to Maj. Gen. Patrick providing an overview of his work. "The informal inquiry was conducted from 31 March 2014 to 4 April 2014 and an initial draft of my report on that inquiry was accomplished on 14 April 2014," he wrote. "On 28 and 29 April 2014 I reopened my inquiry," he continued, and the "final report was completed 30 April 2014." The rest of this memo, including the nature of my complaint, the rationale for reopening the inquiry, and any discussion of its findings, was redacted.[297] The second new piece of information was a letter from Maj. Gen. Patrick to Col. Camerer dated May 22, informing him of the results of the informal inquiry, and providing a copy of the report of investigation (without attachments) for his review "to determine appropriate command action." He was directed to advise his boss "of what command

---

[296] Brig. Gen. Patrick Higby, final response to FOIA 2014-06038-F, September 22, 2014
[297] Col. Randy Hummel, "Informal Inquiry into IG Complaint, Lt. Col. Craig Perry," April 30, 2014

action is taken and provide the required documents" in accordance with AFI 90-301, *Inspector General Complaints Resolution.*[298]

On the bright side, in reviewing my request for documents related to the informal inquiry, the Keesler FOIA requester service center came across a copy of the report of investigation from my earlier CDI at Lackland. Thinking this was part of the package I was seeking, they forwarded the request to the Joint Base San Antonio FOIA requester service center, which released the entire file to me in mid-November 2014. It not only included Lt. Col. McConnell's report of investigation (which I had already received back in March), but almost all the supporting documentation: the two original complaints from Maj. Sprouse and Mr. Kenny; 63 pages of testimony from 20 witnesses, plus both of my sworn statements; and additional exhibits used as evidence. The names of individual subjects and witnesses were of course redacted, but other than that, only 24 pages of the 287-page file were withheld. These included a copy of the letter of reprimand I removed from my superintendent's PIF, and a "print out of EOC" (presumably the MTI School end-of-course survey comment used against her), both of which were withheld under FOIA exemption (b)(6); and the entirety of "Tab I" of the CDI – a 20-page legal review – fully denied under FOIA exemption (b)(5).

My discovery of these documents was fortuitous, offering me a behind-the-scenes look at the actual evidence from my case. They painted a very different picture than what Lt. Col. McConnell portrayed in his report. Not only had he left out favorable testimony that tended to exonerate me, he also misrepresented several statements and omitted critical details that call the credibility and integrity of certain key witnesses into question. Had anyone else actually reviewed this evidence before passing judgment on me? Moreover, considering the JBSA FOIA office provided me Lt. Col. McConnell's report of investigation and almost all its supporting documents, while the Keesler FOIA office fully denied almost every record from Col. Hummel's informal inquiry, these two offices were clearly applying different releasability standards. Unfortunately, by the time I realized this discrepancy, the 60-day deadline to appeal the original FOIA decision had already expired.

---

[298] Maj. Gen. Patrick, "Result of Informal Inquiry Concerning [737 TRG/CC]," May 22, 2014

In January 2015, I contacted the office of my new Congressman, Rep. Will Hurd, about my case. He, too, submitted an inquiry on my behalf, but was no more successful than his predecessor and Senate counterpart in getting a straight answer from the Air Force. He did, however, receive the most thorough and error-filled accounting of my case to date. (I counted at least four mistakes on the first page alone, italicized below.) In a letter dated March 26, SAF/LL again explained how I the "*37th Training Wing* Commander" removed me from command and launched an investigation, which substantiated "three *of the four* allegations" against me. I then filed a complaint with the AETC inspector general, which they referred it to the appropriate command authority. "On *March 25*, 2014, the 2 AF/CC initiated a *CDI* and appointed a senior reserve attorney assigned to 2 AF/JA to serve as the investigating officer."

Maj. Gen. Patrick "elected to do an informal inquiry because of the investigating officer's experience," the letter continued. Col. Hummel "previously conducted important investigations" for 2 AF, and in his civilian capacity was an Assistant United States attorney for the Southern District of Florida. This account again (falsely) asserted the investigating officer substantiated two of the 14 allegations against Col. Liddick, and revealed Col. Camerer verbally counseled her on June 5, 2014. It also added an unexpected twist: "As part of his investigation, the investigating officer independently considered the now-closed 37 TRW/CC CDI and found that he fully concurred with the findings against Colonel Perry (undermined authority, unprofessional relationship, removing LOR)." After cataloging how Col. Camerer rejected my LOR appeal and a separate request for redress (which I'll discuss in the next chapter), the letter concluded,

> *The allegations brought against Colonel Perry were thoroughly investigated twice and reviewed at multiple levels to include legal reviews and [sic] all levels of command. The reviews determined the investigations and follow-on actions were appropriate. There is no credible evidence that anyone in Colonel Perry's chain of command targeted either Colonel Perry or his wife. Colonel Perry's*

actions and questionable judgment warranted his removal from command.[299]

What on earth did any of this have to do with my wife? More importantly, what's this about an independent consideration of my original CDI?

This would certainly explain why the Air Force kept claiming the allegations against me were investigated and reviewed at multiple levels, but it doesn't begin to justify the use of the word "thoroughly" to describe an informal inquiry during which allegations were (allegedly) independently considered. There was nothing thorough about it. Col. Hummel never questioned me about my relief of command or interviewed any other witnesses regarding my CDI, and he collected no new evidence regarding my case. According to his own accounting, the informal inquiry lasted only five days (March 31 through April 4, 2014), then he reopened it for two days at the end of April. Was that when this attorney independently considered my earlier CDI? And why was the Air Force only now coming forward with this claim, nearly a year after the fact? Not for the first time, I got the impression these senior leaders weren't being entirely honest with me, or my Congressman.

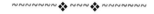

Perhaps Col. Hummel's report of investigation would shed some light on this mystery. In April 2015, I again submitted a FOIA request for the document. I noted how the Air Force had informed three separate members of Congress that the results of that investigation were different from what Maj. Gen. Patrick officially told me. Furthermore, the latest response to a Congressional inquiry asserted Col. Hummel "independently considered" the CDI Col. Camerer used to justify my relief of command, an entirely new claim. I also argued that, since Col. Hummel was duly appointed as an investigating officer, he was not serving in his capacity as an attorney for the 2 AF commander during his informal inquiry, so his report should not be considered attorney work product. Normal practice is to assign a separate legal advisor to assist the investigating officer during such inquiries, and any legal review

---

[299] SAF/LL, response to inquiry by Rep. Will Hurd, March 26, 2015

should be contained in a stand-alone document. Moreover, Maj. Gen. Patrick released Col. Hummel's report to Col. Camerer for review to determine appropriate command action against Col. Liddick, suggesting this report was not, in fact, attorney work product.[300]

The Keesler FOIA requester service center rejected my request as merely an appeal of the earlier determination from September 2014, filed far too late to be considered. So I submitted a request for a different set of records: documents related to Col. Hummel's independent consideration of the 37 TRW commander's CDI, which the Air Force had characterized as a thorough investigation. "Air Force spokespersons have repeatedly claimed allegations against me were thoroughly investigated at multiple levels," I wrote. "These statements are based on the assumption that Col. Hummel independently considered my 37 TRW/CC CDI. Records of such a thorough and independent investigation cannot reasonably be considered attorney work product. If this request is denied, it will indicate Air Force spokespersons provided false or misleading statements to the media and Congress regarding my case."[301]

The Keesler AFB FOIA manager was not amused. "The current request reads like an appeal to the response you received pertaining to this request," wrote Ms. Phyllis Pires, but that deadline had passed in November 2014, so they would not process my request as an appeal of this case. "Additionally, we will not consider this request a new request since we have already processed a request for these same documents, to include any of those in which Col. Hummel was involved," she continued, "and under the FOIA, we are not required to process a request for records more than once." They were therefore closing my request, and would take no further action on it.[302]

Ms. Pires did, however, provide me an inventory of all records reviewed and processed in connection with my original FOIA request, which allowed me to account for the 49 pages that were fully denied. Col. Hummel's report of investigation was 22 pages, while a legal review of his informal inquiry ran four pages. There were nine pages of unspecified attachments, plus a three-

---

[300] FOIA 2015-03636-F, April 20, 2015
[301] FOIA 2015-04042-F, May 18, 2015
[302] E-mail from Ms. Phyllis Pires, "FOIA 2015-04042-F - Duplicate Request/Closure," May 27, 2015

page referral completion report, presumably notifying the AETC inspector general of the results. Finally, 11 pages were a legal review of my separate request for redress under Article 138, UCMJ,[303] which I will discuss in the next chapter. This was useful information, as it confirmed there was a separate legal review, and the 22-page report of investigation should not reasonably have been denied citing attorney work-product privilege.

There was one last recourse to get this report, short of suing the Air Force in federal court: I could file an official FOIA appeal with the Secretary of the Air Force. According to DoD Regulation 5400.7-R, *DoD Freedom of Information Act Program*, paragraph C5.3.3.1., exceptions to the 60-day FOIA appeal time limit may be considered on a case by case basis. Air Force Manual 33-302, paragraph C5.3.3.2. further clarifies, "Any FOIA appeals received after the 60-day time limit are not processed unless the requester provides adequate justification for failing to comply with the time limit." On June 9, 2015, I filed an appeal noting the Air Force had only informed me in March 2015 that Col. Hummel independently considered my CDI, and I had just confirmed a separate legal review had been conducted on his informal inquiry. I argued my late notification of this compelling new information provided adequate justification for my failure to comply with the FOIA 60-day time limit.[304]

Although such FOIA appeals are notionally addressed to the Secretary of the Air Force, they are routed through the same office that originally denied the request. It was actually left up to Ms. Pires to determine the legitimacy of my claims, and her response left no doubt as to where she stood: "We complied with all applicable FOIA guidance in our response to your initial request (#2014-06038-F), and the questions you raised in your June 9, 2015 appeal should have been raised within the 60-day timeline provided in the final response. We will not entertain this appeal nor any future appeals regarding this request; the decision not to process it is final. Your window of opportunity has closed."[305] The absurdity of her logic was staggering: How could I raise a question about Col. Hummel's independent consideration, when I wasn't

[303] E-mail exchange with Ms. Pires, "RE: FOIA 2015-04042-F - Duplicate Request/Closure," May 28, 2015
[304] "Freedom of Information Act (FOIA) Appeal," June 9, 2015
[305] E-mail from Ms. Pires, "FOIA 2015-00136-A - Final Response," July 20, 2015

told about it until months later? And how could I raise a question about the determination his report was attorney work product, when Ms. Pires herself hadn't yet informed me a separate legal review had been conducted?

I can only conclude her office and 2 AF leadership are hiding something, as they clearly had the discretion to consider this appeal. What is it about that report of investigation that's so sensitive? If Col. Hummel did, in fact, independently consider my CDI, it was clearly not the thorough investigation the Air Force claims. Is it possible he didn't fully concur with Lt. Col. McConnell's findings? Moreover, two weeks after completing the initial draft of his report, the investigating officer reopened his inquiry for a couple of days. If he did so in response to feedback from the appointing authority or other members of his staff, and if he then used this opportunity to review my original CDI, his consideration can't really be considered independent. It's not unreasonable to conclude Maj. Gen. Patrick actually instructed Col. Hummel to look into my case – not to ensure due process or assess the credibility of claims against me, but merely so he could say he did, and provide cover for his unwillingness to hold my chain of command accountable. (Alternately, the 2 AF commander may have reopened this informal inquiry after my wife, Caroline, contacted Gen. Rand about my CDI earlier that month, as I'll discuss in the next chapter.)

I also suspect Col. Hummel's report substantiated only one allegation, as Maj. Gen. Patrick confirmed, but the Air Force subsequently overruled the 2 AF commander on the allegation of coercing a gift from a subordinate once my wife filed a lawsuit regarding the wardrobe boxes. Finally, I believe Maj. Gen. Patrick may have appointed a lawyer to conduct the inquiry precisely in order to prevent the subsequent release of his report under attorney work-product privilege. Whatever their reasons for denying my repeated requests, the Air Force is subverting the intent of the Freedom of Information Act, and undermining confidence in the integrity of the chain of command.

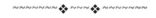

This 17-month odyssey, which began with my initial complaint to the AETC inspector general and ended at the Keesler FOIA office, was far from my only encounter with the Air Force IG complaints resolution process. In addition the complaint I filed with 502 ABW/IG in early June 2014 regarding contracting irregularities, I also filed a complaint with the Air Force IG hotline on June 16, 2014, alleging widespread and persistent abuse of authority by Brig. Gen. (sel.) Camerer and Col. Liddick, as well as failures by AETC/IG and Maj. Gen. Patrick to properly investigate multiple allegations of serious misconduct by my former group commander. SAF/IG acknowledged receipt of my complaint and supporting documentation that same day, and indicated it had been transferred to the Senior Official Inquiries Directorate.

This was an encouraging sign. According to an article which ran on the cover of the *Air Force Times* just weeks later, the chief of that office, Col. Matthew Bartlett, noted an allegation against a senior official "receives the same level of scrutiny as an airman who makes an allegation against a noncommissioned officer." When an IG complaint is lodged against a general officer or general-officer select, Bartlett said, their careers are put on hold whether or not the claims are eventually substantiated. "Any movement comes to a stop," he asserted, including new assignments and promotions. "If they are planning on retiring, that's going to be put on hold by merely filing a credible complaint against a senior official," he said. "About 30 percent of complaints that come into our office are substantiated misconduct. A hundred percent of complaints do impact [their] lives."[306]

And yet, just four days after I filed my complaint, Colonel Camerer pinned on his brigadier general stars at a private ceremony at JBSA-Randolph. He and his wife then proceeded to their next assignment at Ramstein Airbase, Germany, where he now serves as director of plans, programs and analyses for United States Air Forces in Europe and Africa. According to his official biography, Camerer's effective date of promotion was July 3, 2014.[307] If his career was put on hold, it didn't last long. Meanwhile, it took more than a year for SAF/IG to provide a response to my complaint.

"Our apologies for just getting this information to you," wrote an unnamed official from the complaints resolution directorate in October 2015. "After review by SAF IGS and SAF IGQ it was determined that no new or compelling information was

---

[306] Kristin Davis, "Generals breaking the rules: Does rank garner privilege or increased scrutiny?" *Air Force Times*, June 30, 2014
[307] Official biography of Brigadier General Mark D. Camerer, current as of August 2015

presented that warrants further investigation. SAF IGQ closed this complaint on 4 Mar 15."[308] Typically, the complaints resolution process should take no more than 20 calendar days, but these processing timelines may be extended in cases involving senior officials due to "the limited number of investigating officers and unconstrained nature of complaints." Still, it should not have taken them 261 days to determine there was nothing new or compelling in my complaint. Moreover, they didn't bother to notify me at any point during or after the process, as they are required to inform the complainant when complaint analysis is completed, whether or not an investigation is warranted.[309] Not only did SAF/IG fail to live up to the public promises of Col. Bartlett, they also failed to comply with their own formal guidelines.

Perhaps I'm a slow learner, but I gave the military inspector general system one last opportunity to resolve my complaints. I contacted the Department of Defense IG hotline in December 2014, reporting abuse of authority and reprisal by several Air Force leaders. They quickly dismissed most of my allegations, but actually followed up on my whistleblower complaint stemming from the September 2013 social with members of the BMT Triennial Review committee. Nearly a year after AETC/IG dismissed this very same allegation, DoD IG referred my reprisal complaint to the Air Force for further action on February 6, 2015, obliging SAF/IG to formally investigate my claims. The complaint was assigned to the senior official inquiries directorate in April, prompting an Air Force investigator to contact me in late June. He conducted an interview with me on July 10, and requested additional information from me as recently September. He informed me on February 19, 2016, that his investigation was complete, and his report had been forwarded to the DoD IG for review. That review was presumably still ongoing at the time of

---

[308] E-mail response from SAF/IGQ, "RE: EXTERNAL: Re: Complaint against Brig Gen (sel.) Camerer and other 37 TRW senior leaders," October 6, 2015

[309] Air Force Instruction AFI 90-301, *Inspector General Complaints Resolution*, paragraph 4.2.4.1, Table 3.1, and Table 4.2, August 23, 2011

this writing – but after all my experiences with the IG complaints resolution process, I'm not exactly holding my breath for a favorable outcome.

Chapter 13. Redress of Grievance

In the previous chapter, we saw how the Air Force inspector general complaints resolution process failed to address blatant abuse of authority by my chain of command, and only belatedly took up my whistleblower complaint. We also noted how ineffectual Congressional inquiries can be, when representatives are unwilling to confront the Air Force on its misleading claims and demand justice for their constituents. Unlike nonjudicial punishment (Article 15, Uniform Code of Military Justice) and courts-martial, there is no appeals process for administrative actions such as the letter of reprimand I received, even though it effectively ended my career. My ultimate recourse would be to apply to the Air Force Board for Correction of Military Records, a long shot at best.

There was one other option remaining to me, however. One of the peculiar features of the UCMJ is the opportunity it grants military personnel to petition their superiors for redress of grievances. Article 138 reads:

> *Any member of the armed forces who believes himself wronged by his commanding officer, and who, upon due application to that commanding officer, is refused redress, may complain to any superior commissioned officer, who shall forward the complaint to the officer exercising general court-martial jurisdiction over the officer against whom it is made. The officer exercising general court-martial jurisdiction shall examine into the complaint and take proper measures for redressing the wrong complained of; and he shall, as soon as possible, send to the Secretary concerned a true statement of that complaint, with the proceedings had thereon.[310]*

Air Force Instruction 51-904, *Complaints of Wrongs Under Article 138, Uniform Code of Military Justice*, outlines the responsibilities of the officer exercising general court-martial authority: "The GCMA will conduct or direct further investigation as deemed appropriate and will act, based on the facts and circumstances of the complaint and any investigation." In all cases, this senior officer "must inform the member in writing of both the action taken on the complaint

---

[310] 10 U.S. Code § 938 - Art. 138. Complaints of wrongs

and the reasons for that action," and then send the case file to the Pentagon "for Secretarial review and disposition."[311]

I duly filed a request for redress pursuant to Article 138, UCMJ, with Col. Camerer on May 5, 2014. I highlighted the severe flaws in the methodology, analysis, and conclusions of the commander-directed investigation, and accused Col. Camerer of not considering all the evidence presented, "which is arbitrary, capricious, and an abuse of your discretion." I reiterated the disciplinary actions he imposed – LOR, referral officer performance report, opening an unfavorable information file, and filing this derogatory information from my officer selection record for promotion – as well as my removal from command, "were clearly unfair and selective in the application of standards, both in the type of standard applied and in the severity of the penalty imposed." That is, Col. Camerer singled me out for punishment, and imposed a penalty in excess of the investigating officer's recommendation and what he himself levied in previous cases.[312]

My area defense counsel was apparently impressed with my 14-page complaint. "This is one hell of a 138," she noted. "The way this is written, I would compare it to flipping your desk over (papers, computer, and all) on your way out the door. It's very, very direct, but I've gathered that you are not a risk-averse person and you'd prefer to speak your mind. I think you've put together the best case possible, you're aware of the risks and benefits, and you've definitely put out there on the record most, if not all, the concerns you've had over the past several months."[313] But would it make any difference?

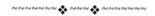

A week later, Col. Camerer responded to my complaint of wrongs. He claimed to have carefully considered the request for redress, reviewing the CDI report of investigation, as well as the various statements, evidence, and character reference letters I previously provided. He even supposedly re-read my original

---

[311] AFI 51-904, *Complaints of Wrongs Under Article 138, Uniform Code of Military Justice*, June 30, 1994
[312] "Request for Redress Pursuant to Article 138, UCMJ," May 5, 2014
[313] E-mail exchange with Area Defense Counsel, "138 Edits," May 2, 2014

response to the LOR. Nevertheless, he decided to deny my request.[314] Considering he's the one who wronged me in the first place, this outcome was not unexpected, but the Article 138 process would hopefully provide a remedy.

Due to a mix-up in my ADC's office, I didn't actually receive this response until June 12, just days before Col. Camerer relinquished command. My attorney next submitted my complaint through legal channels to Maj. Gen. Patrick, Second Air Force commander, on June 30. An officer in the 2 AF staff judge advocate office confirmed receipt the following day: "We anticipate having Col. Bernstein, one of our reservists, review the entire package when she arrives mid-month. She is an O-6 JAG newly assigned to this location, so has no background or history with any personnel involved, but it will be several weeks before she begins her review."[315] Considering how another 2 AF Reserve attorney, Col. Hummell, mishandled my IG complaint a few months earlier, I was not encouraged by this development, or the delay it implied. At what point would the 2 AF commander examine into my complaint and take proper measures for redressing these wrongs?

As it turned out, Maj. Gen. Patrick passed the buck. He relinquished command a month later to Brigadier General Mark Brown, a career finance officer with limited command experience and almost no background in Air Education and Training Command. On August 12, this two-star select informed me he, too, was denying my request for redress. After "carefully reviewing" my complaint, the new guy found the wrongs complained of "do not represent arbitrary, capricious, or clearly unfair applications of administrative actions or standards" by Col. Camerer, "who acted appropriately and within his discretion."[316] It's not clear how he came to this conclusion, however, as no one ever contacted me or any other witnesses to verify my claims or determine the merits of my allegations.

As I discussed in the last chapter, when I submitted a request for documents under the Freedom of Information Act in August, I made sure to ask for a copy of the report from any

---

[314] Col. Camerer, "Request for Redress Pursuant to Article 138, UCMJ," May 13, 2014

[315] E-mail exchange with 2 AF/JA, "Lt. Col. Perry Art 138 Request," July 1, 2014

[316] Maj. Gen. (sel.) Mark Brown, "Request for Redress Under Article 138, UCMJ," August 12, 2014

investigation the 2 AF commander conducted or directed into my Article 138 complaint. The response was revealing: "Personnel in 2 AF Staff Judge Advocate's office stated no inquiry or investigation was ordered in response to your previous Article 138 complaint," I was informed. The only document generated in response to my request for redress was a legal review, which is not releasable as attorney-work product.[317] Presumably this is a reference to the work of the aforementioned Col. Bernstein, who apparently conducted a limited review for legal sufficiency rather than an actual investigation, as seemingly required by AFI 51-904 and the UCMJ. Brig. Gen. Brown's claim to have carefully reviewed my complaint apparently had no basis in reality.

Two weeks after denying my request, the new 2 AF commander visited JBSA-Lackland, where he shared an assortment of clichéd leadership aphorisms he liked to call "Brown's Bag" at a commander's call. Number 10 on the list, "Your intellect can take you to positions that your character cannot sustain," referred to "the seemingly constant news of military leaders failing their core values." He implored airmen to "keep integrity at the forefront of who they are," since our intellect may help us get ahead, but it takes character to "sustain us and make us the leaders needed by our Air Force and the nation."[318] During this commander's call, he alluded to recent stories in the *Air Force Times* about commanders being fired. As I will discuss in a later chapter, my wife, Caroline, and I had been featured on the cover of this periodical two months earlier, and several members of the audience later indicated they had no doubt the general was using my "curious case" to illustrate his point. "You have to ask yourself, why was he fired?" the 2 AF commander reportedly continued. "Officers selected for command must be smart, or else they wouldn't have been given the job. So, his failure must be one of character," he concluded.

"Sir, my jaw just literally dropped," my ADC responded when I informed her of this latest twist. "That's incredible."[319] The officer who just a fortnight earlier rejected my request for redress without bothering to investigate was now seemingly calling my

---

[317] Brig. Gen. Higby, final response to FOIA 2014-06038-F, September 22, 2014

[318] Brig. Gen. Mark Brown, "Commentary: 'Brown's Bag' -- budget and leadership lessons," Air Force Materiel Command official website, July 3, 2014

[319] E-mail exchange with my ADC, "Art 138," August 27, 2014

character into question in front of my former peers and subordinates. Not only was this slanderous and factually inaccurate – none of my alleged offenses involved lapses of character – but publicly disparaging a fellow airman in this way is conduct unbecoming an officer. After declaring that Col. Camerer acted appropriately in relieving me of command, Brig. Gen. Brown behaved entirely inappropriately in front of hundreds of witnesses, undermining confidence in his own judgment and impartiality.

After the 2 AF commander forwarded my Article 138 complaint to the Pentagon for Secretarial review and disposition, I decided to reach out personally to the Secretary of the Air Force. In early September, I sent the Honorable Deborah Lee James an e-mail respectfully requesting she thoroughly review this matter, and grant my request for redress. "I believe the evidence demonstrates that the treatment I received from my former group, wing, and numbered air force commanders was clearly unfair, and that they have conducted themselves in a manner that calls their judgment in my case into question," I wrote, and provided a three-page memorandum supporting these claims. "Please correct this miscarriage of justice," I implored, "which is unfortunately undermining confidence in our Air Force leadership."[320]

The next day, I received a response from the SecAF's senior military assistant, Col. Wayne Monteith. "We have received your note," he confirmed, "and if I follow correctly you have a complaint pending in AF/JA and I assume SAF/IG? If so, what exactly are you requesting? That Sec James review the material you've provided outside of the legal and IG processes, or are you simply looking to ensure she is aware of your position prior to her potentially reviewing your case?" I replied, "the purpose of my note was to bring this complaint to the personal attention of the Secretary, to ensure she is aware that the officer exercising general court-martial authority appears not to have handled it appropriately. I am sure the Secretary reviews hundreds of Article 138 complaints," I continued, "but I suspect few involve cases of such notoriety or complexity." As for acting outside established

---

[320] E-mail to the "Secretary of the Air Force, "Lt. Col. Perry request for redress," September 4, 2014

processes, "my intent was merely to make a protected communication with a member of my chain of command."

The following week, Col. Monteith noted SecAF gets very few Article 138 complaints, "so I have back briefed her on your concerns and we will allow the system to execute due diligence on your package." Despite the "notoriety" associated with my complaint, "that in and of itself does not move the complaint to the front of the line to the detriment of the other pending cases." He also counseled patience with the Air Force IG process, which takes time to work through allegations against senior officers, especially in a case as "complex" as mine. Nevertheless, Col. Monteith assured me, they were "looking at the additional information you previously provided."

I found this last comment puzzling, as I had not provided information to anyone at the Pentagon since my original complaint to Air Force IG in July. The mystery deepened a few days later, when the SecAF's assistant elaborated further: "SAF/IG also reviewed your latest document, as they did a month ago following your communication to CSAF last month."[321] Col. Monteith seemed to be suggesting I had contacted the Chief of Staff of the Air Force, General Mark Welsh, sometime in August. Was this a mix-up of some sort on Col. Monteith's part? Or could this be a case of identity theft? Neither the SecAF's assistant nor SAF/IG ever clarified.

As crazy as it sounds, I suspect someone impersonating me may have sent the CSAF a poison pen letter, in an effort to discredit me in the eyes of senior Air Force leadership. Who would do such a thing? I had probably made my share of enemies by this point, and my repeated complaints against Col. Liddick, Brig. Gen. Camerer, Maj. Gen. Patrick, and now Brig. Gen. Brown provided these senior leaders – as well as their backers – plenty of motive to do me further harm by making slanderous insinuations about my "character." When I later submitted a FOIA request to obtain a copy of the purported communication, however, I was informed the "Office of the Chief of Staff of the Air Force (HAF/ES) and the Chief Executive Communications conducted a search of all record systems that would likely contain the records requested and have

---

[321] E-mail exchange with Col. Wayne Monteith, September 5-12, 2014

failed to identify responsive records;"[322] SAF/IG also came up short in their search.[323] So either Monteith – who has since been promoted to Brigadier General – misled me as to the existence of this communication, or else the Air Force is now trying to cover it up.

Ultimately, Secretarial review and disposition didn't amount to much. Just two weeks after I reached out to the SecAF, the director of the administrative law directorate in the office of the Air Force Judge Advocate General broke the news: "By authority of the Secretary of the Air Force, I have reviewed all matters submitted by you in your request for redress," and "determined that the action taken in this matter" by Col. Camerer and Col. Liddick "was appropriate." The denial of my request for redress was thereby sustained, this civilian lawyer informed me.[324] While her staff may have back-briefed her on my correspondence, Secretary James apparently didn't lift a finger to ensure justice was done in my case, and for all I know remained oblivious of my fate.

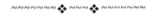

I really wasn't surprised when my request for redress went nowhere. As 2 AF commander, Maj. Gen. Patrick reportedly didn't make a habit of carefully reviewing such cases coming from Lackland, and it appears his replacement may be following in his footsteps. (It's highly likely the two coordinated on my case as they prepared to transfer authority.) To my knowledge, Maj. Gen. Patrick never reversed any disciplinary decisions handed down by his subordinate commanders, Col. Camerer and Col. Liddick. (There's a rumor that Col. Liddick once improperly marked down the enlisted performance report of her executive officer, and this Master Sergeant successfully petitioned to get her evaluation thrown out, but that may simply be an urban legend at BMT.) This is a fundamental flaw in the Article 138 process: after a group or wing commander denies a request for redress and upholds the

---

[322] Tracy Broady, interim response to FOIA request # 2015-05838-F, November 17, 2015

[323] Tracy Broady, final response to FOIA request # 2015-05838-F, November 23, 2015

[324] Conrad M. Von Wald, disposition of Article 138 complaint, September 18, 2014

original punishment, there are few incentives for a general officer further up the chain of command to overrule this lower-level decision, as this would imply a lack of confidence in the subordinate commander's judgment. Rather than holding commanders accountable, the process lends itself to closing ranks around bad decisions.

Then again, sometimes a more senior commander demonstrates the character necessary to make the hard call. In a previous chapter, I mentioned the case of a Master Sergeant who was wrongfully punished for defending his wife from his drunk supervisor. His squadron commander issued him an LOR and marked down his enlisted performance report, while Col. Liddick eliminated him from the MTI corps and denied him an end-of-tour medal. He filed a complaint under Article 138, but Maj. Gen. Patrick summarily denied it. But then something truly unusual happened: over a year later, the AETC commander, General Rand, unexpectedly granted this request for redress, overruling both of his subordinate commanders. This former MTI has since been awarded the decorations he earned, and the EPR reflecting this incident has been removed from his records. While miracles such as these were exceedingly rare at BMT, I had hope that Gen. Rand might be willing to intervene in my case as well.

My wife, Caroline, was the first to appeal directly to the AETC commander. When he met us in November 2013, Gen. Rand asked my wife to send him additional information about her exceptional Key Spouse program. She finally contacted him in early April 2014, apologizing for the delay due to her medical issues and my subsequent removal from command. Before presenting a comprehensive Key Spouse business plan, she apologized for not providing him a more recent update on the current status of the program, but the no-contact order remained in place, "and it is my understanding that the program has unfortunately disintegrated in my absence." Caroline also expressed her concern that our efforts to take care of airmen under my command were taken out of context and used against me during the commander-directed investigation. "I know you are an extremely busy man," she wrote, "but I believe it would be very much worth your while to take some time and seriously look into what is going on in BMT. I think you'd be surprised." Less than 24 hours later, Gen. Rand unexpectedly responded:

Caroline,

Thank you very much for this note and thank you for your contribution to the spouses of the 737 TRSS--your efforts to promote a strong Key Spouse program have been admirable and you should be proud of your team's accomplishments!

You indicated that your and husband's efforts to take care of Airmen and their families may have been taken out of context and used as evidence against your husband in the finding that he created an atmosphere of favoritism. I imagine this has been a very difficult time for you and Craig. I will inquire about your concerns, and have asked the 37 TRW/CC, Col. Camerer, to brief me and AETC/JA team on the findings and conclusions from the appointed Investigation Officer.

You are right, taking proper care of our Airmen and their families is important to me. I sincerely appreciate the support you provided the key Spouse program at the 37 TRW and 737 TRSS. I also hope that your cancer care and treatment is going well.

Sincerely,
Robin[325]

A week later, I followed up with Col. Polly Kenny, AETC staff judge advocate, to update her on my case. I sent her a copy of my responses to my LOR and referral officer performance report for her reference, to provide additional background and context ahead of the meeting with Col. Camerer, which I understand took place later that month. I didn't hear back from her until three weeks later, after after Col. Hummel had completed his informal inquiry into my IG complaint – as well as his supposedly independent consideration of my CDI. "I have inquired and found that your issues are being handled at various levels in IG and command," she wrote; "therefore, Gen Rand and I expect those investigations to run their course." She added, "Gen Rand asked me to reiterate his appreciation of your wife's efforts in support of our

---

[325] E-mail exchange between Caroline Perry and Gen. Robin Rand, "737 TRSS Key Spouse Program," April 7-8, 2014

Air Force." [326]   Apparently the AETC commander wouldn't be intervening in my case, at least not yet.

As 2014 dragged on, I gradually exhausted all my appeals. My various IG complaints had gone nowhere, and my request for redress was denied without even a cursory examination. Repeated Congressional inquiries prompted Air Force leadership to weave an ever-thicker web of lies, which my FOIA request was unable to penetrate. Meanwhile, I was relegated to a low-profile assignment and passed over for promotion. Although my situation seemed pretty much hopeless, I nevertheless refused to give up.

My principal obstacle to rehabilitation was the unwillingness of certain senior leaders to overrule one of their own. It was one thing to reverse Col. Liddick, whose actions were increasingly coming under suspicion since she retired several months earlier. Col. Camerer, on the other hand, had been promoted to the general officer ranks, and he had a powerful patron at Air Mobility Command, so acknowledging my former wing commander had made a mistake in my case might generate blowback for both their careers. However, the release of the witness statements from my CDI in November offered a potential way around this problem. Much of this testimony was not highlighted in the report of investigation, and so was likely never examined by Col. Camerer, Maj. Gen. Patrick, or other senior leaders who reviewed my case. As such, it could essentially be considered new evidence, not readily available when my case was originally decided. Based on this new information, I took another bite at the apple.

On Christmas Eve 2014, I wrote to Gen. Rand to humbly request an act of benevolence. It had been a year since Col. Camerer launched the CDI against me, but a careful examination of the report of investigation and recently released witness testimony called its results into question. I informed the AETC commander how Maj. Gen. Patrick and Brig. Gen. Brown mishandled my complaints, and even his own public affairs officer seemed confused about my case. (More on that in the next chapter.) But as

---

[326] E-mail exchange with Col. Polly Kenny, "AETC/CC meeting with 37 TRW/CC," April 17 and May 9, 2014

I explained to Gen. Rand, I couldn't really fault then-Col. Camerer or other senior leaders for failing to pick up on all the inconsistencies between the report of investigation and the witness testimony. After all, it had taken me days of painstaking analysis to identify the most glaring errors. If the investigating officer had only highlighted more of the testimony in his report – particularly that which tended to exonerate me or reveal critical witnesses as unreliable – it would have been obvious how flimsy these allegations really were.

After making Gen. Rand aware of my many accomplishments during my short time in command, and how I was handpicked by his predecessor for that job following a distinguished military career, I reminded him of how we met:

> *It was in 2006, when you were the 332d Air Expeditionary Wing commander at Balad Airbase, Iraq. I had flown up from Baghdad to brief you on the Air Force Weapons Intelligence Teams, which I then led as part of the 732d Civil Engineer Squadron. During our briefing, the base came under mortar attack, and we took cover under the heavy conference-room table. Unfazed, you insisted I continue my presentation there on the floor. During that tough deployment, when my Airmen and Soldiers suffered three KIAs (including MSgt Brad Clemmons, whose memorial service at Balad you personally attended), I was inspired by the focus and determination you demonstrated that day. I ask you now to grant one of your former 332 AEW "Tuskegee Airmen" an indulgence.*[327]

A couple of weeks later, I received a response from Col. Kenny. She confirmed Gen. Rand received my request, and he had directed her to review the allegations and issues I raised. She asked me to clarify what I meant when I indicated there was essentially new evidence not readily available when my case was originally decided, so I provided an exhaustive catalog of the dozens of errors, omissions, and misrepresentations in the CDI report of investigation. "Although the witness statements were included in the CDI package reviewed by Col Camerer and other senior leaders," I explained, "it's not readily apparent when reading

---

[327] E-mail to Gen. Rand, "Christmas Eve request," December 24, 2014

through Lt Col McConnell's report how disconnected it is from the original testimony." Because of this, "these decision-makers were likely misinformed as to the actual nature of the testimony and the credibility of these witnesses, who Lt. Col. McConnell universally endorsed despite blatant evidence of deception, collusion, and conflict of interest in their statements." Furthermore, "I was unable to highlight any of these significant discrepancies in my various appeals, since I did not have access to the evidence used against me" at that time.[328]

Six weeks later, Col. Kenny unexpectedly dashed my hopes yet again:

> *After receiving your 24 December 2014 request for relief, the AETC Commander tasked us to review your concerns and determine whether the circumstances warranted corrective action. We completed another exhaustive review and reported our conclusions to him. Your concerns have been investigated or reviewed appropriately at the Wing, Numbered Air Force, Headquarters Air Staff (HAF/TJAG), and Secretary of the Air Force (SAF/IG) levels. None of these investigations or reviews support your requested relief. Also, since you are no longer in AETC, the AETC commander cannot take the action you requested. We will forward your request to your chain of command with AETC/CC's recommendation that your chain of command not rescind the Letter of Reprimand or reverse any other personnel actions. If you have any further questions, please refer them to your chain of command.[329]*

This was a particularly cruel betrayal. After so graciously agreeing to consider my appeal, Gen. Rand dispatched a functionary to deliver the bad news. Col. Kenny was now parroting the same tired claim about my concerns being investigated or reviewed at multiple levels, when it's clear there never was any follow-on investigation, and the legal reviews and IG complaint analysis were far from exhaustive. Moreover, if the AETC commander couldn't take the action I requested, why did Gen. Rand bother to direct his

---

[328] E-mail exchange with Col. Kenny, "RE: Christmas Eve request," January 7, 2015

[329] E-mail response from Col. Kenny, "RE: Christmas Eve request," February 20, 2015

staff to review my allegations in the first place? And why add insult to injury by dragging my new chain of command into a matter that didn't concern them? These were scorched earth tactics, seemingly meant to quash whatever hopes of redemption I might have.

An alternate explanation for this abrupt about-face became clear less than a week later, when the Air Force announced the nomination of Gen. Rand to lead Air Force Global Strike Command.[330] Although the AETC commander had no background with nuclear weapons, he would bring his prestige and four-star rank to an organization as badly beset by scandals and poor morale as the one he was leaving. (Ironically, if I had actually taken that assignment I was offered to Barksdale AFB, I would have once again been in his chain of command as part of his AFGSC headquarters staff.) But it wouldn't be prudent for Gen. Rand to go out on a limb for me under these circumstances. The Air Force had long ago closed ranks around my relief of command and career-ending punishments, and any reversal of my fortunes would be embarrassing to those general officers who imposed or endorsed my fate. Whether out of an abundance of caution or an explicit *quid pro quo*, Gen. Rand seems to have sacrificed me to secure the nomination for his next job.

Then again, it's not clear how much real power Gen. Rand exercised as AETC commander, as he was caught between a rock and hard place. On the one hand, his boss, Gen. Welsh, seemed disinterested in granting me any relief. (The blogger behind "John Q. Public" admitted even he made a personal appeal to the Chief of Staff of the Air Force "to take an interest in this case, given how many serious and systemic problems it manifested," but that appeal "fell on deaf ears."[331]) Welsh may also have opposed opening up the can of worms that BMT had become in the wake of the Lackland sex scandal, particularly given how his words and

---

[330] Brian Everstine, "Rand nominated to be first four-star Global Strike chief," *Air Force Times*, February 26, 2015
[331] John Q. Public, "As Fired Commander Prepares Memoir, More Signs That All is Not Well at Lackland," *John Q. Public*, March 14, 2016

deeds seemingly facilitated the excesses of the Camerer/Liddick regime.

On the other hand, Gen. Rand took charge of AETC at a time when its headquarters staff remained fully committed to the policies that got them into this mess in the first place. His director of staff, Col. Shane Courville, commanded BMT when then-Brig. Gen. Patrick was running the local wings, and his legal advisor, Col. Kenny, previously served as Maj. Gen. Patrick's staff judge advocate. Once the 2 AF commander became the AETC vice in 2014, the likelihood of holding leadership at Lackland accountable for abuse of authority or other offenses became even more remote. It was simply not in the interest of Gen. Rand's staff to dig too deeply into the problems at BMT, and they likely would have opposed any initiatives by their boss to do so.

However, once Lieutenant General Darryl Roberson assumed command of AETC in 2015, he apparently launched his own inquiries into the command climate at Lackland. The preliminary findings were reportedly not at all positive. For example, a draft report described Col. Liddick as the worst possible selection that could have been made as BMT commander, while her choice of a group superintendent with no BMT experience was similarly awful. It also supposedly acknowledged that no one from the wing commander on down listened to input from enlisted members. It is unlikely these inquiries will ever be officially acknowledged, but at least the current AETC leadership finally appears to be asking the right questions about what went wrong at Lackland.

Chapter 14: Legal Remedies

In the last two chapters, I discussed all the measures I took to secure justice via official channels. I filed a request for redress through my chain of command, and multiple complaints with various inspectors general. I petitioned my representatives in Congress, and appealed directly to a four-star commander and even the Secretary of the Air Force. None of my efforts seemed to make a bit of difference.

Caroline, on the other hand, took a different approach. I already mentioned how she followed up with General Rand regarding the Key Spouse program, and she previously reached out to several other senior leaders on my behalf. Although we had not been married long, my lovely and talented wife had already made a favorable impression on a number of general officers, who were more than willing to put in a good word for me. Oddly, their entreaties seemed to fall on deaf ears at the Pentagon and Joint Base San Antonio, as if certain key leaders had already made up their minds about me even before I was relieved of command. It also quickly became apparent that Colonel Camerer, who had recently been selected for promotion to Brigadier General, felt he could act with impunity in my case, for he apparently had his own four-star in his corner. Nevertheless, my clever Caroline still had a few tricks up her sleeve.

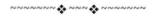

Remember how Col. Liddick pressured me to give her over a dozen wardrobe-size boxes for a do-it-yourself move she was planning after she retired in June 2014? Not only was this completely unethical, and a violation of federal law, but it also brought my wife into the mix. You see, those boxes weren't mine; they belonged to Caroline, who purchased them at her own expense before we were married. She never wanted to part with them in the first place, since she planned to re-use them whenever we had to move again. And after I was relieved of command, she wanted her property back.

When Col. Camerer requested I be moved out of the local area as soon as possible, I was soon notified of a new assignment at Barksdale Air Force Base, Louisiana. I was ordered to report there by the end of May, even before Col. Liddick was scheduled to retire, so we would presumably be moving before she would – that is, if I didn't get out of the assignment in the meantime. It was only fair that my boss return the boxes to us, since we needed them sooner than she did, and she shouldn't have taken them in the first place. When Col. Liddick finally agreed to rescind my no-contact order in early May, imposing in its place a more limited restriction from coming into the BMT headquarters building where she worked,[332] I was finally able interact with my former subordinates, and attend events such as the base-wide Master Sergeant promotion release party on May 22 to congratulate a few lucky members from my former squadron. I also contacted the BMT warehouse managers to arrange for me to pick up whatever moving boxes Col. Liddick left behind.[333]

On May 9, Caroline sent my group commander a note requesting the return of her property. "Debbie," it began, "Now that you've done everything in your power to ruin my husband's career, I no longer feel the stress and pressure of your inappropriate and unreasonable demands on us." Caroline continued, "During Craig's short tenure as one of your unfortunate subordinates, you repeatedly exercised undue command influence on him, on us, for your own personal gain. As you were his boss, we were both fearful of reprisal if we rebuffed your repeated, self-serving and illegal demands – but since you have managed to have him relieved of command, your tenure of fear and intimidation is now over."

After noting how Col. Liddick repeatedly expressed frustration at not being selected for wing commander or promoted, and having to move her own household goods upon retirement because her husband wanted to "make some money" off the government, Caroline pointed out how she "began to systematically harass both of us to forcibly gift" her those boxes, in violation of federal law. "As a person who has repeatedly moved," my wife continued, "you know the value of said boxes – otherwise you would have just gone out and bought them yourself." Instead, Col. Liddick seized the opportunity to prey on one of her subordinates, and made a point of inquiring about the status of our unpacking at every opportunity. "So, I am respectfully requesting either the

---

[332] Col. Liddick, "No Contact Order," May 9, 2014
[333] E-mail exchange with Jim Steele, "Warehouse boxes," May 21, 2014

return of all 17 boxes and their bars, or reimbursement" at their current fair market value.

Not surprisingly, Col. Liddick didn't respond to this request, so Caroline sent her a follow-up message on May 20. "Debbie," she again addressed the Colonel, "This is my second and final email to you regarding my wardrobe boxes and bars you still have in your possession." My wife noted her original offer had been more than fair, giving Col. Liddick two viable options and ample time to comply. This time, Caroline issued an ultimatum: If Col. Liddick did not immediately comply with her request, and resolve this matter to her liking, "I will be taking legal action against you in civil court," she wrote. Again, my boss ignored this appeal, leaving Caroline no choice but to follow through on her threat.

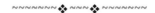

To say Col. Liddick misjudged Caroline would be an understatement. On the one hand, my boss was overheard in her office referring to my wife as a "wetback" – a crude racial slur with no basis whatsoever. (For the record, Caroline was born in Minnesota, and is of Nicaraguan – not Mexican – descent.) On the other hand, my boss knew very well how exceptional my wife is – well dressed, of course, but also smart and savvy. After she finished medical school in Houston, Caroline attended the South Texas College of Law, and she is quite familiar with the state legal system. More importantly, she knows plenty of attorneys willing to represent her *pro bono*. As it turns out, it was actually a high-school classmate of mine, Melanie Cogburn, of Haddad Legal Group in Austin, Texas, who agreed to take the case.

She filed a lawsuit in Bexar County court on May 30 against Deborah Liddick, demanding restitution through either the return of the boxes or the cost of replacement, as well as damages for mental anguish "as a result of Colonel Liddick's tortious conduct" and attorney's fees. "To add insult to injury," the petition claimed, "Colonel Liddick engaged in her illegal campaign to snap up the [...] boxes free of charge while actively conspiring to remove Lieutenant Colonel Perry from his command without cause." While "padding the file" during October and November 2013, "she ensured the procurement of the wardrobe boxes immediately before his removal and months and months before the date when she would actually need the boxes, June 2014." Col. Liddick was therefore "guilty of duress and undue advantage," the plaintiff's attorney concluded.

Filing a lawsuit was one thing; formally notifying Col. Liddick proved to be quite another. Suspecting she would try to avoid service, Ms. Haddad arranged for a private process server to approach her in a place we knew he could find her: at the Lackland parade grounds just prior to the start of the weekly BMT graduation ceremony. However, when he arrived at the spot in the venue parking lot where Col. Liddick usually waited before parade, she was nowhere to be found. Someone had obviously tipped her off, and a handful of airmen – including CMSgt Sutherland, the group superintendent; Maj. Sprouse, who had assumed command of the 737 TRSS after helping get me fired; MSgt Pickett, the group commander's favorite flunky; and Nancy Conley, the group protocol officer – seemed to be running interference. CMSgt Sutherland confronted the process server and demanded he surrender the legal documents, while the rest of this crew apparently kept a lookout for my wife. Once the coast was clear, they signaled to Col. Liddick, who was waiting in her staff car nearby, and briskly escorted her into the venue.

The way Col. Liddick later told the story, she was concerned for her safety that Friday morning. She claimed Caroline had been spotted in the crowd wearing a wig, which she implied was a crazy disguise meant to deceive her staff. (She neglected to mention my wife was a cancer patient who recently lost all her hair.) Col. Liddick also accused the process server of approaching her in the middle of the graduation ceremony, in front of thousands of spectators, in order to embarrass her. By Sunday, the BMT commander decided she needed a personal security detail. She told some folks she thought my wife was crazy and she was afraid of her, while her official excuse was that these armed guards were necessary to "avoid the drama" of her last week in command. However, she reportedly asked Lt. Col. Gallagher, 323 TRS commander, if she could avoid service of process by surrounding herself with Security Forces personnel. He was himself a Security Forces officer, and she apparently asked him to coordinate this request with Lt. Col. Scott Foley, commander of the local cop squadron.

Col. Liddick was assigned a protective detail the following week, which was a prominent feature of all her public appearances leading up to her retirement ceremony on Monday, June 9. Her staff handed out pictures of Caroline to these defenders, so they could keep an eye out for my wife in case she tried to crash the party. This ludicrous waste of taxpayer resources was completely unnecessary, as Caroline was neither crazy nor a threat to the group commander's safety, as my former boss undoubtedly knew. Moreover, Col. Liddick used her official government position to direct her subordinates and leverage overextended law enforcement assets for her own personal benefit, an unethical abuse of authority. In any case, my wife was fully aware of what she was up to, and could afford to simply wait her out.

And that's precisely what she did. The morning after Col. Liddick relinquished command and retired from the Air Force, the process server arrived at her residence on base, where the former group commander and her husband were busy packing their household goods into a waiting moving truck. He came bearing a flower arrangement, so Terry mistook him for a deliveryman and invited him in. Debbie seemed pleased by the prospect of receiving this unexpected bouquet, but her joy was short-lived when she realized what was really going on. After the process server completed his task, Terry reportedly asked if they could at least keep the flowers. "No," he replied, "these are for someone who deserves them."

Meanwhile, word of Caroline's lawsuit began to spread. Haddad Legal Group issued a press release about the case on June 6, and *Air Force Times* picked up the story the following day. "Liddick could not be immediately reached for comment," the author noted, but an AETC spokesman confirmed the Air Force was aware of the lawsuit. "It is clearly a civil matter," he said, "and, as is appropriate, a civil court will decide on the outcome."[334] Caroline soon had the chance to tell her story in her own words on a military spouse blog. "I might be the first spouse to ever sue her husband's commander in civil court," her provocatively titled article began. "This is the story of why."

After I was removed from command, Caroline explained, no one in my chain of command ever checked on us – "not the first sergeant, not his boss, not the wing commander, not anyone." Despite paying lip service to the Key Spouse program, group and wing leadership seemed to be punishing me for our efforts to be engaged in the lives of my subordinates, and they abandoned us during our greatest time of need, knowing full well Caroline was

---

[334] Kristin Davis, "Spouse to husband's former boss: Return moving boxes or pay up," *Air Force Times*, June 7, 2014

struggling with multiple serious illnesses. "That's when we knew we had to take matters into our own hands," she declared.

Caroline noted how my commander began pressuring us to give her our wardrobe boxes – "the kind of high-end moving supplies for which the military will not pay" – nine months before she was set to retire. "We thought it odd that she needed them so far in advance, but it later made sense" when she removed me from command just a month after taking our property. "I understand that my actions may seem petty or vindictive to some," Caroline conceded, "but it's not about the money – it's the principle of the matter." She sued my commander "to shed light on a much larger problem: an environment where O-6s can punish airmen of all ranks, enlisted and officers alike, on a whim and without justification, but where these same senior leaders can violate all sorts of rules and regulations and never suffer any consequences." In the end, Caroline "was simply doing what was right – for our airmen and for our Air Force." And she'd do it all again.[335]

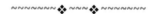

It's not like I didn't give the Air Force a chance to handle this situation properly. Months before Caroline took matters into her own hands, I had already filed a complaint with the Air Education and Training Command IG alleging, among other things, that Col. Liddick had coerced the offering of a gift from me – namely, those wardrobe-size moving boxes. These allegations were referred to the Second Air Force commander, Maj. Gen. Patrick, who appointed an attorney on his staff to conduct an informal inquiry into this matter. Although I provided him written evidence Col. Liddick improperly asked for and acknowledged receipt of these boxes, the investigating officer nevertheless found this allegation unsubstantiated. In a resolution letter addressed to me, dated May 22, Maj. Gen. Patrick confirmed this finding.

However, this is not at all what the Air Force later told several members of Congress. In July 2014, they asserted that a "thorough" commander-directed investigation substantiated two "technical trivial issues," including that the 737 TRG commander "asked for and accepted moving boxes from the Perrys." Moreover,

---

[335] Caroline Perry, "I Sued My Husband's Commander," *SpouseBUZZ.com*, June 17, 2014

according to the letter, "37 TRW/CC verbally counseled the 737 TRG/CC about the potential perception that could have been created regarding the moving boxes."[336] Eight months later, the Air Force provided additional details: it was the 2 AF investigating officer who substantiated the two allegations; the 2 AF commander concurred with his findings; and the verbally counseling occurred on June 5.[337]

What are we to make of this discrepancy? There's no reason to believe Maj. Gen. Patrick made a mistake when he notified me he found this allegation unsubstantiated; his legal advisors reviewed the report of investigation, as well as (presumably) the resolution letter outlining its findings, so this wasn't a typo. Furthermore, he doesn't appear to have changed his position in the wake of Caroline's lawsuit. By the time the 2 AF staff judge advocate mailed the resolution letter to my area defense counsel on June 9, *Air Force Times* had already published a story on the lawsuit, and she actually assumed Ms. Cogburn was my attorney. If Maj. Gen. Patrick had changed his mind in the meantime, his staff would doubtless have updated the resolution letter to reflect this fact before sending it to me.

So if 2 AF didn't substantiate this allegation, as the Air Force contends, who did? When Caroline sent Col. Liddick those e-mails requesting her property back, my commander was understandably irritated. She clearly saw no problem with taking those wardrobe boxes from us, which she considered a gift of no real value since (she assumed) the government paid for them during one of my military moves. She would likely have complained to her boss, Col. Camerer, as well as their legal advisor, Col. Oler, about my wife's supposed harassment, but it's unlikely they would have seen eye to eye with her on this issue. But the lawsuit – coupled with Col. Liddick's extraordinary efforts to avoid service of process – was a game-changer. Col. Camerer may very well have decided at that point to warn his subordinate "about the potential perception that could have been created regarding the moving boxes." He wouldn't need any prompting from the 2 AF commander to recognize the advisability of distancing himself from the defendant in this case. And although his office could not represent the defendant in the civil suit, Col. Oler might have offered her some free legal advice: just give the boxes back.

---

[336] Response to inquiry by Rep. Gallego, July 23, 2014
[337] Response to inquiry by Rep. Hurd, March 26, 2015

This would explain why, over the weekend of June 7-8, with her family in town for her retirement ceremony, Col. Liddick and her husband actually unpacked all the wardrobe boxes she took from us and returned them to where she found them – the 737 TRSS warehouse, where we had been storing them since the BMT children's fall festival. Rather than informing Caroline or Ms. Cogburn of this fact directly, however, Col. Liddick had the legal office contact the plaintiff's law firm over the weekend. Unfortunately, Melanie didn't get the message until the following week, by which time my former commander had already been formally notified of the pending lawsuit. No wonder she seemed so surprised when the process server showed up at her home: she probably thought she had settled this issue by returning the boxes. On the contrary, surrendering this property, without first working out some agreement with the plaintiff or her attorney, amounted to an admission of guilt in the eyes of the law.

Col. Liddick's capitulation left the Air Force no choice but to concede my claim against her regarding the moving boxes. But this created a dilemma, since Maj. Gen. Patrick was on the record rejecting this allegation just three weeks earlier. The Air Force could have simply told the truth, and admit it was Caroline's lawsuit that inspired the verbal counseling and the return of misappropriated property. But this would have further eroded confidence in Maj. Gen. Patrick and the IG complaints resolution process. Instead, someone in the chain of command decided it was easier just to mislead Congress about the findings from the 2 AF informal inquiry. I have no idea if this lie originated at Keesler AFB, JBSA-Randolph, or the Pentagon, and I don't know how many airmen were complicit in the conspiracy to cover up the truth about this issue. But whoever was behind this deception obviously didn't anticipate anyone would call them on it.

Thus ended Col. Liddick's tenure at BMT: not with a bang, but a whimper. After caving to Caroline's demands, she relinquished command on Monday morning and retired from active duty, under the watchful eye of well-armed Security Forces personnel patrolling the perimeter of the brand-new Recruit/Family Inprocessing and Information Center. Col. Camerer presented her another Legion of Merit medal, and credited her efforts with laying "the foundation of success" for her successor.

"Today we're better off because of your service," he laughably declared. "You will walk away from here today without a title, but you will have something more valuable: You'll have a testimony of distinguished service."[338] But it's not at all clear whose testimony he was referring to with these comments.

As she prepared to bid farewell to BMT, Col. Liddick was featured on the cover of the base paper, offering her reflections on her time in command. "It's been a great 25 years," she said. "I always tell people find something special about every assignment. Not every assignment is going to be perfect, but find one thing and then you can look back and say, 'wow, I had a great career.' It's [sic] goes by fast." Col. Liddick didn't specify what her "one thing" was, only that there had been challenges and rewards. "I thought when I came here it would be like my previous group job" as a maintenance group commander, she confessed, "but we had to implement significant changes here" at BMT. Nevertheless, "I wouldn't change a thing about the last 21 months. I'm very proud about what we've accomplished," she concluded. "The trainees have a safe training environment and are being properly trained," she added. "Our MTIs do a great job of making the trainees understand and live by the Air Force Core Values," by treating them with dignity and respect. "It starts right here in BMT. In the end, we are a better organization because of all those changes."

Col. Liddick said watching first-hand how civilians are transformed into airmen made her job as BMT commander the most rewarding of her career. "I see what our MTIs produce every week over an eight-week period," she said. "They take these civilians who come into training who can barely march, often with no military background, and develop them into really motivated Airmen." By the time they graduate, the airmen "seem like they stand about two inches taller," and their families couldn't be prouder. "I see the final product and I know it doesn't happen on its own," she noted. "There are so many people in this group that make this machine move."

When asked what "footprints" she would leave on BMT, Col. Liddick cited only two. First, she modified the training schedule to provide the trainees an extra hour of sleep each morning. "It's a better quality of life for our MTIs and probably for their spouses," she noted, plus it meant she wouldn't have to get up

---

338 Mike Joseph, "New commander takes the lead of Basic Military Training," AETC official website, June 11, 2014

so early for physical training. Second, Col. Liddick allowed members of the 322 TRS "Drum and Bugle Corps" to march down the "bomb run" during their graduation parade. "It's like the Super Bowl of BMT, marching down the bomb run and doing eyes right," she said. "Now every Friday the band marches down the bomb run. It's a beautiful sight and I'm proud of that."[339]

A few months earlier, Col. Liddick had been profiled by her college alumni magazine, and she provided additional insights into her BMT experience. The primary focus of her command was ensuring the success of the new recruits, and making sure that everyone was safe. "That's your job as a commander," she stated. The group commander enjoyed the day in, day out routine of monitoring basic training: "I say that every day is different, but every week's the same." What she enjoyed most, however, was watching the growth of individual recruits. "When I see where they have come over the last eight weeks, it's tremendously satisfying." As the 737 TRG commander, she noted, it "helped that I am someone who believes in doing things by the book. If you are fair and consistent and you train folks to understand the rules and meet your expectations, and hold them accountable, you are going to succeed." Nevertheless, changing BMT culture proved to be "a slow process," Col. Liddick acknowledged. "I say it's like turning the Titanic, slowly."[340]

Her various interviews offered some revealing insights into Col. Liddick's leadership philosophy, such as it was. She often touted the importance of teamwork, yet in practice she demonstrated almost no teambuilding qualities, and she made little effort to help her subordinates understand her expectations. As Col. Liddick explained to one of my colleagues, she didn't mentor, she didn't do lunch, she only gave feedback after the fact. While her focus on trainee safety, dignity, and respect was admirable, in practice this translated into overprotecting these recruits from the beneficial stresses basic training is meant to induce, with worrying effects on their resiliency and discipline. Despite her passing praise for the MTIs under her command, her true passion was for the trainees: while @DebbieLiddick routinely tweeted about her interactions with these new recruits, for example, she never once mentioned any other airman. Charged with moving big rocks in

---

[339] "Basic military training commander to conclude 25-year Air force career," June 6, 2014
[340] "Commanding Presence," p. 7-11

transforming the organizational culture at BMT, Col. Liddick instead focused on the little things, and took a by-the-book approach to an environment where the book was being completely rewritten. This maintenance officer seemed to perceive BMT as nothing more than a machine, powered by MTI cogs turning out interchangeable airmen widgets. Her analogy to the captain of a doomed luxury liner couldn't have been more apt, if unintentionally ironic: rather than skillfully navigating BMT through treacherous waters, Col. Liddick busied herself rearranging deck chairs on a sinking ship.

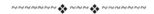

Heading off into retirement was bittersweet for Debbie Liddick. She officially claimed her decision to retire was a personal one, so she could spend more time with her husband, Terry. While she was BMT commander, they only saw each other about every three months because of his work requirements. "We built a house in South Dakota in 2011 and we've been dreaming about living up there and enjoying our life together," she told the base paper. "I made this decision last summer. It was difficult at first because I knew I'd be leaving the Air Force."[341] On the other hand, she admitted to my wife and others how bitterly disappointed she was to retire as a colonel, short of her ultimate career goal.

Rather than build upon her background as a maintenance officer, or leverage whatever leadership skills she managed to acquire during her 25-year Air Force career, Debbie Liddick dusted off her undergraduate degree in retirement. She had studied mathematics to qualify for a Reserve Officer Training Corps scholarship, and was one of only three math majors in her graduating class at Wilkes University. "Out of the three people, I was not the smartest," she admitted in an interview with her alumni magazine, adding, "Getting the math degree was one of my biggest challenges in life. But it gave me the confidence that I could do anything."[342] Ironically, this is the very subject she now tutors to similarly mediocre students at Black Hills State University.

---

[341] "Basic military training commander to conclude 25-year Air force career," June 6, 2014
[342] "Commanding Presence," p. 8-9

Meanwhile, Camerer and Liddick haven't been missed much down at Lackland. When an ex-MTI going by the Reddit username "Banuvan" revealed the BMT commander had retired, another user was relieved: "Thank fuck. She was awful," he wrote. ("Your thoughts are shared by many," Banuvan tactfully replied.) On the other hand, when asked about my curious case, which had recently appeared on the cover of the *Air Force Times*, this MTI was unequivocal: "LtCol. Perry was railroaded for being a good commander," he declared.[343]

---

[343] "I was an MTI from 2009-2014 amid the entire scandal," July 18, 2014

Chapter 15: Flirting with the Fourth Estate

The press was slow to grasp the festering situation at Basic Military Training. Although publications like the *San Antonio Express-News* and *Air Force Times* had been quick to expose lurid details of the Lackland sex scandal, and report on the dozens of court-martial proceedings that ensued, the media paid scant attention to the incompetent rollout of the bewildering array of initiatives meant to transform BMT. With the exception of a few articles published in 2013,[344] there was seemingly no recognition that the implementation of the Woodward report recommendations, Air Education and Training Command add-ons, and local policy changes were having unintended consequences, and creating a worrying new set of problems at JBSA-Lackland.

This journalistic neglect suddenly ended in late May 2014, after both publications obtained the results of the survey of Military Training Instructors conducted by RAND Corporation the previous summer. The headlines were as sensational as they were overdue: "Lackland drill instructors rip leaders, say they fear recruits," wrote Sig Christenson, while Kristin Davis revealed MTIs were "scared to train."

The Air Force immediately went into damage control mode. When asked for comment, Col. Camerer conceded the myriad changes implemented at BMT hadn't come without trouble. However, he argued, "We've gone a long ways to fixing the things that you're talking about," noting that surveys in January and April 2014 had produced "vastly different" results from the earlier RAND report. "So, were we in a tough spot in July of last year? Yes, we were," he admitted. "I need my MTIs to know we listen to them," the wing commander explained. "It's understandable that people in the organization, that that's stressful for them, and that they feel like they didn't get a lot of voice in that. Well, they didn't get a lot of voice in that," he acknowledged. Just three weeks before he relinquished command, Col. Camerer offered a surprisingly honest

---

[344] Kristin Davis wrote a couple of articles for *Air Force Times* in June 2013 about an MTI who claimed he was unfairly punished, and another in September 2013 suggesting BMT reforms may have gone too far.

self-assessment: "Did we get it all right, a hundred percent? No? Is it all 100 percent correct today? No."[345]

Col. J.D. Willis, AETC deputy director for technical training, claimed officials were so concerned with the number of MTI complaints about the critique boxes, they went back and reviewed the nearly 1,900 critiques dropped since BMT first began emphasizing this means for trainees to report misconduct. "Our initial concern, especially from my perspective, was maybe leadership was overreacting and had created a different problem," he admitted. However, the review showed the majority of comments were actually positive, he said, and less than three percent were allegations of MTI misconduct. While a third of these were found "not to be a problem," the rest "were dealt with" with various administrative actions, "so the MTI understands you crossed a line."

BMT leadership was subsequently told to communicate those numbers to instructors, Col. Willis added. "They have a perception, too. The MTIs are working off partial information and knowledge. By giving them the picture, we took away the mystique. What we have seen is a changed perspective. I think they have less concern about that," he explained. Col. Willis conceded MTIs were still working long hours and facing months without leave and extended tours of duty. "There is no way to have that work pace and not have a negative impact on the quality of life," he noted, but these concerns largely "were due to manning issues, which we have been addressing. We're well on our way and getting very close." Finally, he was encouraged that the overwhelming majority of MTIs surveyed were prepared to report a fellow instructor for sexual assault or other crimes. "By and large, they are willing to do the right thing," he said. "I'm hopeful we'll see those responses get stronger the next time we're able to administer a survey. Time will tell. Culture change is one of the more challenging things any institution does."

BMT leadership had no problem finding willing collaborators to defend the transformation initiatives. MSgt Jeremy Pickett, the MTI School commandant, said BMT was turning out more aware airmen. "We're really focusing on treating each other with dignity and respect," he said. "We really want to promote an environment of professionalism," he added. "A lot of changes were

---

[345] "In survey, Lackland drill instructors rip leaders, say they fear recruits," May 29, 2014

taking place," noted an MTI School instructor. "They were good changes. Just like any change, it takes a little bit of time and adaptation. It created some stress for some people," he explained. "Trainees don't have more power," however, but are merely "given additional avenues to report misconduct." Based on his experience, there was no reason to worry: "I have had major critiques dropped on me before and I've been investigated before. As long as MTIs are not doing anything wrong, they are going to be cleared. As long as no misconduct is actually taking place, the instructor is put right back with their flight and the training carries on," he assured gullible readers.[346]

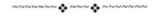

General Rand launched a counteroffensive days later, when he reported the results of a climate survey from April 2014. He denied the July 2013 MTI survey had been repeated, but the new poll showed morale at BMT was on the uptick. "We are better than we were a year ago, and I expect we will be better a year from now," the AETC commander concluded. "There is still room for improvement," he continued, but "our training instructors are adapting the way we expected." Today's MTIs are "hitting a home run," he said. "I know you can fool a four-star some of the time but you can't fool a four-star all of the time. In my entire career I have never served with better [noncommissioned officers] than the ones now serving as MTIs." AETC was standardizing policy so MTIs know what is expected of them. "We're going to make sure they know what the right thing is. If they do the right thing, they'll have nothing to worry about," Gen. Rand explained. He disputed charges that overzealous leadership was punishing MTIs for minor infractions. "I would argue steps taken have reduced the number of infractions," he claimed, noting that, of the 168 proven cases of misconduct in the last year, half resulted in verbal counseling; 43 MTIs received letters of counseling; 16 were issued letters of reprimand; and only four were released from MTI duty, compared to a historical average of seven to eight a year. Gen. Rand also didn't believe that watered-down basic training is turning out ill-

[346] "Survey shows Lackland MTIs 'scared to train'," May 29, 2014

prepared airmen. "I'm not buying for one second that training is easy and that trainees are driving the train out there," he said.[347]

In a separate interview, Gen. Rand said BMT was "on the right glide path." The recent climate assessment showed 92 percent of respondents felt they understood and were part of the mission; nine of every 10 said they worked in a professional environment with an atmosphere of dignity and respect; more than eight in 10 said corrective training for poor performance was fairly enforced; and more than 95 percent of respondents strongly agreed or agreed that BMT was free of sexual harassment, sexual assault, malpractice and abuse. "Now, we're not happy. We'd like to see that 100 percent," Gen. Rand said. "We're not declaring victory," Rand said. "We're just telling you we're in a far better place today than we were two years ago." He added that instructors "have every reason to believe that they're going to be successful" as long as they follow the rules. Finally, he reiterated that training had not become easier. "I have never had a fellow commander, either my peer or one of my subordinate commanders, complain to me about the quality of our trainees coming out of Lackland," Gen. Rand said. "So I think the idea that somehow training has suffered, I would not accept that. I would say that I think our trainees are leaving here as professionally trained as they ever have in our Air Force history," he added. "I'll bet my reputation on it, and you can quote me on that."[348]

Sadly, these journalists failed to follow up on the can of worms they had opened. For example, Col. Camerer suggested there was another survey in January 2014, but the AETC commander mentioned only the April climate assessment, an apples-and-oranges comparison to the more in-depth, tailored RAND appraisal. In fact, all indications are the January poll was a reprise of the July 2013 questionnaire, which was scheduled to be administered every six months. If the results of that second survey in January really were "vastly different," as Col. Camerer claimed, then Gen. Rand almost certainly would have acknowledged and discussed them. The truth is, not much had changed in the meantime, and the second iteration of the RAND survey likely showed little improvement in MTI attitudes. When Col. Willis

---

[347] Kristin Davis, "Newest climate survey results show MTI morale improving," *Air Force Times*, May 30, 2014
[348] Sig Christenson, "Top general says Lackland morale on upswing," *San Antonio Express-News*, June 1, 2014

stated he was hopeful these responses would get stronger the next time they administered a survey, it begged the question: when do you expect that will be, exactly?

Gen. Rand's statistic on MTI discipline also strain credulity. Col. Liddick bragged she had eliminated over 80 MTIs by late 2013, and I have no doubt she released more than four airmen from MTI duties for alleged misconduct in her final year as BMT commander. (I was able to document four such cases in earlier chapters, and I'm sure there were many more.) While such an improbably low disqualification rate would in fact be below historical averages, the general didn't provide any context for the 43 LOCs and 16 LORs. With only 439 instructors on duty at that time, this amounts to well over 10 percent of the MTI corps receiving derogatory paperwork in a single year. If this pace were to continue over their entire 3.5-year tour, we would expect nearly a third of all MTIs to walk away from BMT with blemishes on their records. This sure sounds like MTIs were being punished for minor infractions by overzealous leadership.

While the RAND survey story represented a missed opportunity for the media to further investigate what was going on at Lackland, it was soon overshadowed by a much more compelling story. The following day, *Air Force Times* finally broke "the curious case of Lt. Col. Craig Perry."

"Leader tried to reach out; investigation cites favoritism." This was the subtitle of "Relieved of command," an online article by Kristin Davis telling the story of how my wife and I involved ourselves in the lives of airmen and families at our new command, yet our seeming acts of kindness were characterized as favoritism and fraternization. Caroline, who responded to the author's inquiries via e-mail, was quoted extensively throughout the article. She wrote that, when I heard I was being put in charge of a BMT squadron, "he was a little concerned, since he wasn't all that familiar with enlisted basic training." However, "he knew Air Force leadership wouldn't have selected him for this opportunity if they didn't think he was up to the challenge – and besides, he was excited to tackle this critical mission." When no one from my squadron or the group made an effort to welcome us, Caroline made it her mission to resuscitate the Key Spouse program in the unit. She noted how I made every effort to reach out to all the sections in the squadron, and her efforts were later praised.

This type of behavior seemed in keeping with the recently published Air Force Instruction 1-2, *Commander's Responsibilities*, which requires leaders to be aware of issues that could affect the climate and morale of their units, both on- and off-duty. "Commanders have the unique authority and responsibility to engage in the lives of their subordinates, where appropriate, to improve quality of life, promote unit morale, and ensure all members are treated with dignity and respect," the instruction states. In a May 21 news release, Gen. Mark Welsh, Chief of Staff of the Air Force, called the most important job as commanders "is to take care of the sons and daughters our nation has entrusted to us."

Nevertheless, I was removed of command in December 2013, pending the outcome of a command-directed investigation. The *Air Force Times* obtained a copy of the report of investigation, whose testimony of favoritism contrasted with character reference letters later written in my favor. The author highlighting the ambiguity of the investigating officer's conclusions, and she also noted how I allegedly clashed with Col. Liddick and may have been playing favorites when I removed an LOR from my superintendent's personnel information file. Again, however, the investigating officer merely recommended counseling and remedial training, and my colleagues wrote letters on my behalf saying my performance was no different from my peers.

In an e-mail statement, Col. Camerer merely reiterated he lost confidence in my ability to lead the squadron. His wing public affairs officer refused to comment on my case, but noted commanders "are not supposed to provide an atmosphere where there is any preferential treatment. It's supposed to be equal and unilateral across the unit. There cannot be an appearance of a better relationship with one than another. This is a business. Commanders have to ensure they are taking care of business equally." (Did this Air Force spokeswoman really just compare commanding a military unit to managing a business?)

Ms. Davis also reached out to a retired Air Force Lieutenant Colonel for another perspective on my case. "If you're going to be relieved for things like favoritism, it should be a clear-cut case. They do not sound like clear-cut cases to me," wrote Tony Carr, a former squadron and deputy group commander. "As a commander, I would always reserve the right to invite my superintendent over to my home or my chief master sergeant," he said. "I've had troops to my house when they were alone. It's an Air Force tradition that has deep roots. Having someone over to your home as a leader is a good thing to do, especially around the holidays," Mr. Carr said. "I'm speaking in generalities without knowing the details of the case. But it would surprise and alarm me if the Air Force would relieve someone from command for what is considered normal social interactions or taking care of people the way we encourage commanders to do." This retired officer lamented the rise of the "helicopter parenting model" within the Air Force. "I think we've been pushing too far. If we're doing that – and we are – we shouldn't turn around and hold any commander to a weird standard. That should not and would not be the normal basis for someone being relieved. It's alarming if that happens."

At the time this article was published, I was still awaiting reassignment to Barksdale AFB, Louisiana, and had been issued a career-ending punishment. Still, Caroline said she was hopeful my chain of command would take another look at my case. "It feels like our entire world has fallen apart these last five months," she said. "I think the hardest part is just not understanding what happened."[349]

The reaction to this article was immediate and overwhelming. Within a few days, *Air Force Times* readers recommended it over *32 thousand times* on Facebook, causing this story to quickly go viral. That Monday, it received more comments than any other story on their website,[350] and made the "Early Bird Brief," a military-focused daily news summary. A family friend quickly set up a "Team Perry" community page on Facebook, to which they posted this and other articles related to my case. Colleagues and former subordinates came out of the woodwork to express support in this and other online venues, and airmen I barely remembered attested to my leadership qualities based on their interaction with me from years before. When I returned to work at Fort Sam Houston the following week, complete strangers came up to me and declared they would gladly work for me

---

[349] Kristin Davis, "Relieved of command," *Air Force Times*, May 31, 2014

[350] @AirForceTimes, June 2, 2014

someday. My curious case quickly became a topic of discussion in squadrons across the Air Force, and it was reportedly even debated within academic circles at Air University, at Maxwell AFB, Alabama. While some online commentators seemed incredulous, or insisted there must be more to the story, no one who claimed to be familiar with my case expressed the view that I deserved the punishment I received. Views about Col. Liddick and Col. Camerer, on the other hand, were decidedly less favorable.

The buzz surrounding this story only intensified a week later, when it was featured as the cover of the *Air Force Times* weekly print edition, available on newsstands at commissaries and base exchanges at U.S. military installations around the world. A portrait of Caroline and me, dressed up for the MTI Association honors banquet the previous fall, was plastered across the cover of every issue, with the caption: "Officer's wife says his career was derailed because they were too friendly with enlisted. The Air Force says he undermined his boss. The curious case of Lt. Col. Perry."[351]

Kristin Davis rewrote her "Relieved of command" article for the print edition, offering additional details and sources. "Case shows fine line between friendship and favoritism," read the subtitle to an even more incisive analysis into "the perplexing gray area of officer-enlisted relationships, where relaxed protocols can become inappropriate conduct, in reality or in perception." According to the author, Caroline "pins her husband's troubles on basic training leadership, whom she says distorted their squadron outreach work, portraying it as favoritism and fraternization with the enlisted airmen they were charged with caring for." She noted I arrived JBSA-Lackland "at a time when it had been defamed by a very public sexual misconduct scandal that had plagued basic military training for two years. An outside survey of instructors there at the time revealed low morale, little trust in leadership and waning job satisfaction. Dozens of MTIs had been investigated on allegations ranging from unprofessional relationships with basic training graduates to rape of recruits."

An AETC spokesman, Col. Sean McKenna, provided a revealing statement for the print edition of this story. "By all accounts, the Perrys were successful in engaging in the lives of their subordinates," he wrote in an e-mail dated June 4. We "fostered a healthy Key Spouse Program, one that was recognized

---

[351] "On newsstands this week," *Air Force Times*, June 8, 2014

and highlighted" by my wing commander to the AETC commander. "As a couple, they demonstrated their commitment to their squadron families in a number of different acts. All were good examples of the types of behavior we admire in our commanders and in all Air Force members." However, these efforts were unrelated to the reasons I was relieved from command, according to Col. McKenna. "A commander directed investigation substantiated serious accusations that Lt. Col. Perry made derogatory statements about his immediate commander, decided not to investigate alleged misconduct against one of his favored subordinates, and removed a letter of reprimand, issued by his group commander, from the same subordinate's Personnel Information File. His actions communicated a fundamental misunderstanding of the definition of unprofessional relationships, the way unprofessional relationships can create perceptions of favoritism, and the impact his actions had on good order and discipline in his squadron and within the group." The bottom line, McKenna said, was that "ultimately, his superior commander and his unit lost faith in his ability to command the squadron."

This version of the story highlighted how unexpected my change of fortunes was. The investigating officer recommended my boss hold me "administratively accountable," and that I commit myself to correcting the problem. However, Caroline noted, I was never given the chance. Caroline also claimed I was not counseled prior to my abrupt removal from command, but the AETC spokesman countered, "It's a commander's prerogative as to the number and levels of counselings given to subordinates prior to issuing an LOR or any other type of discipline."

This updated account revealed I would be staying in San Antonio under an Exceptional Family Member Program deferment due to Caroline's health, but clarified the fallout from my commander-directed investigation was not limited to me. Although the report said no one benefited from my alleged favoritism, a "Blue Rope" MTI who I allegedly singled out for special treatment was moved from his Deliberate Development instructor job to a training squadron, where he has been performing administrative duty, while my former superintendent was eliminated from the MTI career field and received a letter of counseling for behavior that helped to "create the impression of impartiality."[352] Ironically, the final section of this two-and-a-half page article was featured next to the recent *Air Force Times* interview with Gen. Rand, retitled "AETC chief: Basic trainees not 'driving the train'," about a climate survey supposedly showing improved MTI morale.

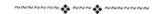

The print edition of the "Relieved of command" article also featured the conclusions of a Naval War College professor who reviewed my case. Captain Michael Junge studies investigations in which officers are relieved of duty, and like dozens of readers who commented on the original *Air Force Times* story, he believed I was unjustifiably punished for doing what the military has long demanded of its best commanders. In a sidebar to the article labeled "Expert's Review," he notes the investigating officer's findings that ultimately led to my sacking could have just as easily been used to clear me.[353] His complete analysis is reprinted below:

> *Allegation 1: The investigator writes conflicting information and opinions. I could easily use all of the investigator's words to make the allegation unsubstantiated. [...] For me, the key piece is this – did LtCol. Perry obey his commander's orders. If so, then nothing was undermined. We don't have to like our seniors, there's no rule or regulation requiring it, and none of the comments rise to the level of disrespect. I might hate my boss with a passion, but if I do what I am told, that is respecting command authority.*
>
> *Allegation 2: This is a pissing contest over a fun run? Seriously? Here there is potential for undermining command authority...but again, not proven and in this case unsubstantiated. That said, the rationale reads the same as Allegation 1.*

352 Kristin Davis, "Relieved of command," *Air Force Times* (print edition), June 10, 2014
353 Kristin Davis, "Expert's Review," *Air Force Times* (print edition), June 10, 2014

Allegation 3: With all the redactions that one is difficult to follow...but I am unconvinced. The guidelines for the USAF in this case mean that a commander should not ever socialize in any form with a subordinate. That's just not realistic, or what the regulations state or intend. The perception existed...but those who let themselves be sidelined by the perception bear blame. Of note, LtCol. Perry was counseled and addressed the situation. Yet it was still held against him. Bad form for USAF to do so.

Allegation 4: While unsubstantiated it comes down to the same as 1 and 2. Sure, he said something, maybe, but what did he do?

Allegation 5: In this case, again the investigator is all over the place in statements. LtCol. Perry did something he believed was authorized and the investigator acknowledges that the wrong action was not willful. Also, the Group Commander in this case doesn't recall something, but that same defense didn't work for LtCol. Perry in all other cases.

This is a pretty poor investigation that doesn't, in my mind and limited by the redactions, substantiate any of the allegations and does not in any way support relief of command. Unfortunately, the relief is done and there's nothing that can fix LtCol. Perry's career.[354]

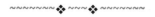

"Relieved of command" turned the typical narrative on its head: this was no mere "dog bites man" tale of a flawed squadron commander whose serious misconduct or gross incompetence prompts a loss of confidence among his superiors. Rather, it painted a picture of an officer whose career was derailed seemingly because he and his wife were too friendly with enlisted members. The article left readers wondering if I had really done anything wrong, or if my firing was collateral damage of the toxic leadership environment at Lackland. I will be forever grateful to Kristin Davis,

---

[354] E-mail from Captain Michael Junge, "LtCol. Perry Investigation," June 2, 2014

the author of this article, for bringing my story to light, and framing a debate about the proper role of squadron commanders in the lives of their airmen. My "curious case" is continuing to reverberate across the Air Force thanks in large part to the work of this journalist.

But she was not the only author to take up my cause. Amy Bushatz at *SpouseBUZZ.com* explored the fraternization angle, noting the word on the street at Lackland is that, "if you're an officer, hanging out with or paying special attention to enlisted folk is going to get you canned." She noted that I was "doing stuff that generally makes him and his wife sound like the dream command team": a commander and spouse "that actually care, that take the time to build the relationships the Air Force and other services have labeled as key to a good command climate and the opposite of toxic leadership." She conceded that some pieces to this puzzle were missing, but likened my career-ending punishment to "burning down the house because you saw a garden spider." While "there is a line where fraternization between the commander and, particularly, lower enlisted service members should be kept to a minimum," there is also interaction that helps – "interaction that is vital, that makes troops better at their jobs and keeps families happy because they feel cared for and noticed. That's the stuff we want to keep around. And that's what is hurt when stories like this one scare you into questioning what you can and cannot do."[355]

Susan Reynolds, winner of the 2014 Joan Orr Air Force Spouse of the Year award, chose not to write about me at all. "While I am saddened for a man that was a shining example of what AF leadership should be," this author was instead writing about my wife "and the Queen Bee that bullied her," Col. Liddick. Caroline became a "solution spouse" who enthusiastically tackled problems affecting family members, but she was "stung" by a fellow female leader. The author was most fearful that, "if spouses don't align themselves with what commanders want, then their service member's career could be damaged," and the Key Spouse program will fail. "Queen Bees have no place in our military. They have no place in our family support. This is a time to recognize good leadership instead of hinder it."[356]

---

[355] Amy Bushatz, "Don't Hang With Enlisted? The 'Fraternization' Line," June 2, 2014

[356] Susan Reynolds, "Home Front Operations: Queen Bees," *Fayetteville Observer*, June 17, 2014

A brave Senior Airman (and part-time novelist) from South Carolina wrote a letter to the *Air Force Times* in response to the "Relieved of command" article. "While the Air Force is plagued with rising suicide rates and ever-decreasing morale," he wrote, "it's critical for commanders to maintain positive relations with their subordinates. Or is it?" In this day and age, "it's dangerous to be a leader in the USAF." For example, my supposedly "disparaging" comments at a staff meeting "make it seem that the Air Force wants 'yes' men and commanders who keep their heads low." He concluded, "If I ever get injured, I'll tell my commander not to visit me in the hospital. God forbid he gets relieved of command because of 'fraternization' charges for sending me flowers or a get-well card."[357]

Finally, Michelle Zook wrote a couple of blog posts for *Clash Daily* referencing my situation. The first was a sort of "Dear Boss, I quit" letter to Gen. Welsh. "Those of us who appreciate good commanders are especially concerned regarding the curious case of Lt. Col. Craig Perry and his wife, Caroline, going on down at Lackland, and wonder just who can be trusted in command if this is the way a man who was – by all appearances – a great commander will be treated." She truly believed "there is a command climate so entrenched in the Air Force that a modern day Robin Olds" – a legendary, if unorthodox, leader from the Vietnam era – "would have quit as a junior captain rather than deal with it." With the constant turmoil, box-checking, and other nonsense, "It's getting harder and harder to keep drinking the blue Kool-Aid, much less to pass it down to the next generation."[358] Her second post concerned a cultural shift in the military, particularly within an Air Force already experiencing increased scrutiny over sexual harassment and personnel issues. "The issues at Lackland – whether the aftermath of the sexual assault scandals there or the curious case of former squadron commander Lt. Col. Craig Perry – have further done their damage." She concluded, "Military culture is important to all Americans, regardless of whether or not they have served, because a toxic environment and distrust in leadership creates an

---

[357] Senior Airman James Ticknor, "Case of Lt. Col. Perry," *Air Force Times* (print edition), June 23, 2014
[358] Michelle Zook, "'Dear General': Time to Rethink Some Things in the Air Force," *ClashDaily.com*, June 18, 2014

inherent weakness in American force projection. It weakens American foreign policy."[359]

By far the most prolific advocate for my cause was Tony Carr, the retired Air Force officer interviewed for the original *Air Force Times* article on my curious case. Writing for the *John Q. Public* blog, this former Lieutenant Colonel began his career at BMT as an enlisted member, before earning his commission and becoming a C-17 pilot. He finished his career as a squadron and deputy group commander, but soon realized he couldn't have much of an impact on the issues affecting the Air Force while still in uniform. After his retirement, he somehow found time to write frequent and lengthy blog posts on military issues, as well as maintain an active Facebook and Twitter presence, all the while pursuing a doctor of jurisprudence degree at Harvard Law School.

JQP wasted no time weighing in on my case, immediately framing the discussion with this insightful headline: "Did Lackland Trade Recruit Abuse for Toxic Leadership?" Commenting on the *Air Force Times* article that went viral just days earlier, Tony Carr wondered whether the outrage airmen were expressing over this seeming injustice was an overreaction, or if they were "peering through the veil of official action and accurately glimpsing toxic leadership?" He argued that "loss of confidence" was the most critical turn of phrase in a case like this one, as it begs the question: "how does one commander lose confidence in the ability of another – especially one carefully groomed and hand-picked for his assignment and on the job for such a brief time that he hadn't even had a performance report yet?" I clearly wasn't inept, or a criminal, he noted, and I hadn't been given the chance to change my approach to command. So what explains my firing? "Given the absence of a reasonable explanation for what looks like a questionable firing of a high-caliber, high-performing, well-regarded, hand picked commander," my boss could simply have wanted rid of me, and wielded her authority to manufacture my removal.

---

[359] Michelle Zook, "Major Crises? Huge Shifts in Military Culture Raise Concerns," *ClashDaily.com*, June 25, 2014

Commander-directed investigations allow the Air Force to have it both ways, the author explained, "by relieving a commander and destroying a career without having to ground its actions in the kind of proof that should be required." He dismissed each of the allegations from my CDI in turn, noting in particular how Col. Liddick's comments about my supposedly "cozy" relationship with my superintendent smacked of sexism. "Something doesn't add up," he concluded. "Often, when things don't add up, abuse of power lurks in the background." He noted that many regarded Col. Liddick a toxic leader, and that sources who spoke to him "directly or through online interactions about Liddick did so under the condition of anonymity, fearing harsh reprisal if their identities were discovered." He added, "it seems maybe it's easier to get fired at Lackland for being a good commander rather than a poor one."

"Firing commanders is not something we should shy away from," Tony Carr continued, "and in fact it probably doesn't happen enough." But it can't be "based on fiat, whimsy, or preference," and the firing official better have a good reason he or she can publicly explain, as we "are entitled to understand how the system failed to select the right person or how the right person became the wrong person." How could the fortunes of an officer change so quickly? Such pathology, the author concluded, seems likely to have arisen from toxicity. "It might just be that Perry's biggest infraction was his failure to surrender his intellectual freedom when he took the reins of a squadron in dire need of his brand of demonstrative, relationship-driven leadership. It might be that his second biggest crime was caring more about his airmen than his boss thought was appropriate. If these are his biggest infractions, it's fair to question whether Camerer fired the wrong commander, and whether in doing so, he raised new questions about his own judgment." My case should be reopened, he argued, "this time with Liddick and Camerer included within the scope of the investigation," and Congress should "renew its interest in Lackland and exercise its oversight authority."[360]

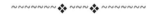

---

[360] Tony Carr, "Loss of Confidence: Did Lackland Trade Recruit Abuse for Toxic Leadership?" *John Q. Public*, June 1, 2014

Tony Carr followed this *tour de force* with another painstaking analysis less than two weeks later, "a case study in the use and abuse of power, with important implications for the future of the U.S. Air Force." Rejecting the AETC statement on my relief of command, featured in the print edition of the *Air Force Times* article, he argued my CDI "quite simply doesn't say what AETC claims." He notes that several witnesses were actually complainants whose statements were presumably biased, and "there are direct and unresolved contradictions in the key facts" used to substantiate the allegation that I undermined Col. Liddick's authority.

The allegation regarding unprofessional relationships "was almost exclusively about the hurt feelings of a small number of people rather than anything Perry did to cause those hurt feelings." Its most alarming aspect was its focus on my relationship with my senior enlisted leader. "Perry would have been a fool to not rely on her professional advice, and would have been an even bigger fool to marginalize her role in squadron affairs for fear of hurting the feelings of more junior members who might disagree with her recommendations or his decisions." But it's safe to say the Chief of Staff of the Air Force spends inordinate amounts of time with the Chief Master Sergeant of the Air Force, and they and their families socialize from time to time. Even Col. Camerer "is known to spend considerable time with his senior enlisted advisor – even more than he spends with his Vice Commander – and to socialize with him often." This is a clear double standard, which "is best understood as a form of gender discrimination exercised by Liddick and endorsed by [...] Camerer." The author notes the negative perceptions adopted in this case would be invalid had my superintendent been male rather than female, and Col. Liddick's use of that term "cozy" has implications that should have been investigated for their role in this case. "It's almost as though Perry's compliance with Liddick's demands only intensified her desire to push him out of command."

Then, "almost as if starving for comic relief, the CDI enumerated a third substantiated allegation laughably unsupported by the evidence." Tony Carr concludes it's clear "the CDI should not have substantiated this allegation, Liddick should not have endorsed the CDI with such a grave error, and Camerer should not have relied upon it in making his decision to relieve Perry. Then again, it's possible Perry wasn't actually relieved on the basis of the CDI at all." The author noted the "perverse

314

circularity" of Col. Liddick's testimony that she did not trust me: "Liddick ordered an investigation, supplied testimony to it which was then used to substantiate allegations she made, and then used the resulting report to fire someone. The mind boggles to understand how this would not be a case of the fox guarding the hen house." She needed a way to justify firing me, "so it seems she used the CDI process to fulfill a pre-determined result on the basis of a pre-judged perception of guilt," and her boss went along for the ride. What the analysis reveals is "the use of ideas and perceptions to manufacture facts, rather than the use of facts to formulate ideas. The no-mistake firing of a highly regarded commander is a fallacy so departed from logic that it is only explainable by the abuse of power."

Indeed, "to the extent the CDI supplies actionable findings, they've got much more to do with the overall environment at Lackland than with Perry or his former squadron." Ironically, "Liddick herself was showing favoritism toward some of Perry's subordinates while accusing him of the same behavior," allowing them to bring down their own commander by co-opting my boss. Although Col. Liddick testified she did not trust my superintendent, she reassigned her to the same role in another squadron, suggesting she was either inept or dishonest. And the issue with the wardrobe boxes (discussed in the last chapter), resulting in a civil suit and extraordinary measures to avoid service of process, "fit within the emerging rubric of a toxic leader running amok."

As for Col. Camerer, many have suggested that with his own promotion close at hand, he "didn't want to jeopardize his own advancement or his legacy at Lackland by inviting portrayal of a climate of conflict, ineptitude, or misconduct cultivated by his group commander." This would explain why he allowed the "amateurish" CDI to stand, and ignored its "startling revelation about Liddick not trusting Perry – something that would have jumped off the page when viewed by any military commander." If Col. Liddick had predetermined to fire me, and the CDI was nothing more than a pretense, "this means every public statement made about the firing has been fundamentally dishonest." The AETC press release is contradictory, and my list of counter-claims was mishandled. "It would appear all involved are determined to ride out any negative press coverage, continue to stonewall, and move on with their careers, knowing that each medal, promotion, and reassignment will legitimize that they must have been right and Lt.

Col. Perry – as well as his family and the troops in his squadron negatively impacted – must have been wrong."

This scenario "casts a long shadow over what it will mean to be a commander in the future," the author concludes, and if this case stands without a second look, "the Air Force will take a giant leap toward institutional failure." Beyond Lackland, my case is also dangerous because it undermines the incentive to strive for command; it could degrade the performance of those brave enough to accept command; and, most critically, it will create paranoid leaders. "Imagine a dog that expects it will be beaten by its owner, but doesn't know when that beating will come. Such a dog is skittish, jumpy, and tentative. Such a dog is constantly looking over its shoulder. This is the kind of commander that will prevail and become common in an Air Force adopting this Lackland standard: circumspect, guarded, defensive, and constantly looking backward." This debacle could also put the Key Spouse program and the notion of commanders taking care of families at grave risk. "One thing that is not in question is that Air Force commanders, particularly those in or approaching command at squadron level, are watching events at Lackland very closely. The chilling effect is noticeable and could fundamentally and rapidly alter the calculus of command."[361]

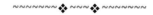

Capitalizing on our 15 minutes of fame, Caroline wrote a couple of pieces of her own for publication. In the previous chapter, I discussed how she explained her lawsuit against Col. Liddick as a matter of doing what's right to hold senior leaders accountable.[362] She followed with a letter to the *Air Force Times*, which appeared alongside SrA Ticknor's commentary. Since our appearance on the cover of that periodical, she wrote, "dozens of Air Force spouses have approached me with concerns about placing their service member's career in jeopardy by taking care of airmen in their units." She felt the most important lesson to be learned from our situation is "you should always take care of your airmen, no matter what." She lamented that our efforts to engage

---

[361] Tony Carr, "The Case Study of Craig Perry and the Future of Command in the U.S. Air Force," *John Q. Public*, June 14, 2014
[362] "I Sued My Husband's Commander," June 17, 2014

in the lives of my subordinates were used against me, "but that was only a pretext." The "official explanations don't add up," and the "evidence against my husband is unconvincing." She encouraged readers to go back to their squadrons and "and establish and implement the strongest Key Spouse program possible. Engage in the lives of your airmen and their families. Treat everyone the same and treat them all very well. It is the right thing to do, and if my husband and I had to do it all over again, we would take care of them just the same – because we did nothing wrong."[363]

I finally went on the record in late June 2014, in an interview with a reporter from the *Military.com* website. "It came as quite a shock when my boss called me into her office the day after Christmas, and told me I was being removed from command because I was under investigation," I was quoted in the article. "I had no idea what the allegations were, and my boss claimed she didn't know either. She had her deputy escort me out of the building to an office on a remote part of the base, and it was several weeks before anyone told me what the allegations were," I said. "One of the hardest things about this ordeal was the way my wife, Caroline, and I were abandoned by my chain of command. My commander, the first sergeant, nobody ever checked on us to see how we were doing. Worse, my boss bullied any of my fellow squadron commanders who reached out to me, and the wing commander made it clear to them that he didn't appreciate the letters of support they wrote in my defense," I explained.

I naturally disputed the allegations against me, and the results of the "formal months-long Air Force investigation." In response, an Air Force spokeswoman, Rose Richeson, regurgitated the earlier AETC statement featured previously in the *Air Force Times*, adding, "All of the allegations were thoroughly reviewed and investigated at multiple levels and the reviews determined the investigations and follow on actions were appropriate." Col. McKenna reiterated, "This is in no way associated with a commander taking care of his people. We in the Air Force encourage communication with subordinates. The specific allegations were not fraternization but more favoritism," he claimed. "The reports that he was relieved from command because he engaged in the lives of his subordinates are incorrect."

---

[363] Caroline Perry, "Case of Lt. Col. Perry," *Air Force Times* (print edition), June 23, 2014

I suggested the Air Force established an overly prosecutorial atmosphere in the wake of the Lackland sex scandal, which prompted the Air Force to scrutinize and intensely crack down on superior-subordinate relations at the base. While I applauded and strongly supported the efforts to combat sexual misconduct, I wondered if the Air Force was over-correcting or going too far. "The Lackland staff judge advocate set up a 'prosecution task force' to go after all the MTIs who had committed crimes," I was quoted as saying, "but that pool had pretty much dried up by the time I assumed command last July. But rather than stand down, they just kept going after MTIs for increasingly minor policy violations. It created an atmosphere of fear and isolation which persists to this day," I concluded.[364]

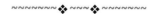

I was encouraged when *Fox News* immediately reposted the *Military.com* article on their website,[365] suggesting my situation was finally getting the national-level attention I thought it deserved. However, no other news outlets picked up the story, and media interest in my curious case soon began to wane. A staff writer at *The Washington Post* informed me he didn't feel my case rose to the level of national news for his paper's audience, while a media insider I spoke with got similar responses from her contacts at *The New York Times* and *Boston Globe*. She tried pitching them a "shifting military culture in a landscape of sexual misconduct and discrimination" hook, but the mainstream media seemed to consider my case too "inside baseball" to be relevant to national issues.

Local San Antonio media initially showed much greater interest in my situation. Caroline and I spoke with a reporter from the *San Antonio Express-News* on more than one occasion, and he initially seemed very interested in our story, as well as that of Lt. Col. Valenzuela. However, he soon became preoccupied with the Veterans Affairs scandal and Bowe Bergdahl case, and later offered an unconvincing explanation for dropping the ball. "I wish we could have gone forward with your story, and I am grateful for you

---

[364] Kris Osborn, "Commander Says He Was Fired for Helping Airmen," *Military.com*, June 27, 2014
[365] *Fox News* reprint of Kris Osborn article, June 27, 2014

wanting to explain it to me. Your trust, honesty and courage was obvious, and I respect that. I ran the reporting by my boss and he felt it was a dispute between your [*sic*] and your superiors that did not touch on some larger issue that would get it into the paper. Nonetheless, what happened is a sorry thing."[366]

A local television reporter who attended the same high school as me put in a good word with a colleague at her station, *WOAI News 4*, and he reached out to Caroline's attorney after she filed the lawsuit. We soon began discussing my case, and it was clear this investigating reporter was interested: "We REALLY want to tell your story," he wrote me, "and we are hoping doing so will benefit you as well." He contacted the Air Force for comment on the feature he was producing, and brought a cameraman out to our home to film an interview in late June. But he, too, ran into an insurmountable obstacle, when his producers insisted they needed additional people to make assertions similar to ours before they'd run his spot on the air. I informed him how incredibly difficult it would be to get other active-duty airmen to go on the record, but I somehow managed to convince a former colleague to sit down for an interview. Nevertheless, his producers wouldn't budge. "Again, I'm sorry we haven't been able to air the story... feel awful about it. But this does happen occasionally... the editorial process here has many layers and often they require much more than just one individual or couple's allegations to launch a story," he wrote.[367]

Another news outlet that failed to follow through on a story was *Stars and Stripes*, the legendary armed forces daily. Although officially managed within the Department of Defense, the newspaper is editorially independent, and often features stories critical of the Air Force. A reporter first interviewed me in mid-July 2014, and she later spoke to a couple other officers from BMT. She also reached out to AETC and other Air Force sources about my story before interviewing me again at the end of August. We continued exchanging e-mails through October, when she indicated she had finally submitted her piece to her editors. It took more than a month for her to receive feedback on her draft, and she sent me a list of follow-up questions in December. I immediately answered these just over an hour later, but I have not heard a word from her since then. In the meantime, she published over 50

---

[366] E-mail exchange with *Express-News* reporter, February 20, 2015
[367] E-mail exchanges with *WOIA News 4* reporter, June 16 and July 14, 2014

articles in *Stars and Stripes* before leaving that publication to take a job as a senior editor at *Air Force Magazine*, the journal of the Air Force Association.

I am no fan of conspiracy theories, and I certainly wouldn't want to damage my own credibility by indulging in baseless speculation, but ... seriously? One San Antonio journalist famous for his hard-hitting stories about the Air Force writes off my tale as a difference of opinion, not touching on some larger issue. Another investigative reporter is stymied by his producers, who suddenly set the bar for broadcast incredibly high. A print journalist works on a story for over five months before ceasing communication with me, then lands a great job at a publication often dismissed as a propaganda arm of its namesake military service. You don't have to wear a tinfoil hat to wonder if the Air Force brought pressure to bear on each of these news outlets to quash their stories. So much for freedom of the press.

One year to the day after I assumed command of the 737th Training Support Squadron, *John Q. Public* struck again. His latest blog post raised new questions about Col. Camerer and the command climate he cultivated at Lackland, as the Air Force closed ranks rather than providing explanations. Instead of providing an explanation that would help airmen understand and learn from the situation, the Air Force stonewalls and dismisses its critics as uninformed. Yet a continuous stream of disturbing facts, claims, and allegations had poured out of Lackland over the past several weeks. The author noted how the subordinates I allegedly favored were all punished for their supposed association with me, while Col. Camerer overused CDIs to hound his own subordinates. More worrisome was the inconsistency with which he addressed misconduct, making sure my career was irremediably wrecked, yet punishing others far less severely for more serious alleged offenses. While Col. Camerer may have taken these steps because he was actually dissatisfied with me for some reason, more plausibly he "was just out of touch enough that he lacked the foundation to challenge Liddick when she set her sights on making an example out of the one commander who seemed intelligent and confident enough to challenge her toxic and totalitarian leadership style." Having sided with her initially, he may have calculated that reversing course would make him look inept or jeopardize his pending promotion.

Whatever the rationale behind Camerer's actions, the Air Force seemed increasingly confused about it, judging by the various statements made about my case. "Given the obvious institutional misgivings reflected in the variance between official statements, the obvious question is why the Air Force doesn't simply admit the Lackland situation is a mess and initiate a new investigation." The reason is simple: "this decision has been bought at the highest levels, meaning senior officials will lose face if they change course." My CDI "turned out to be little more than well-dressed gibberish, but the generals who adopted it can ill afford to forsake it, lest they appear to have been inept in the first place."

Why does this matter? First, "Perry's situation has been more like something out of a bad movie script than what should be expected of the world's best Air Force." Considering "Lackland nearly unraveled a few years ago because of the abuse of power running unchecked within BMT," the problems at Lackland haven't been solved. Second, "the Air Force can't provide national defense if it doesn't attract and retain motivated officers and NCOs to lead airmen, and it will not attract capable leaders if they are not treated fairly." But there's "something deeper and uglier going on here." In the author's opinion, I was guilty of daring to occasionally disagree with my immediate superiors, an "intellectual insolence" that led to my professionally annihilation. In contrast to the once-cherished traditions of intellectual freedom, senior Air Force officers had recently begun demanding of their subordinates "not just conformity of action, but conformity of thought." Such a dangerous corruption of organizational climate could bring down the entire Service.[368]

As Tony Carr explained, the Air Force offered a dizzying array of explanations as to why I'd been fired. You'll recall that the CDI in my case substantiated three allegations: that I undermined Col. Liddick's command authority by commenting on her involvement in my squadron; that I engaged in unprofessional relationships with three personnel in my organization, including fraternization with my superintendent; and that I removed an LOR from my superintendent's personnel information file in violation of

---

[368] Tony Carr, "Closing Ranks: New Questions, No Answers in Lackland Firing Scandal," *John Q. Public*, July 2, 2014

policy. When Col. Camerer formally reprimanded me, however, he dropped the charge of fraternization, and merely accused me of creating the appearance of unprofessional relationships and favoritism with unspecified subordinates. I also "wrongfully" made statements and "wrongfully" removed an LOR from a PIF, according to the paperwork I received.

Col. Camerer later clarified that I hadn't "done anything illegal, immoral, or anything like that," but he refused to further comment on the reasons for my relief. When an investigative reporter reached out to the Air Force for comment, he received the following statement from AETC public affairs on behalf of Col. Camerer:

> It's been widely reported that Lt. Col. Perry's relief of command was related to his and Mrs. Perry's efforts to care for and support Airmen assigned to his squadron. Let me be very clear, there is no link between their actions to care for and support Airmen assigned to his squadron and my decision to relieve Lt. Col. Perry of command.
>
> I've been a wing commander for almost 4 years, at two different wings, and have supervised over 70 squadron commanders. All of these commanders endeavored to care for their Airmen and their families, and most did the same types of things the Perrys did to care for Airmen and families. None, including Lt. Col. Perry, were relieved of command because they provided support to their Airmen or their families.
>
> On reaching my decision, I clearly communicated the reasons for his relief, in a written reprimand to Lt. Col. Perry. The misrepresentation of the facts surrounding Lt. Col. Perry's relief have left some commanders and their spouses fearful that commonly accepted practices to support and care for Airmen and their families might result in unfair disciplinary action or relief of command, but nothing is further from the truth. Again, let me be very clear, Lt. Col. and Mrs. Perry's efforts to care for and support Airmen and families assigned to his squadron had no bearing on my decision to relieve Lt. Col. Perry of command.[369]

---

[369] Statement from Col. Camerer, June 19, 2014

Meanwhile, Col. McKenna, chief of AETC Public Affairs, began advancing an alternative narrative. In the statement he provided the *Air Force Times* for the print edition of my story in early June, the three substantiated allegations from my CDI and LOR morphed into something unrecognizable. Comments I allegedly made about my commander were now described as "derogatory," when they were nothing of the sort. My removal of an LOR from a subordinate's PIF was characterized as a slight against my commander, rather than a violation of policy. And no mention whatsoever was made of unprofessional relationships – merely a reference to my decision not to investigate alleged misconduct by a supposedly favored subordinate. This was a remarkable development: AETC had effectively thrown out an entire substantiated allegation, changed the basis of another, and completely mischaracterized a third. There is literally not a single element of McKenna's statement that is true.

Later that month, Col. McKenna further whitewashed my CDI, when he stated the specific allegations were not fraternization, but favoritism. Had he actually read the investigating officer's conclusions? Rose Richeson introduced another exaggeration, claiming that all of the allegations against me were thoroughly reviewed and investigated at multiple levels, with the reviews determining the investigations and follow on actions were appropriate. It was only months later, when the Air Force claimed Col. Hummel had "independently considered" my original CDI, that this statement finally made sense. They were pretending that an informal inquiry into a separate matter, whose report of investigation they refuse to release, represented a thorough investigation confirming my guilt. That's their story, and they're sticking to it.

Air Force senior leaders also made passing references to my curious case. When questioned about "the squadron commander at Lackland who got fired for knowing what was going on in his troops' lives," Chief Master Sergeant of the Air Force James Cody insisted supervisors ought to know when they've crossed the line. "To me, it's not as gray," he said. "You know when it's gone unprofessional. When you're doing things that just aren't appropriate, that you wouldn't do for anybody else, when you're doing things that you wouldn't say out loud. That point where it becomes unprofessional [is] where you wouldn't want anybody to know what you were doing." [370] Considering I did nothing inappropriate, I offered to do the same for everyone, and I made no secret of what I was up to, it's not entirely clear what the CMSAF was talking about.

The other public commentary on my case came from the 2 AF commander, Brig. Gen. Brown, who called my character into question shortly after dismissing my request for redress under Article 138, UCMJ. I discussed this incident in a previous chapter, and *John Q. Public* tackled the topic as well in a blog post. "For Brown to reveal his thoughts about a case he adjudicated in such an open forum is a prospect riddled with privacy and process concerns," Tony Carr wrote. "But the *way* Brown used the information went to a level beyond troubling. If the reports are accurate, it was obnoxious and ultimately unacceptable." He suggests Brig. Gen. Brown may have violated Article 133, UCMJ, by "using insulting or defamatory language" about a fellow military officer. "But his remarks having achieved escape velocity from the planet of fact, it's not clear what moral or legal space those remarks now inhabit."[371]

After about a month in the media spotlight, my star began to fade. Apart from the occasional mention in a *John Q. Public* post, my curious case was no longer getting much attention in the press. That didn't stop the *Air Force Times* from naming me one of the top "USAF newsmakers of 2014," however. In a short write-up, Kristin Davis reported how I had settled into a new job at the Joint Information Operations Warfare Center at JBSA-Lackland, a welcome change after months spent in limbo. But all my inspector general complaints, requests for redress, and Congressional inquiries had gone nowhere, and I anticipated being passed over for promotion and forced to retire.[372]

---

[370] Stephen Losey, "Cody: 18-month overhaul starts with new feedback form," *Air Force Times*, June 16, 2014

[371] Tony Carr, "General Reportedly Disparages Fellow Officer: a Teachable Moment About Mistakes and Character," *John Q. Public*, August 28, 2014

[372] "USAF newsmakers of 2014," *Air Force Times*, January 4, 2015

More recently, another reporter from the *Air Force Times* revisited my curious case upon the occasion of my retirement. "My appeals were obviously going nowhere, and the Air Force had no intention of leveraging my background and training," I said in an e-mail to the author, "so I decided it was time to go ahead and retire." I added, "I should be at Air War College right now, and pinning on O-6 next year." I revealed I was writing a memoir about my recent experiences, and how they relate to the Lackland sex scandal and the current Air Force leadership climate. "I've been able to gather dozens of stories of airmen who were wronged without recourse, and I'm painting a compelling picture of cover-up and corruption," I explained – a preview of the book you're reading now.[373]

---

[373] Stephen Losey, "Controversially fired Lt. Col. Perry retires, plans memoir," *Air Force Times*, November 3, 2015

Chapter 16: Keeping Friends Close

During my first weeks in exile after the launch of my commander-directed investigation, I had plenty of time to mull over what I might have done wrong, and consider how to defend myself against allegations still unknown. Concerned I might soon be out of a job, I reached out to several former colleagues in the Intelligence Community for moral support. As I wrote to one of my mentors,

> *After all I've been through these last few years, this latest setback is incredibly discouraging. I felt like I'd been doing a pretty good job as commander, getting the mission done while taking care of my airmen. I've also earned the respect of my fellow squadron commanders, most of whom were among the top performers in their career fields with prior command experience before BMT. They're joined by an all-star cast of CMSgt superintendents and SMSgt shirts, plus more Captains and Majors than you can shake a stick at. But this high-powered leadership team has often been frustrated in its efforts to innovate and think outside the box. For many of us, it feels like we're being set up for failure, and we'll be lucky if we emerge from BMT with our careers intact.*
>
> *Still, I'm hopeful I can overcome this latest obstacle. I am confident whatever allegations I'm facing are unsubstantiated, and I can't imagine how anything I've done would warrant relief from command. But I can't help but worry that some sort of example is being made of me ... early retirement may very well be in my future in 2014! I guess I'll have to keep my fingers crossed that the intel community will welcome me back after the dust settles.*

Major General Jim Poss, who retired in 2012 as the Assistant Deputy Chief of Staff, Intelligence, Surveillance and Reconnaissance – at the time, the Air Force's highest-ranking intelligence officer – soon responded to my plea for help, asking me to call him to discuss my situation. I first worked for this Mississippi native on the Air Combat Command staff at Langley Air Force Base, Virginia, where he served as director of intelligence beginning in 2006. This general officer was instrumental in my selection to lead the Air Force's first-ever weapons intelligence teams in Iraq later that year, and his endorsement helped me secure a position as director of operations at a National Security Agency field site in Alaska a couple of years later. Upon my completion of that tour, Maj. Gen. Poss brought me to the Air Staff to serve as executive officer for his boss, Lieutenant General David Deptula, AF/A2, just before he retired. It was there at the Pentagon that I was first selected for command, of the 29th Intelligence Squadron at nearby Fort Meade, Maryland.

As I was wrapping up a rehearsal for my change-of-command ceremony in late June 2011, just days before I was to assume command, Maj. Gen. Poss called to break some terrible news: the 70th ISR Wing commander had put my assumption of command on hold, and requested an investigation against me for alleged misconduct. This was my first brush with the arbitrary and capricious nature of certain Air Force senior leaders. Unfortunately, it wouldn't be the last.

Although we had met in high school, Caroline and I struggled to maintain a long-distance relationship – she lived in Houston, while I was in San Antonio – in the era before the Internet and cell phones. I foolishly moved on with my life, and we soon lost track of each other. We eventually married other people, but as fate would have it, neither of these marriages worked out. My first wife filed for divorce in October 2009, while I was stationed up in Alaska. She soon returned home to San Antonio, but seemed uninterested in actually following through with the divorce, since I was supporting her financially while she continued receiving healthcare and other benefits as my military spouse. It was only after I pressed the issue that a Bexar County judge finally declared us divorced on December 1, 2010. Because it was my ex-wife who brought the case to court, her attorney was responsible for drafting the final decree of divorce based on the judge's notes. However, the plaintiff continued dragging her feet through the following summer. The final decree – reflecting a December 1st effective date of divorce – was only signed on June 15, 2011, and I didn't receive a copy for my records until late July.

That spring, I was selected for squadron command at Ft. Meade. This was quite an honor, and I was very excited about getting to lead my fellow intelligence professionals supporting the

National Security Agency mission. In preparation for this assignment, I attended the Air Force ISR Agency squadron commander's course in April 2011 at Joint Base San Antonio-Lackland. After my divorce the previous year, Caroline and I had become engaged, and my high school sweetheart joined me in my hometown that week as my fiancé. Ironically, my class was invited to attend a Basic Military Training graduation parade at the end of the course, but I skipped this to travel up to Cannon AFB, New Mexico, to participate in a dedication ceremony for a fallen comrade. The local wing was renaming a street in honor Captain Kermit Evans, my weapons intelligence flight operations officer who was killed in Iraq during my last deployment. Little did I know, I would be back at BMT as a squadron commander a couple of years later.

As the date of the 29 IS change-of-command ceremony approached, I made arrangements to drive across town from the Pentagon to Ft. Meade to familiarize myself with my new unit and its mission. I knew the current commander, Lt. Col. Eduardo "Mo" Monarez, from our time together at Langley AFB, where he served as then-Brig. Gen. Poss's executive officer. I also took time away from the office to attend change-of-command ceremonies for my new wing and group commanders at Ft. Meade, and I accompanied my Air Staff boss, Lt. Gen. Larry James, to this post for a visit. When I mentioned to a colleague at the Pentagon that I would once again be spending the day at Ft. Meade, she jokingly suggested I was "brown-nosing" my new leadership. Ironically, Maj. Gen. Poss teased me as well when I mentioned I would be out of the office for another ceremony. So I thought nothing of updating my Facebook status to read, "Spending another day at the fort tomorrow, brown-nosing my future chain of command." Unfortunately, this clever bit of self-deprecating humor would soon come back to haunt me.

My new boss was to be Lt. Col. Mike Downs, with whom I had worked a decade earlier at the 32d Air Intelligence Squadron at Ramstein Airbase, Germany, when we were both captains. He had recently assumed command of the 707th ISR Group, and would be attending a group commander's course at Maxwell AFB, Alabama, immediately before the 29 IS change of command. He would be presiding over that ceremony on his first day back in the office, June 27, 2011, but he hadn't found time to catch up with me before departing for his weeklong course. Too late, I realized he had no idea I was divorced from my ex-wife, whom he had met years earlier in Germany. As he prepared his remarks for the ceremony, he would undoubtedly pull my personnel records, but these still reflected my ex-wife as my dependent, since I could not officially update my marital status without the signed final decree of divorce. So on Sunday, June 19, I called my old friend to explain my predicament, and ask whether it would be appropriate to introduce Caroline to my new squadron as my fiancé under these circumstances.

Lt. Col. Downs seemed to take the news well. He didn't lecture me or shut me down, but he did say he wanted to check with the wing staff judge advocate before giving me any further advice on my situation. He immediately followed up in an e-mail: "Thanks again for the call and I know on top of being an AF superstar, you're a human and you've got a personal life & some tough issues to deal. Again, I'll get back to you later in the week re: how to proceed."[374] Unfortunately, the staff attorney he consulted informed the new wing commander, Col. Mary O'Brien – and then all hell broke loose.

Although I had clearly explained how I was legally divorced, and merely awaiting court documents to correct my personnel records, Col. O'Brien jumped to the conclusion I had brazenly confessed to adultery, with both a wife and a fiancé. She immediately began searching for any incriminating information she could find on my Facebook page, whose privacy settings then (regrettably) allowed friends of friends to see my status. There she found the post about me "brown-nosing" my future chain of command, which she somehow felt impugned her character. She also came across a random song lyric I posted – a line from "Summertime," by Sublime – which she incorrectly interpreted as a threat against my ex-wife. She requested my assignment as 29 IS commander be put on hold, and asked my current boss, Lt. Gen. James, to launch an investigation into my conduct. And she did all this within just three short days of that initial phone call, without anyone ever bothering to talk with me to clear up her idiotic misunderstanding.

I was flabbergasted that an Air Force senior leader would so badly mishandle an issue like this. Although I didn't know Col. O'Brien well, I had met her once before, during an Air Force Senior ISR Officer conference at AFISRA headquarters the previous December. I happened to know she wasn't the AF/A2's first choice

---

[374] E-mail exchange with 707 ISRG commander, "29 IS CoC," June 19, 2011

to take command of the 70 ISRW, but I assumed she would have the professional courtesy and judgment commensurate with her rank to not make such a rash decision without at least talking to me first. As a Lieutenant Colonel selected for squadron command, with 17 years experience and an impeccable record, I deserved at least that much respect. Or at least, so I assumed. What I hadn't counted on was an officer only a few years senior to me so sensitive to the slightest hint of impropriety that she would carelessly toss me aside, as if none of that mattered.

My Air Staff boss was no better. Rather than defend me against Col. O'Brien's baseless allegations, or assure her he would get to the bottom of this matter himself, Lt. Gen. James outsourced the inquiry to the Air Force District of Washington. Following in the footsteps of the legendary Dave Deptula – whose contribution to the 1991 Desert Storm air campaign earned him a reputation as a brilliant innovator – Larry James seemed completely out of his depth as head of the Air Force ISR enterprise. The way he threw his executive officer under the bus didn't go unnoticed among his peers at the Pentagon, who were already put off by this unimpressive yet overconfident space officer. Rather than contact me himself, my supervisor directed Maj. Gen. Poss, who was on leave at the time, to notify me I was under investigation.

At the request of Lt. Gen. James, the local 11th Wing commander directed an investigation, appointing one of my Air Staff colleagues, Col. Tom Bailey, as investigating officer. I was accused of everything from adultery to conduct unbecoming an officer and a gentlemen – and when my ex-wife later filed an inspector general complaint that I was not providing adequate financial support, they tacked on an additional allegation. But there was no basis for any of these claims, and the investigating officer soon found each of them unsubstantiated, concluding that Col. O'Brien had overreacted. Although the 11 WG staff judge advocate concurred with his findings,[375] the wing commander, Col. Ken Rizer nevertheless recommended I be counseled for something

---

[375] E-mail from 11 WG/JA to Col. Tom Bailey, "CDI ROI to A2," July 27, 2011

331

or other – I'm not entirely sure what, since he never provided me the required notification of the final CDI results.[376]

So what was to be done? On July 28, Lt. Gen. James informed a handful of colleagues – including Col. O'Brien, Maj. Gen. Poss, and Maj. Gen. Bob Otto, the new AFISRA commander – that my investigation was "pretty much wrapped up," and they "need to develop a plan for what's next" for me. He tasked Col. Mark Westergren (a fellow Olmsted Scholar) and Col. Monica "Stretch" Midgette "to take lead and work options with the right folks." In response, Maj. Gen. Otto noted the new squadron commander candidate list should be published in two weeks. "We'll work an early look with Mary to find the right fit," he assured his boss, suggesting they were expecting someone else to take command of the 29 IS – before even reading the report of investigation.

Maj. Gen. Poss replied to the AFISRA commander the next morning. "We're trying to see if the JAG/IG will let Mary see the investigation results. There's debate whether we can let her see it because Mary was the complainant and was a witness. It's important that she see [it] because the investigating officer did not substantiate any of the complaints. This may impact her decisions." My mentor was urging caution and deliberation, but Maj. Gen. Otto had already made up his mind. "Beyond the investigation, the fact that she saw Craig's very unprofessional posting on facebook (referencing her) and the whole issue you cite leaves significant questions about his judgment which led to a loss of confidence in his ability to effectively command," he responded. "But more information to make fact-based decisions is goodness (if permissible)." Maj. Gen. Poss ended this e-mail exchange on a prophetic note: "Copy all - just want to make sure she has all the facts. Don't need this coming back to bite us later."[377]

When I sent a note to my supervisor, Lt. Gen. James, the following Monday, asking for an update on the CDI, he was evasive. "We're still awaiting the final sign out of the CDI by the 11th Wing," he wrote a couple of days later, "so until that happens, I don't want to get in front of the process. Once that's done, we'll do everything possible to move forward." He added, "Maj. Gen. Otto should get in

---

[376] SAF/IGQ, "Commander-Directed Investigation (CDI) Guide," July 7, 2006, paragraph 7.1

[377] E-mail exchange between Lt. Gen. Larry James, Maj. Gen. Jim Poss, and Maj. Gen. Bob Otto, "EYES ONLY: Lt. Col. Perry," July 28-29, 2011

touch with you soon as well."[378] The new AFISRA commander did just that on July 5, informing me over the phone that Col. O'Brien had disregarded the results of the CDI, and neither he nor any of her superiors were willing to overrule her. But it's just as well, he reassured me, since I obviously wouldn't want to work for a commander who held such a grudge against me.

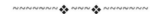

When I was selected for command at Ft. Meade, I requested permission to move closer to my new assignment, since the commute from Alexandria, Virginia, would be over 35 miles each way. But as Caroline and I were preparing to move to Laurel, Maryland, my assignment was canceled. Thankfully, the Air Force honored its promise to pay for my relocation, but it would be a while before I would be gainfully employed again. In the meantime, I was detailed to the Air Force Intelligence Analysis Agency at Joint Base Anacostia-Bolling for several months, while I awaited reassignment.

To avoid any perception they were treating me unfairly after my CDI cleared me of misconduct, Maj. Gen. Poss apparently ensured I was added to the list of intelligence squadron command candidates for the following year, published in mid-August 2011.[379] I wrote him a note thanking him for whatever part he played in making sure my name stayed on the squadron command list, and his response was magnanimous: "You've taken tremendous risks for our country and produced tremendous results," he replied. "It's the least we could do. Don't let this get you down. You're a superb officer."[380] However, when Lt. Gen. James sent an e-mail to the "A2 Team" congratulating the squadron commander candidates from his staff, he somehow failed to mention me, his former executive officer – but he did highlight another officer who had already been selected for command: my replacement at the 29 IS. Although Lt. Gen. James ranked me the "#3 of 43 O-5s on A2 staff," he didn't

---

[378] E-mail exchange with Lt. Gen. James, "CDI results," August 1-3, 2011

[379] PSDM 11-71, "CY12 14N Intelligence Sq/CC Candidate Selection Results," August 16, 2011

[380] E-mail exchange with Maj. Gen. Poss, "RE: Sq/CC Candidates," August 22, 20111

recommend me for command on my officer performance report, which he signed on August 2, severely undermining my chances for future selection.[381] Furthermore, he is rumored to have informed Col. O'Brien he would not look favorably on anyone who hired me for squadron command. That fall, she apparently relayed this warning to several of her fellow wing-level hiring authorities, and she may even have informed them I was an adulterer, despite the CDI findings.

So it came as a surprise when I received an unsolicited offer to compete for command of a Basic Military Training squadron in late 2011.[382] This was my first indication that I hadn't been selected to command an intelligence squadron that cycle, but I wasn't ready to give up on that dream just yet. When I contacted both Maj. Gen. Poss and now-Brig. Gen. Mark Westergren in November 2011, both assured me there was no "whisper campaign" against me within the intelligence officer community. I decided to hold out another year to compete one last time for command within my career field. How different things might have turned out if I hadn't passed on that first BMT opportunity!

Maj. Gen. Poss came through for me yet again when he found me a job at United States Cyber Command, collocated with the National Security Agency at Ft. Meade. The chief of staff there was a fellow intelligence officer, Maj. Gen. David Senty, an Air Force Reservist who worked for the Central Intelligence Agency when not on active-duty orders. He actually lined me up to become USCYBERCOM's first-ever liaison to CIA, but he retired by the time I actually began working at Ft. Meade at the end of October 2011. His replacement, Rear Admiral Peg Klein, had different plans for this position, so I was reassigned to the USCYBERCOM intelligence directorate. It's just as well, I figured, since the daily commute to Langley would have been a real drag!

This turned out to be one of the best assignments of my Air Force career. After a brief stint in the cyber-targeting division, the USCYBERCOM Joint Intelligence Operations Center commanding officer, Navy Captain Mark Jarek, selected me as his chief of operations. For the next 15 months, I was given virtually free reign to implement his vision for the CYBER JIOC, a 400-person

---

[381] Lt. Gen. Larry James, AF Form 707, *Officer Performance Report (Lt thru Col)*, August 2, 2011
[382] E-mail from Lt. Col. Mark Delvecchio, "Basic Military Training Command Opportunity," November 11, 2011

organization composed of civilians, contractors, and members of all five uniformed military Services (including the Coast Guard). Together with the division chiefs and a small support team, we pursued dramatic mission realignment to better posture the J2 to support cyberspace operations. I was also able to develop a compelling case for increased J2 manpower requirements, normalize integration of reserve military forces, and manage countless administrative tasks with minimal disruption to the mission.

Most of all, I felt valued and respected. CAPT Jarek was a phenomenal commanding officer, who assembled a capable team of leaders and empowered us to succeed. Although all the division chiefs outranked me, my boss ensured I had the resources necessary to be effective, making difficult but necessary changes for the good of the organization. He neither micromanaged operations nor abdicated responsibility for the tough decisions, but rather focused on the "big rocks" appropriate for his level of command. And he took care of his people. After less than a year on the job, he ranked me his "#1/20" field-grade officers, and the director of intelligence, Rear Admiral Sam Cox, called me his "#1/8 O-5 joint officers," with a "phenomenal impact across [the] J2 directorate!"[383] Moreover, the admiral provided me a coveted "definitely promote" recommendation to the Colonel central selection board, two years below my primary zone.[384] Although I wasn't selected at that time, I felt as if my career was finally getting back on track after the 29 IS fiasco.

And yet, the Air Force intelligence community didn't seem to notice. Although my name again appeared on the intelligence squadron commander candidate list in 2012,[385] I was once again passed over for command. Col. Midgette, who managed intelligence officer assignments at Air Staff, later confirmed I had received bids from hiring authorities that time around, but none of them were high enough to get matched. On the other hand, another Air Force intelligence officer who worked with me on the USCYBERCOM J2 staff was selected for command, despite my

---

[383] CAPT Mark Jarek and RADM Samuel Cox, AF Form 707, *Officer Performance Report (Lt thru Col)*, June 4, 2012
[384] RADM Samuel Cox, AF Form 709, *Promotion Recommendation*, P0612B board (2012)
[385] PSDM 12-62, "CY13 Intelligence Officer (14N) Squadron Commander Candidate Selection Results," July 13, 2012

higher stratification from the same senior rater, RADM Cox. The admiral contacted Maj. Gen. Poss, a colleague with whom he had worked years earlier, for recommendations on how he could assist me in advancing my career.[386] My mentor apparently revealed to him I had been blacklisted within my career field, not only because of the unsubstantiated allegations addressed by the CDI the previous year, but also undocumented rumors outside the scope of that investigation. Apparently there was a "whisper campaign" after all.

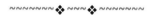

Nevertheless, several months later I was unexpectedly selected to command a BMT squadron down at JBSA-Lackland. Making good on a recommendation from the recently completed Woodward report, Air Education and Training Command filled BMT command billets in 2013 with high-potential officers. After being blacklisted within my own career field for two years running, I imagine I was among the better qualified intelligence officers not yet selected for squadron command, making me a prime candidate for AETC consideration. Yet I was apparently the last of the new BMT squadron commanders notified of my selection, suggesting some negotiations went on behind the scenes before my career field managers agreed to release me for this assignment. Some of my colleagues undoubtedly still questioned my suitability for command after the 29 IS fiasco, and so probably opposed giving me a second chance at BMT. Pushback from my fellow intelligence officers may have stemmed from a different source, however. There were those within my career field who knew I had been unfairly denied a command opportunity in 2011, and rumor has it some of them felt I had paid my dues at USCYBERCOM – so much so, they intended to credit me for a squadron command tour based on my excellent performance in that joint assignment. Whatever the reason, I would finally be getting my long-awaited opportunity to command.

Yet within a year, I was again the subject of a commander-directed investigation, removed from my position while I awaited the results of what I hoped would be a quick and fair process. Based on the results of my first CDI two years previously, I had

---

[386] E-mail from RADM Cox to Mag. Gen. Poss, September 24, 2012

every reason to hope this latest investigation might go my way as well. This was my state of mind when I received that phone call from Jim Poss in January 2014. Now retired, he commiserated with my plight, and lamented my obvious bad luck at again finding myself at odds with my chain of command. He couldn't help but wonder why female O-6s seemed to have such a hard time getting along with me, but when he learned Col. Liddick was a maintenance officer, that cleared up any confusion in his mind about my current predicament.

After I was finally relieved of command a couple of months later, I again contacted Maj. Gen. Poss for advice. I explained how I had already filed an IG complaint, and was considering an Article 138 request and perhaps a Congressional for good measure, but I knew I would have an uphill fight on my hands to straighten out my records in time for the upcoming O-6 promotion board. "If you think you're right, then by all means fight this," he replied, suggesting the IG and Article 138 were my best bet. "Congressionals never work out and just get you bad visibility all the way up to the CSAF," he cautioned. "To be honest, I wouldn't pin my hopes on the O-6 board even if you do win," he continued. "I don't think you'll have time to get this out of your record before the board," he concluded, and even if I did, I would either have a weak officer performance report or an "OPR removed due to IG direction" form to account for my time in squadron command. And that was assuming I could get a "definitely promote" recommendation out of my next chain of command.[387]

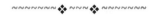

After my abortive relocation to Barksdale AFB was canceled, I was in a hurry to find a new job before the accountability date for the upcoming Colonel board. Wherever I was assigned at that time would determine who wrote my promotion recommendation, and I figured my chances would be better if I worked anywhere other than the 37th Training Wing. My next-door neighbor happened to be the executive officer for the AFISRA commander, and he graciously helped expedite my reassignment to that organization ahead of the deadline. On June 12, 2014, I signed into my new unit, the Joint Information

---

[387] James Poss, LinkedIn message, April 2, 2014

Operations Warfare Center, a branch of the Joint Staff collocated with the AFISRA headquarters on Security Hill. However, my senior rater would be the AFISRA commander, Maj. Gen. Jack Shanahan.

The following week, I attended the 37 TRW change of command ceremony, held in conjunction with the weekly BMT graduation parade. SSgt Josh Hite, the 2012 "Blue Rope of the Year," was the "Commander of Airmen" that morning, and his wife, Melanie, invited Caroline and me to sit with her family in the infield, just feet away from the "bomb run" where marching airmen pass in review. This was my first parade since my removal from command six months earlier, and I was excited to once again observe this time-honored spectacle. The program featured several special events, including a tribute to the 326th Training Squadron superintendent, CMSgt Reginald Murrell, on the occasion of his retirement; the transfer of authority between Col. Camerer and Col. Trent Edwards, presided over by Maj. Gen. Patrick; and a final salute to the outgoing wing commander by a formation of Military Training Instructors, led down the "bomb run" by CMSgt Sutherland – an unusual sight, considering the BMT superintendent was the only member of this "MTI mass" not wearing a campaign hat. The reviewing official, Col. Camerer, addressed the crowd at the end of the ceremony, telling the MTIs in attendance that he respected each and every one of them. This ironic statement echoed a sentiment he expressed in his final interview as 37 TRW commander: "We have the finest NCOs our nation has to offer molding and training our newest Airmen. They're the ones doing the job day in and day out, and they're doing it spectacularly. The proof is in the Airmen we're producing."[388]

Following the parade, I shared about 20 of the photographs I took that morning with my friends on Facebook. Soon afterward, the "Team Perry" administrators reposted a handful of these pictures to their Facebook page, crediting me as the photographer – but adding comments critical of Col. Camerer, CMSgt Sutherland, and others involved in my curious case.[389] This apparently didn't go over well with my former chain of command, as I would soon learn.

---

[388] Mike Joseph, "37th TRW ceremony to bid Camerer farewell, welcome Edwards," JBSA official website, June 20, 2014
[389] "Team Perry" Facebook posts, July 20, 2014

Late on the afternoon of June 30, I was summoned to Maj. Gen. Shanahan's office. This was not a social call, or an opportunity to introduce myself to my new senior rater. No, I was there to receive yet another no-contact order. As I stood there before his desk, he notified me I was hereby directed to refrain from entering any 737th Training Group facilities, attending any official BMT functions or events, and "taking or providing photos of Air Force personnel for publication without permission of personnel in the photograph." The AFISRA commander claimed this order was "necessary to safeguard and protect the morale, good order and discipline, and usefulness" of members of JBSA-Lackland and the 37 TRW, and would remain in effect for six months unless he said otherwise. "Prior to issuing this order," he added, apropos of nothing, "I have carefully considered the legal review concerning your situation."[390]

It was deeply disappointing to me that such a senior leader in the Air Force ISR community would so easily roll over on one of his own. Rather than pushing back against the local training wing and AETC leadership, or soliciting my side of the story before taking such drastic action, he simply did their bidding, based on nothing more than the same flawed legal reasoning that railroaded me in the first place. Unlike the senior leaders in my former chain of command, who felt obligated to close ranks around the bad decisions of their subordinates at Lackland, Maj. Gen. Shanahan had no skin in this game. He could easily have told his AETC counterparts to pound sand, or delayed taking action until he had a chance to look into my case on his own. Instead, he blindly toed the party line, coming down on the wrong side of an issue that did not concern him or his command, and which he clearly did not understand.

The next morning, I sent an apologetic note to my neighbor, the general's executive officer. "I am so sorry that happened yesterday," I wrote, "and I'm mortified that 37 TRW leadership dragged your boss into this. I can't begin to explain why the new group and wing commanders felt this order was necessary. I am happy to have finally found a new home here on Security Hill, and I have absolutely no desire or intention to go back to BMT ever again. For some reason, they seem to have confused my legitimate

---

[390] Maj. Gen. John N.T. Shanahan, "No Contact Order," June 20, 2014

grievances with their predecessors as a threat against them or their organizations. I suspect they're getting bad counsel from the JAG, who previously advised Col. Camerer and Col. Liddick." I asked him to please extend my apologies to Maj. Gen. Shanahan.

When I informed my area defense counsel of this latest development, she contacted her colleagues in the Lackland legal office, who confirmed these restrictions came about because of the "Team Perry" posts crediting me as the photographer. "That was what prompted them to draft this order," she wrote. "They do not want that to happen again." Her opinion was that this was a lawful order, and she advised me to comply. "Do not post any photos to your Facebook timeline depicting Airmen who do not explicitly provide you permission to post them. This applies to all Airmen – background or foreground, in uniform or not. Restrict the ability of third parties to download photos from your timeline, and if this means limiting who can view your photos, so be it. You can still be liable if you do not restrict people's ability to download photos of Airmen who haven't provided you permission to post their pictures. Don't give any photos, either publicly available or personally owned, to media outlets if you don't have the permission from the Airman to do so. The consequence for any of these actions is an investigation that could result in further action against you, up to a court-martial." She conceded there could potentially be an argument that specific parts of the order are overbroad on First Amendment grounds, "but what is your remedy?"[391]

Nevertheless, the prohibition on taking or providing photos of Air Force personnel for publication without permission was an unnecessarily broad, and arguably unconstitutional, restriction on my liberty. As written, it applied to pictures of any airman (not just those assigned to 37 TRW) taken anywhere in the world (not just there at Lackland) at any time (not just during my current assignment), whether or not I was even aware they were in the Air Force. The order did not specify what was meant by "publication" (did this apply to posts on my personal Facebook timeline shared only with friends?), or how "permission" might be demonstrated (did "tagging" the subject imply consent?), and took no account of my intent in taking or providing the photo. Technically, sharing photos of my late grandfathers during their Air

---

[391] E-mail exchange with Area Defense Counsel, "Lt. Col. Perry NCO," July 15, 2014

Force careers would violate this order, since I didn't obtain their permission before they passed away. I was also theoretically barred from posting photos from my last promotion ceremony, without first tracking down every person pictured in the background to secure their consent. And it wasn't clear if this order applied retroactively, to pictures I had already posted.

What had I really done to deserve this new set of restrictions? I attended a public event that was open to any member of the community with base access, but I created no disturbance nor disrupted the festivities. I took photos that morning, as did countless parents, family members, and friends of the graduating airmen. (In some of my pictures, you can actually see members of the 37 TRW public affairs staff photographing the ceremony, while employees of Basic Video Productions are actually contracted to videotape BMT graduation events.) I posted some of my photos to Facebook, but I'm sure I wasn't alone among the thousands of people in attendance who did this. Someone else then downloaded a handful of my pictures and used them for their own purposes – tell me again how this became my responsibility? If the "Team Perry" administrators had instead used an official photograph of the events that day, or a snapshot taken by one of the parents, would these photographers have been held responsible for somehow impairing the "usefulness" of the subjects pictured? Of course not. This wasn't about the source of the photos so much as it was about trying to assert control over me and my behavior.

Just because I swore to uphold and defend the Constitution as a member of our armed forces, doesn't mean its protections no longer apply to me as an airman. While military members are rightfully limited, for the sake of good order and discipline, in what they can say about their superiors and other military members, this no-contact order stripped away my basic First Amendment rights as a citizen. This was typical of the type of overreach I'd recently come to expect from Air Force leadership.

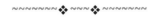

I was initially wary of pushing back against this ridiculous no-contact order, since I didn't want to further alienate my new senior rater, from whom I still naively hoped to receive a favorable promotion recommendation. And I really had no desire to trespass upon BMT or go around photographing airmen; after all, there were plenty of folks willing to feed me and Caroline information about what was going on over on the training side of base without me needing to trespass. When a fellow intelligence officer, who until recently had served as the 322d Training Squadron director of operations, invited me to her promotion ceremony at the BMT Pfingston Reception Center at the end of July, she waved me off when she realized 737 TRG leadership might cancel her ceremony if I tried to attend. But after I received the Air Force response to the initial Congressional inquiry by Representative Pete Gallego in late July, which failed to address his questions and made troubling new claims, I brought this latest restriction to my Congressman's attention. "I am an Air Force officer who has served his country honorably for almost 20 years now," I explained. "I am an intelligence professional with a Top Secret security clearance, and have routine access to highly sensitive information, sources, and methods as part of my duties." It was "completely unreasonable for me to be subjected to such petty and vindictive restrictions," I concluded.[392]

In response to another inquiry by Rep. Gallego, the Air Force blamed the victim. The chief of the "Congressional Inquiry and Travel Division" recounted how the AFISRA commander "regarded the order as necessary to safeguard and protect the morale, good order and discipline" – but not the "usefulness" – of the local military community, and a review found the order "legally sufficient, necessary and appropriate." To date, however, "Colonel Perry has not requested the AFISRA/CC to approve any specific exception or modification, or to rescind the order."[393] So, while the Air Force made no comment on the content of this no-contact order, and defended its issuance as sufficient, necessary, and appropriate to safeguard something or other, they suggested these continued restrictions were my own fault because I hadn't asked the person who issued them to reconsider.

The opportunity to test this theory soon presented itself. In early September, I was invited to attend the retirement ceremony of TSgt Jeff Jordan, a former Master MTI assigned to the 321st Training Squadron, on October 2. As I discussed in a previous chapter, Col. Liddick arbitrarily deprived him of a stripe and his campaign hat nearly two years earlier. Because the

---

[392] E-mail exchange with Congressional staffer, July 28, 2014
[393] Col. Yetishefsky, reply to inquiry by Rep. Pete Gallego, September 9, 2014

ceremony was being held in the 321 TRS airman training complex, I couldn't attend unless my restriction on entering 737 TRG facilities was lifted.

On September 18, I respectfully requested Maj. Gen. Shanahan rescind the no-contact order, but he refused. The AFISRA commander did, however, invite me to request exceptions on a case-by-case basis, so I specifically asked to attend TSgt Jordan's ceremony. "It is my understanding," Maj. Gen. Shanahan replied, "that TSgt Jordan does not personally know you and he was not expecting you to attend his retirement ceremony." Under these circumstances, he concluded, "your request is hereby denied."

Huh? I don't know where the general was getting his information from, but he had clearly been misinformed. Caroline and I knew both this airman and his fiancé, and both of them were expecting us to attend – in fact, I was one of fewer than 20 personnel specifically addressed on the electronic invitation sent out by the event organizer. After explaining all this to my senior rater, I added a conciliatory note: "I'm sure they'll understand why you were advised to deny this request."

Maj. Gen. Shanahan immediately backtracked. "Based on your reply and new information provided by TSgt Jordan," he replied, my request to attend his retirement ceremony was approved. However, my attendance "may be disconcerting for some of the other invitees," he cautioned. "As I trust you will appreciate," the general continued, "any disruptions would be viewed as highly detrimental to the guest of honor and his family on this special day. Accordingly, if your attendance appears to be detracting from TSgt Jordan's ceremony, professional courtesy may dictate an early departure."[394]

I almost felt sorry for Maj. Gen. Shanahan during this whole ordeal. He had again been lied to and embarrassed by 37 TRW leadership, who obviously hadn't bothered to get their facts straight before effectively accusing me of trying to crash this party. (TSgt Jordan later informed me his first sergeant actually contacted him to confirm he knew me, but he pushed back, asking if he needed to account for everyone on the guest list.) The ceremony itself went off without a hitch, and none of the other invitees seemed disconcerted by our presence – not even the new deputy 737 TRG commander, Lt. Col. Christopher Fuller, the senior-most

---

[394] E-mail exchange with Maj. Gen. Shanahan, "Request to rescind no-contact order," September 18-30, 2014

officer present. (Neither the squadron nor group commanders showed up.) As much as TSgt Jordan wanted to trash the "Butcher of BMT" who ruined his career, he kept his remarks professional, and there were no other disruptions. The guest of honor even welcomed us to the reception following the ceremony, and one of his family members later posted pictures from this event of Caroline and me on Facebook.

Ironically, we also received an invitation to attend the annual Blue Rope Ball a few weeks later. Because this was not an official BMT event, and wasn't held in a 737 TRG facility, there was no official obstacle to our attending. However, when the president of the Military Training Instructor Association got wind we might be coming, he sent a message to the "Team Perry" administrators. "While I cannot force you to stay away," he wrote, mistakenly assuming I was the page administrator, "I would respectfully ask that you do so. Given the events of the past year I think it would be appropriate if you do not attend any of our events." As it turned out, we were out of town that weekend and couldn't attend. But it would have been fun to see how certain folks reacted to our presence.

"Facebook is the spawn of the devil," Maj. Gen. Poss once told me, warning of the dangers social networking poses to intelligence professionals like us. Considering how this site contributed to the loss of my first squadron command opportunity, and the imposition of a no-contact order after I was fired from my second, he may have a point. Certainly, the "Team Perry" phenomenon became a source of tension with my Air Force chain of command.

In early September 2014, the administrators of that Facebook page published a series of posts about my former group commander, Debbie Liddick, highlighting inconsistencies in her public persona. They compared her various media interviews, LinkedIn profile, and Twitter tweets, with the image she cultivated while commanding BMT. This retired officer was not at all pleased by this negative publicity, and she reportedly complained to her former colleagues that I was invading her privacy. That was a laughable accusation, considering all of these sources were accessible to the public online, given Ms. Liddick's privacy settings on those social networking sites. Moreover, I wasn't the administrator of the "Team Perry" page, a fact the Air Force independently confirmed.

Nevertheless, Liddick's allegations made their way to the Pentagon, then rolled back down my chain of command to Security Hill. Rather than deal with me directly, AFISRA leadership asked the deputy JIOWC director, Navy Captain Scott McClure, to question me about this "Team Perry" activity. He summoned me to a meeting with the JIOWC personnel director, another Navy captain, on September 15, and quickly got to the point: Was I behind the "Team Perry" page? When I denied responsibility, he expressed relief, noting I seemed too intelligent to get caught up in something like that. This naval aviator then quickly changed the subject, inquiring after Caroline's health, and checking to make sure I was doing all right with all the stress we'd been under. I explained how my wife had almost died undergoing an experimental medical procedure the previous month, while I was attending training up in Norfolk, Virginia. These two officers were visibly alarmed they hadn't heard anything about this, and surprised by how well I seemed to be holding up, and they both pledged to pray for Caroline. (They also asked if I was getting the support I needed, which led to note how unresponsive the AFISRA Key Spouse program had been, as I will discuss below.)

In November, "Team Perry" posted a copy of the referral officer performance report Col. Liddick issued me earlier that year, but accidently failed to redact the last four digits of her Social Security Number on the form. I was in Tampa, Florida, at the time attending a course at the Joint Special Operations University, when I received a phone message from my boss asking me to call CAPT McClure immediately. He told me he'd again been contacted by Air Force authorities, who wanted me to ask the "Team Perry" administrators to take down the offending document. Why they didn't just contact "Team Perry" directly, I have no idea.

Debbie Liddick, on the other hand, did send a message to the "Team Perry" administrators: "I would appreciate it if you would black out my last four of my SSN from Lt. Col. Perry's OPR. My SSN is considered Personally identifiable information (PII). If you don't know how to handle/protect PII then Google it or ask Lt. Col. Perry."[395] She inexplicably addressed this message not only to the page administrators, but also to my mother, who she

---

[395] Facebook message from Debbie Liddick to "Team Perry," November 14, 2014

incorrectly assumed was somehow responsible for the page. For the record, the Air Force considers the SSN in any form, including truncated to the last four digits, to be PII,[396] but this is not a universal standard across the federal government or industry. (I Googled it.) Nevertheless, "Team Perry" immediately removed the referral OPR, and posted an apology to the page.[397]

This wasn't the last time I ended up getting talked to about "Team Perry" posts. In early January 2015, CAPT McClure again called me to his office. After asking about Caroline's health, he informed me my activity on "Team Perry" was not going unnoticed in certain Air Force circles. He had been told I had "liked" a comment someone else made on that page, about kicking some other person's ass. (I honestly have no idea what he was talking about, and I never was able find the comment he mentioned.) CAPT McClure also mentioned that several days after he called me to his office in September, he noticed "Team Perry" published a post about that conversation.[398] He was very diplomatic about it, acknowledging that someone else might be using my account to "like" stuff, and that Caroline or someone else I talked to could have tipped off the "Team Perry" administrators about our conversation. But he cautioned me that all this Facebook activity was making me look bad, and he recommended I move on.

Tired of being blamed for stupid stuff I didn't do, I took his advice, and refrained from "liking" or commenting on any further "Team Perry" posts until I retired several months later.

When the *Air Force Times* broke my story at the end of May 2014, there was a mixed reaction within the Air Force ISR community. Many of my colleagues spontaneously reached out to me to commiserate, and literally hundreds of former coworkers and subordinates "liked" the "Team Perry" page supporting my cause. Included in this number were at handful of retired Air Force general officers, colonels, and senior civilians, as well as dozens of field-grade intelligence officers with whom I had worked over the

---

[396] AFI 33-332, *Air Force Privacy and Civil Liberties Program*, paragraph 5.4
[397] "Team Perry" Facebook post, November 14, 2014
[398] "Team Perry" Facebook post, September 21, 2014

years.   Notably absent from the "Team Perry" bandwagon, however, were any sitting intelligence squadron commanders or active-duty senior leaders.   In fact, several of my O-6 friends who had been privately offering encouragement after I was removed from command stopped conversing with me altogether once the media got ahold of my story.   One of my peers sent a personal note explaining that she couldn't "like" the "Team Perry" page since her husband was a sitting commander – "I have to very careful of optics," she wrote – but she wanted me to know she really felt for me and wished she could do more.   I'd like to think this was a common sentiment among those who remained silent.

On the other hand, there was a genuine outpouring of support from airman at BMT.   "When I found Team Perry on Facebook, it gave me a glimpse of hope," one former subordinate later wrote me.   "I believed every word that Team Perry presented on your behalf.   I believed, because it was happening to me as well, and no one would do one damn thing about it." She continued, "To this day it truly bothers me that no one advocated for me and my issues.   You brought it to people's attention, and they listened to you, but nothing happened."   Another MTI wrote, "As odd as it seems, your situation gave me strength.   I figured if it happened at your level, things were wrong and I had to fight the broke system.   See you were a mentor and didn't even know it!   Thank you for that."

Caroline experienced her own ostracism within my professional community.   The wife of one of my former colleagues – whom she had met when I was stationed at the Pentagon – was a freelance writer for *Military Spouse Magazine*, and she contacted my wife for an interview soon after our online story went viral.   However, she never did publish an article, claiming her editors didn't find it newsworthy – even after my wife was featured defending her husband on the cover of the *Air Force Times*.   Caroline was arguably the best-known military spouse in the world at that particular moment, but this made her anathema to many of her peers.

For example, an acquaintance whose husband worked at AFISRA headquarters, Heather Walrath, unexpectedly launched a broadside attack in response to one of Caroline's Facebook posts.   "I dare to say that there is no other 'company' that takes care of its people as well as the United States Air Force," she wrote, "and it has been my experience that the Air Force is made up of a huge number of good people constantly putting their service for their fellow airmen above themselves. It is a good place, a great family. I hope you find what you are looking for somewhere else, because you continue to make it clear that the Air Force is not a family you want to be a part of. Good luck to you wherever you endeavors and skills take you. As for me, it continues to be an honor to be a part of this fantastic organization. It is bigger than me, bigger than you, and will forever be a special place for the elite few that still chose to serve."

My wife's response was classic Caroline, and worth repeating at length. "I had no idea you felt that way since I haven't heard from you during this whole ordeal," she began, and although she appreciated the support, she didn't need anyone to feel sorry for her. "I know it must be difficult to know what actually happened since we haven't talked in these last six months," Caroline continued, "and all you have to go on is the media, rumors, and conjecture," but "I have never said that I didn't want to be part of the Air Force family." On the contrary, she wrote, "I love the Air Force as does my husband," so "it is incumbent upon us to do something when we see an injustice, an abuse, or corruption." Not knowing when to quit, Mrs. Walrath persisted. "I certainly understand your devotion to stand by your husband even when mistakes have been made," she replied, but it "pains me deeply to see something I love and respect dragged through the mud." Needless to say, these two aren't friends anymore.

But perhaps the most inexcusable rejection of all came from the AFISRA Key Spouses themselves. Caroline had already met the commander's wife, Laura Shanahan, as well the AFISRA director of staff's spouse, Shiela Williams, at a Lackland officers' spouses' club event the previous year, while I was still in command. These two ladies were responsible for the headquarters Key Spouse program, for which Maj. Gen. Shanahan was an outspoken advocate. He even published one of his trademark "Shanagrams" on this program in August 2013, reiterating to his subordinates that "our real strength comes from our people" and "the family is front and center." He noted that, with just a little investment of time by unit leadership and volunteers, the Key Spouse program "can make the difference between a good and a great organization," and he helpfully provided his wife's e-mail address and a link to the AFISRA spouse's group Facebook page.[399]

---

[399] Maj. Gen. Shanahan, "SHANAGRAM #6: The Key Spouse Program," August 15, 2013

We weren't surprised when no one welcomed us to AFISRA after I reported for duty, given the notoriety surrounding my curious case. But when Caroline tried to contact Mrs. Shanahan and Mrs. Williams, she received no response, and they even blocked her from the AFISRA Key Spouse Facebook page they administered. In September 2014, I reached out to Mr. Williams, a senior civilian with whom I had worked at various points throughout my career, and who had even gone out of his way to attend my change of command ceremony the previous summer. We were friends on Facebook at that time, so I sent him a message asking for his wife's contact information so Caroline could get in touch with her about the AFISRA Key Spouse program. His response? "Sorry, no craig."

I was completely blindsided by this reaction. Was Mrs. Williams not involved in the program? I asked. Is there someone else we should reach out to? "Caroline could really use the support of her fellow spouses after all that we've been through," I wrote. "It almost feels like we're being isolated on purpose. Is there some issue we're not aware of?"[400] Crickets. I mentioned this snub to my leadership at the JIOWC soon afterwards, and I received an unexpected phone call from the AFISRA director of staff later that day. Mr. Williams inquired after Caroline's health, and offered his wife's e-mail address and phone number. Yet when Caroline again attempted to contact Mrs. Shanahan and Mrs. Williams, she still received no response, and her husband "unfriended" me on Facebook shortly thereafter. Apparently taking care of people and their families wasn't as big a priority in my new command as we'd been led to believe.

It was never very realistic for me to hope I might be selected for promotion to Colonel less than a year after my relief of command, and the odds became longer and longer as the date of the board approached in November 2014. My promotion folder would feature my most recent officer performance reports, with the hateful referral OPR sitting on top. It would also contain the letter of reprimand that triggered that derogatory evaluation, as

---

[400] Facebook message exchange with Ken Williams, September 12-13, 2014

well as the memorandum reflecting my de-selection for senior developmental education. The most important document in the officer selection record, however, would be my promotion recommendation form, signed by my senior rater, Maj. Gen. Shanahan.

In the best-case scenario, the Air Force would have acknowledged I was wronged, rescind my LOR and remove it from my OSR before the board met, and pull the referral OPR from my records. In this exceedingly unlikely scenario, there was a remote chance that Maj. Gen. Shanahan would give me a "promote" or "definitely promote" recommendation on my PRF, and I might actually be selected by the board. By late summer, however, it was clear this simply wasn't going to happen, as all my appeals had been denied or ignored.

Another option outlined in an Air Force instruction was for the "wing commander or issuing authority, whichever is higher," to direct early removal of my LOR from the OSR prior to the promotion board, but this should only be considered in "rare instances, as an exception to policy."[401] Since the LOR was issued to me by the 37 TRW commander, it wasn't clear if Maj. Gen. Shanahan had the authority to do this, and on top of that he would have to give me a positive promotion recommendation. However, there was nothing in my interactions with my senior rater that suggested he would consider such a course of action, and it was highly doubtful he would be willing to push me for promotion over some other, less controversial officer unless the Air Force first admitted it made a mistake in my case.

Maj. Gen. Shanahan removed all doubt as to his opinion of me in early October, when he presented me my PRF. He told me he had "no choice" but to recommend I not be promoted because of my LOR and unfavorable information file. "Do not promote Lt. Col. Perry this board," he wrote on the form, "due to his pattern of misconduct which resulted in an LOR and removal from scheduled training." Specifically, he claimed I "[c]reated appearance of unprofessional relationship/favoritism with subordinate personnel," and "[w]rongfully removed LOR from subordinate personal information file which was not his authority to do so."[402] Beyond the awful grammar, these comments did not reflect the

---

[401] AFI 36-2608, *Military Personnel Records System*, August 30, 2006
[402] Maj. Gen. Shanahan, AF Form 709, *Promotion Recommendation*, P0614C board (2014)

findings of my commander-directed investigation or resulting LOR, as I explained to him in an e-mail.

First of all, there was no evidence of a pattern of misconduct on my part; on the contrary, the investigating officer noted after Col. Liddick counseled me for some act, "no other incidents of this behavior were noted," suggesting there was no such pattern. Secondly, he wrote that I "wrongfully" removed a document without authority to do so, but that was simply not true. "Sir, by now I hope you've realized that the way my case has been handled is highly irregular," I wrote, before providing a brief overview of my frustrating case. "More recently, you yourself experienced similar frustration in dealing with 37 TRW regarding my case," I reminded him, "when someone apparently misinformed you about my relationship with a retiring NCO," TSgt Jordan.

Finally, his claim that he had "no choice" but to issue a "DNP" recommendation was nonsense. Given my distinguished record, "I believe I still have much to offer the Air Force and the ISR community," I wrote, "but I cannot be effective while my family and I continue to be neglected, slandered, and abused. As you know," I continued, "this mistreatment has persisted even after my reassignment to your command, as I have been needlessly subjected to a no-contact order, and every attempt by my terminally-ill wife to communicate with headquarters Key Spouses has been ignored or rejected."[403] Not surprisingly, my senior rater disregarded this appeal.

My last recourse was to write a letter to the central selection board. "You may already be familiar with my 'curious case,'" my letter began, a reference to the media attention my unfair treatment over the past year had garnered. "It is truly an unbelievable story: After relieving me of command without clear cause, my chain of command subjected me to arbitrary and capricious administrative actions, while the Air Force has repeatedly failed to observe due process in resolving my complaints." I explained how I came to be selected for command, and the circumstances that lead to my removal. "Had my mistreatment ended there, I probably wouldn't be writing this letter now," I continued. I next recounted how "my chain of command seemed determined to destroy my career," while Air Force leaders had "closed ranks around the questionable decisions

---

[403] E-mail to Maj. Gen. Shanahan, "PRF correction," October 17, 2014

by my immediate chain of command." I urged them to consider my entire service record when evaluating my suitability for promotion, as my selection for command at BMT was no accident. "The wrongs that have been done to me are clearly unfair, and have seemingly ruined my once promising Air Force career," I concluded. "But it's not yet too late to correct this injustice."[404]

The results of this board were entirely anticlimactic when they were released in February 2015. I wasn't surprised when I didn't find my name on the promotion list, but the promotion statistics from this board only added insult to injury. You see, the selection rate for officers in a non-rated operations career field like mine, who attended (or were selected to attend) senior developmental education in residence, was 100 percent. In other words, had I not been removed from command and reprimanded, there is virtually no doubt I would have been promoted to Colonel – regardless of whether I received a "promote" or "definitely promote" recommendation from my senior rater.

When enlisted airmen engage in significant misconduct, meriting nonjudicial punishment or worse, commanders and courts-martial can reduce them in rank, taking one or more stripes as punishment. I was never accused of anything so serious, and was merely subjected to administrative actions, yet the Air Force essentially redlined my next promotion without due process. The financial implications of this preemptive rank reduction are sobering. An O-6 with over 22 years of service (which is about when I would have expected to pin on) makes about $1,236 more in salary and housing allowance per month than an O-5 with the same time in service. Compound this over the length of my career – which would likely have been several years longer as a full-bird Colonel, with additional active-duty service commitments for promotion and school attendance – and the difference is considerable. And it only gets worse in retirement, as I can expect to receive 63 percent less in retired pay over the next 30 years than if I punched out a few years later as an O-6. That's a difference of over a million dollars – all for a few flimsy, not-quite-proven allegations.

One name I was surprised to see on the list that year was Lt. Col. Matthew McConnell, the officer appointed to conduct my commander-directed investigation. It's not that I question his suitability for promotion, but rather the appropriateness of him

---

[404] "Letter to the Central Selection Board (CSB)," November 5, 2014

influencing my fate while we were both competing for promotion to Colonel in our primary zone. Even worse, we were also in competition with each other for wing-level stratification, as well as "definitely promote" recommendations from our senior rater at the time. This was an obvious conflict of interest that should have precluded Col. Camerer from appointing him as investigating officer. It is indeed ironic that Lt. Col. McConnell noted a witness in my case had something to gain personally from how a particular activity was conducted, when the investigating officer himself stood to benefit from the outcome of this CDI.

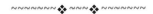

Being passed over for promotion in my primary zone was a demoralizing blow, but it didn't necessarily spell the end of my career. I could continue on active duty as on O-5 until I reached 28 years of service, and I would be given the opportunity to compete again and again for promotion. However, the percentage of those selected above the zone each year was miniscule, so I would have to find some way to distinguish myself from my peers.

Such an opportunity seemed to present itself in August 2014, when the Olmsted Foundation invited me to attend an annual political science symposium at the United States Air Force Academy. The topic for the 56th-annual "Academy Assembly" in February 2015 was U.S.-Russia relations, and I was one of several Olmsted Scholars with background in the region asked to participate on a panel with prominent foreign-policy experts, including the keynote speaker, former U.S. Ambassador to Russia Michael McFaul. I would also lead roundtable discussions with the cadets on my experience as the first-ever Air Force scholar in Russia. I was really looking forward to seeing some of my former colleagues again, and perhaps vacationing with Caroline for a few days in Colorado Springs.

And then, suddenly, I was disinvited. The head of the USAFA political science department, Col. Cheryl Kearney, sent me a note on January 13, just three weeks before the event, asking me to give her a call. A fellow intelligence officer, she claimed she was initially unaware of my circumstances, but someone in the philosophy department brought to her attention the fact that I'd been relieved of command. She told me she wanted "to set the cadets up for success," so it was best that I not be part of a leadership roundtable, as this would open up all sorts of questions for them. I was later informed I had inadvertently set this chain of events in motion myself, when I contacted someone at the Academy seeking feedback on my commander-directed investigation. When Col. Kearney learned of this, she apparently brought it to the dean of faculty, Brig. Gen. Andrew Armacost, who decided it would send the wrong signal for me to serve as a roundtable leader. They initially considered allowing me to attend in some other capacity, but ultimately opted to cancel my invitation altogether.

The Olmsted Foundation was well aware of my curious case before they extended the invitation, so they naturally came to my defense. The vice president of the Foundation, a USAFA alumnus and retired fighter pilot, expressed his strong opinion to Col. Kearney that the Air Force had screwed up but was unwilling to admit it. He reportedly compared my case to that of Brig. Gen. (ret.) Terry Schwalier, whose career was unfairly cut short after the Khobar Towers bombing in 1996. In an e-mail to me, he noted, "No one said life would be fair and it is clear to me that there is a crisis of leadership in DoD and all of the Services," and it was a shame my wife and I got caught in the crossfire when our hearts were in the right place. "Rest assured that you have in no way caused any discredit on The Foundation," he consoled me. "Things just happen sometimes."[405]

When I was invited to participate in this Academy Assembly, I saw a light at the end of the tunnel, a way to begin redeeming myself and put what happened the previous year behind me. But the Air Force wouldn't let me move on. They concluded my experience as an Olmsted Scholar in Russia was less important – even in a purely academic setting – than whatever success I experienced during my brief tenure as a squadron commander. This was a shame, since the Academy could have approached this as a teachable moment for their cadets, or simply instructed me to exercise discretion while in Colorado Springs. Instead, they effectively signaled to their cadets that ours is a one-mistake Air Force – all the more ironic, as none of the allegations against me concerned my character or any behavior that violates the USAFA Honor Code. And this decision was just the latest made with absolutely no input from me.

---

[405] E-mail exchange with Olmsted Foundation vice president, "USAFA Assembly," January 14, 2015

Did my lack of success as a squadron commander really negate my 19 years of service leading up to that debacle? Were those three years of my career spent learning Russian and earning a master's degree really of no further use to the Air Force? Where was the "reset" button for my career?

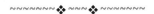

Rather than traveling to Colorado for the Academy Assembly in early February, I found myself consulting with another mentor of mine about my career options. Maj. Gen. "Dash" Jamieson was my commander in the 32d Air Intelligence Squadron at Ramstein Airbase, Germany, more than a decade earlier, and our paths had occasionally crossed in the years since. She suffered her own career setbacks along the way, but managed to persevere and earn a second star in 2013. I hoped she could offer some advice for what I ought to do next. I felt I still had a lot to offer the Air Force, I explained to her, but after everything that happened, perhaps it was time for me to retire already. I could always try to find a job as a contractor or government civilian in the Intelligence Community or cyberspace field, I reasoned, or else I might join the Foreign Service. Caroline and I were willing to relocate back to the East Coast or overseas, as my hometown had taken on some bad associations recently.

Maj. Gen. Jamieson made some inquires to determine whether there was a plan to move me that summer, so I could get a fresh start away from my current command. (AFISRA had been re-designated 25th Air Force in October 2014, and realigned under Air Combat Command). She apologized that she couldn't bring me up to Joint Base Langley-Eustis, Virginia, where she was director of intelligence at Air Combat Command headquarters, as there weren't any positions available on her staff. Moreover, based on her conversations with officials at Air Force Personnel Center and other senior intelligence officers, no one else had expressed an interest in hiring me.

As it turns out, that wasn't entirely true. Unbeknownst to Maj. Gen. Jamieson, another general officer had in fact asked that I come work for him, to leverage my particular background and skills against his command's mission set. However, this by-name request apparently wasn't well received at the Pentagon, since such prestigious assignments are typically reserved for officers with a potential for future promotion. It looked as if I would be stuck in San Antonio indefinitely, should I choose to remain in the Air Force.

When Gen. Rand denied my Christmas Eve appeal a few weeks later, I was done. As I discussed in an earlier chapter, this was a particularly cruel rejection. After his staff strung me along for more than six weeks, the AETC commander suddenly claimed he was in no position to help me, then went out of his way to dissuade my current chain of command from helping me either. The announcement of his nomination for a prominent new position just days later was icing on the cake. This was the last straw, an unambiguous signal that the Air Force I had faithfully served for over two decades had no further use for me. The following day, I put in my papers to retire.

Getting out of the Air Force turned out to be easier said than done. Retirement applications typically take about four to six weeks to process, but I was still waiting to hear something two months later. When I checked on the status of my application, AFPC informed me they were awaiting an officer grade determination package from my 25 AF leadership. This process allows commanders to recommend applicants retire in a lower grade than they currently hold, based on their last period of "satisfactory" service. If Maj. Gen. Shanahan were contemplating such a step in my case, he would have to notify me in writing and give me 10 days to respond before proceeding with this recommendation. However, since I had already served in the grade of Lieutenant Colonel for over three years by the time I assumed command at JBSA-Lackland, I would presumably still retire in this grade in any case. Thankfully, when I contacted the 25 AF director of staff, Mr. Williams, about this issue, he reassured me an officer grade determination was not needed, and my retirement was approved a week later.

When I first put in for retirement, I was at a low point in my career. I wasn't feeling much like celebrating, and I didn't see the point of conducting a ceremony. But when Maj. Gen. Jamieson graciously agreed to officiate this event – which coincided with a trip she was making down to San Antonio in early August for official business – I resolved to go through with it after all. I wanted this day to be memorable, and not just another mundane gathering inside a nondescript room on a military base, so I booked a local venue with deep significance for me as a San Antonio native: the historic Japanese Tea Garden in Brackenridge Park, near the neighborhood where I attended school growing up.

My chain of command continued dragging its feet regarding my retirement right up to the end. It wasn't clear whether Maj. Gen. Shanahan would approve my retirement medal until he signed it just days before my ceremony, then 25 AF scheduled their change of command, followed by a promotion ceremony for the outgoing commander, for the same date – August 3 – as my event. Luckily, Maj. Gen. Jamieson was able to pull off these early afternoon engagements and still preside over my retirement later that day. After being so unfairly treated within the Air Force ISR community over the past several years, it was incredibly gratifying to be honored by the highest-ranking USAF intelligence officer on my last day in uniform.

The turnout for this event, held under a shady pagoda overlooking the beautiful gardens below, was much higher than I dared expect, especially given the extreme heat that August afternoon. My family naturally came out in full force, as did Hamant Kalidas, a friend who drove in from Houston to offer a stirring rendition of the National Anthem. In addition to my current JIOWC leadership and a senior civilian from the 25 AF staff, the front row also featured Col. Glenn Palmer and CMSgt Ken Williams, both retired. I was particularly pleased that some of my former subordinates agreed to participate in the ceremony. MSgt Art Ayala, who once led the 737 TRSS personnel processing flight, was the narrator for this event, and two "Blue Rope" MTIs – SMSgt Ricardo Chavez and MSgt (sel.) Luis Mercado – conducted a moving flag-folding ceremony in honor of my retirement from active duty. They were joined by a couple of members of the 25 AF staff who selflessly volunteered to help out.

"It is such a blessing to me," I noted in my remarks, "if I have to finish my career anywhere, that I do it here in San Antonio." I loved growing up in this city, but I knew I wasn't going to spend my whole life there. "I was eager to go out and see the world, and continue my education, and hopefully do something that felt important, like I was making a difference," I explained to the audience. "And I have to say, the Air Force gave me all of that. I can't be more grateful [for] the opportunities the Air Force has given me." After briefly recounting my career highlights, I noted how the service helped me develop as a leader. For example, as a young intelligence officer, I learned that if you're preoccupied with building PowerPoint slides for the headquarters, "and not focused on the operational units that actually need that intelligence to go out and kill people and break things, you're doing it wrong."

My ultimate leadership opportunity was as a BMT squadron commander. "It was an awesome responsibility," I acknowledged, "and so far as I know, I've not heard any indications that I wasn't doing a good job" in accomplishing the mission. I also focused on staff development, increasing unit cohesion and esprit de corps, and improving the family support network. "Rumor has it, morale improved during my few short months in command," I noted, "so I believe we left the 737th Training Support Squadron better than we found it." The audience, which included several airmen profiled in this memoir, seemed to agree.

During the ceremony, I received a touching gift commissioned by an anonymous group of MTIs. It featured a distinctive campaign hat of a master instructor, and designated me as an honorary member of this elite cadre. The inscription reads, "Title of Honorary MTI presented to Lt Col Craig M. Perry, in grateful appreciation for his dedication, service, and zealous advocacy to the MTI corps. Champion of Integrity, Service, and Excellence." SMSgt (ret.) Howie Watkins presented this memento, along with the two flag-folding "Blue Ropes" in attendance.

In my remarks, I didn't hesitate to address the elephant in the room: "Caroline likes to say that everything happens for a reason. And if I'm being honest with you, when I was relieved of command last year, it took us a while to figure out what the reason could possibly be." In the end, we came to realize "there must be a reason all this happened to us, and this is it: It's time to move on to bigger and better things." I would start by going back to school, then maybe find a job. "In the meantime, I think I might take a little bit of time to work on a book I've been writing about my recent experiences," I hinted. But there's one thing I was sure of: "I have no regrets about the way I led my squadron, or the manner in which I served my country."

However, I did confess to one mistake I wished I could fix: "I would have married the love of my life much, much sooner." I couldn't thank Caroline enough for standing by me after all we'd been through. "We promised to have and to hold each other for better or for worse, in sickness and in health, for richer or for poorer ... and we've experienced all that in the last few years," I joked. "But I wouldn't trade one moment with you." Not surprisingly, Caroline pretty much stole the show that day. Maj.

Gen. Jamieson praised her for her impact on the airmen and families of BMT, as well as the teamwork she and I demonstrated. When my wife came forward to affix my retirement pin on my uniform – short-sleeve blues, owing to the heat – she experienced déjà vu: "You know, last time I was up on a stage pinning something on it was your commander's badge," she recalled, "but I don't see it … it must have fallen off."

Moments later, it was her turn to be honored. The officiating officer presented Caroline the obligatory certificate of appreciation – signed, with no apparent sense of irony, by a couple of general officers who figured prominently in my premature retirement. The next presentation was much more personal, when a couple of Air Force wives stepped up to honor this former Key Spouse Mentor. They read letters from some of the folks whose lives she touched, and presented her a collage of photos of her time at Lackland. Not to be outdone, Caroline had an unexpected presentation of her own. As the emcee announced the end of the ceremony, she shouted out, "Wait, I have something for you!" She unveiled a portrait she had secretly painted of the two of us, an uncanny reproduction of our favorite wedding-day photograph.

I ended my remarks with a quote from the legendary Colonel John Boyd, who used to say each of us will come to a fork in the road, and "you're going to have to make a decision about which direction you want to go."

> *If you go* that *way you can be somebody. You will have to make compromises and you will have to turn your back on your friends. But you will be a member of the club and you will get promoted and you will get good assignments. Or you can go* that *way and you can do something – something for your country and for your Air Force and for yourself. If you decide you want to do something, you may not get promoted and you may not get the good assignments and you certainly will not be a favorite of your superiors. But you won't have to compromise yourself. You will be true to your friends and to yourself. And your work might make a difference. To be somebody or to do something. In life there is often a roll call. That's when you will have to make a decision. To be or to do? Which way will you go?*

"Looking back on my career," I concluded, "I am proud of which way I went. I did something, and I never compromised myself."

Before I stepped off the stage, I recited the closing words of the Airman's Creed, which I felt summed up my career: "I am an American Airman. Wingman, Leader, Warrior. I will never leave an Airman behind, I will never falter, and I will not fail."

Chapter 17: Beyond Basic

With the departure of Debbie Liddick and Mark Camerer from Lackland in 2014, there were high hopes among the airmen left behind that the local command climate would improve. Colonel Liddick retired in early June, surrounded by armed guards and faint praise from the wing commander, before heading off to obscurity in South Dakota. Col. Camerer relinquished his post less than two weeks later, followed immediately by a promotion ceremony at JBSA-Randolph presided over by the Air Education and Training Command boss, General Rand, and his predecessor, General Rice. He was off to bigger and better things in Germany, seemingly unaffected by the formal complaints still pending against him. It is perhaps some consolation, then, that Brig. Gen. Camerer has reportedly struggled in his new job, where he quickly earned a reputation as an arrogant and abusive staff officer. To paraphrase a "Brown's Bag" aphorism, his connections have apparently taken him to a position his character cannot sustain.

In choosing replacements for these notoriously toxic leaders, AETC had an opportunity to avoid the mistakes of the past. However, the first officer they selected to lead Basic Military Training, Col. David Coley, actually turned down the opportunity, choosing instead to retire from the Air Force. AETC's second choice was drawn from the same playbook used to select her predecessor: a female officer with experience as an AETC group commander. Unlike Liddick, however, Col. Michele Edmondson led a training group at Vandenberg AFB, California, where she reported directly to the Second Air Force commander, Maj. Gen. Patrick. The new wing commander, Col. Trent Edwards, was an AETC veteran as well, the former wing king at Maxwell AFB, Alabama.

In tone and temperament, both of these leaders seemed like huge improvements over the noxious Camerer and Liddick. Yet the policies they implemented were hardly distinguishable from those of their predecessors. For example, on his first full day in the office after assuming command, Col. Edwards' issued a prohibition against audio or video recording any official meetings or conversations within the 37th Training Wing unless all parties consented. He claimed this order was "designed to encourage the free expression of ideas and communications" within the wing,[406] but it was more likely meant to keep subordinates from holding their leadership accountable, as several of us had tried to do under the previous regime. Not surprisingly, this ill-conceived policy had unanticipated results, as we will see below.

The following week, Col. Edwards and his staff convinced my new commander to impose a six-month no-contact order on me, merely for taking photos at a public event. As I discussed in the preceding chapter, the "Team Perry" Facebook page reposted some of these pictures, adding new captions about folks such as the BMT superintendent, CMSgt Sutherland, who contributed to my relief of command. The no-contact order was supposedly to protect the "usefulness" of members of the command, a not-so-subtle reference to the subjects of these photos – and an inadvertent admission that CMSgt Sutherland and others were merely tools, whose utility could be damaged by someone pointing out their utter unsuitability for their current positions.

The new 737th Training Group commander, Col. Edmondson, no doubt supported such unwarranted restrictions on me, and must have lobbied to maintain them a few months later when I asked to attend a retirement ceremony on her turf. She or her staff lied about whether I had been invited or even knew the retiree, setting my two-star boss up for embarrassment in a desperate attempt to keep "Public Enemy #1" away from BMT. Still, Col. Edmondson initially seemed like an improvement over her predecessor, if for no other reason than she wasn't Col. Liddick. She came across as much more open-minded and approachable, and her husband was involved in various family support activities.

Col. Edmondson immediately distanced herself from the BMT five-kilometer races over which Liddick demanded control, allowing 737 TRSS personnel to manage these fundraising events. In the process, the newly renamed "Raptor Private Organization" jettisoned the t-shirt vendor Col. Liddick favored, and implemented a plan we developed to lower the cost of entry for trainees. (The vendor later filed complaints and threatened a lawsuit for breach of contract, claiming Col. Liddick had promised him this business. However, she had no authority to make such promises, and there

---

[406] Col. Trent Edwards, "Policy on Recording Conversations for Permanent Party Members Assigned to the 37th Training Wing," June 23, 2014

was no written contract in place. Apparently, he "hitched his wagon to the wrong star" after all.)

It didn't take long, however, for the BMT command climate to revert to its previous malaise. The counterproductive policies and procedures of the Camerer/Liddick era remained largely intact, no matter how much lipstick the new leadership tried to put on that pig. In the absence of any true reforms, or even acknowledgment they had a problem, the pervasive toxic leadership environment soon reasserted itself, and Col. Edmondson's true colors eventually came out. As one of my former colleagues noted, at least with Col. Liddick you knew where you stood, as she made no effort to conceal her disdain for her subordinates; Col. Edmondson, on the other hand, would smile to your face, then stab you in the back. Another officer told me this group commander was the most inauthentic person she had ever met, a sentiment echoed by several of Caroline's fellow spouses.

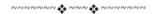

While both Col. Edwards and Col. Edmondson revealed themselves to be flawed leaders, they were not the unmitigated disasters Camerer and Liddick proved themselves to be, and both were soon rewarded for their efforts. Col. Edwards was selected for promotion in January 2015, but allowed to remain in place at Lackland after his position was upgraded to a one-star billet. Before the stand-up of Joint Base San Antonio, a Brigadier General had led the 37 TRW, but that billet moved to JBSA-Fort Sam Houston with its incumbent, then-Brig. Gen. Patrick, when he assumed command of the newly established 502d Air Base Wing in 2009. Finally recognizing the folly of entrusting the Air Force's largest training wing to a Colonel, AETC swapped the O-7 billet of the 81st Training Wing commander for the O-6 leading the 37 TRW. Brig. Gen. Edwards pinned on his new rank in May 2015.

Unlike her predecessor, Col. Edmondson was selected for wing command, of none other than the 81 TRW at Keesler AFB, Mississippi. She departed Lackland in early June 2015, before completing a year as 737 TRG commander. In fact, she served less time in this position than any BMT commander in the previous three decades. Such a short command tour is not common in the Air Force, as it offers insufficient time for the leader to accomplish much in his or her assignment, and too-frequent turnover at the top can compromise organizational effectiveness. Col. Edmondson had only been at BMT for about six months when she was selected for her next job, and had not yet received an officer performance report reflecting her performance to date. (At that point, her most notable achievement was simply not being Liddick.) Under ordinary circumstances, such an officer wouldn't even be considered for wing command so early in the current command assignment.

All of this begs the question: Why would AETC put forward Col. Edmondson as a potential candidate for wing command in 2014, when she had only just begun her current command tour at BMT? After all, she had been passed over by the wing command selection board in 2013, while she was in her final year of group command at Vandenberg. If her commander and rater at the time, Maj. Gen. Patrick, was adamant she should have been given a wing based on her strong performance in that assignment, he likely would have arranged to move her to AETC headquarters or some other staff job where her subsequent selection for wing command wouldn't cause so much disruption. Instead, she was put in charge of the largest training group in the Air Force, coming off one of the most tumultuous periods in its history, when stability and solid leadership were sorely needed. Pushing Col. Edmondson to wing command under such circumstances makes little sense as deliberate career progression.

So why was Col. Edmondson removed from BMT so early? My guess is Maj. Gen. Patrick, who had since become AETC vice commander, pursued this course of action to protect a vulnerable subordinate. Perhaps he sincerely hoped she would be able to clean up the mess Col. Liddick left behind, and might have left her in charge the 737 TRG for a full two years if she appeared to be making significant progress. But when it became clear she would be unable to quickly undo the damage of the Camerer/Liddick era, her mentor may have opted to pull the plug on her assignment so as to salvage her promising career. Maj. Gen. Patrick couldn't simply reassign her without prompting questions about her performance, but her selection for a higher-level command wouldn't raise many eyebrows. If my theory is correct, Col. Edmondson was pushed for wing command to keep BMT from tarnishing her career, as it had those of so many other officers.

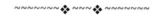

Another officer whose career didn't survive a command tour at BMT was my former colleague, Lieutenant Colonel Dat Lam. A Vietnamese refugee, Dat had distinguished himself in the Air Force, and was serving as commander of the 627th Civil Engineer Squadron at Joint Base Lewis-McChord, Washington, when he was selected for command of the 322d Training Squadron. In response to Maj. Gen. Woodward's call for high-caliber, well-qualified officers, he was one of half a dozen chosen to assume command at BMT in 2013. Like Lt. Col. Liz Valenzuela, however, he was a frequent target of harassment by Col. Liddick, who seemed to think he was not as intelligent as his peers. But like Liz, Dat was able to put an end to the most egregious threats and intimidation from his boss, after he informed her he no longer trusted her and so was recording their conversations.

Lt. Col. Lam was among the several squadron commanders who filed inspector general complaints against Col. Liddick, and he wrote a character reference on my behalf when I was removed from command. Dat even came to visit me in my windowless office across base while I was awaiting news of my fate, the only one of my peers to do so. Nevertheless, he and his wife, Rissa, drifted away from Caroline and me after I was relieved of command. Our two spouses got together only once more before the *Air Force Times* broke my story at the end of May 2014, and Rissa stopped communicating with my wife altogether on June 25, the very day Caroline was planning to meet with a 322 TRS Military Training Instructor who may have had information helpful to my case. Dat ordered his subordinate to have no further contact with us, and neither he nor his wife has spoken to us since. They likely feared the backlash he would suffer if he appeared too close to us.

Lt. Col. Lam developed a reputation as a commander who was tough on the trainees under his care. He often expressed the opinion that, with all the reforms implemented in the wake of the Lackland sex scandal, BMT had sacrificed intensity for safety, producing airmen who were less disciplined, respectful, and resilient than in previous years. He believed in the shock value of basic training, and encouraged his MTIs to subject new recruits to stressful situations on at least three occasions during their short time at Lackland: pickup night, when they first arrived at Lackland; shakedown, a very loud and intense dorm inspection attended by the squadron commander; and their first time through the dining facility, where they were required to sit at attention while eating. The intent of such tactics was to inoculate trainees to stress, not through abuse and mistreatment but by imposing the kinds of useful stressors – *eustress*, as opposed to *distress* – necessary to build "warrior airmen of character." Feedback from graduating airmen was generally positive, and many praised Lt. Col. Lam for his leadership by example, especially during daily physical training. However, his time-honored tactics may have seemed cruel or mean-spirited to some trainees, and they were at odds with the myriad restrictions implemented under Col. Liddick.

Complaints soon began to trickle in to group leadership, from both trainees and other commanders and enlisted leaders. When Col. Edmondson asked Lt. Col. Lam to brief her on what he was doing to make his squadron the best at BMT, he seemed excited to share with her his unorthodox approach to training. However, it soon became clear she did not approve of his methodology, and she was actually there to get to the bottom of the complaints. The following day, Lt. Col. Lam informed his staff they were no longer allowed to yell at trainees or make them sit at attention during meals, and they would only train according to the most basic standard, nothing more. With tears in his eyes, he announced he had just been trying to make a difference, but he didn't want to put anyone's career in jeopardy.

Late in 2014, Lt. Col. Lam was again selected for command, of the 60th Civil Engineer Squadron at Travis AFB, California, where he and his family would relocate after his current BMT command tour ended in 2015. Whatever his leadership at Lackland thought of him, Dat was obviously still well enough regarded within his own career field to be offered yet another coveted leadership assignment, his third straight. Just weeks later, however, his BMT career began to unravel. In early December, an entire flight of trainees was transferred out of the 322 TRS to a sister squadron, supposedly because they did not feel comfortable reporting misconduct up their chain of command. This was a highly unusual development. When BMT leadership receives such critiques, blame typically, falls squarely on the flight's instructors, whose campaign hats are often removed while their alleged misconduct is investigated. However, there were indications the MTIs also shared this perception of their squadron leadership, suggesting a broader problem within this unit.

The following week, Col. Edmondson launched a commander-directed investigation against Lt. Col. Lam over allegations he abused his subordinates and restricted them from reporting alleged misconduct within the squadron. This behavior apparently came to light after a member of the 737 TRG staff received multiple trainee critiques about the 322 TRS commander. When no action was taken at Lackland to address these complaints, he eventually contacted his colleagues at 2 AF regarding his concerns. However, unlike in my curious case, Dat was allowed to remain in command while this investigation proceeded. Such an arrangement is not unusual when the commander is suspected of relatively minor misconduct that affects only a small number of subordinates. For example, Lt. Col. Valenzuela was left in command each time she was investigated over trivial matters, and I arguably should have been afforded the same courtesy during my CDI.

However, this seemed an odd way to handle an inquiry into allegations against the 322 TRS commander, who was rumored to have engaged in widespread abuse and intimidation. But rather than remove the officer accused of fostering the potentially unhealthy command climate, BMT leadership instead removed an entire flight of his subordinates. (Ironically, after being granted asylum in another squadron, these refugees went on to distinguish themselves in January 2015 as a BMT "Honor Flight" – and their new MTIs were recognized as 37 TRW "Performers of the Week" for saving them from disaster.) On the other hand, when a 322 TRS senior noncommissioned officer was accused of telling trainees not to use the critique system, he was removed from the squadron pending investigation. Col. Edmondson supposedly advised Lt. Col. Lam not to communicate with this wayward MTI, but the squadron commander apparently continued checking on him on a weekly basis, demonstrating a loyalty that belied his reputation for mistreating subordinates.

Col. Edmondson assumed command of BMT just as my "curious case" was making headlines, raising troubling questions about how the bogus allegations against me were handled. Although she subtly distanced herself from her predecessor, and slowly seemed to be improving the command climate at BMT, when rumors of misconduct by another squadron commander began to circulate, she seemed hesitant to take decisive action. Perhaps she was concerned Lt. Col. Lam's removal from command pending investigation would jeopardize his next command, and she almost certainly wanted to avoid following in the footsteps of Col. Liddick. She may also have feared firing another squadron commander would lead to a reprise of the "Perry situation," a public relations disaster.

For their part, my fellow BMT squadron commanders probably figured lightning wouldn't strike twice, and so there was little chance any of them would be relieved after my debacle. Such a perspective missed the entire point of my "curious case," which had little to do with my removal from command – and everything to do with the ridiculous reasons cited for my relief, the unjustified destruction of my career, and the Air Force's stubborn unwillingness to admit mistakes were made. Moreover, two wrongs don't make a right. Justice would not have been served by failing to properly discipline wayward BMT commanders, just because things went south the last time the chain of command tried it. Rather, it is the very perversion of justice in my case that made the handling of allegations against the 322 TRS commander so troubling. Any further public relations disaster could have been avoided by simply exonerating me.

Not surprisingly, the investigation against the 322 TRS commander initially failed to turn up much evidence of wrongdoing. With Lt. Col. Lam still in place, any witnesses to misconduct would naturally be hesitant to speak out against their commander. More troublingly, there was said to be a recording of Lt. Col. Lam encouraging his MTIs to reduce the number of trainee critiques, which he reportedly felt were making him and the squadron look bad. If true, this would be evidence of unlawful restriction on protected communications. However, the purported witness was apparently unwilling to come forward due to the prohibition on recording conversations the wing commander, Col. Edwards, implemented months earlier.

Suppression of potential evidence of wrongdoing was a predictable result of promulgating a no-recording policy, which contradicted state and federal "one-party consent" laws. This was cruelly ironic. After the Woodward report found barriers existed to trainees reporting allegations of sexual assault, sexual harassment, unprofessional relationships, maltreatment, and maltraining, hotline phones and comment boxes were installed across the BMT campus, and 2 AF implemented a formal alleged misconduct reporting process to ensure trainees and students were not abused or mistreated. Yet less than two years later, in an apparent effort to protect senior leaders from embarrassment, the wing commander perversely stifled reporting of abuses against his subordinates.

Although this ill-advised policy expired in September 2014, it seems not everyone got the message. The damage was done.

At one point, when the new 2 AF commander was visiting Lackland, he and Col. Edmondson were overheard discussing Lt. Col. Lam's CDI. Although this investigation had so far failed to substantiate the allegations against the 322 TRS commander, Maj. Gen. Brown allegedly reassured the group commander she could always fire Dat and say it was for "loss of confidence." Whatever the reason, Lt. Col. Lam was suddenly removed from command and temporarily reassigned on February 12, 2015. The wing refused to comment on the ongoing investigation, but released a confusing statement: "we want to alleviate any concerns that this investigation or the commander's temporary reassignment is not related to sexual misconduct."[407] To underscore his presumption of innocence, Dat was allowed to attend the Air Mobility Command squadron commander's course at Scott AFB, Illinois, later that month, in anticipation of his follow-on assignment. Unfortunately for him, circumstances would prevent him from relocating to California that summer as expected.

Lt. Col. Lam was ultimately relieved of command on April 9, but the official explanation for his firing downplayed his personal culpability. Col. Edmondson lost confidence in his ability to command due to his "repeated inability to enforce compliance with expectations and standards within his squadron," according to an official AETC statement, and his airmen failed to provide trainees opportunities to report alleged mistreatment. "Lt. Col. Lam's subordinate leadership team continued to negatively affect morale and violate standards and training expectations while under his command," the statement continued. "Command is a privilege," the statement reminded readers. "When commanders fail to meet the Air Force's expectations and standards, senior leaders have the responsibility to address the performance and hold them accountable."[408]

The hypocrisy of this statement was staggering, particularly as it pertained to Lackland. Col. Camerer and Col. Liddick repeatedly failed to meet the Air Force's expectations and standards, yet senior leaders never addressed their performance or

---

[407] Jeff Schogol, "Training squadron commander temporarily reassigned," *Air Force Times*, February 23, 2015
[408] Jeff Schogol, "Training squadron commander relieved of command," *Air Force Times*, April 10, 2015

held them accountable – the reported verbal counseling of my boss for "the potential perception that could have been created regarding the moving boxes" notwithstanding. Instead, these toxic leaders were rewarded with an unwarranted promotion and prestigious medal, respectively, despite having created a poisonous command climate that persisted even beyond their departure. Their legacy lived on in many corners of BMT, where several squadron commanders adopted a harsh – some might say tyrannical – style, treating their subordinates with suspicion and disdain and reproducing the toxic leadership environment Col. Liddick fostered. Ironically, many of these officers seemed to be playing against type, ignoring their natural temperaments and previous command experience to fit in at BMT during the Camerer/Liddick era. Those two Colonels took such a brutal approach to alleged misconduct, it's not at all surprising some BMT squadron commanders were worried about critiques coming out of their squadron.

This tendency grew markedly worse after my relief of command, as my unfair treatment encouraged many of my former colleagues to become even more insular and distrustful of their superiors, subordinates, and each other, with even more incentive to suppress any signs of dissatisfaction within their units. As one witness to events in the 322 TRS later relayed to me, unlike other organizations where squadron commanders develop camaraderie, BMT was "just a bunch of officers drowning in a lake," where "there was only one life raft, and they were all willing to push each other down to get to it."

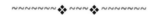

Col. Liddick's signature initiative was the consolidation of MTI on-the-job training into a single unit, the 323d Training Squadron. As I discussed in previous chapters, once MTI students graduated from the schoolhouse in my old squadron, they would accomplish a sort of internship at the 323 TRS, under the guidance of experienced MTIs qualified as trainers. These "apprentice" MTIs remained administratively assigned to the 737 TRSS for as long as three months after graduation, until they demonstrated sufficient proficiency to be deemed "training qualified" and permanently reassigned to one of the line squadrons. During this period, trainers and instructor supervisors in the 323 TRS were entirely responsible for the training plan, but if a new MTI required any counseling or disciplinary action, they would be sent back to the schoolhouse rather than handled on the spot by those familiar with the situation. This was but one of the unanticipated (but entirely predictable) consequences of Col. Liddick's brainchild, an organizational "Frankenstein's monster."

The commander of this "trainer" squadron, Lt. Col. Chad Gallagher, was arguably the most experienced and well-qualified officer who reported to BMT in 2013. This prior-enlisted airman commanded half a dozen Security Forces units before arriving at Lackland, and he was the only one in our group promoted to Lieutenant Colonel ahead of his peers. Chad and I were alone in earning Bronze Stars on deployment, and he, too, was selected to attend senior developmental education in residence – in fact, his follow-on assignment was to Air War College. For all his credentials, however, Lt. Col. Gallagher was clearly worn down by his time in command at BMT. Like Liz, Dat, and me, Chad frequently found himself at odds with Col. Liddick, and he was initially one of her most outspoken critics. However, he soon saw the writing on the wall, and learned to pick his battles with our boss more carefully.

Like other commanders, Lt. Col. Gallagher had his share of run-ins with Col. Liddick over disciplinary issues. I remember him discussing a particular case where an MTI had engaged in some misconduct, and Chad determined he deserved a certain level of punishment based on the circumstances of the case. Col. Liddick disagreed, however, and pressured him to levy harsher punishment. When he refused to submit to her borderline-unlawful command influence, she pulled the case up to her level and hammered the MTI in her usual style.

When I was removed from command, Lt. Col. Gallagher and his wife, Loretta, welcomed Caroline and me to their home for a New Year's Eve party, and he made sure the investigating officer, a fellow cop with whom he had previously worked, was fully aware of Col. Liddick's guidance on personnel information files. On the other hand, Loretta soon began bad-mouthing my wife, and Chad declined to write a character reference letter on my behalf. The Gallaghers had no further contact with us after I was relieved of command, and Lt. Col. Gallagher didn't hesitate to arrange a Security Forces detail for Col. Liddick during her final week in command, ostensibly to protect her from my wife.

Between the toxic leadership of Col. Liddick, and the demands of managing the "trainer" squadron, Lt. Col. Gallagher earned a reputation as a bit of a tyrant. Morale in his squadron was reportedly some of the worst at BMT, and esprit de corps among the "Mustangs" remained weak, reflecting poorly on squadron leadership. Although his MTIs were more experienced and better qualified than the average line instructor, the 323 TRS often didn't measure up to other squadrons in terms of producing new airmen. Interaction between Lt. Col. Gallagher and new recruits seemed awkward and inappropriate to some observers, and according to sources who worked in this and other BMT squadrons, trainees graduating from the 323 TRS were more likely to complain about how they thought BMT was going to be harder. They didn't feel the sense of accomplishment they expected before arriving at Lackland.

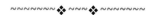

When my position as 737 TRSS commander unexpectedly became vacant in 2014, Col. Liddick didn't hesitate to pick a replacement in her own image. Lt. Col. Jill Murphy already had orders to accompany her husband to JBSA-Randolph that summer, where she expected to be assigned to the AETC headquarters staff. Instead, Col. Liddick selected this fellow maintenance officer to take command of my former squadron. When we heard this officer was coming into town on a house-hunting trip in late April, Caroline and I invited her out to dinner so we could advise her of the challenges she would confront at BMT. Jill claimed never to have met Col. Liddick, but acknowledged her new boss had a reputation within the maintenance community as a toxic leader, which she wrote off as typical of fighter aircraft maintainers. Lt. Col. Murphy assumed command from my treacherous, self-serving operations officer, Maj. Sprouse, in early June, and it wasn't long before she began displaying some of the same leadership flaws as the officer who hired her.

My squadron's family support network quickly unraveled after Caroline and I were barred from BMT, and it has never recovered. Lt. Col. Murphy doesn't welcome each new class of MTI School students like we used to do, and she has apparently made no effort to reach out to families in her squadron. Several wives who served as Key Spouse in other BMT squadrons turned down the opportunity to reprise this role after their husbands were reassigned to the 737 TRSS. Despite our exile from BMT, numerous spouses continue reaching out to Caroline rather than seeking support from their own Key Spouse or commander's better half, and she's often invited to attend luncheons off base with women who weren't even assigned to my squadron.

One wife who did volunteer as 737 TRSS Key Spouse found herself so isolated within the squadron, she felt compelled to post a plea for help on a MTI spouse social networking page: "I have absolutely no support with the 737th to try to reach incoming families...my rosters are all out of date so if [you're] new or your husband is currently assigned to the school house either teacher or student please let me know so I can add you to our facebook page and get you on our email list for our monthly news letter. TIA! [I'm] trying to reach out the best I can with what little support I have :/"

In addition to appearing uncaring and disinterested, Lt. Col. Murphy has also gained a reputation as an arrogant, transactional leader. She is reportedly abusive to her subordinates, and she quickly alienated her fellow squadron commanders with her condescending, unfriendly style. When Lt. Col. Valenzuela's wife, Bunny, arranged with Col. Edmondson to conduct the annual BMT children's holiday party at the Pfingston Reception Center, she was chewed out for not coordinating with the squadron commander on the use of her building. (After all, it was Jill who attended the dedication ceremony for this facility in July 2014.[409]) On the bright side, Lt. Col. Murphy didn't make the same mistake I did in trusting her squadron key leaders. She coordinated the transfer of the duplicitous Maj. Sprouse to another squadron, and almost managed to get rid of SMSgt Walls as well. After all the lies they told to get me fired, these co-conspirators likely soon realized the grass isn't always greener on the other side.

Lt. Col. Murphy also ruined Thanksgiving for BMT squadron commanders and their families. As I discussed in an earlier chapter, the 737 TRSS commander would traditionally accompany a couple of trainee flights to the Cypress Grille in Boerne, Texas, along with their squadron commander, and each officer would bring along his or her family to join the festivities. Lt. Col. Murphy expressed concern that family members were enjoying a free meal, and the group staff agreed, concluding that this long-standing practice violates federal ethics standards regarding gifts

---

[409] Mike Joseph, "Basic Military Training opens new reception center; honors past, looks to future," AETC official site, July 31, 2014

from outside sources. Not wanting to force squadron commanders and other senior leaders to spend Thanksgiving without their families, they delegated the responsibility for chaperoning to other BMT staff members already on shift that day. However, this is a misinterpretation of the relevant regulation, which creates an exception for social invitations from non-prohibited sources – those not seeking to do business with, or regulated by, an Air Force agency – where no fee is charged to any in attendance.[410] While this regulation doesn't specifically address whether the government employee can bring a guest, there is nothing in the policy that would indicate this is unethical. Furthermore, they are disregarding the intent of the hosts. The owners of this establishment were well aware that the squadron commanders would be bringing family members as they had in previous years, and expressed no objection to sharing Thanksgiving with a few more military dependents. When I informed Cypress Grille about the policy change, a manager replied, "I just want to feed a bunch of people for free, what is the harm in that? I hope they will work it out and that those that want to attend can."

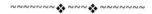

In September 2014, the U.S. Government Accounting Office issued a report card on the implementation of recommendations from Maj. Gen. Woodward's 2012 commander-directed investigation. While the Air Force had fully executed 39 of these initiatives, the rest remained incomplete. Improving video surveillance in the dormitories and increasing Military Training Instructor staffing were in the works, but plans to shorten the duration of Basic Military Training to eliminate "white space" in the schedule had been postponed repeatedly. The GAO found the Air Force also had not done enough to ensure candidates from across all career fields would be considered for command of BMT squadrons, and it had taken no action whatsoever to develop and institutionalize a more effective incentive program for MTI duty. Most troubling, the service had not fully established an oversight framework to evaluate the effectiveness of its actions. Without

---

[410] 5 C.F.R. § 2635.204(h)

such controls, the GAO concluded, the Air Force will not know whether to sustain these efforts or undertake different actions.[411]

The media reaction to news that the Air Force wasn't doing enough to fix what went wrong at Lackland was reminiscent of the classic scene from "Casablanca," where the French official claimed to be shocked (shocked!) to find gambling going on in Rick's Café Américain. The usual suspects wrote articles on the subject,[412] and one editorial board even called on the Air Force to implement the GAO's "common sense recommendation."[413] But for those of us familiar with BMT, the GAO assessment came as no surprise whatsoever. Despite Gen. Rice's apocryphal observation that he had "zero percent confidence we got this 100 percent correct," Col. Camerer, Col. Liddick, and their successors treated with suspicion and contempt any effort to provide constructive feedback by those of us actually implementing Woodward report recommendations.

Although they had no reliable method of evaluating their progress, the Air Force seemed to be randomly picking which Woodward report initiatives to take seriously. For example, rather than implementing a more effective incentive program for MTI duty, the Air Force actually considered cutting special duty assignment pay by $150 per month. [414] Designated a "developmental special duty" in 2014, the MTI career field was no longer soliciting volunteers or offering additional inducements such as points towards promotion. Since such special-duty assignments take airmen away from their normal jobs, many consider them career-killers,[415] and MTI duty was considered even

---

[411] United States Government Accountability Office, "GAO-14-806: DOD Needs to Take Further Actions to Prevent Sexual Assault during Initial Military Training," September 9, 2014, p. 2

[412] Wyatt Olson, "Results unclear for new sex assault safeguards at Air Force facilities," Stars and Stripes, September 9, 2014; Sig Christenson, "Report: Changes underway after Lackland AFB scandal," *San Antonio Express-News*, September 9, 2014; Kristin Davis, "GAO: No way to tell if changes at basic are working," Air Force Times, September 13, 2014

[413] Express-News Editorial Board, "Air Force should act on GAO report," *San Antonio Express-News*, September 11, 2014

[414] Stephen Losey, "Special pays may be reduced for MTIs," *Air Force Times*, May 9, 2014

[415] Stephen Losey, "Commands will choose airmen for special duty jobs," *Air Force Times*, July 16, 2013

less desirable in the aftermath of the Lackland sex scandal. The Air Force's failure to ensure those chosen to serve as MTIs were properly incentivized seems puzzling.

Another recommendation the Air Force failed to implement properly was the selection of squadron commanders. The GAO found the 2013 and 2015 rotations were selected from a pool that consisted of all career fields, but the Air Force did not know whether they would be given this priority of choice in future commander selections.[416] This analysis ignores the 2014 rotation altogether, when officers handpicked by Col. Liddick and Col. Camerer were installed as BMT squadron commanders. In addition to Lt. Col. Murphy, the new 319 TRS commander was also a spousal accommodation (the wife of an incumbent 37 TRW squadron commander), while the third was a former squadron operations officer whom Col. Liddick favored. This is not to say these officers were unqualified to command; on the contrary, all three were presumably screened as squadron command candidates within their respective career fields, and at least one has since earned a reputation as a relatively effective BMT commander. However, the process used to select them made no effort to ensure they were among the highest-caliber and best-qualified officers available.

Another startling revelation was buried in an appendix to the GAO report. The Air Force claimed to have developed an MTI survey to gather feedback on work experiences and misconduct in the BMT environment. According to an unspecified Air Force instruction, this survey was to be conducted twice a year, but it did not identify a timeline for its rollout, and the Air Force said it had not yet implemented this tool.[417] If such a survey sounds familiar, that's because Air Education and Training Command had in fact administered a RAND Corporation survey in July 2013 and again in January 2014. As noted in a previous chapter, AETC covered up the alarming results of these questionnaires, which revealed just how miserable the MTI corps had become during the Camerer/Liddick era. Rather than acknowledge this abortive effort to take stock of MTI attitudes, the Air Force lied to Congress instead.

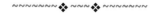

---

[416] GAO report, p. 19

[417] GAO report, p. 58

Among the last of the Woodward report initiative to be implemented was tightening up the BMT curriculum to reduce "white space" on the training schedule. Gen. Rice didn't immediately embrace this recommendation, noting that course content was under review via a separate initiative, which would determine the appropriate BMT course length.[418] By the time the BMT Triennial Review committee met in September 2013, however, Chief Master Sergeant of the Air Force James Cody could confidently declare, "we are walking out of here with a seven-and-a-half week program." Rather than disrupt the established technical training pipeline by shipping graduating airmen off to their follow-on training schools one week earlier, AETC would keep them at Lackland for a brand-new course of instruction. Setting aside the time-honored methods that had produced generations of American airmen, the Air Force would now try something radically different: a touchy-feely social experiment with far-reaching implications for the future of air power.

This so-called "Capstone Week" was the brainchild of CMSAF Cody, who previously served as AETC Command Chief under Gen. Rice. Even before the publication of the 2012 Woodward report, Chief Cody claims he had a conversation with the Chief of Staff of the Air Force, Gen. Welsh, about how to reduce downtime in the BMT schedule and get character lessons to stick better.[419] "Our Basic Military Training today does a tremendous job developing young men and women into Airmen," he acknowledged, but "as we looked at the current structure, we saw an opportunity to further enhance those Airmanship skills with a final week focused entirely on character development. These are core skills every Airman needs to be successful in our Air Force."

The AETC commander, Gen. Rand, naturally embraced the concept. "We developed Capstone Week to better prepare Airmen for their first assignments by reinforcing our core values of integrity, service and excellence through an interactive environment emphasizing character development, the profession of arms, and our Air Force heritage," he announced. "The course focuses on the importance of every Airman treating each other with respect and dignity, better preparing them to become skilled warriors ready to do our nation's business." The AETC Command

---

[418] AETC Commander's Report to SecAF, p. 42
[419] Kristin Davis, "Reinventing basic: Graduation comes earlier; 'real life' schooling follows," *Air Force Times*, February 17, 2015

Chief echoed this sentiment. "BMT's Capstone Week will ensure Air Force basic training remains a center of excellence and our Airmen remain the best fighting force in the world," CMSgt Gerardo Tapia said. "It's a fantastic and innovative way to ensure we prepare Airmen to become men and women of character – great wingmen, leaders, citizens and warriors. This is not going to be the 'last' week of BMT, but rather the first week of the rest of their Air Force careers."[420]

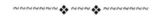

Planning for this transition week began while I was still in command, and it fell to my squadron to rearrange the BMT schedule and curriculum to accommodate the change. Standing up a new formal AETC course was out of the question given the bureaucracy involved, so "Capstone" was simply incorporated as the last block of the basic BMT course. The traditional parade marking BMT culmination was moved up a week in the schedule, but since the newly minted airmen technically wouldn't have graduated yet, AETC initially considered renaming this event the "Airman's Parade." (Thankfully, they quickly abandoned this idea.) Following the parade, airmen would be reassigned to a different squadron for their final week at BMT, where they would learn about wingmanship, resiliency, leadership and followership, sexual assault prevention and response, the warrior ethos, and balancing their personal and professional lives, all in an even more relaxed environment than BMT had become of late.

It is indeed ironic Col. Liddick selected the 326 TRS – commanded by her least-favored subordinate, Lt. Col. Liz Valenzuela – to serve as the transition squadron. But she didn't see a lot of other options. Most other line squadrons already had special missions assigned: the 320 TRS and 331 TRS train "battlefield airmen," the 322 TRS hosts the BMT Drum and Bugle Corps, and the 323 TRS is the "trainer" squadron. Meanwhile, the 324 TRS was scheduled to shut down, so the only other option was the 321 TRS, which had recently relocated into a brand-new Airman Training Complex and shared a dining facility with the 323 TRS. And so, the most unlikely of BMT squadron commanders was

---

[420] Tech. Sgt. Joshua Strang, "Air Force BMT introduces innovative Capstone Week," AETC official website, January 23, 2015

given the high-profile task of transitioning her squadron to the "Capstone" construct.

Not surprisingly, Liz proved herself more than capable of the task. The 326 TRS routinely produced more on-time graduates, suffered a lower number of trainee injuries, and required fewer ambulance calls for suicidal ideation than the other line squadrons. Such quantity did not come at the expense of quality, however, as the 326 TRS also generated plenty of distinguished graduates and honor flights. The secret to Liz's success was simple: she treated her MTIs and trainees with dignity and respect. Unfortunately, when it came to abusing this squadron commander, Col. Edmondson picked up where her predecessor left off, continuing to harass Liz for her support of "Team Perry" and other perceived nonconformities. The wing commander's wife, Vanessa Edwards, echoed that sentiment to Liz's spouse, Bunny, suggesting she would be better off leaving her wingman, Caroline, behind. When it became clear Lt. Col. Valenzuela's leadership approach was producing superior results, Col. Edmondson didn't praise her subordinate, but rather criticized her for not sharing her techniques with others. And for all the media interest in the "Capstone Week" story, the chain of command ensured neither the 326 TRS nor Lt. Col. Valenzuela was ever credited for the phenomenal job they did in pulling off this transition.

Unlike BMT, where MTIs provide virtually all instruction, whether academic or practical, "Capstone Week" would be run by contractors. As a logistics readiness officer, Lt. Col. Valenzuela was quite familiar with government contracting regulations, and she soon became alarmed by the approach AETC was taking towards this program. In April 2014, Col. Liddick provided a tour of the 326 TRS to a representative of Franklin-Covey, a potential bidder for the "Capstone" contract. Considering a statement of work hadn't even been drafted at that point, it sure seemed like the BMT commander was offering this vendor an unfair advantage. (I filed a complaint on this issue with the 502 ABW inspector general in June.)

This contract was ultimately awarded later that year to Crew Training International, which "will be responsible for all instructors, facilitators, courseware developers and is expected to develop and deliver approximately 31 hours of instruction/facilitation per week. They will develop scenario-based video modules addressing decision making as it relates to the character and mission related expectations for Air Force

379

airmen. In addition, they will create a supplementary program to train-the-trainer in all courseware and presentation methods.[421] CTI partnered with a production company, Running Pony, to develop videos for the contract, as well as support scenario development work with actors, filming, and editing. According to their managing partner, "The use of video will make this critical information much easier for prospective Airmen to understand and integrate into everyday behavior."[422]

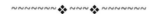

The trainees who would comprise the first "Capstone" class arrived at Lackland in late January 2015. "I think it is truly revolutionary, what we're doing," Col. Edmondson gushed to the media. "It's a totally different form of learning for these airmen, it is an investment in their future as airmen." The wing commander agreed. "Capstone isn't about the here and now, Capstone is about the future, and we have the ability to fundamentally shape the future of our enlisted force over the next 10 years," said Col. Edwards. "In order to change behavior, we have to change the way our airman think about professionalism, themselves and the Air Force." Col. J.D. Willis, AETC deputy operations director, also had high hopes for the new program, which "has the potential, certainly, to be an historic change from BMT and really for our Air Force in how we shape our airmen."[423]

As the dates of the initial "Capstone Week" approached, the Air Force media blitz intensified, replete with hyperbole and mixed messages. Describing BMT as "fast-paced," with "so much going on," CMSAF Cody noted trainees "don't have a lot of time to reflect and internalize and take a deep breath before we put them in the technical training pipeline." This five-day seminar would offer a reset button for airmen emerging from "the fog of BMT" – an awkward analogy likening BMT to warfare. At the same time, Cody noted a more professional training environment had emerged at Lackland, where it was no longer necessary to tear down a recruit

[421] BMT Capstone explanation of contract, CTI official website
[422] "CTI and Running Pony Productions team up to train Airmen," *Inside Memphis Business*, November 19, 2014
[423] Sig Christenson, "Air Force launches a big change in basic training," *San Antonio Express-News*, February 7, 2015

in order to build him or her into an airman. "While that might have been a philosophy expected in the past, it is not conventional wisdom today. There's no reason to break them down. We're taking them as who they are and where they're at, we're acknowledging that, and we're building them up," he said. Nevertheless, Gen. Rand insisted, BMT was not getting any easier. "Generationally, everyone probably thinks that. I think that our basic military training is as professionally done and as tough as we've had it and these airmen are as prepared as they've ever been."

The opening day of "Capstone" would be a multimedia spectacle, according to Col. Edwards. It would begin with an inspirational video on the significance of the oath of office, followed by a big reveal: "out from behind the screen walk the MTIs in their campaign hats. They take them off, walk up to the trainees and shake their hands – not as MTIs but as equals." This would be a time to "grow them, to mentor them, to solidify that foundation," the wing commander continued. "It's like orchestrating a movie and you have to get it right. It's the wow factor. You've got to capture them on the first opportunity on the first day. This is different. This is not BMT."[424]

No it is not. While acknowledging BMT had changed in recent years, becoming more accommodating and less intense, these senior leaders simultaneously portrayed this environment as still too stressful for today's young airmen, as if they were precious snowflakes unable to fully comprehend the character lessons being imparted by their MTIs. The proposed solution was a mind-boggling tableau reminiscent of the "Wizard of Oz," with instructors emerging from behind the curtain to turn good order and discipline on its head. One can only imagine the reaction of the bewildered airmen in the audience, wondering if they were in Kansas anymore.

When the first-ever "Capstone Week" finally began on March 23, 2015, the local Lackland leadership – Col. Edwards, Col. Edmondson, CMSgt Sutherland, etc. – weren't the only senior leaders on hand. The AETC commander, Gen. Rand, traveled across town to address the airmen, and even share a meal with these most junior enlisted personnel. One officer who was not given a chance to properly address the airmen that first day, however, was their

---

[424] Kristin Davis, "Reinventing basic: Graduation comes earlier; 'real life' schooling follows," *Air Force Times*, February 17, 2015

squadron commander, Lt. Col. Valenzuela. This disconnect did not go unnoticed by the *John Q. Public* blog, which published a scathing indictment of this ill-conceived attempt to micromanage character development.[425] Not surprisingly, several of the airmen in this inaugural class later exhibited disciplinary issues that required them to be washed back to repeat the experience the following week. Needless to say, Lt. Col. Valenzuela insisted on addressing her airmen on the first day from then on out, and this particular problem didn't recur during her remaining time in command.

This wasn't the only way the chain of command marginalized the 326 TRS commander regarding "Capstone Week." For example, her MTIs participated in the delivery of classroom instruction, but were sometimes called away for other military duties. Lt. Col. Valenzuela always ensured another qualified instructor was available to stand in for the missing MTI, but the contractors didn't appreciate the disruption, and complained to the 37 TRW program manager. When Liz objected to this interference in the management of her squadron, the chain of command came down firmly on the side of the contractors. It quickly became clear who was running this dog and pony show.

A week after Lt. Col. Valenzuela relinquished command of the 326 TRS in early May, Gen. Rand renamed the course – but AETC delayed announcing this rebranding until a new BMT commander was on board. Col. William Fischer assumed command of the 737 TRG on June 5, having moved across town from JBSA-Randolph where he had served as chief of the Airman Assignments Division at Air Force Personnel Center. Unlike Col. Liddick and Col. Edmonson, both of whom were graduated group commanders before coming to Lackland, Col. Fischer had only recently pinned on O-6, and his leadership experience appears much more limited than his most recent BMT predecessors.[426] The explanation for this unorthodox personnel move may have something to do with Gen. Darren McDew, the former Air Mobility Command boss. McDew likely crossed paths with Fischer in 2002-03, when he was wing

[425] Tony Carr, "Capstone: Accelerating the Decline of Air Force Basic Training," *John Q. Public*, March 27, 2015
[426] Colonel William D. Fischer official biography

commander at Scott AFB, Illinois. Rumor has it, the general recommended Fischer for his new job at BMT, much as he once sponsored the notorious Col. Camerer for a Lackland assignment.

Col. Fischer's first order of business was to put his mark on the week formerly known as "Capstone." "The name Airmen's Week reflects the idea that the week belongs to the Airmen as they go through the program," the new BMT commander announced. "We encourage them to take ownership of their first professional military education experience." Feedback from the first several thousand attendees had been very positive, he noted. "Airman after Airman has stated that they feel better equipped for the challenges of the Air Force after taking the course," Fischer said. "However, the Airmen have also made suggestions to improve the training. We take that feedback very seriously because it helps us identify where we need to refine lessons to reach our target audience," he added.

"We created an opportunity to enhance Airmanship skills in a post-BMT week, focused on character development," Col. Fischer continued. "BMT teaches them what they must know, be able to do and how to behave," he explained, while "Airmen's Week teaches them to think critically. The course strengthens their resilience and makes them more self-aware," giving them the opportunity to self-reflect and self-actualize in order to internalize the Air Force core values. The wing commander, Brig. Gen. Edwards, reiterated the party line. "Airmen's Week reinforces the fact that an environment of professionalism, dignity and respect is absolutely mission critical," he said. "Ultimately, we hope to give our Airmen the strength, character and resiliency to make decisions that are consistent with our Air Force core values. The goal of Airmen's Week is to produce more professional, resilient Airmen, inspired by our heritage, committed to the Air Force core values, and motivated to deliver airpower for America."

However, measuring the success of this program won't be quick or easy, Col. Fischer acknowledged. "Our measure for success is not a test score this week, but better Airmen for the operational Air Force," he said. "We look forward to feedback from the field on how the program is doing."[427] While it's heart-warming to hear BMT leadership taking the advice of brand-new airmen so seriously, and soliciting feedback from the operational Air Force on

---

[427] TSgt Joshua Strang, "Airmen's Week: Transition from trainee to Airman," U.S. Air Force official website, June 17, 2015

the quality of their graduates, they've shown far less patience for such critiques coming from experienced MTIs and officers at Lackland. But what do we know about airmanship?

Airmen's Week soon provided the backdrop for a new product launch. Originally published in 1997, the "Little Blue Book" was a small, bound pamphlet explaining Air Force core values, but it was soon phased out to save money. After floating the idea of adding "respect" to the established core values (integrity first, service before self, excellence in all we do), Gen. Welsh announced the Air Force would resume issuing an updated version of the "little blue book" to new airmen.[428] In late August, the top three Air Force leaders – Secretary James, Gen. Welsh, and CMSAF Cody – converged on Lackland to hand out copies of *America's Air Force: A Profession of Arms* to students just before they completed Airmen's Week. "What's in this document is nothing new to Airmen," the Chief of Staff explained, "but is a reminder that service to one's country is no ordinary calling." Chief Cody described this book as "a guide to the meaning of service and the principles that make us so strong."[429] (Of note, this document elevated "respect" to a position above the Air Force core values, asserting it "is at the root of the Profession of Arms and bonds every Airman who voluntarily serves."[430]) Soon, computer desktops across the Air Force enterprise featured a new icon, a shortcut to an electronic version of the "Latest Blue Hymnal," as *John Q. Public* sardonically dubbed this unwelcome propaganda.[431]

A few weeks later, the *San Antonio Express-News* published a front-page story on Airmen's Week under the headline, "Holding the High Ground." It offered an uncritical behind-the-scenes look at this so-called "core values course," designed to help young airmen

[428] Brian Everstine, "Air Force to bring back 'little blue book' as standard issue," *Air Force Times*, April 3, 2015

[429] AETC Public Affairs, "SECAF, CSAF, CMSAF present new 'Little Blue Book'," AETC official website, August 27, 2015

[430] Department of the Air Force, *America's Air Force: A Profession of Arms*, August 26, 2015

[431] Tony Carr, "CMSAF Shows He Can Get Results When It Matters Most (To Him)," *John Q. Public*, September 2, 2015

"identify and hold the ethical high ground" in the very place that was "ground zero" for a notorious sex scandal almost four years earlier. The author noted videos used in Airmen's Week are based on real incidents, but none addresses what happened right there at Lackland – or that the worst offender was assigned to the very squadron where these airmen now train. For some reason, the online version of the article was renamed, "At Lackland, core values course is basic," an ironic editorial choice given how the BMT curriculum was gutted to carve out this weeklong colloquium. The newspaper also replaced the print-edition photo of MTIs leading trainees with a publicity shot from the recent visit by the Air Force leadership triumvirate. As an added bonus, clicking on the link to the article automatically downloads a digital copy of *America's Air Force: A Profession of Arms*.[432] The Air Force couldn't have asked for better publicity than this gullible puff piece.

Meanwhile, time-honored traditions continued to unravel at BMT. Col. Edmonson discontinued the award of "Honor Flight" and "Warrior Flight" streamers to graduating trainee flights, on the grounds that these coveted designations fostered unhealthy rivalry among MTIs. While her critique has some superficial merit, she failed to consider how MTIs might use this competition as a motivational tool for encouraging teamwork and excellence among the trainees. Teamwork took another hit in July 2015, when BMT launched a new initiative: gender-integrated "Heritage Flights." For their last week of training before the graduation parade, trainees are reorganized according to their projected career fields into one of 14 new flights, each named for a former Chief Master Sergeant of the Air Force or other enlisted hero. "It's about preparing them to work as part of a team," said Dr. Munro, 737 TRG training director. "We are preparing the Airmen for the active duty Air Force they will experience and how it operates day to day." The deputy group commander, Lt. Col. Fuller, added, "It makes no real difference to military training instructors who they are training and how they form up. We train great Airmen, bottom line."[433] But team integrity does make a difference. Until the advent of Airmen's Week, MTIs had 8.5 weeks to mold dozens of raw recruits into airmen, who proudly marched together during their graduation

---

[432] Sig Christenson, "At Lackland, core values course is basic," *San Antonio Express-News*, September 16, 2015

[433] SSgt Marissa Garner, "Air Force BMT implements gender-integrated Heritage Flights," JBSA official site, July 24, 2015

parade. Now MTIs send their flights off to field training during week five, and these not-quite-airmen are then dispersed into unfamiliar groupings just as they're getting the hang of things. Breaking down unnecessary gender barriers is a laudable goal, but sacrificing esprit de corps for the sake of a few days of co-ed marching is a dubious way to go about it.

After everything BMT has been through these last several years, it remains an extremely dysfunctional environment. While many of the structural shortfalls and leadership failures that contributed to the Lackland sex scandal were adequately addressed, others problems were misdiagnosed or overcorrected. Through it all, Air Force leaders have steadfastly refused to have an honest conversation about what went wrong, and whether the cure they administered is any better than the disease. They've ignored or whitewashed the results of surveys designed for this very purpose, going so far as to deny such a polling instrument even exists. They've punished and marginalized those of us who stood up for our subordinates or offered constructive feedback about ill-conceived policies. They've rewarded those who abused their authority or betrayed their fellow airmen, in the process making a mockery of each and every Air Force core value.

But there's no need to take my word for it – simply review the comments the MTIs themselves provided during the Camerer/Liddick era, as faithfully reported in the media. Unfortunately, things haven't gotten much better since then. One of my former MTI students, who arrived too late to participate in those RAND surveys, shared her observations with me. "Being a MTI was the best job the Air Force asked me to do," she wrote. "However, the period I was at Lackland has been the most miserable time of my life and Air Force career. I loved my Air Force up until that point. Now, I can't wait to retire." This senior NCO felt the environment at BMT "went unchecked for too long," where MTIs had the mentality that, "because they were treated like shit, then they will in return treat everyone else like shit." But two wrongs don't make a right, she noted. "If you spoke out, you were silenced one way or the other," she continued, and leadership seemed to take care of only a chosen few.

"If I could tell the bigger Air Force leadership anything I wanted without repercussion," she continued, "I would shake my head at them and say: 'Shame on you!'" She felt they should be embarrassed for allowing BMT leadership "to negate that environment in such a way that someone with so much passion and a bright future would be dwindled down to where they feel defeated, disenfranchised and question their sanity." Agencies meant to protect airmen, such as the inspector general or military equal opportunity office, are a joke, she said, as they trust the words of a toxic leaders over complainants with valid, tangible proof of wrongdoing. "That is not the Air Force I signed up for. This is not the Air Force I can advocate for. This is not the Air Force I would allow my own children to enter."

The perspective of a prior-enlisted officer at BMT wasn't much better. "Coming back as a flight commander, for the first time in my 12 years of service I felt I didn't want to be part of the USAF anymore," she wrote, "because I didn't believe in what we were doing or the quality of airmen we were sending out" into our shrinking Air Force, which "desperately needed each airman to be of the highest caliber and come out firing on all cylinders." She also worried we were doing the trainees a disservice by not mentally preparing them properly. "I found myself in some very stressful situations during my career and I always attributed my instincts to stay calm and collected came from my experience in BMT." When she volunteered to come back to Lackland, she imagined "leading and working with a cohesive team to accomplish the mission," but instead it seemed careerism was all that's really left. "I don't want to be part of that. Good riddance, no regrets here."

Chapter 18: Men Biting Dogs

Mine is undoubtedly a curious case: a relatively distinguished Air Force officer relived of command for no compelling reason, whose career was subsequently destroyed without any clear misconduct on my part. Squadron commanders are fired from time to time, of course, often for conduct clearly unbecoming an officer entrusted with the responsibility and authority of command. Most of the time, their firings don't make headlines, for the very simple reason that the relieved commander probably deserved what he or she got. Unless the alleged offenses are egregious in some way, the media tends to ignore such "dog bites man" stories as routine and unremarkable.

But my story was different, as the front page of the *Air Force Times* made perfectly clear: this was no ordinary relief of command, but rather a "man bites dog" tale that begged further explanation. Sadly, since my relief of command grabbed headlines in 2014, it has become increasingly clear this was not an isolated incident, but rather the proverbial tip of a rather large iceberg against which the Air Force appears to be foundering. Other examples of toxic leadership and abuse of authority soon emerged, including similar stories of commanders wrongfully relieved. For me, these cases were like déjà vu all over again.

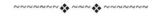

In February 2014, the commander of the 19th Airlift Wing, Col. Patrick Rhatigan, relieved Lt. Col. Blair Kaiser of command of the 30th Airlift Squadron, an active-duty C-130 unit embedded with the Wyoming Air National Guard. He had been in command only 12 weeks when he was dispatched to Afghanistan to command an expeditionary airlift squadron, but a unit climate assessment before he deployed suggested he had been performing well so far. During the five months Lt. Col. Kaiser was leading airlift operations in a combat zone, his operations officer was left in charge of the 30 AS, with full command authority over the squadron. So it came as a complete surprise when, just weeks after he returned from this successful deployment, Lt. Col. Kaiser was fired without explanation. Months later he was reassigned to a staff job at Air Mobility Command headquarters, at Scott AFB, Illinois, and issued a referral officer performance report, despite never having been counseled, admonished, reprimanded, or punished in any way.[434]

When Senator Mark Pryor (D-AR) later inquired into this situation on Lt. Col. Kaiser's behalf, the response the Air Force provided raised more questions than it answered. It informed him that, five days after Lt. Col. Kaiser was relieved of command, Col. Rhatigan launched a commander-directed investigation into several allegations against him, regarding matters raised in an inspector general complaint by a member of his squadron. "Although the CDI did not uncover specific instances of misconduct by Lieutenant Colonel Kaiser," the Air Force letter conceded, "the decision to remove him from command was not changed." In other words, this retroactive investigation provided no excuse for having relieved this commander.

So why was he fired? According to the official response to a Congressional inquiry, the group commander, Col. Johnnie Martinez, relieved Lt. Col. Kaiser of command for the following reasons: "issues regarding overall climate within the 30 AS and concerns about officer and enlisted fraternization, [and] alleged alcohol consumption within 12 hours prior to flight duties." But it was Rhatigan, not Martinez, who made this decision, as an e-mail from the wing commander's legal adviser made clear. Moreover, Lt. Col. Kaiser had just returned from a 20-week deployment, so if the 30 AS command climate deteriorated in his absence, responsibility ought to rest with Lt. Col. Tyson Willis, the officer left in charge. It turns out it was Willis himself who lodged the allegation regarding alcohol, based on a misunderstanding of a simple clerical error in the flight log. It was quickly determined Lt. Col. Kaiser had not violated the rule about drinking before flying, and Col. Martinez reportedly admitted this even as he delivered the bad news about his relief of command. Yet the Air Force later cited this false rumor as a reason for the squadron commander's removal, shamefully sullying this pilot's professional reputation.

Unfortunately for Kaiser, his operations officer was considered a protégé of then-Lt. Gen. Darren McDew, the 18th Air Force commander. Moreover, Col. Rhatigan had also taken a personal interest in Lt. Col. Willis, offering him career advice while

---

[434] Tony Carr, "Another Commander Sacked: is the Air Force in an Unrecognized Ethical Tailspin?" *John Q. Public*, July 27, 2014

he was sitting in for the 30 AS commander.[435] In an e-mail to Lt. Gen. McDew in early February, the wing commander expressed concern about the command climate in the 30 AS. Col. Rhatigan noted he felt Lt. Col. Kaiser was "not the right commander to turn that climate around," but he believed his understudy "has the right temperament and leadership abilities to turn this squadron around" – a dubious assertion, considering he had been in charge of the 30 AS since the previous August. McDew apparently had no objections, so Rhatigan relieved Kaiser the very next day, and installed Willis as permanent commander shortly thereafter.

Ironically, this position turned out to be anything but permanent. On August 25, 2014, Col. Rhatigan relieved Lt. Col. Willis of command as well, citing a "loss of confidence" in the airman he had so recently recommended for the job. This was reportedly the fifth officer Col. Rhatigan fired from leadership positions in just six months, seriously calling into question the judgment of this senior leader.[436]

John Q. Public naturally championed the cause of Lt. Col. Kaiser, as he had my own curious case. "Not only was there no fire, there wasn't even enough smoke for a faint signal," Tony Carr wrote about this pilot's relief of command. "The burden is not on Kaiser – just as it wasn't on Craig Perry at Lackland – to prove sainthood or to knock down every rumor or innuendo uttered by any disgruntled subordinate or peanut gallery member."[437] In another post, this author noted the tendency of wing commanders to consult more-senior leaders before making a decision to relieve a subordinate of command. However, once general officers further up the chain of command "buy" that decision, "there's no real chance for a course correction if it turns out to have been a bad call," since the general "can also be seen as wrong for having 'picked' or 'groomed' or 'pushed' such a questionable candidate."[438]

---

435 Tony Carr, "Raging White: The Jettisoning of Lt. Col. Blair Kaiser and the Air Force's Ethics Problem," *John Q. Public*, August 6, 2014
436 Tony Carr, "Another One Bites the Dust: 'Amateur Hour' Continues in AMC with Continuous Unexplained Firings," *John Q. Public*, August 26, 2014
437 Tony Carr, "Ready, Fire, Aim: the Dangerous Habit of a Corrupt Chain of Command," *John Q. Public*, July 28, 2014
438 Tony Carr, "Jammed Controls: the Systemic Reasons Why Bad Firings Usually Stick," *John Q. Public*, July 30, 2014

Ironically, it was Gen. McDew who seems to have played this role in both our cases. You'll recall, this is the same general officer who sponsored my former wing commander, Col. Camerer, and he is believed to have protected him from the consequences of his toxic leadership at the 37 TRW. Gen. McDew similarly provided top-cover for Col. Rhatigan, first as 18 AF commander, then later as leader of Air Mobility Command. (In another bizarre twist, Gen. McDew's legal advisor as AMC commander was none other than Col. Lisa Turner – the very same staff judge advocate who abused her authority at AETC in response to the Lackland sex scandal.) "This situation reeks of ethical compromise, and fits into a pattern across the larger force" Carr concluded. "As important as individual justice is the cases of Blair Kaiser, Craig Perry, and others, of paramount importance is the processes used to determine their fates. When our processes begin to resemble too closely those employed by our enemies, we have reason to worry."[439]

Lt. Col. Lance Annicelli assumed command of the 9th Physiological Support Squadron at Beale AFB, California, in June 2014. He inherited a unit with considerable morale and climate issues, which he immediately set out to improve. He apparently got results, as the 9th Medical Group commander, Col. Jody Ocker, recommended the 9 PSPTS be recognized as the 25th Air Force Outstanding Squadron of the Year. She also praised the unit's performance under Annicelli in early February 2015, writing that "PSPTS is VERY deserving of recognition." One week later, however, she met with the 9th Reconnaissance Wing commander, Col. Douglas Lee, to discuss what she later described as "serious concerns about command climate issues within the 9 PSPTS and the very dangerous risk to flight safety," including possible acts of intimidation, bullying, and retribution within the squadron. The wing commander then gathered his staff, including his staff judge advocate and the inspector general, to determine Annicelli's fate.

After the meeting, Col. Ocker informed her subordinate she was temporarily relieving him from command for approximately

---

[439] "Raging White: The Jettisoning of Lt. Col. Blair Kaiser and the Air Force's Ethics Problem"

two weeks, on the basis of a specific and egregious allegation. She also told Lt. Col. Annicelli she was ordering a CDI into this allegation, but if it proved unsubstantiated, he would be returned to command. He was ordered to stay away from his squadron for the duration of the investigation. The very next morning – Friday the 13th, as it so happened – Col. Lee reportedly visited the 9 PSPTS and announced to the squadron he had personally removed their commander due to "toxic leadership." An hour later, Col. Lee informed Lt. Col. Annicelli he had overridden Col. Ocker, and decided to make his relief permanent even before the results of the CDI were known. That afternoon, he gathered together the other 9 RW squadron commanders and informed them he had relieved their colleague for "toxic leadership."

Rather than confine her CDI to a specific accusation, Col. Ocker ordered the investigating officer to look into "all aspects of allegations regarding toxic leadership by the 9 PSPTC/CC," without actually defining what was meant by this charge. Given that the wing commander had already pronounced judgment on Lt. Col. Annicelli as a toxic leader, it is inconceivable an inquiry conducted by one of his subordinates (the deputy Mission Support Group commander) and overseen by another (his staff judge advocate, who was present when the decision was made to remove Annicelli) would reach any other conclusion. The investigating officer apparently informed Col. Ocker of the testimony of certain witnesses while the CDI was still going on, which she in turn revealed to members of the squadron, tainting the course of the investigation. He also cherry-picked witnesses, and cited weak, inappropriate evidence, without giving Lt. Col. Annicelli the chance to rebut the testimony against him.

In the end, the CDI report stipulated Lt. Col. Annicelli didn't cause the squadron's problems, and leadership issues existed at all levels within the unit, not just the front office. While this squadron commander obviously failed to get buy-in for his hard-nosed leadership style from all his subordinates, there was no suggestion he abused his authority in any way, calling into question his censure as a toxic leader. On the other hand, there is reason to believe it was the wing commander who better deserved this label. One officer wrote to Tony Carr, "I have never witnessed such a dysfunctional leadership team. When I first started attending meetings, I was amazed at how tense other O-6s were around [Lee]. Everyone appeared on edge and feared getting dressed down in public." Another 9 RW insider complained to a U.S.

Senator that, "soon after taking command of the 9 RW, Col. Lee made many comments during staff meetings and daily stand-up briefings suggesting he wouldn't hesitate to fire a squadron commander if he wasn't happy with them."[440]

Like me, Lt. Col. Annicelli filed a request for redress under Article 138, Uniform Code of Military Justice. After a *pro forma* rejection by the wing commander, his complaint made its way to Maj. Gen. Jack Shanahan, 25 AF commander – the very same officer then serving as my senior rater. Not surprisingly, the general dismissed this request on July 27, 2015, finding that "Colonel Ocker did not abuse her authority or act arbitrarily, capriciously, or unfairly" in removing Lt. Col. Annicelli from command, and in fact she acted reasonably "based on her loss of confidence in [his] ability to safely command the unit." This is wrong on two counts. First, this wasn't the reason he was fired, as both his group and wing commanders made clear. Second, it wasn't Col. Ocker who relieved Lt. Col. Annicelli of command, but rather her boss, Col. Lee. Nevertheless, "Shanahan (undoubtedly with the considerable help of his lawyer) found legally nimble ways to neglect all of the evidence indicating Lee, and not Ocker, had done the firing, choosing instead to close ranks, protect the image of the chain of command, and double down on a corrupt and unfair process," Carr concluded.[441] Another commander at Beale AFB subsequently filed an inspector general complaint alleging Col. Lee lied to the 25 AF commander about who made the decision to fire Lt. Col. Annicelli, to avoid charges of violating Article 37, UCMJ, by exercising undue command influence. In the process, he may have violated Article 107 by providing false or misleading official statements as to his involvement.[442]

Lt. Col. Annicelli "was doomed to professional ruin on the basis of an allegation alone, and he's never even been told who made it or what he was claimed to have done," opined another *John Q. Public* blog post. "After two decades of committed service, he wasn't even afforded the basic dignity of a fair process. He was promptly abandoned at the whim of a colonel whose decision

---

[440] Tony Carr, "Fire, Ready, Aim: The Sacking of Lt. Col. Annicelli," *John Q. Public*, July 30, 2015
[441] Tony Carr, "Sidestepping Evidence, General Dismisses Fired Commander's Appeal," *John Q. Public*, August 3, 2015
[442] Tony Carr, "Spinning Out of Control: Another Beale Commander Claims Senior Officer Abuse," *John Q. Public*, August 31, 2015

couldn't be questioned without embarrassing the chain of command that empowered him." The author continued,

> *Through silence and inaction, the Air Force is encouraging and even incentivizing abuse of power. Commanders are governed by no meaningful checks or limits on their use of administrative sanctions such as relief, reprimand, and downgraded performance reports. Unlike courts-martial and nonjudicial punishment proceedings, firings and reprimands are not subject to meaningful standards of evidence or process safeguards. This has created a massive punishment loophole for power addicts to enforce not just the rules, but their own stylistic preferences, through a fascist doctrine of total obedience and obliterated agency. The chain of command holds sole authority over whether to question its own decisions, creating a crippling power imbalance and an endemic conflict of interest that leads to corrupted outcomes. It also strangles dissent, robbing the Air Force of a badly needed internal discussion among leaders.*

"The Air Force is running a 'trust us' system," the author concluded, "without doing the things necessary to deserve that trust."[443]

In a previous chapter, I examined the cases of former squadron commanders who were wrongly punished in the wake of the Lackland sex scandal. A similar thing happened a few years later, once again based on events that transpired at Joint Base San Antonio. This time, however, the tale had a much more tragic ending.

The story actually began back in 2004, when an Air Force recruiter, Technical Sergeant Eric Soluri, was accused of assaulting his ex-girlfriend in Waltham, Massachusetts. His local chain of command declined to pursue the matter, but civilian authorities pressed charges. By the time the case finally went to trial in 2006, TSgt Soluri had been reassigned to Lackland AFB, where he served

---

[443] Tony Carr, "Something About This Firing Doesn't Add Up," *John Q. Public*, August 18, 2015

as an instructor at the Air Force Recruiting School. A Massachusetts court found him not guilty of assault and battery, but did convict him of threatening to commit a crime, a misdemeanor. He received a six-month suspended sentence, of which he spent 14 days behind bars.

Such a conviction and sentence would typically have serious repercussions for an airman's career. However, his supervisors did not record this incident in his enlisted performance reports, and his squadron commander even pushed this high-performing noncommissioned officer for promotion in early 2008.[444] Soluri was allowed to reenlist the following year, and stratified as the #4 Master Sergeant in the 37th Training Wing by none other than Brig. Gen. Patrick. Not surprisingly, after returning to his primary Security Forces career field, Soluri was promoted again in 2010 and his ascent culminated when he sewed on Chief Master Sergeant in December 2013 – having been designated the #1 Senior Master Sergeant in 12th Air Force by then-Lt. Gen. Rand. By this point, Chief Soluri had returned to Lackland, assigned now to the 802nd Security Forces Squadron.

Chief Soluri's past came back to haunt him in 2014, while he was deployed to Afghanistan. Someone tipped off the 502d Air Base Wing commander, Brig. Gen. Robert LaBrutta, about a subordinate who rapidly rose through the ranks despite a 2006 conviction, so this senior leader immediately launched an investigation. He ordered the Chief to return home early from deployment, and reassigned him to JBSA headquarters. This inquiry found the Chief had properly disclosed his conviction to his chain of command at the time of the incident, and his leadership was under no obligation to make the conviction a part of his service record, even though this might have resulted in his discharge. Air Force instructions also did not require civilian convictions to be documented in enlisted performance reports, and Soluri's leadership chose not to "take the conviction into account when stratifying him for promotion against his peers," an Air Force spokesman, Col. Sean McKenna, noted. "His commanders made permissible discretionary decisions during that period not to document his civilian conviction or jail time in any of his formal military reports," he concluded.

---

[444] Kristin Davis, "Tech made chief in 7 years despite 2006 conviction," *Air Force Times*, October 27, 2014

Nevertheless, the Chief of Staff of the Air Force, Gen. Welsh, "has directed a review of Air Force instructions to make sure this doesn't happen again," Col. McKenna continued. "As we've stated throughout the process, military members must adhere to the highest standards of integrity and professionalism, including holding each other accountable, regardless of when the misconduct occurred," he said.[445] Perhaps responding to this exercise of undue command influence by the CSAF, Brig. Gen. LaBrutta decided to hold CMSgt Soluri accountable – even though he had long ago been made to answer for his actions. This wing commander retroactively punished CMSgt Soluri for a crime committed over a decade earlier – long after the statute of limitation had expired – issuing this airman a letter of reprimand and denying him a Bronze Star medal for his recent service in Afghanistan. Furthermore, LaBrutta reportedly threatened the Chief that if he did not retire, he would have him demoted – then he apparently forbade him from conducting a retirement ceremony. Adding insult to injury, Col. McKenna announced Soluri would retire in a lower pay grade, since he had not served as a Chief for at least three years. Thankfully, Soluri was able to obtain a time-in-grade waiver to retain his current rank in retirement.

Another airman involved in this drama wasn't so lucky. Lt. Col. Chris de los Santos commanded the 345th Training Squadron from 2008 to 2010, and was responsible for reenlisting MSgt Soluri in 2009. According to regulations then in effect, commanders had total selection or non-selection authority when it came to reenlistment, and they could grant waivers to airmen who were otherwise ineligible due to a civil court conviction or five or more days "lost time." Commanders were under no obligation to consult with their superiors or the base legal office before making such a decision – it was left entirely to their discretion.[446]

Despite having formally cleared CMSgt Soluri's commanders of any wrongdoing, Brig. Gen. LaBrutta was nonetheless determined to hold de los Santos accountable somehow. This officer had been selected for promotion to Colonel, in 2013, and he assumed command of the 673rd Logistics Readiness Group at Joint Base Elmendorf-Richardson, Alaska, the

[445] Kristin Davis, "Chief to retire at lower grade after probe of 2006 conviction," *Air Force Times*, January 31, 2015
[446] AFI 36-2606, *Reenlistment In The United States Air Force*, November 21, 2001

following year. When he was questioned about his handling of the Soluri case, Col. de los Santos officially stated he had not consulted with the legal office back in 2009, but he apparently told his new wing commander he had. This was a minor, likely inadvertent discrepancy, with no bearing whatsoever on the case – but it was enough for Brig. Gen. LaBrutta to accuse this group commander of lying.

The 502d Air Base Wing commander apparently convinced his counterpart in Alaska, Col. Brian Bruckbauer, to fire Col. de los Santos in February 2015. His career suddenly in ruins, this officer had little choice but to retire – but because he had so recently pinned on O-6, he was discharged from the Air Force at a lower grade. Sadly, Lt. Col. (ret.) de los Santos didn't take his capricious reversal of fortune well. This phenomenal leader, who once seemed on track to someday become a wing commander, took his own life in October 2015. He was laid to rest at Arlington National Cemetery the following February, survived by his wife and two children.

During the Lackland sex scandal, Gen. Rice punished several former commanders for supposedly mishandling disciplinary actions against certain subordinates, who subsequently went on to engage in more serious misconduct. The Air Force later determined the AETC commander and his legal advisor, Col. Turner, had abused their authority, and the Senate rejected her nomination for promotion. Meanwhile, Brig. Gen. LaBrutta persecuted a former commander – not for allowing an allegedly bad airman to go on to do worse things, but for permitting a good airman to redeem himself after making a single mistake. This arguably represents a more egregious abuse of authority, yet Brig. Gen. LaBrutta was nonetheless nominated for promotion in February 2016. He will soon pin on a second star: one for each career he ruined in his unconscionable witch-hunt against Soluri.

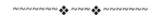

While the notoriety of JBSA-Lackland has gradually receded from the headlines, another Air Education and Training Command base has emerged as a new hotbed of scandal. Laughlin AFB, in Del Rio, Texas, is home to the 47th Flying Training Wing, which conducts specialized undergraduate pilot training. This is one of several such wings within 19th Air Force, which was reestablished in 2014 to oversee all AETC flying training units from its headquarters at JBSA-Randolph. Student pilots are typically newly commissioned officers, college graduates in their early twenties, while many trainers are "first assignment instructor pilots" who only recently earned their own wings through this same 52-week program. Consequently, the differential in rank, age, and experience between instructors and student pilots is considerably less at Laughlin and other pilot training bases than that between MTIs and trainees at BMT, or even most technical training instructors and junior airmen.

The first public sign of trouble at Laughlin emerged at the end of April 2015, when Maj. Gen. Michael Keltz, 19 AF commander, unexpectedly resigned. He had been the convening authority for an Article 15 (nonjudicial punishment) hearing at Laughlin AFB three weeks earlier, during which he made inappropriate comments about the defendant. [447] According to witnesses, the general criticized this company-grade officer for his life choices and relationships, and reportedly scolded the officer for appearing "drunker than 10,000 Indians" in a photograph. Later in this diatribe, he modified this insult to "drunker than 10,000 sailors," but the damage was done. It's not clear if he realized his mistake on his own, or if he came to this conclusion in response to complaints about his racially insensitive remarks. Either way, the AETC commander, Gen. Rand, accepted his resignation and request for retirement, but did not dig into the unfolding crisis at Laughlin.[448] He also withdrew the offer of nonjudicial punishment against this young Captain, an instructor pilot later identified as "IP7." Nevertheless, 47 FTW commander, Col. Brian Hastings, reinitiated Article 15 proceedings a few weeks later, this time upholding the punishment despite an alarming lack of evidence.[449]

This crisis had been brewing since at least the previous year, precipitated in part by the update of AETC Instruction 36-2909 in December 2013. Rewritten in the wake of the Lackland sex scandal, *Recruiting, Education, and Training Standards of Conduct* defined the expectations for professional and unprofessional relationships between recruits, trainees, and students, on the one

---

[447] Stephen Losey, "Comments end 19th Air Force commander's career," *Air Force Times*, May 4, 2015
[448] Tony Carr, "General's Resignation Hints at Deeper Problems," *John Q. Public*, May 1, 2015
[449] John Q. Public, "Broken Wings: the Cautionary Tale of IP7," *John Q. Public*, February 1, 2016

hand, and their recruiters, instructors, and other permanent-party staff on the other. While these strict rules make some sense in the context of BMT, where the power differential between MTIs and trainees is extremely high, they seem less appropriate when applied to environments with more mature or experienced learners – say, the MTI School, or officer pilot training – where the faculty barely outranks the students.

Among the new provisions was an obligation for faculty and staff with knowledge of an alleged violation to "immediately report the allegation to an appropriate authority." The instruction defines knowledge as any "awareness of an allegation," however obtained – witnessing the offense, statements by third parties, course surveys, etc. – and "does not require a belief in the accuracy or truth of the allegation." This reporting requirement, designed to prevent instructors from turning a blind eye to each other's misconduct, instantly created a culture of informants, where anyone who hears anything – even a rumor they believe to be false from a source with no direct knowledge – is obliged to report it. To get the word out about these changes, AETCI 36-2909 further requires all training commanders to ensure all personnel are "briefed on the relevant provisions of this instruction upon their arrival, and at least annually thereafter."

Col. Hastings didn't get around to announcing the AETCI 36-2909 updates at Laughlin until late July 2014, when he briefed them at a commander's call. The following day, according to *John Q. Public*, several officers were called in for questioning in connection with a suspected unprofessional relationship involving a male instructor and female student, who had dated before assuming roles that made any further romance unlawful. In the course of that inquiry, investigators found text messages indicating other instructors might have had knowledge of the suspected relationship but not reported it. Their cellphones were seized and searched, and they were later punished based on this evidence. However, the conduct at issue took place before they were aware of a duty to report on rumors of impropriety, and the wing commander's mass brief "looks more like a ham-handed attempt to establish the foundation for a planned crackdown than a good faith attempt to create the right kind of climate."

John Q. Public cataloged the absurdity of this new AETC policy. It requires airmen to view each other with suspicion and encourages the propagation of unreliable information, which together "stand to erode trust and upend good order and discipline." Even worse, it "incentivizes backstabbing and discord while discouraging the type of open communication required to discern and address actual disciplinary problems." It is "inconsistent with every principle of wingmanship and resiliency the Air Force claims to cherish, and removes any incentive for rule violators to self-redeem after they've made a mistake." Moreover, "there's also the problem of how anyone accused of violating the reporting requirement can raise a defense," as anyone testifying on behalf of the accused would incriminate themselves. "This makes the charge practically indefensible, and thus legally problematic from a due process standpoint." Finally, the same officer who certified this policy as lawful – Col. Polly Kenny, AETC staff judge advocate – was later responsible for advising Gen. Rand as he considered appeals from officers punished under the reporting rule, an incredible conflict of interest.

"But even if Kenny created a rule that was strictly legal," the author concluded, "it has to be one of the single dumbest ideas in modern military history. If your enforcement mechanism requires airmen to not just relay gossip like maids at a market, but to debase themselves and their teams by reporting every stray vagary overheard at the water cooler to the chain of command, then you don't have much of a rule. This should have occurred to everyone involved before the rule was published. The fact it didn't is just the latest evidence that the Air Force is incapable of effectively administering its own justice system."[450]

The events at Laughlin finally made national headlines in September 2015, thanks to investigative reporting by *John Q. Public*. This blog's principal author, Tony Carr, is a retired Air Force pilot pursuing a law degree at Harvard, so he was especially qualified to expose the questionable legality of this "witch-hunt in the desert." It began in 2014 with a suspected unprofessional relationship between an instructor pilot and a student, which in turn led investigators to identify nearly a dozen officers involved in similar shenanigans. The inquiry was soon broadened to include bystanders who failed to intervene, prompting agents from the Air

---

[450] Tony Carr, "Air Force Witch Hunt Punished Officers for Failing to Report Relationship Rumors," *John Q. Public*, October 3, 2015

Force Office of Special Investigations to begin seizing cellphones of those under suspicion, opening an entirely new can of worms.

This dragnet ultimately identified four pilots (including "IP7") who were suspected of drug use, based on private text messages they exchanged amongst themselves containing various pop-culture references to illegal substances. With no evidence of actual wrongdoing, investigators referred these officers to their chain of command for disciplinary action. They were suspended from flying, placed on administrative hold, barred from their squadrons, and preventing from interacting with teammates for months while their commanders considered their fates. All four voluntarily submitted to drug tests, which they passed, and investigators turned up no other corroborating evidence or witness testimony indicating actual drug use. At that point, the government should have dropped these cases for lack of credible evidence.

Instead, Air Force officials pursued nonjudicial punishment against one of the officers, charging him under Article 112a, UCMJ: Wrongful use, possession, etc., of controlled substances. In February 2015, he challenged this allegation in a public hearing, and convinced the presiding two-star general (none other than   Maj. Gen. Keltz, before he resigned) to throw out the charges. This pilot has since returned to flying status and moved on with his career. The other three alleged co-conspirators, on the other hand, weren't so lucky. Rather than drop this ridiculous persecution, Col. Hastings issued each of them letters of reprimand instead. As we've seen in my case, there is no meaningful recourse to challenge or appeal an LOR, and the career of any officer receiving such paperwork is effectively finished. Since these pilots couldn't be convicted or offered nonjudicial punishment, "their chain of command opted to abandon the law altogether and destroy them administratively" rather than admit it had made a mistake or simply couldn't prove these allegations.[451]

Tony Carr soon uncovered even more lawlessness in this scandal. One officer ("IP7") was instructed not to speak to anyone about his case, a clearly illegal order that interferes with his ability to mount a defense, seek counseling, obtain legal representation, or confide about the issue with family and trusted friends – not to mention communicate with his Congressional representatives, a right guaranteed under Title 10, Section 1034 of the U.S. Code.

---

[451] Tony Carr, "Witch-Hunt in the Desert: Careers Destroyed in Laughlin Cellphone Grab," *John Q. Public*, August 26, 2015

When the accused officer allegedly broke this order by speaking to someone, he was issued nonjudicial punishment, making this bad situation worse. Another officer found himself unable to purchase a firearm, months after the investigation into his alleged drug use ended without criminal charges, much less a conviction. His name had been flagged in the National Instant Criminal Background Check System, presumably as "an unlawful user of [...] any controlled substance," implying he was actively engaged in ongoing drug use. When he made his chain of command aware of the problem, they took no action to restore his Second Amendment rights.

There were also problems with the search warrants used to seize and search these officers' cellphones. They were overly broad, and not based on a reasonable suspicion a crime had been committed. When one officer refused to unlock his mobile device and requested legal representation, the OSI agents told him he couldn't leave the interview without revealing his password, and gave him the impression his chain of command was giving him a lawful order he must follow. Not only did the agents violate this officer's right to due process by denying him counsel, they also infringed his Fifth Amendment right against self-incrimination. Finally, resorting to administrative action against the officers when it became clear they could not be successfully prosecuted constituted an end-run around their Sixth Amendment right to due process. Lacking sufficient evidence to prove them guilty in court, their commanders simply found a different way to punish them. At the same time, none of these officers had their security clearances suspended, suggesting their commanders didn't find them all that untrustworthy, and perhaps didn't even consider them drug users.[452]

Moreover, the Air Force never bothered to search the homes or automobiles of the accused. If their chain of command seriously suspected these airmen of using and distributing drugs, argued *John Q. Public*, "it would be something like prosecutorial malpractice to not obtain warrants" to search for additional evidence. "The fact it was never attempted means one of two things: either the prosecutor and commander didn't think there was enough probable cause to sustain a warrant, or they were afraid of the implications of searching and finding nothing. Either

---

[452] Tony Carr, "West Texas Salem: Civil Liberties Trampled in Abusive Criminal Probe," *John Q. Public*, September 3, 2015

way, the inability to amass enough evidence to go to court should have been the end of the matter.[453]

So, why are they being destroyed? "Because the chain of command can't be wrong," Tony Carr concluded. "Having wagered its credibility in an initial gambit to hound these officers, it can't admit having made a mistake without losing that credibility. This is always seen as unacceptable because it costs generals their stars, disturbs cherished narratives about being tough on misconduct, and tarnishes a justice process that is already in jeopardy of wholesale reform."[454]

It was only a matter of time before members of Congress registered their concern about the injustices being uncovered at Laughlin. On September 15, 2015, Representatives Duncan Hunter (R-CA) and Adam Kinzinger (R-IL), both veterans with reputations for holding the military accountable on matters of individual justice, sent a letter to the Chief of Staff of the Air Force. Noting how investigators had "painfully misunderstood" the evidence in this case, these Congressmen asked some tough questions about the Laughlin dragnet. They then put Gen. Welsh on the spot to answer for the results of that probe: "We also ask that the Air Force state whether it believes the actions taken against the pilots is warranted based on text messages, obtained from private cellphones, without any additional corroborating evidence."[455]

Within a few days, other news outlets picked up the story of these hapless pilots, offering additional details of their offending text messages, which seemed to boast of using and distributing drugs such as ecstasy and marijuana. Some of the pilots texted about a weekend trip to Las Vegas, where the Miley Cyrus song "We Can't Stop," including lyrics about "dancing with Molly," became an inside joke. In other texts, the officers laughed about getting high on prescription medication and "popping pills" and "smokin' bud."

---

[453] John Q. Public, "Disgraced 2-star Sounds Off on Miley Gate, Raises New Questions," *John Q. Public*, January 18, 2016

[454] "West Texas Salem: Civil Liberties Trampled in Abusive Criminal Probe," September 3, 2015

[455] Tony Carr, "Congress Demands Answers from Air Force on Laughlin Witch Hunt," *John Q. Public*, September 16, 2015

This was juvenile banter, to be sure, but not meant to be read literally. There is no evidence any of them ever used drugs, and in fact one of the pilots is a Mormon who doesn't even drink alcohol and rarely consumes caffeinated beverages. "I can't imagine a scenario in which a group of Air Force officers would be texting about engaging in criminal acts if that's what they actually had done," one of the pilots later wrote his commander. "Maybe I'm naive in this regard, but it makes no sense to me." An attorney for one of these officers agreed. "As anyone who is not tone-deaf to popular culture would readily recognize," he wrote, these text messages were quoting lyrics from rap songs. "To think that the use of such language is indicative of drug use makes zero sense."[456]

In an extraordinary development, Gen. Welsh actually met with Reps. Hunter and Kinzinger about this issue in early October, and subsequently ordered a new investigation into the Laughlin debacle.[457] "There's no question how serious Gen. Welsh is taking this," a spokesman for one of the Congressmen said. "He committed to going back and taking a good, long look at this," and he reportedly vowed to return to Capitol Hill to brief both lawmakers within four and six weeks.[458] An Air Force spokesman later confirmed the Air Force Inspector General had begun "an inquiry of the investigative process and the procedures used to administer any adverse personnel actions" at Laughlin, and upon completion of that inquiry, "a general officer will independently review the final adjudication and resulting outcome of each member's administrative case." He added, "Commanders are expected to hold members accountable for their actions, while ensuring due process and equitable treatment are appropriately applied in every case," and they take this responsibility very seriously. "An allegation of mistreatment is reviewed at multiple levels and the Laughlin cases are no exception."[459] Where have we heard that before?

---

[456] "Shane Harris, "Air Force Grounds Pilots for Quoting Miley Cyrus, *The Daily Beast*, September 18, 2015
[457] Tony Carr, "Welsh Meets Personally with Congressmen, Reportedly Orders Inquiry Into Laughlin Witch Hunt," *John Q. Public*, October 11, 2015
[458] Jeff Schogol, "Welsh vows review of three Laughlin pilots punished for text messages," *Air Force Times*, October 13, 2015
[459] Jeff Schogol, "Miley Cyrus song crashes Air Force pilots' careers," *Air Force Times*, October 19, 2015

~~~~~~~ ❖ ~~~ ❖ ~~~~~~~

But if accountability, due process, and equitable treatment are the objective, Air Force commanders keep missing the mark. After the *Air Force Times* ran a front-page story about the Laughlin trio fired for texting, Gen. Welch sent an e-mail to his wing commanders sharing his thoughts on the issue. "We've captured the Air Force's culture and standards in AFI 1-1," an Air Force instruction on required standards of conduct. "We all know 24 hours a day, 7 days a week, on and off-duty, Airmen have signed up to live up to Air Force Standards and Core Values. Through all the different ways in which Airmen communicate and interact, respect and dignity are essential. It doesn't matter whether it's in person, by text, twitter, or the latest social media app, we are all personally accountable for what we say and post." In one stroke, the Chief of Staff of the Air Force declared airmen have no reasonable expectation of privacy, even in non-public places and interactions. Rep. Hunter expressed concern about the impact Welsh's doctrine might have on morale. "There's no way this kind of 'zero privacy policy' creates an environment where people will go fight for you."[460]

It didn't take long for this policy to be put to the test. The following month, the 47 FTW chief of public affairs and another airman posted comments on a publicly accessible Facebook page referencing LSD use. Under the "Miley Gate" precedent, later endorsed by Gen. Welsh, such seemingly innocuous banter can easily be twisted into probable cause of criminal activity. A spokesman for Rep. Hunter was quick to note the similarities between this incident and the "Molly Three": "To be fair and apply the same standard evenly and consistently, we believe it's prudent for the AF to begin an investigation to determine possible drug use/collusion among the individuals identified, and possibly others," he wrote to senior Air Force officials. "It is not our desire to make this request. However, the AF needs to fairly apply its

---

[460] Tony Carr, "In Message to Wing Commanders, Welsh Declares 'Zero Privacy' Doctrine For All Airmen," *John Q. Public*, October 21, 2015

406

standards for investigations. Presumably, somebody is picking and choosing what/who gets investigated and what/who doesn't."[461]

Not taking the hint, Col. Sean McKenna, the chief of AETC Public Affairs, offered the following response: "The comment by the PA member was posted in response to a friend's comment," he said. "47th Flying Training Wing leadership have spoken with the individual and they are handling the matter appropriately."[462] This prompted another letter from Rep. Hunter to Gen. Welsh, highlighting the apparent hypocrisy of the Air Force reaction. "General Welsh, I know you are committed to resolving the case of the Laughlin pilots," he wrote. "And I know you are committed to avoiding the creation of a double standard, or even the appearance of one. But both of the situations that I have raised should underscore to the Air Force the magnitude of your decision in the case of the Laughlin pilots and the precedent it will set."[463]

Although the SAF/IG investigation and general-officer review of the "Molly Three" cases were completed as scheduled by late November, Gen. Welsh sat on the results for several weeks, prompting another Congressional inquiry. [464]   Just before Christmas, however, the Air Force finally released its ruling, declaring the alleged misconduct regarding improper drug use was not sufficiently substantiated by the evidence, so the three pilots would be reinstated.[465] "The commitment to a just outcome is a credit to Gen. Welsh," Tony Carr noted at the time, "but also a signal of the plainness and clarity of the wrongness and injustice manifested in the situation." How a miscarriage of justice like this could have happened in the first place, and what is being done to prevent its recurrence, remained unresolved questions.[466]

---

[461] Tony Carr, "In Social Media Posts, Laughlin Leaders Appear to Discuss Dropping Acid," *John Q. Public*, November 19, 2015
[462] Jeff Schogol, "Hunter asks Welsh about Laughlin PAO's LSD Facebook post," *Air Force Times*, November 23, 2015
[463] Tony Carr, "Congressman Warns CSAF to Avoid 'Creation of Double Standard' in Laughlin Review," *John Q. Public*, November 23, 2015
[464] Tony Carr, "Congress Presses CSAF for Answers on Miley Gate," *John Q. Public*, December 10, 2015
[465] AETC Public Affairs, "Final ruling on Laughlin pilot misconduct released," AETC official site, December 23, 2015
[466] Tony Carr, "Laughlin Pilots to Get Wings Back, Drug Reprimands to be Rescinded," *John Q. Public*, December 23, 2015

It took another six weeks for the Air Force to release the report of investigation, which unfortunately revealed SAF/IG had failed "to conduct an inquiry into whether correct processes and procedures were followed to determine the disposition of disciplinary actions," as Gen. Welsh directed. For example, the only witnesses interviewed were the very commanders and attorneys whose decisions were under review. Moreover, the IG didn't question why OSI was directed to lead an inquiry into relatively minor drug use allegations, and it ignored highly incriminating statements by the wing commander, Col. Hastings. The Laughlin staff judge advocate comes across as incompetent in the report, while the former 19 AF commander, Maj Gen Keltz, applied inappropriate disciplinary standards to instructor pilots and their students. The investigation also exposed Gen. Welsh and his staff as directly involved in the disposition of these matters, creating a fundamental conflict of interest for this inquiry ordered by the Chief of Staff of the Air Force. "This report represents the failure of the current leadership team to wrestle with an obvious ethical crisis in the ranks," *John Q. Public* concluded. "More distressingly, it represents an effort to conceal that such a crisis exists."[467]

More troubling, AETC did not actually restore the *status quo ante* for this trio as expected, and no apparent action has been taken to hold the former wing commander, Col. Hastings, accountable for his wrongful punishment of "IP7" and the other pilots. "The Air Force has had a chance to abridge this sad story by tearing some of the more unfortunate pages out and writing a new story ... a better one about doing the right thing, accepting the loss of face, punishing the *actual* wrongdoers no matter their ranks or positions, and learning important lessons for the future," Tony Carr wrote. Unless Gen. Welsh and the AETC commander change course, "that better story will never be written. We'll be stuck telling a much more regrettable tale instead."[468]

In the end, this seeming exception – the half-hearted exoneration of airmen accused of wrongdoing – merely proved the rule: "Gen. Welsh is unwilling to admit that the Air Force over which he presides has a problem with command abuse and overzealous prosecution," Tony Carr wrote. For an officer who

---

[467] John Q. Public, "Anatomy of a Whitewash," *John Q. Public*, February 5, 2016
[468] Tony Carr, "Molly Hangover: Pilots Still Grounded After Being Cleared of Drug Use," *John Q. Public*, January 6, 2016

built a public persona around his love for airmen, the Chief of Staff's actions – and inactions – speak much louder than his words. "Mark Welsh does not care about you unless you're in his personal circle," Carr concluded.

Needless to say, the members of Congress who demanded justice for the "Molly Three" were not amused. "I think perhaps we were too quick with our praise for General Welsh in this case," a spokesman for Rep. Hunter wrote. "The Air Force seems to make a habit of infuriating members of Congress for all the wrong reason and I'm just shocked that they are hanging their hat on this Laughlin issue, just to protect a few egos and toxic bands of leadership."[469] *JQP* issued a warning to airman considering a career in the Air Force: *Caveat emptor.* "Individual justice is a dead letter in today's Air Force. It's time for reform, and Congress should take the first step toward reform by demanding the Air Force set aside every charge against IP7 and restore his record to its *ex ante* condition." Unfortunately, there is little reason to expect this will happen, which is why "dark days lie ahead for America and her Air Force."[470]

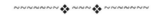

"Miley Gate" was not the first time members of Congress pressured Gen. Welsh into investigating senior-leader misconduct. During an Air Force weapons and tactics conference at Nellis AFB, Nevada on January 10, 2015, the vice commander of Air Combat Command, Maj. Gen. James Post, reportedly told the audience, "if anyone accuses me of saying this, I will deny it ... anyone who is passing information to Congress about A-10 capabilities is committing treason." The previous year, Air Force leaders had decided to retire several weapon systems, including the A-10 "Warthog" attack aircraft, due to budgetary pressures. However, many critics felt this close-air-support platform remained essential to national security, and was in fact then actively engaged in airstrikes on Islamic State terrorists. "This is a continuation of the party line that anyone who disagrees with CSAF's choices is reacting emotionally. It's a tactic to trivialize opponents, now

---

[469] Tony Carr, "Welsh Defies Congress, Turns Back on Wronged Laughlin Pilot," *John Q. Public*, January 28, 2016
[470] "Broken Wings: the Cautionary Tale of IP7," February 1, 2016

complete with a traitor label heaped on top," noted the *John Q. Public* blog. "This is a big deal if it's true. Generals hold the power to destroy lives and ruin careers. If speaking against your chain of command is considered treasonous by senior leadership, we should be concerned about the abuse of power to hound the perceived traitors." Moreover, restricting military members from communicating with Congress would violate federal law.

Air Combat Command initially defended Post's remarks. "The general's use of hyperbole in his comments during a recent discussion with attendees at a Tactics Review Board at Nellis were intended to communicate a serious point: the Air Force decision on recommended actions/strategic choices for the constrained fiscal environment has been made and the service's position communicated. While subsequent government debate will continue at the highest levels as those recommendations and other options are evaluated, our job as Airmen is to continue to execute our mission and duties – certainly our role as individual military members is not to engage in public debate or advocacy for policy."[471]

Members of Congress were not amused. Senator Kelly Ayotte (R-NH) declared she was "deeply disturbed" by the reported comments. "The Constitution defines treason as levying war against the United States in providing aid and comfort to our enemies," she said in a statement. "How could members of the armed forces exercising their lawful right to communicate with Congress be providing aid and comfort to our enemies? If the facts are on the Air Force's side regarding its efforts to prematurely divest the A-10, what does the Air Force fear?" Sen. John McCain (R-AZ), chairman of the Senate Armed Services Committee, called on the Secretary of the Air Force to investigate the reported comments. [472] In response, the Air Force Inspector General launched a formal investigation into the matter on January 22. Sen. Ayotte pressed Gen. Welsh during Congressional testimony the following week, asking if he found comments attributed to Maj. Gen. Post "acceptable." "I support any airman's right to discuss anything you'd like to discuss with them," Welsh replied. "My job is

---

[471] ADI News Services, "Post's comments send chill through Air Force ranks, A-10 panics ISIS," *Arizona Daily Independent*, January 15, 2015

[472] Brian Everstine, "2 star's 'treason' comments spark call for an investigation," *Air Force Times*, January 22, 2015

to wait until the facts are known," he added.[473] A month later, Sen. Ayotte eagerly awaited the results of this probe. "I am sure you would agree that we must unambiguously defend the lawful right of service members to communicate with Congress," she noted in a letter to the Secretary of the Air Force.[474]

The results of the investigation confirmed what critics complained of all along: Maj. Gen. Post did use the word "treason" during his remarks, which "had the effect of attempting to prevent some members from lawfully communicating with Congress," in violation of the 10 U.S. Code § 1034 and DoD directives, "whether that was his intention or not," according to an ACC press release. Consequently, on April 9, the ACC commander, Gen. Hawk Carlisle, fired his deputy and issued him a letter of reprimand.[475] This LOR "likely signals the not distant end of Post's career, and almost certainly disqualifies him for further advancement," *JQP* noted, which "seems appropriate to most observers."

However, "Lurking within the investigation and the events leading to it are clues gesturing toward deep-set problems of senior leadership, institutional climate, and transparency," Tony Carr wrote. He noted Gen. Welsh was aware of the controversy surrounding the ACC vice commander's remarks as early as January 13, yet he took no action to discipline the wayward general or renounce his chilling statements. It was Secretary James, not Gen. Welsh, who launched the IG investigation more than a week later, and neither the SecAF nor the CSAF commented publicly about the matter after Gen. Carlisle took his action.[476] It took another two weeks before they issued a tepid memorandum reminding airmen of military whistleblower protections.[477]

The reports of the death of Maj. Gen. Post's career were greatly exaggerated, however. While he was under investigation for his "treason" comments, the ACC vice commander was

[473] Martin Matishak "Senator presses Air Force chief on A-10 'treason' comments," *The Hill*, January 28, 2015
[474] Martin Matishak, "Republican senator wants update on A-10 'treason' probe," *The Hill*, February 25, 2015
[475] Jeff Schogol, "Two-star fired for 'treason' rant against A-10 supporters," *Air Force Times*, April 10, 2015
[476] Tony Carr "Air Force 'Treason' Debacle Reveals Deeper Problems," *John. Q. Public*, April 16th, 2015
[477] Tony Carr, "Months After Treason Remarks, Air Force Issues Ho-Hum Restriction Memo," *John Q. Public*, May 15th, 2015

dispatched to Maxwell AFB, Alabama, to mentor new wing and group commanders."[478] After his relief from this position, he was kicked upstairs to become the Air Staff director of current operations. This outcome speaks volumes about the misplaced priorities of Air Force leadership: While the 19 AF commander was ushered into retirement following his racially insensitive remarks, another two-star general received no more than a slap on the wrist for denouncing as treasonous the exercise of a fundamental right by American airmen. While loyalty, compliance, and conformity are signal qualities of military organizations, *JQP* warned, they can create a fascist culture when taken to the extremes Maj. Gen. Post seemed to advocate.[479]

---

[478] Tony Carr, "Maj Gen Post Mentors Future Wing Commanders at USAF Charm School," *John Q. Public*, April 18, 2015
[479] Tony Carr, "Creeping Fascism in the (un?)American Air Force?" *John Q. Public*, January 17, 2015

Chapter 19: Military Injustice

While Air Force general officers can apparently weather reprimands with no ill effects, such administrative action is typically disastrous for more junior officers like myself or the "Molly Three." But such bureaucratic punishments pale in comparison to sentences the Air Force has sought when prosecuting allegations of sexual misconduct at courts-martial. Perhaps the most lasting legacy of the Lackland sex scandal is the myth of a sexual assault epidemic in the military, and the extraordinary measures implemented to combat this overhyped phenomenon.

For example, TSgt Aaron Allmon, a combat photographer stationed at Minot AFB, North Dakota, faced up to 130 years in prison for unwanted sexual contact with four women – allegations that amounted to no more than a few kisses and a half-dozen touches, plus a series of reported inappropriate comments of a sexual nature. After a pretrial Article 32 hearing in December 2014, the investigative officer scolded the prosecution. "Given the sheer volume of charges in this case, and the apparent tendency of that volume to artificially exaggerate the criminality of the accused, it is entirely possible that the trial judge will simply dismiss the offending specifications," he wrote. "In many of the individual specifications," he continued, "it could be argued that the accused was not so much motivated by sex or a desire to humiliate or degrade as simply being socially maladroit and crass."

"The full weight of the military chain of command has come down on Aaron because the chain of command has abandoned justice and elected expediency," one of his attorneys noted. "Because of the hypersensitivity associated with real sexual assault cases, the Air Force in particular has overreacted against Aaron in a manner that is absolutely an injustice but is also degrading the esprit de corps of unit cohesion all across the military. Even assuming all the charges are true, which they are not, this conduct as charged would warrant nonjudicial punishment, not the highest level of action at a general court-martial where Aaron could lose all his retirement benefits and go to jail." The defendant's sister estimated she would spend $200,000 on her brother's legal defense, which includes a former sheriff's deputy as investigator, a civilian lawyer and a former Army judge advocate who took the case *pro bono*.[480]

This case prompted *John Q. Public* to question whether any airman accused of a sex-related infraction could expect a fair process.

> *For years, the Air Force and its sister services have been hounded by Congress for their failures to address sexual misconduct. That hounding has translated into intense political pressure that threatens the interests of the bureaucracy, which has in turn amplified it to a level capable of warping justice.*
>
> *When everyone from the President and Secretary of Defense to the service chief and local command chain is constantly and relentlessly insisting that sexual misconduct be dealt with swiftly and severely, and when rhetorical habits have eliminated any distinction between types and degrees of sexual misconduct, it arguably becomes nigh on impossible for an accused member to expect that his fate will be shaped by a fair-minded, objective prosecutor. It also makes it less likely that a panel of truly impartial jurors can be seated, given that such panels are comprised of airmen subject to the same message bombardment that seems to be pushing prosecutors and commanders into questionable decisions.*[481]

Ultimately, TSgt Allmon was acquitted of charges of sexual assault, sexual harassment, and making threats, but was convicted of making sexual comments to two female airmen and lying to the OSI agents. He was sentenced to 30 days confinement and demotion to Staff Sergeant. His attorney plans to appeal the judge's ruling, noting that Air Force leaders have "overreacted in the name of political correctness."[482]

---

[480] Rowan Scarborough, "Aaron Allmon case makes Minot Air Force Base ground zero in military's new gender wars," *The Washington Times*, November 5, 2015

[481] Tony Carr, "Minot Airman Faces Life in Prison for Being 'Socially Maladroit'," *John Q. Public*, November 7, 2015

[482] Phillip Swarts, "Minot tech sergeant acquitted of sexual assault, found guilty on lesser charges," *Air Force Times*, November 20, 2015

Perhaps the most salacious tale of misconduct by an instructor pilot at Laughlin AFB was that of Captain Chris Hill. He carried on an illicit affair with one of his female students while his wife struggled with a difficult pregnancy, then brought his mistress along with him on a trip to San Antonio with his wife and newborn daughter. As investigators closed in on him in 2014, he buried an external hard drive, an iPad, and a cellphone near a hangar at Del Rio International Airport, on which forensic experts found incriminating photographs.[483] Capt. Hill pled guilty in November 2015 to engaging in an unprofessional relationship with this student, involving adultery and sex on federal property (in his Laughlin office). He also admitted to having sex with an enlisted airman while deployed to Guam in 2012, and fraternizing with two other female enlisted members when stationed at Minot AFB, North Dakota, between 2010 and 2012. In addition, he failed to obey a no-contact order, made a false official statement to an investigating officer, and obstructed justice for (literally) burying evidence of his crimes.

Although he was facing over 20 years in prison for these charges, the judge sentenced him to only three months confinement, as well as dismissal from the Air Force and forfeiture of all pay and allowances. However, he will only serve 45 days due to pre-trial agreement.[484] While Capt. Hill's conduct was clearly unbecoming an officer and gentleman, dismissal seems a particularly harsh sentence given the crimes he committed. For a military officer, this is the equivalent of a dishonorable discharge, and carries with it severe consequences. In many states, dismissal is recognized as a felony sentence, and federal law precludes dismissed officers from carrying firearms. For these reasons, this sentence is ordinarily reserved for the most severe, usually violent, criminal offenses.

More troubling is the question of whether Capt. Hill was able to mount an adequate defense. The witch-hunt at Laughlin

---

[483] Sig Christenson, "Air Force pilot to serve 45 days in sex, obstruction case," *San Antonio Express-News*, November 16, 2015
[484] 19th Air Force Public Affairs, "Laughlin AFB instructor pilot court-martialed," AETC official site, November 17, 2015

created an environment of fear and intimidation, which dissuaded witnesses from participating in the legal defense of their wingmen. Leaders made public statements that seemed to prejudge the guilt of accused officers, while those under investigation were sometimes issued no-contact orders preventing them from enlisting witnesses. Some officers who dared to write character reference letters allegedly saw their performance reports downgraded. [485] In the case of Capt. Hill, multiple potential witnesses declined to help explicitly because they feared retribution from their chain of command, and this was a factor in his decision to plead guilty to the charges rather than defend himself at trial. While it's tempting to write this off as an isolated incident, *John Q. Public* warned this problem could be much scarier: "the service's top officer has cultivated a kafkaesque environment of institutional paranoia that stands to distort every instance of the justice process across the entire enterprise."[486]

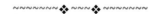

With the repeal of the "Don't Ask, Don't Tell" policy in 2011, homosexuals were at last allowed to serve openly in the military. Unfortunately, it was only a matter of time before service members would find themselves accused of crimes involving gay sex. Perhaps the highest-profile prosecution to date is against Lieutenant Joshua Seefried, a founder of OutServe – an advocacy group instrumental in the repeal of "DADT" – in 2010. This U.S. Air Force Academy graduate is facing court-martial on charges of wrongful and abusive sexual contact and forcible sodomy in a case scheduled to go to trial on August 22, 2016, at Fort Meade, Maryland.[487]

These charges stem from allegations by a Marine officer that Seefried performed sexual acts on him in a New York hotel room in 2012, while he was intoxicated and unable to give consent.

---

[485] Tony Carr, "Bombshell Report: Laughlin Reprisal Campaign Destroyed Anyone Providing Support to Witch Hunt Targets," *John Q. Public*, October 4, 2015

[486] Tony Carr, "How the USAF's Toxic Climate is Degrading Military Justice," *John Q. Public*, November 20, 2015

[487] Michael K. Lavers, "Gay Air Force lieutenant court martial trial scheduled," *Washington Blade*, March 11, 2016

However, a U.S. Coast Guard officer who was also present claimed that the encounter was fully consensual. "We got into bed – the three of us," he testified at a pre-trial hearing. "I believe [the Marine] was a willing participant," he added. The military investigator who presided over a pair of Article 32 hearings concluded there was insufficient evidence to prove the allegations against Seefried, and a court-martial would most likely result in the defendant's acquittal.

Nevertheless, the Air Force insists on pursuing this prosecution. Maj. Gen. Darryl Burke, commander of the Air Force District of Washington, has twice ordered the case to go to trial, and Secretary James reportedly denied Seefried's request to resign his commission in lieu of court-martial. Such an outcome is not surprising to observers such as Eric Montalvo, a retired Marine Corps attorney. After years of political pressure from Congress and the White House to address sexual assault in the military, "10 times out of 10 it's going to get referred to a general court martial," Montalvo said. "It doesn't even have to be a straight faced allegation because I've seen all kinds of craziness coming through the system now," he said. "And so the pendulum has swung to the absurd and in my opinion a lot of true victims are getting lost in this shuffle because the amount of nonsense coming through the system is beyond belief."[488]

Another questionable case that only recently made headlines is that of Major Michael Turpiano. I met this intelligence officer in late 2014, when he introduced himself to me while I was eating lunch at a fast-food restaurant near JBSA-Lackland. He recognized me from the cover of the *Air Force Times*, and noted my curious case had become a cautionary tale among the officers in his squadron. Previously a communication officer, Maj. Turpiano had been cross-training into the intelligence career field at Goodfellow AFB, in San Angelo, Texas, when his own tragic story began.

In March 2013, Maj. Turpiano came under investigation when his ex-girlfriend, an Air Force civilian, filed a complaint with

---

[488] Lou Chibbaro Jr., "Air Force Sec'y reportedly won't drop case against gay lieutenant," *Washington Blade*, December 22, 2015

OSI that he raped her, claims that were ultimately found to be false. But she wasn't the only alleged victim in this relationship. Maj. Turpiano also filed an unrestricted report against his ex with the local sexual assault response coordinator. The SARC considered Maj. Turpiano's allegation sufficiently credible that he was assigned a special victims counsel, and an Air Force mental health provider later diagnosed him as having experienced adult sexual abuse. (Disturbingly, the SARC continued to represent his accuser throughout this process, an obvious conflict of interest.) However, Air Force authorities were much more interested in the crimes this officer supposedly committed.

In addition to the civilian complainant, a female student reported her class leader, Maj. Turpiano, sexually abused her, and a couple of other female students also claimed he touched them inappropriately.[489] Once the initial allegations came to light, the 315th Training Squadron commander immediately put Maj. Turpiano on administrative hold just days before he was scheduled to graduate. He also issued this class leader a no-contact order covering 38 personnel, effectively isolating him from his support networks and potential defense witnesses. While the commander later whittled this list down as the investigation dragged on, he only removed names as students graduated and departed the local area. (At the time, he claimed he issued this order for the safety of the other students, but he later stated it was because it appeared a witness had been coached.) The squadron commander reportedly dropped in on OSI interrogations on several occasions to encourage witnesses to denounce Maj. Turpiano, and he also allegedly questioned witnesses separately in his own office. Finally, both the squadron and group commanders discussed details of this ongoing investigation with several classes of students, creating a hostile work environment for the accused, who had since been reassigned to the wing headquarters.[490]

One of these witnesses later wrote a statement about her interrogation, which offers a harrowing glimpse of OSI intimidation tactics. The agent began by asking this second lieutenant if she was

---

[489] *Air Force Sexual Assault Court-Martial Summaries*, p. 40 (Note: The official summary incorrectly states "a female officer reported she was sexually harassed by Maj Turpiano.")

[490] Maj. Michael Turpiano, IG complaint against 17 TRG and 315 TRS commanders for abuse of authority, creating hostile work environment, and privacy violations, July 3, 2013

involved in a relationship with anyone at Goodfellow AFB. When she answered "no," he accused her of lying, and suggested she was in fact in a relationship with Maj. Turpiano. The agent threatened to write the witness up for making a false official statement, at which point she asked for a lawyer, but he denied her request. Switching gears, the agent then expressed concern that Maj. Turpiano had sexually assaulted the witness, but when she denied ever having been sexually assaulted in her life, her interrogator told her he didn't believe her.

The special agent eventually advised her of her rights and asked if she wanted a lawyer. When she said "yes," the agent left the room for several minutes, then returned with her squadron commander. After being back-briefed on the details of the interrogation, the commander entered the room and sat next to his subordinate, while the OSI agent continued trying to convince her to change her statement. Her commander piled on, telling her she appeared to be untruthful, and she would feel better if she told OSI the truth. He eventually got up and left the room, but the OSI agent continued questioning her for some time before recalling she had already been read her rights and requested a lawyer. Her interrogator released her to her squadron commander, who confirmed she was not going to do anything to hurt herself before giving her the phone number for the local area defense counsel.[491]

This story is personally unsettling for me. As a former Air Force intelligence officer, I had hoped my schoolhouse wouldn't engage in the same sorts of buffoonery seen at Lackland and other training bases. Moreover, Maj. Turpiano's squadron commander was actually a friend of mine, who I served with in Korea and again at the Pentagon. I never would have imagined someone like him engaging in this kind of conduct. Then again, Goodfellow is an AETC base, a training environment particularly susceptible to shenanigans such as these. Ironically, if Maj. Turpiano hadn't introduced himself to me that day, I'd have had no clue such egregious injustice was occurring at my alma mater, which begs the question: Where else are airmen experiencing such shocking abuses of authority?

During this ordeal, Maj. Turpiano filed a pair of complaints against his chain of command with the 17th Training Wing inspector general, which were referred to the wing commander for

---

[491] "Statement of events occurring 6 Apr 13 at Goodfellow AFB," October 15, 2013

action. She directed only an informal inquiry into this matter, which not surprisingly found his allegations against the group and squadron commanders unsubstantiated.[492] When Maj. Turpiano petitioned Maj. Gen. Patrick in March 2014 to launch his own investigation into the handling of this case, the 2 AF commander conducted only a cursory legal review of the 17 TRW informal inquiry. He claimed to be "satisfied that the issues have been sufficiently examined and there is no need for further investigation."[493]

It wasn't until July 2014, after he had been reassigned to JBSA-Lackland, that Maj. Turpiano's new commander preferred charges against him. He was accused of physical and sexual assault of his civilian ex-girlfriend; abusive sexual contact against a female officer; and conduct unbecoming an officer for wrongfully touching fellow students and being drunk and disorderly in their presence.[494] By the time his case finally went to trial at Lackland in January 2015, however, these charges had been reduced to one specification of sexual assault and four specifications of assault consummated by a battery.[495] Although Maj. Turpiano was acquitted of all charges related to his ex-girlfriend and the female officer whose allegations set off the witch-hunt against him, he was found guilty of assaulting two other students.

Upon closer inspection, however, it's not clear any crimes actually occurred. The first incident allegedly happened while Maj. Turpiano was "dirty dancing" with a fellow student at a nightclub off base, when he supposedly touched her breast. According to a clemency request his lawyers submitted after the trial, if this alleged contact happened at all, it "was either accidental or consensual," or at a minimum, "Maj. Turpiano had a reasonable mistake of fact about whether she consented based on the circumstances." Although this alleged victim denied it at trial, Maj. Turpiano testified that she had reached over and grabbed him

---

[492] 17th Training Wing commander, "Response to IG Complaint re: Allegations of Abuse of Authority, Hostile Work Environment and Privacy Violations Against the 17 TRG/CC, 315 TRS/CC and 315 TRS/CCF," August 30, 2013

[493] E-mail exchange between Maj. Turpiano and Maj. Gen. Patrick, "Command/OSI Misconduct Concerning Victims of Sexual Assault," March 1-31, 2014

[494] Charge sheet, July 10, 2014

[495] *Air Force Sexual Assault Court-Martial Summaries*, p. 40

between his legs while they were dancing. She continued dancing with him after this alleged assault until he left the dance floor, and danced with him again later that evening. Another witness testified it seemed like she was having fun, and this alleged victim never reported any assault until she was interrogated by OSI – and even then, her sworn statement differed significantly from her subsequent court testimony.

The second incident allegedly occurred at a local bar, where Maj. Turpiano supposedly hugged another student against her will. Although there were several witnesses present, none claimed to have seen this purported assault, which was again not reported until OSI launched their probe. While not admissible at trial, Maj. Turpiano passed a polygraph regarding both these incidents, adding credence to his version of events.

In their clemency request, Maj. Turpiano's attorneys also objected to the OSI misconduct, including keeping witnesses for unreasonably long times in the interrogation room (up to 10 hours, in one example); threatening witnesses with criminal charges such as obstruction of justice, false official statement, or perjury unless the witness implicated Maj. Turpiano in additional misconduct; yelling and verbally abusing witnesses; and telling them exactly what to write in their statements. They also accused the prosecution of failing to disclose favorable information to the defense. One witness who experienced abuse at the hands of OSI later recanted his sworn statement, telling prosecutors "they should consider anything in his written statement suspect," and even pointing out a specific example of what he called "erroneous information" contained in his written statement. However, the prosecution never informed the defense of this retraction, and the judge declined to grant relief based on this law enforcement misconduct.

For his alleged offenses, Maj. Turpiano was sentenced to three months confinement, forfeiture of pay, and dismissal from the Air Force. "We respectfully submit that a dismissal, which is for all intents and purposes a dishonorable discharge, is unduly severe for the offenses of which Maj. Turpiano was convicted," his lawyers later wrote. "Again, had the allegations in those two specifications been the only accusations against him, it is likely that they would have been resolved by nonjudicial punishment under Article 15,

UCMJ rather than a general court-martial."[496]   This was, quite simply, a travesty of justice, yet the convening authority, Brig. Gen. LaBrutta, refused to grant clemency.   Given the shocking abuses documented during the investigation, prosecutorial misconduct leading up to the trial, and the glaring mismatch between the alleged offenses and the sentence adjudged, this case seems ripe for reversal on appeal.

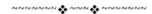

Maj. Turpiano wasn't the only airman to stand trial for sexual crimes at JBSA-Lackland in early 2015.   An even more notorious case went to court-martial on January 20, involving a former Military Training Instructor accused of raping three women. Master Sergeant Mike Silva was the last of the MTIs to face prosecution in the wake of the Lackland sex scandal, during which a handful of instructors were accused of rape and sexual assault, and dozens more were found to have engaged in unprofessional relationships with trainees and students.   By the time this case finally went to trial, however, the Air Force had managed to secure a rape conviction against only one other MTI, SSgt Luis Walker. It was the Walker case that launched an Air Force-wide witch-hunt, yet none of the dozens of other defendants since then was found to have engaged in similarly heinous crimes at BMT. "United States v. MSgt Michael Silva" seemed to offer one last opportunity to put a serial rapist behind bars.

The similarities between these two cases didn't end there. MSgt Silva was alleged to have raped a trainee in and around the same recruit housing and training facility – Building 9210 – where SSgt Walker later committed his crimes. MSgt Silva hired a civilian attorney to assist in his defense, who previously represented Walker during his court-martial – although he never advised his new client of this unfortunate coincidence. In an even more ironic twist, MSgt Silva would receive an identical sentence as his notorious predecessor, perversely bookending this sad chapter in Air Force justice.

---

[496] Terri Zimmermann and Capt. Arthur Vaughan, "Clemency Request ICO *United States v. Major Michael Turpiano, U.S. Air Force*," June 10, 2015

What made the Silva court-martial unlike any other MTI prosecutions that came before was the timeframe of the allegations. The crimes MSgt Silva stood accused of committing didn't occur during the troubled recent era at BMT. Rather, he supposedly raped a trainee back in 1995, when he was just a Senior Airman. This former trainee first came forward in October 2012, months after the Lackland sex scandal made national headlines, when she reported her alleged assault to the AETC sexual assault hotline. Her story changed several times, however, before this case went to court-martial, where she accused MSgt Silva of raping her not once, but twice. One night, she testified, SrA Silva woke her up in the open-bay barracks, told her to put on her physical training clothes, and took her to his personal vehicle. When she expressed concern about being alone with him, this MTI supposedly told her he would take care of her and she did not have to worry. SrA Silva then allegedly raped her in the front seat of his car – and again a few days later in an unspecified dark room. She claimed SrA Silva told her if she reported what happened, either nobody would believe her or it would follow her around for her whole career. In addition to these alleged crimes at Lackland, Silva also stood accused by two ex-wives of raping them during their marriages – first in North Carolina in the early 1990s, then again in 2007, when he was stationed in Wyoming.[497]

None of these alleged victims appeared at an Article 32 evidentiary hearing in February 2014,[498] but they provided damning testimony when the case finally went to trial nearly a year later. Although these were essentially "he said, she said" allegations, with no physical evidence or corroborating witnesses, the prosecution painted a compelling picture to bolster their case. According to a newspaper account of the trial, the new recruit who accused MSgt Silva of raping her nearly two decades earlier was "outstanding" before she joined the Air Force, "throwing two paper routes as a kid, taking advanced classes in school, playing guitar and singing in a choir. She also had family in the military and couldn't wait to serve," the author wrote. Her mother described her as "vivacious," "strong" and "determined" when she shipped off to BMT at age 18, but she "was not the same girl" after coming home. "She just didn't know what she was going to do anymore,"

[497] *Air Force Sexual Assault Court-Martial Summaries*, p. 67
[498] Sig Christenson, "Rape hearing runs 30 minutes," *San Antonio Express-News*, February 24, 2014

her mother told the court. Her husband and mother both described her as "paranoid and hypervigilant, staying in her house more often than not, struggling to sleep and distant from her children," claiming to fear Silva or someone else was observing her.

When she took the stand, this alleged victim said she "knew the enemy could do bad things," but she felt she had been betrayed by a fellow airman. "I used to have a hate for Michael Silva in my heart, and I don't like that," she told the jury panel of five officers and three senior NCOs. One of MSgt Silva's ex-wives wrote in an unsworn statement read to the jury that she "was extremely anxious around authority figures," made a lot of mistakes in her job and struggled to be intimate with her new husband since her alleged rape. "I became emotionally flat," she wrote. Prosecutors said MSgt Silva choked and overpowered his victims during their alleged assaults, and they sought a life sentence for these offenses.

MSgt Silva wasn't called to testify during the trial, and appeared to show no emotion as the jury handed down its sentence at the end of his nearly two-week trial. He had been convicted of raping both the trainee and his second wife, but acquitted of the oldest charge. During the punishment phase of the trial, the defendant's sister tearfully told the jury her brother was a good father, and so devoted to his parents that he returned home from an overseas tour to care for his dad, a retired Army sergeant major; his mother has also lived with him since suffering a heart attack. "He's always been taking care of everybody," she said. In an unsworn statement, which allowed him to take the stand without being cross-examined, MSgt Silva expressed sorrow to the Air Force, his family, and even the jury. He did not, however, apologize to any of his alleged victims, maintaining his innocence until the end. His government-appointed attorney noted MSgt Silva was a father, the son of a career soldier, and an Air Force veteran on the rise who had been selected for promotion to Senior Master Sergeant.

On the other hand, the recruit he was convicted of raping told the jury this former MTI "is not the Air Force," and with a guilty verdict rendered, she no longer has to be scared.[499] MSgt Silva was sentenced to 20 years confinement, a dishonorable discharge, total forfeiture of all pay and allowances, and reduction in grade to E-1. He is currently incarcerated at Fort Leavenworth,

---

[499] Sig Christenson, "Lackland instructor gets 20 years in prison in rape cases," *San Antonio Express-News*, January 30, 2015

Kansas, and could be eligible for parole after serving one-third of his sentence, or just under seven years.[500]

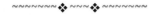

This portrait of Mike Silva as a sexual predator and serial rapist is wholly at odds with the man his friends, family, and coworkers knew. During his nine years as an MTI – first at Lackland and then at Officer Training School at Maxwell AFB, Alabama – Silva touched countless lives. Yet no other recruits ever accused him of inappropriately touching them, let alone committing such a horrific crime as rape. On the contrary, most remember him as a caring and engaged leader, who became a lifelong mentor to many of his former trainees. At least one of them went on to become an MTI himself, even following in Mike's footsteps from BMT to OTS. After growing up on the "tough streets" of Washington, DC, this MTI now praises the Air Force for saving his life. Gen. Welsh honored him at the Air Force Association's Air and Space Conference in September 2015, one of several "heroes" he introduced onstage.[501] But the Chief of Staff didn't mention that this exceptional airman considers his own MTI, then-SSgt Silva, to be a father figure who had a tremendous positive influence on his career. His own hero is now sitting in prison for crimes he likely did not commit.

MSgt Silva's defense attorneys had their work cut out for them at trial. They were facing an experienced Lackland prosecution team, and special victims counsels represented two of the alleged victims. Although none of their allegations was particularly convincing on its own, together they appeared to establish a pattern of crimes extending over a decade and a half. Moreover, because one of his accusers was once his trainee at BMT, this former MTI was presumed guilty by association with the scandal that had so recently gripped the Lackland community.

Moreover, the military judge in this case seemed biased against the defendant throughout the trial. She told the jury that the inability of the former trainee to credibly answer questions was a result of fatigue rather than dishonesty. She also suggested this

---

[500] *Air Force Sexual Assault Court-Martial Summaries*, p. 67
[501] U.S. Air Force, "2015 Air and Space Conference: Air Force Update with Gen. Mark A. Welsh III," September 16, 2015

alleged victim may have been assaulted at a different time and place than her testimony indicated. An observer in the courtroom saw the judge making faces when defense counsel asserted her client's innocence, and on another occasion she lost her temper with defense counsel in front of the jury. When the prosecution seemed unsure as to where one of the alleged rapes occurred, the judge declared, "it had to have happened somewhere."[502] Such behavior was highly prejudicial to the defense, and probably prevented MSgt Silva from receiving a fair trial.

Furthermore, critical evidence that might have exonerated MSgt Silva wasn't available during his court-martial. For example, OSI didn't properly interview two instructors who helped SrA Silva push the trainee flight to which an alleged victim was briefly assigned. The female MTI in charge of the "brother" flight later signed an affidavit stating she had never "witnessed any inappropriate interactions between Mike and a female trainee," nor had she ever heard any gossip in the squadron to that effect. She also denied SrA Silva ever attempted to gain entry into the dorms after lights out.[503] Another airman provided a sworn statement confirming he shadowed SrA Silva as he pushed this flight, his first as a member of the BMT staff before attending the MTI School. As he was not yet signed off to be with the flight by himself, he never left SrA Silva's side during that period: "We would meet in the morning for Roll Call and work all day until lights out and would leave at the same time in our separate vehicles," he declared. He, too, denied ever seeing SrA Silva behave inappropriately.[504] The prosecution also didn't turn over any of the alleged victim's medical or training records for a critical six-day period, which may have left the jury with the impression SrA Silva had access to her during that time.

Finally, the defendant's attorneys failed to request critical records during discovery, and they opted not to present certain evidence that might have discredited prosecution witnesses. Apparently overconfident about the outcome of the trial, they declined to put their client on the stand, likely hurting their own case. Since the verdict was announced, however, more evidence

---

[502] Defense Counsel, "Clemency Request, AB Michael Silva," September 21, 2015
[503] Affidavit from SrA Silva's MTI teammate, June 24, 2015
[504] Statement from SrA Silva's MTI student, May 26, 2015

has been uncovered that casts this outcome even further into doubt.

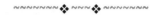

Let's begin with the simply incredible rape allegations by the BMT recruit. According to her official records, she arrived at Lackland on Wednesday, September 20, 1995, where she was initially assigned to SrA Silva's flight in the 322 TRS. Three days later, she reported to the base hospital complaining of pain in her Achilles tendon, a preexisting condition exacerbated by running at BMT. She was issued crutches and removed from training, then presumably reassigned to medical hold across base at the 319 TRS. She returned to training in a different squadron, the 331 TRS, on September 29, but went back to the hospital and the 319 TRS the following month for other medical issues. She was ultimately discharged from BMT on November 7, after less than seven weeks in the Air Force.

Alarmingly, it's impossible to reconcile the trainee's account with the extremely short period of time – only three nights – she spent in the 322 TRS before her injury. For example, she stated she was wearing physical training clothes during the initial assault, but this uniform likely wasn't issued until Friday. Furthermore, it was standard policy in those days for an MTI of the same gender to sleep in the dormitory with the flight during their first couple of nights at BMT, meaning SrA Silva would have had no access to these trainees at that time. (He would actually have been in their brother flight's dorm on those evenings.) She claimed she was raped again "a few nights after" the initial attack, but there simply wasn't enough time for both assaults to occur before she was removed from Silva's flight on Saturday morning.

This former trainee's account of the alleged assaults doesn't add up, either. She claimed the first attack occurred in a well-lit parking lot, just yards away from the recruit housing and training facility. She testified her MTI led her to his two-door personal vehicle (SrA Silva drove a four-door Geo Prizm back in those days), where they initially sat talking in his car. He then supposedly asked her to come around to his side of the vehicle, so she exited the passenger door and walked to the driver's side, where she allegedly found him sitting with his pants already down. At this point, she presumably could have run away from him in this compromised position, or cry for help from the nearby squadron building. Instead, she testified she got on her knees and performed oral sex – yet incredibly, under cross-examination, this alleged victim claimed not to remember whether her assailant was circumcised or not. Finally, her MTI supposedly pulled her into the front seat of his vehicle (not an easy task for a 6'4" man in a compact car) and raped her, all while the car door remained open. He then somehow returned her to her locked and guarded dorm unnoticed.

Her account of the second alleged rape is equally suspect. A few days later, she testified, her MTI again summoned her to come downstairs after hours, ostensibly to perform charge-of-quarter duties. He supposedly led her out to his car again, but this time he drove her somewhere. Telling her to keep her eyes closed, her assailant led her into a dark, windowless room, where she allegedly could not see anything around her. Nevertheless, he supposedly managed to brush her hair, remove her Battle Dress Uniform, rape her multiple times, and get her dressed again – all in this pitch-black environment. He then drove her back to the squadron and dropped her off at the curb outside the building, leaving her to find her own way back upstairs to her dorm. Whether this alleged incident occurred "at a residence," as the press reported,[505] or in a supply shed near the squadron building – as the prosecution also insinuated – is anyone's guess.

Moreover, this former trainee's various accounts betray a startling unfamiliarity with standard BMT procedures, reinforcing the perception she was not being entirely honest in her recollections. For instance, she claimed her MTI selected her as an element leader on her first night at BMT. That's simply not how things are done, however; such leadership positions are not chosen on pick-up night, and it's exceedingly unlikely an 18-year-old with no prior Junior Reserve Officer Training Corps experience would be singled out for this honor. Furthermore, she testified her bed was at the back of the dorm bay, but element leaders sleep near the MTI office, further suggesting she made this detail up. She also claimed she was called down to perform charge-of-quarter duties before the second rape, but there's no way she would have been trained for such responsibilities so early in her BMT career. Significantly, no one could explain how this trainee managed to get in and out of

---

[505] Sig Christenson, "Lackland instructor guilty in recruit's 1995 rape," San Antonio Express-News, January 29, 2015

her dorm without the female MTI, the dorm guards, or anyone else noticing.

Finally, not a single witness corroborated any of the alleged victim's statements. MSgt Silva claimed he has no recollection of this particular trainee whatsoever, and not one of the twenty trainees interviewed during the investigation remembered any unusual incidents during that time. The alleged victim accused SrA Silva of stalking her at BMT, saying he escorted her to the 331 TRS to introduce her to her new instructor, then dropped in from time to time to keep an eye on her in the 331 TRS chow hall. However, her 331 TRS instructor testified nothing like this ever happened. Moreover, the 331 TRS was located three-quarters of a mile away from the 322 TRS back in those days – not exactly a convenient detour for an MTI busy pushing a flight, with an MTI student watching his every move. She also claimed SrA Silva approached her at the chapel in civilian clothes, and he supposedly introduced himself to her uncle, a county sheriff who was in town visiting. However, this purported witness also denied this incident occurred, and he believed she would have told him or other authorities if she had experienced such unlawful actions by her MTI. Even more disturbing, the former trainee testified she revealed her alleged rape(s) to a doctor at the base hospital, but he refused to do anything about it. However, this physician testified that no female trainee ever reported to him she had been raped – and if anyone had made such a report, he would have notified law enforcement immediately.

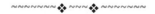

There are numerous other inconsistencies in this alleged victim's account. In her first statement to OSI in 2012, she denied ever telling anyone else about what happened to her at BMT, not even her mother or first husband, who she met at Lackland. During her trial, however, her mother testified her daughter did tell her about the rape when she returned home from BMT. It strains credibility that this alleged victim would have forgotten this confession, or that her mother never asked how she was dealing with this trauma over the next 17 years. The accuser later admitted to investigators she had in fact told one other person: a fellow trainee she met in the 319 TRS. Unfortunately, this potential corroborating witness had died in July 2008.

In another bizarre twist to an already dubious tale, this alleged victim offered addition details about her brief stint in the Air Force on a Facebook page dedicated to the memory of her deceased BMT wingman. In a series of posts between 2010 and 2013, she carried on a one-sided conversation with "her best friend in the Air Force" about the "fun times we had at our squadron," and "all our fun goofy times in the USAF." ("No one messed with us," she wrote the dead girl's mother in another post.) She made no allusions to her alleged rape until late 2011, when she complained of having bad dreams. "You literally stood next to me when for no reason [but] to intimidate he would show up at our squadron," she wrote, an apparent reference to her alleged rapist. "SMSGT. now what a reward for such an evil person," she continued, suggesting the man she believed attacked her was already an E-8. (MSgt Silva wasn't selected for promotion to that rank until 2013, but this promotion was later red-lined due to her allegations against him.)

Although she was medically discharged in early November 1995, this former trainee remembered spending that Thanksgiving in San Antonio with her "USAF Bestie." She said a Hispanic family "took us for the day," treating them to a trip to the grocery store and sightseeing on the downtown River Walk. She claimed to have pictures of the two of them in their Air Force battle-dress uniforms on Thanksgiving Day, suggesting she participated in "Operation Home Cooking," a program where trainees are matched with local families for the holiday. However, the author of these posts was no longer in the service by this point, according to her official records. She also bragged about "looking sharp in our Blues" when she and her wingman attended sporting events in town, another odd contention considering she probably wouldn't have been issued the more formal blue uniform after fewer than four weeks of training, nor would she likely have been allowed to depart base. She repeatedly claimed to have pictures from those events packed away somewhere in her home, but she could never seem to find these keepsakes, and she never shared any photos of herself in uniform. However, family members of the deceased airman apparently have no recollection of her ever wearing blues, and she apparently never spoke of a friend who was raped at BMT.

In her final post on this memorial page, nine months after reporting her alleged rape, she thanked her dead friend for helping her years ago, "when I did all I knew to do to save my USAF career and stay safe from him hurting me again. I will stay strong to change things so others are safe," she declared, hinting at her new calling as an advocate for survivors of military sexual trauma. She subsequently confided in other alleged victims who had made a name for themselves in the survivor community, and she began closely following the activities of Jennifer Norris, a retired airman who became an outspoken advocate for fellow rape victims, as well as the case of Ruth Moore, a Navy veteran who was awarded $405,000 in retroactive disability benefits in 2014. Given her history of mental instability and self-promotion, the prospect of cashing in as a survivor of military sexual trauma must have seemed a tempting incentive to simply invent her own victimization.

In April 2012, she alluded to her alleged perpetrator in a comment on another Facebook page: "It's been almost 18yrs ago for me and I have had a good life but like I said it will never go away and he is now a Chief Master Sgt." In September 2012, she volunteered additional details about her alleged assault:

> *The person who sexually assaulted me was my [MTI]. When I reported it to a [doctor] at Wilford Hall Medical Center because I realized the flashbacks I was having were causing me to blackout. I told him I just needed him to tell me how to stop passing out after flashbacks because I couldn't risk my career! He looked straight at me and said we aren't going to talk about that. I was discharged for migraines, which the [doctor] admitted to me I didn't meet the criteria for that diagnosis but he would recommend discharge because I wasn't going to ruin his career. My [MTI] literally stalked me until discharge. The last thing he said to me is "Are you going back to your home of record?" I stayed home for Christmas and moved away. For years, it's affected my life. I didn't tell anyone for many reasons after being discharged. I've been working on this issue to be taken care of. I recently found a promotion list, he is now a CMSgt and stationed a few hours from me. It's taking senators to stop him now! Thanks to help at the VA I'm doing much better. They changed a diagnosis a civilian doctor gave me of bipolar disorder, realizing my symptoms were from [military sexual trauma] and [post-traumatic stress disorder]. Nightly nightmares, anxiety attacks, flashbacks and sleep deprivation is devastating to a person. Thank You God for giving me the strength to do what I said I would do the night it happened, that is not let him win and one day see that he*

ends up in Leavenworth. Please let everything myself and those backing me be successful in holding him responsible for his actions.

However, this account appears to be false in almost every detail. Her doctor testified at trial that no female trainee ever reported a rape to him. Moreover, she again described her rapist as a Chief Master Sergeant, now stationed near her home in the Pacific Northwest – a description that does not at all match MSgt Silva, who had lived in San Antonio since 2009, and was never stationed anywhere near her since she left BMT. No other airmen named "Silva" was promoted to Chief that year, and none of her former MTIs ever achieved that rank, suggesting she was simply making this story up.[506]

The following month, she posted this on a Facebook page: "I was raped while active after reporting I was diagnosed within 24hrs with a medical condition I do not have. Never allowed to speak with or submit a statement to the [medical evaluation board] and appealed my discharged while my perpetrator stalked me." She elaborated further in March 2013: "I wasn't having unprofessional or sexual conversation with my superior. Simply put, I was following orders in regulation military issued clothing. I said no, I was trying to rationalize with the person, still being professional saying sir and saying anything my shocked, scared and horrified mind could think of. I said everything I could think of, yet I was still raped." According to her later testimony, she was asleep and undressed before the first alleged incident. Ironically, in the same post she wrote, "To be willing to be the reason someone may be imprisoned and traumatize not only the accused but their family is again the act of an evil, sick person with no conscience."

Ominously, MSgt Silva wasn't the first person this woman accused of raping her. Prior to enlisting in the Air Force, she claimed her stepfather had sexually assaulting her as a child, and he served four years in prison for this crime. She later testified at his parole hearing in January 1996, just months after her discharge

---

506 Bob McCarty, "Is Accuser's Facebook Update Riddled With Inaccuracies?" *BobMcCarty.com*, September 23, 2015

from the Air Force. When she divorced her first husband – an airman she met at Lackland – in 2002, she apparently claimed he was mentally and physically abusive, and implied he raped her during the marriage. However, her ex-husband was ultimately awarded custody of their five kids, suggesting the judge in this case was not convinced. She is now married to an Army veteran who she says was medically retired with 90 percent disability due to traumatic brain injury and post-traumatic stress disorder. Over the years, she has frequently posted on social networking sites about the difficulties she and her family faced obtaining medical care through the VA system.

The reliability of this alleged victim was cast further into doubt by her brief career as a psychic medium. In 2009, she advertised her services on Twitter, including "psychic readings and help with anything from past, present, and future," as well as "hauntings." She charged $60 per hour for calls to her "hotline," but she offered discounts to members who signed up on her website. As a blogger who's been following this case sardonically noted, if this woman who waited 17 years to report a rape were truly psychic, "shouldn't she have known in advance if she was about to become the victim of a horrible crime?" [507] When questioned about this business venture during MSgt Silva's trial, however, she denied any involvement, further perjuring herself.

Reading through her various social networking entries, this alleged rape victim comes across as unstable and prone to exaggeration. She claimed to have pursued a singing career in Nashville, and described herself on her Twitter profile as a "Country Music singer, mother, wife to my hero husband who is a wounded soldier!" "My husband and I are more fortunate than the Dugars [sic]," she wrote in a Facebook comment about a family made famous by reality television, since "we both don't have to work and don't worry about finances." (Although she's given birth to seven children, she only has custody of one.) Elsewhere, she noted she liked to gamble in Las Vegas and vacation in Oahu, a lifestyle financed entirely by their government benefits.

She also boasted of being educated in criminal justice, medicine, and psychology, and she was supposedly completing her doctorate in psychology, but she never mentioned where she went

---

[507] Bob McCarty, "Social Media Postings Reveal Much About 'Psychic Medium' Who Accused AF Basic Training Instructor of Sexual Assault," *BobMcCarty.com*, September 26, 2015

to school to earn her purported degrees. (In fact, it's not clear she has any sort of college degree.) The only work experience she referenced, apart from her brief stint in the Air Force, was as a "registered nursing assistant" for four years – but during the trial, she testified she had no medical training whatsoever. Finally, she conspiratorially claimed her seventh child was "killed" in the hospital shortly after his birth in late 2011, without further elaborating as to the supposed cause or taking any apparent action to hold anyone responsible for this alleged crime. It would appear she turned this tragic loss into yet another opportunity to draw attention to herself, a disturbing pattern that has manifested itself on countless occasions throughout her troubled life.

Sadly, this BMT trainee wasn't the only woman who came forward alleging MSgt Silva raped her. His first wife claimed he had sexually assaulted her during their brief marriage, while he was a C-130 crew chief at Pope AFB, North Carolina. However, she didn't report this at the time, and in fact only accused her ex-husband of rape after OSI contacted her two decades later regarding his other alleged crimes. Moreover, her behavior during their marriage raised serious doubts about her reliability. According to Silva's 1992 petition for divorce, his wife abandoned him, committed adultery, wrote bad checks, abused illegal drugs, and neglected and endangered their toddler son.[508] Silva was awarded temporary custody, but as their divorce dragged on, the mother allegedly kidnapped their child and took him to Puerto Rico. Later that year, she was found guilty back home in Texas of two counts of theft of government property. When their divorce case finally went to trial, she refused to consent to a drug test, so the court awarded Silva full custody of their child. Thankfully, the jury in MSgt Silva's court-martial didn't find this alleged victim credible, and they acquitted him of her assault.

MSgt Silva wasn't so fortunate with the other ex-wife who accused him of rape. On May 2, 2007, this active-duty Senior Airman came into the OSI detachment at F.E. Warren AFB, Wyoming, to report an incident that occurred on April 28. In a written statement she provided the following day, she noted she

---

[508] Decree of Divorce (No minor children), May 16, 2007

was separated from then-Technical Sergeant Silva at the time, so she went to her husband's house that evening hoping to discuss their marital troubles. The conversation didn't go as well as she hoped, however. As she was preparing to leave, MSgt Silva allegedly grabbed her hand, led her to the bedroom, and proceeded to sexually assault her, despite her crying and desperate pleas for him to stop. Realizing she couldn't resist, she became submissive and reluctantly consented to intercourse, which she described as "agreeable to both parties."

Elsewhere in her statement, she conceded she didn't think her husband knew to stop when she cried out, as if he didn't truly hear her. On the other hand, she alleged he had done this once before during their separation, and he had also previously choked her while they engaged in sexual activity, to the point she couldn't breathe and had to struggle to alert him to her distress. Although it was "very difficult to come through and report this," she wrote in her statement, "I can rest knowing that I did my part in preventing this from happening to other women."[509]

TSgt Silva was called in later that day to make a statement about this incident. According to his version of events, their sexual activity that evening was entirely consensual and mutually satisfying. He claimed his wife intended to stay the night at his house, but she decided to go back to her dorm when she realized she didn't have a change of clothes for church in the morning. Their interaction over the following days seemed amicable, he wrote, until she became upset over ownership of their car.[510]

The night before his wife made her first statement to OSI, she apparently called MSgt Silva's mother and told her, "I'm going to ruin your son's career." On the other hand, she reportedly informed the sexual assault nurse examiner who processed her rape kit that the sex was consensual. Moreover, according to notes from her original OSI interview, she told agents she took her own clothes off, said something along the lines of "okay" to the sexual activity, and engaged in consensual – including oral – sex.[511]

On May 7, his wife returned to OSI to formally recant her allegation:

---

[509] SrA Silva, AF IMT 1168, *Statement of Suspect/Witness/Complainant*, May 3, 2007
[510] MSgt Silva, AF IMT 1168, May 3, 2007
[511] AFOSI Detachment 805 special agent interview notes, May 2, 2007

I do not feel after reading Article 120 [rape definition under the UCMJ] that the situation reported to OSI meets the criteria of this allegation. I consented to intamacy [sic] with Michael Silva. I only thought it necessary to report since my leadership advised it was the right steps to take. I had no intention of reporting this, I had wanted to put this behind me. [The first sergeant] asked if Mike was forceful or had aggressive behavior in intimacy. I wasn't aware this was headed toward rape charges. I didn't know where this fit. I know Mike has an aggressive & controlling personality, but I don't feel that rape depicts our situation.[512]

OSI closed the investigation and declared her allegations unfounded, and these two were soon divorced.

Yet nearly six years later, his ex-wife changed her story yet again. In early January 2013, she offered a series of statements to OSI that significantly differed from her earlier accounts. Admitting she had difficulty recalling everything she said earlier, she nevertheless introduced new details she hadn't mentioned before, when the incident was presumably still fresh in her memory. This time, she accused TSgt Silva of "forcefully" removing her clothing, and of stating he was trying to get her pregnant. She claimed not to recall if they engaged in oral sex, and she made no mention of discussing their plans for the next day. She lamely tried to explain away her previous statement the sex was consensual, and asserted her only regret was not being strong enough to prosecute her ex-husband back in 2007[513] – somehow forgetting she had freely and voluntarily recanted her allegations less than a week after making them.

Two years later, she told yet another version of this tale on the stand during MSgt Silva's court-martial, helping convict her ex-husband of the very crime she once definitively disavowed. Why would this woman flip-flop on such a serious issue? One possible motive is money. When she became pregnant with her second child, she applied to separate from the Air Force, but a medical evaluation board found she was eligible for retirement based on mental health treatment in connection with her alleged 2007 rape. She also convinced the VA she was a victim of military sexual

---

[512] SrA Silva, AF IMT 1168, May 7, 2007
[513] SSgt ____, AF IMT 1168, January 3, 2013

trauma and post-traumatic stress disorder. During the trial, however, she admitted under cross-examination that she never disclosed she had recanted her original claim. By securing her ex-husband's conviction, she created a pretext to continue receiving these fraudulent benefits.

After the trial, this alleged victim submitted a letter to Maj. Gen. Brown, 2 AF commander, claiming she had never been the victim of violence prior to her marriage to MSgt Silva, and that he caused her subsequent mental problems. Frankly, these were lies as well. She had indeed sought mental health treatment and claimed prior abuse before they married, and since their divorce she has enjoyed a full social and professional life.[514] She apparently has no remorse for condemning her former husband to prison for a crime he didn't commit.

Just three months after the conclusion of MSgt Silva's court-martial, Joint Base San Antonio highlighted three victims of sexual assault who were using their voices to advocate and help fellow survivors. They were featured in a full-page spread in the base paper, accompanied by a photo with a T-1 Jayhawk at JBSA-Randolph. The local Sexual Assault and Prevention Response victim advocate arranged this publicity stunt, providing these women a "survivors' flight" with the theme, "Soaring Over The Storm: The Survivor's Story," to show solidarity for other victims. In this article, a Chief Master Sergeant shared her sexual assault experiences. "I hope that people will start having real conversations about sexual assault," she said in the interview. "Sexual assault occurs in many different ways to many different people," she noted. "There are predators that you would not expect or suspect." In her case, "a lot of people were saying, 'No way, he could never have done that,'" yet her alleged assailant "had multiple victims spanning many years." Nevertheless, the Chief said she had no intention of coming forward with her survivor story until after this noncommissioned officer was convicted and sentenced at a military trial at JBSA-Lackland.

---

[514] Defense Counsel, "Response to Amended SJAR – AB Michael Silva," November 5, 2015

The NCO she appears to be describing is MSgt Silva, who was indeed confronted by an additional accuser during his court-martial: a Chief Master Sergeant and former MTI, who claimed the defendant sexually assaulted her over a decade earlier. While the government could not charge MSgt Silva with this particular crime due to the statute of limitations in effect at the time, they did use her salacious account to reinforce their narrative of the defendant as a violent sexual predator. As a former MTI in the wake of the Lackland sex scandal, MSgt Silva was undoubtedly presumed guilty by some in the courtroom – including, perhaps, the military judge who oversaw his trial. Introducing such highly prejudicial testimony from a seemingly upstanding active-duty airman likely further swayed the jury to put aside their remaining doubts about the reliability of the alleged rape victims. Under the faulty premise that, where there's smoke, there's fire, they appear to have convicted MSgt Silva of rape based largely on accusations of an altogether different crime, one for which he was never charged.

This Chief actually met MSgt Silva back in 1995, when she was a trainee in his BMT squadron. (Ironically, she graduated just days before the recruit who later accused him of rape arrived at Lackland.) When she returned to BMT as an instructor in 1999, she briefly worked with SSgt Silva, but he was soon reassigned to Maxwell AFB. He would return to Lackland on business from time to time, and on one of these visits his accuser invited him to her apartment. There they sat on the couch as he played guitar, until she began kissing him. At this point, their stories diverge. According to her account, she became uncomfortable for some unspecified reason and asked him to leave, but he sexually assaulted her as he was exiting her apartment.[515] MSgt Silva, on the other hand, asserts they continued talking for a while after kissing, then he left without incident.

There are several reasons to be skeptical of the Chief's account. First of all, there's no evidence SSgt Silva was in town during the time frame she described – between her divorce in the summer of 2002, and the beginning of her relationship later that year with her current husband. Although SSgt Silva did come to San Antonio both before and after this period, the alleged victim may have fudged the dates to avoid the appearance of cheating on either her ex- or future husband. Furthermore, her account of the supposed assault seems highly dubious. She testified SSgt Silva

---

[515] CMSgt ____, AF IMT 1168, April 26, 2013

pinned her to the floor and choked her in the entryway to her ground-floor apartment, with the front door standing wide open, while his guitar was slung across his back.

Moreover, this alleged victim was unable to provide critical details of this incident. She seemed unclear as to whether she was violated orally or digitally, for example, and she could not remember whether she verbalized her objection, or if her alleged assailant said anything, or even how long the incident lasted. The special agents interviewing her noted she was unsure if her lack of memory "was due to the fact that she was near the point of unconsciousness because of how traumatic the event was or because the event occurred so long ago."[516] They were clearly leading the witness, as the Chief had said nothing in her statement about almost blacking out or feeling traumatized by the incident.

The Chief told her interviewers she didn't report the incident because there was no physical evidence, so it would be her word against her alleged assailant. She also said she did not want the facts of the incident to become public knowledge among her peers and subordinates. Nevertheless, she did tell several colleagues about this incident over the years, beginning with her best friend. When questioned, however, this witness claimed she was told only that SSgt Silva choked her, not that she'd been sexually assaulted.[517] The alleged victim later told another female MTI about this, and she claimed this colleague admitted she'd experienced a similar situation with Silva. But her confidante said nothing of the sort in her statement to OSI, and denied even knowing the defendant very well. On the other hand, she did confirm the alleged victim told her about the incident, after supposedly spotting MSgt Silva at the 2011 Blue Rope Ball. The witness wrote, "seeing him must have reminded her of something she had never told me before," prompting her to share her sordid tale.[518] But MSgt Silva didn't attend that event – after all, he wasn't a Master MTI, and didn't receive invitations to this or other Blue Rope get-togethers – so this testimony wasn't particularly credible.

The OSI agent conducting her initial interview observed the alleged victim was nervous about moving to the same area as MSgt Silva when she was reassigned to Lackland later that year. This seems odd, as they were previously stationed together in San

---

[516] OSI interview of CMSgt _____, AFOSI Form 40, April 26, 2013
[517] Witness #1, AF IMT 1168, September 6, 2013
[518] Witness #2, AF IMT 1168, June 12, 2013

Antonio between 2009 and 2011, apparently without incident. In her statement, the accuser noted her San Antonio realtor – another former MTI – mentioned MSgt Silva lived in the same neighborhood where she was house-hunting in early 2013. She supposedly said she didn't want to live anywhere near her alleged assailant, prompting the realtor to volunteer that the defendant liked to choke girls. When he was questioned by OSI, however, this witness denied they had such a conversation – but he did confirm he heard rumors the defendant choked a girlfriend in the late 1990s, and he also stated Silva told him in 2001 or 2002 that his ex-wife accused him of choking her up in Wyoming.[519] Neither of these allegations is credible, however, as OSI surely knew, since the ex-wife's accusation didn't happen until 2007, and the ex-girlfriend informed OSI that Silva never behaved this way towards her.

The inconsistencies in this testimony suggest possible collusion among the witnesses, all of whom were current or former MTIs. OSI agents contacted the Chief in April 2013, after they heard rumors she may have once been romantically involved with MSgt Silva. The others witnesses weren't interviewed until June or later, however, allowing plenty of time for the alleged victim to back-brief these corroborating witnesses. OSI may also have encouraged her to embellish her allegation with incriminating details. As we've seen in this and other cases, special agents are notorious for leading witnesses to confirm prosecution narratives. Alternately, this alleged victim may have simply made up this tale to get back at MSgt Silva for rejecting her advances back in the day. Whatever her motives, she unexpectedly showed up in MSgt Silva's office during the investigation, presumably to discuss the allegations against him or offer support. Out of the blue, she began asking him if he remembered what he had done to her in her apartment over a decade earlier. It was later revealed she was wearing a wire during this encounter, a clumsy attempt by OSI to solicit an admission from the target of their investigation.

The pivotal role this Chief played in MSgt Silva's conviction has sharply divided the MTI community. She has had a phenomenally successful career in the Air Force, achieving the highest enlisted rank in a mere 17 years. Yet the man she accused was well regarded in his own right, and friends who knew them both weren't quite sure whom to believe. Even those inclined to give this Chief the benefit of the doubt, however, have been puzzled

---

[519] OSI interview of Witness #3, AFOSI Form 40, June 6, 2013

by how she handled her sexual assault allegations. Why, for example, did she suddenly start sharing her story with colleagues in 2011, after remaining silent for nine years? Could this have anything to do with the sex scandal that was just then emerging at Lackland, with its rumors of MTI misconduct? Furthermore, why were none of the witnesses she named able to corroborate key elements of her testimony?

Significantly, the Chief was neither a victim of nor witness to the alleged crimes for which MSgt Silva faced court-martial, and so was under no legal or ethical obligation to cooperate with investigators and prosecutors. Why, then, did she volunteer to wear a wire and take the stand during his trial? And after doing so much to seal MSgt Silva's fate, why would she then deny having testified against him? Suspicions about the Chief's true intentions only intensified following the court-martial, when she became an outspoken advocate for sexual assault survivors at Joint Base San Antonio, appearing several times in the base paper to promote awareness. Given so many troubling inconsistencies in her allegations, it's not at all unreasonable to suspect she may have invented her story of survival at MSgt Silva's expense.

Rape and sexual assault are an ugly business, and inherently difficult to prosecute. Balancing a defendant's presumption of innocence and right to a fair trial, on the one hand, with our sympathy for those violated in such an intimate and personal way, on the other, is always challenging. In the absence of corroborating witnesses or physical evidence, securing justice in such cases is an even more fraught proposition, which often comes down to the credibility of the accuser. My intention here is not to trash the reputations of those women who came forward, and I am not at all unsympathetic to survivors of sexual crimes. (My own wife, Caroline, was herself a victim of a brutal kidnapping and rape.) I am also not suggesting that alleged victims are prone to lie about sexual assault. On the contrary, conventional wisdom finds less than 10 percent of rape allegations are provably false.[520] But

---

[520] Jason Richwine, "That 'Only 2 to 8 Percent of Rape Accusations Are False' Stat Is Extremely Misleading," *National Review*, April 6, 2015

even if the majority of such allegations are valid, untrue claims are occasionally made, and at least some of those convicted of these crimes are actually innocent.

Sadly, the temptation to exaggerate or fabricate in rape cases has been exacerbated in the Air Force by an unhealthy climate cultivated in the wake of the Lackland sex scandal. The prosecutorial frenzy gripping the service puts enormous pressure on OSI to uncover crimes and for commanders to prefer charges. Supposed victims are harassed and intimidated into lodging complaints, often turning seemingly innocent or unintentional behavior into something awful. Some have less charitable motives, such as revenge, a desire for attention, or even financial incentives. Others undoubtedly suffer from mental disorders that cloud their judgment or memory. Perhaps this explains why, despite the enormous efforts to identify and prosecute MTIs accused of violent sexual crimes, only three cases resulted in conviction, one of which was later overturned on appeal. At the end of the day, all the Air Force had to show for their efforts to curb sexual assault at BMT was the imprisonment of SSgt Walker – the notorious sexual predator whose appalling crimes launched the scandal at Lackland in the first place, and MSgt Silva – the final victim of a witch-hunt that long ago ran out of criminals to persecute.

In a clemency request to the 2 AF commander, Maj. Gen. Brown, MSgt Silva made an impassioned appeal for mercy. "I feel that my court martial guilty verdict was decided prior to it even beginning," he wrote. "The fact that I had previously been a Military Training Instructor, resulted in my immediate connection to the current BMT sexual assault scandal and the political witchhunt began yet again." The Lackland sex scandal "had nothing to do with me," he asserted, noting he "never once received any negative feedback" as an MTI from either students or superiors. There is "so much political pressure to end military sexual assault and prove to Congress that the military is handling these cases," he continued, but "what they fail to see is there are innocent service members such as myself that are falsely accused and unjustly convicted." He ended his appeal with a quote from Thomas Aquinas: "as a matter of honor, one man owes it to another to manifest the truth."[521] Unfortunately, Maj. Gen. Brown was not that man; he rejected this plea for clemency, much as he dismissed my earlier request for redress.

---

[521] MSgt Michael Silva, "Clemency Request," September 13, 2015

Although the hype regarding a supposed sexual assault epidemic in the military seems a bit overblown, and the pendulum appears to have swung a bit too far in favor of "special" victims and prosecutors at the expense of those accused, retaliation is still an unfortunate reality for many survivors. In 2015, Human Rights Watch issued a report on such retaliation within the U.S. military, including extensive interviews with alleged victims and the results of a 2014 RAND Corporation military workplace study. Of the women surveyed who reported unwanted sexual contact to military authorities, 62 percent claimed they experienced negative consequences. More than half of those women said they were ostracized or bullied, while about a third suffered an adverse administrative action or professional retaliation. Eleven percent claimed they experienced punishment for an infraction after reporting a sexual assault, typically minor "collateral misconduct" such as underage drinking or adultery.[522]

On the other hand, we must assume that at least some of those service members who reported unwanted sexual contact were not being entirely truthful. According to official statistics, there were 6,131 reports of sexual assault in the Department of Defense in fiscal year 2014.[523] Even if we stipulate that the rate of false reporting is less than 10 percent, this still means that in perhaps several hundred of these cases, someone was wrongly accused of a crime. And yet, almost none of these faux victims are actually prosecuted for perjury. Civilian accusers (such as those who framed MSgt Silva) are not subject to court-martial under the UCMJ, while many commanders and prosecutors are hesitant to go after military members for lying about sexual assault, as this might discourage real victims from coming forward in search of justice. As a result, it is virtually unheard of for an alleged victim to face punishment for perjury.

That makes the case of Airman Basic Jane Neubauer all the more remarkable. Shortly after she arrived at Keesler AFB,

---

[522] Human Rights Watch, "Embattled: Retaliation against Sexual Assault Survivors in the US Military," May 18, 2015
[523] *Department of Defense Annual Report on Sexual Assault in the Military, Fiscal Year 2014*, May 1, 2015

Mississippi, in 2013, Air Force OSI recruited her as a confidential informant to infiltrate a local drug ring. She claimed she was raped while working a case, but authorities soon began to suspect this alleged victim wasn't telling the truth. The Air Force insists Neubauer was ordered to cease her undercover activities before this crime allegedly occurred, and she was later arrested for marijuana use and busted for driving under the influence with drugs in her car. This airman subsequently failed out of technical training, and was sent to a mandatory drug treatment program.[524]

When the Air Force formally charged AB Neubauer with lying about her rape (among other crimes), hers became a *cause célèbre* among victims' rights advocates. For example, Jennifer Norris, who was herself sexually assaulted at Keesler in 1997, rallied around this latest supposed survivor. "Here we are in 2014 and I am reliving what happened to me all over again at Keesler AFB except this time it isn't me," she wrote on her blog. "This time I am the one helping the airman who reached out for support because of the backlash that came with reporting a military sexual assault." The author continued, "We start out having to prove that we are not lying when instead it should be the offender who should be proving that they didn't do it"[525] – a novel interpretation of the "innocent until proven guilty" principle enshrined in the Sixth Amendment to the U.S. Constitution. Only, this time around, the alleged victim really was lying– and Jennifer Norris later quietly deleted her blog post without issuing a retraction.

In March 2015, AB Neubauer pled guilty before a special court-martial to a total of six charges and 18 specifications, including making 10 false official statements related to her alleged sexual assault. According to court documents, she engaged in consensual sexual intercourse with an airman on the evening of July 26, 2013, staying out past curfew at his residence until around 1:30 the next morning. In the meantime, her unit realized she was missing from the dorms, and began trying to locate her. She initially claimed she was in her dorm room the whole time, then she reported to a local hospital to request a rape kit. During the following days and weeks, she made several false statements about what had occurred, and who her alleged assailant was. She falsely

---

[524] Jacob Siegel, "Spies, Lies, and Rape in the Air Force: An Undercover Agent's Story," *The Daily Beast*, March 4, 2014
[525] Jennifer Norris, "Military Sexual Assault Comes Full Circle at Keesler Air Force Base," May 1, 2014

claimed her assailant impregnated her, going so far as to present a bogus pregnancy test to support her tale. She also asked the airman with whom she had sex to lie about their activities that night. For this and other offenses, she was sentenced to a bad-conduct discharge, forfeiture of $12,372 in pay, and confinement for four months – reduced to 84 days in accordance with a pre-trial agreement.[526]

Unfortunately, this case is the exception that proves the rule. Because of her status as an OSI informant, AB Neubauer's claim to have been raped on the job was potentially damaging to this investigatory agency. It was in their interest not only to assert they had suspended their relationship with her before the alleged assault – a convenient claim impossible to verify – but also to expose her as a lying, drug-using criminal. In this context, prosecuting this airman for falsely crying rape may have merely been a means to deflect criticism from the controversial OSI informant program, rather than an effort to hold perjurers accountable for pretending they were sexually assaulted.

No survivor of sexual assault should face retaliation for reporting this crime. At the same time, holding alleged victims accountable for their own collateral misconduct is not necessarily improper – and punishing them when they completely fabricate their victimization is essential to ensuring justice and maintaining good order and discipline. Bearing false witness in such cases not only ruins the lives and careers of those falsely accused, it also makes it harder to believe real sexual assault survivors when they're telling the truth.

---

[526] United States Air Force Court of Criminal Appeals, United States v. Airman Basic Jane M. Neubauer, United States Air Force" (ACM S32308), March 10, 2016

Chapter 20: Getting Back on Track

As curious as my particular case turned out to be, it is representative of a much larger, and more troubling, set of issues confronting the United States Air Force. This renowned institution remains the most powerful military organization the world has ever seen, whose overwhelming capabilities and unparalleled combat success have reassured our allies and deterred our most dangerous enemies for generations. Yet all is not well with our nation's air arm.

For many observers, the Air Force started to veer off track at least a decade ago, when the exigencies of the "Global War on Terror" began to distort its mission and sense of purpose. Amid conflicts in Iraq and Afghanistan, where so many soldiers and Marines were giving their last full measure of devotion, the Air Force struggled to remain relevant, both on the battlefield and inside the Beltway. Airmen were deployed to war zones as "in lieu of" forces, offering boots on the ground for various tasks – such as collecting and analyzing intelligence on improvised explosive devices, a mission I led in Iraq in 2006-07 – to free up troops for other purposes. USAF vastly expanded its airborne intelligence, surveillance and reconnaissance coverage, and increasingly provided armed overwatch with manned and remotely piloted aircraft. The Air Force eagerly accepted contingency "GWOT" funding for all manner of indulgences, no matter how tangential to the war effort. Yet these myriad initiatives weren't enough. In 2008, Secretary of Defense Bill Gates fired both the Secretary and the Chief of Staff of the Air Force, ostensibly for failing to manage the nuclear enterprise properly.

Before he was sacked, General T. Michael Moseley introduced the "Airman's Creed," which he hoped would "reinvigorate the warrior ethos in every Airman of our Total Force."[527] Parroting the "Soldier's Creed," it somewhat defensively asserted American airmen are "warriors" who have answered their nation's call, every bit as much as their Army and Marine Corps counterparts. Rather than remaining faithful to our proud Air Force heritage, however, this new corporate statement of beliefs displaced all existing Air Force-related creeds, including time-honored recitations associated with noncommissioned officers,

---

[527] General T. Michael Moseley, "CSAF presents Airman's Creed," Seymour Johnson AFB official site, April 25, 2007

senior NCOs, Chief Master Sergeants, first sergeants, even Military Training Instructors. Simultaneously, the Air Force rushed a new Airman Battle Uniform into service, retiring the standard battle-dress uniform worn by generations of U.S. armed forces. While airmen initially welcomed ABUs – which we were explicitly instructed not to starch or hot-press, and whose boots do not need polishing – these uniforms are devoid of insignia identifying the member's command and squadron, further eroding esprit de corps. (Moreover, they've proven ineffective in combat, and have since been replaced by the "MultiCam" camouflage pattern for airmen and soldiers deploying to the Middle East.[528])

It was in during this era that Basic Military Training changed its curriculum to focus on a new kind of airman – one who is a "warrior first."[529] As I discussed in an earlier chapter, the hasty expansion of enlisted accession training in 2008 directly contributed to the crisis that followed, as insufficient resources were allocated to properly train new recruits and supervise their transformation into "Warrior Airmen of character." The overreaction by Air Force leaders to the resulting Lackland sex scandal soon revealed just how badly the service had lost its way – and subsequent events sadly confirm this scandal was no anomaly, but rather part of a disturbing trend afflicting the entire Air Force, where toxic leadership and abuse of authority are becoming ever more pervasive.

Our modern-day Air Force has become almost unrecognizable to many veterans. It's not the new-ish technology being employed these days that causes airmen of a certain age to become disoriented. After all, military aviation has always embraced the latest innovations to achieve a decisive advantage over our adversaries. And it's not the groundbreaking personnel policies regarding gays in the military or women in combat, which are long overdue concessions to equality of opportunity and efficient resource utilization. It's not even "kids these days," as if the latest generation of recruits are somehow inherently unsuited to the profession of arms. No, the difference those of us who served in uniform during previous decades most often note about the current Air Force climate is a lack of effective leadership.

---

[528] TSgt Jess Harvey, "Officials to issue new camouflage uniforms to deployers," Air Forces Central official site, January 30, 2011
[529] "Air Force Basic Military Training Fact Sheet," BMT official site, July 19, 2011

For years now, our service's senior leaders have failed to address the most pressing problems confronting the Air Force, instead focusing their attention on superficial or extraneous issues. They refuse to hold general officers and other senior officials accountable for their actions, fostering a toxic environment where reprisal and abuse of authority are rampant. At the squadron level, commanders are hamstrung by excess regulation and micromanagement by their superiors, while supervisors are encouraged to concentrate more on their own careers than accomplishing the mission and developing their subordinates. While junior airmen may lack discipline or seem entitled, this has less to do with how they were raised growing up than how they have been trained and led in the Air Force – first at BMT, then in technical training, and finally during their first duty assignments. Instead of camaraderie, mentorship, and leadership by example, they are all too often confronted by apathy and self-interest, where Core Values and the "Airman's Creed" seem more like empty slogans than words to live by.

What can be done to get the Air Force back on track? A good place to start would be at the "Gateway to the Air Force." Under intense political pressure during the Lackland sex scandal, Air Force leaders misdiagnosed the problems at BMT, and applied inappropriate and counterproductive solutions. Having uncovered egregious misconduct by a handful of MTIs, local leaders implemented a series of common-sense reforms, and the Woodward report offered additional recommendations to prevent a recurrence of such abuses. But these sensible steps weren't enough to satisfy critics. The group and wing commanders were sacrificed for political expediency, ushering in the tragic reigns of Col. Camerer and Col. Liddick. Burdensome new reporting requirements were imposed at the wing, numbered air force, and major command levels, while Air Education and Training Command needlessly tinkered with BMT personnel requirements. General Rice and his staff judge advocate abused their authority by wrongfully punishing several former commanders, a pattern repeated by his subordinate senior leaders and their legal advisors. The former AETC command chief, now the Chief Master Sergeant of the Air Force, even used this crisis as an opportunity to implement his pet "capstone" project at BMT.

Taken together, this bewildering array of purported improvements radically changed BMT – but not for the better. While trainees are certainly safer today from the predatory advances of wayward MTIs, their instructors have been rendered much less effective at transforming civilians into airmen. MTIs are no longer allowed to employ time-honored tactics, techniques, and procedures proven to break down new recruits and build them back up as brothers and sisters in arms. Reorganizing the BMT curriculum so newly minted airmen can graduate early and sit around discussing Air Force core values with contractors – in an even less stressful environment further removed from their original instructors and wingmen – seems like a solution in search of a problem. The result of these ill-conceived social experiments is already obvious across the Air Force, where first-term airmen are reporting for duty unprepared for success in the armed forces.

BMT is broken, to be sure, but it's not too late to get "back to basics." While the Woodward report recommendations were generally sound, most of the supplemental transformation initiatives were poorly planned and executed, and ought to be rolled back as soon as possible. Begin by abandoning "Airmen's Week" as a stand-alone course of instruction, and instead fold its learning objectives – along with the associated 326th Training Squadron – back into the basic course. The integrity of trainee flights should be maintained for the duration of BMT, reinforcing the importance of team integrity and esprit de corps throughout all phases of training. If greater gender integration is a goal, this can be easily accomplished through more co-ed training events, rather than forming hokey "heritage flights" just in time to march in the graduation parade.

Balance must be restored to the BMT instructor cadre as well. Increasing the minimum grade requirements for MTIs and squadron superintendents created an unsustainable manpower model. Over the years, high-performing Staff Sergeants (E-5s) have proven themselves more than capable of performing MTI duties, whereas Master Sergeants (E-7s) have no business leading individual trainee flights as novice instructors. Given the size and billet structure of BMT line squadrons, Senior Master Sergeants (E-8s) are fully competent to serve as senior enlisted leaders, and both these and the group superintendent position should always be filled by qualified MTIs. (Similarly, diamond-wearing Master Sergeants can easily handle first-sergeant duties in units of this size.) The consolidated "trainer squadron" is another concept that has outlived its usefulness. Standardizing on-the-job training of new MTIs doesn't require they all be assigned to the same unit during their apprenticeship. On the contrary, it's much more effective to send these instructors to their line squadrons at the earliest opportunity, where they can be mentored by qualified in-house trainers and supervisors, rather than gutting these squadrons of experienced personnel to man the 323d Training Squadron. Finally, BMT must produce enough Master MTIs to maintain continuity and fill key leadership positions, and these "Blue Ropes" ought to be empowered to provide greater oversight of training operations. Company grade officers, on the other hand, should be reduced in number and redesignated as assistant operations officers (ADOs), allowing MTI instructor supervisors to once again earn their duty titles as section chiefs.

Above all, we must trust MTIs to do their job. Given the robust vetting process now in place for this developmental special duty, only the highest-caliber noncommissioned officers are being considered as instructor candidates, and the MTI development process has been sufficiently recalibrated to leave no doubt as to standards and expectations. In a dynamic training environment like BMT, MTIs must be allowed to improvise and innovate as the situation dictates, tailoring their instruction to the needs of an increasingly diverse recruit population. Moreover, as highly trained and well-qualified professionals, they ought to be given some benefit of the doubt when accused of minor misconduct by trainees, and always treated as innocent until proven guilty. That is not to say that trainee complaints shouldn't be taken seriously; on the contrary, all credible allegations must be fully investigated to ensure trainee safety and good order and discipline. But the immediate removal of an MTI at the mere hint of impropriety demoralizes the instructor cadre and emboldens disgruntled trainees, who will soon find the operational Air Force doesn't provide them anonymous comment boxes around every corner. Trainees must always be treated with dignity and respect – but then again, their instructors are no less worthy of such treatment.

In hindsight, the Lackland sex scandal seems wildly overblown. Initial reports of several dozen MTIs engaged in sexual misconduct with scores of trainees turned out to be false. Only a third of the MTIs prosecuted were proven to have engaged in sexual activity with trainees under their control, an inexcusable betrayal of trust in such an environment. On the other hand, most MTIs who faced courts-martial during this period were found to have done nothing more serious than have consensual sex with graduated airmen in student status – a serious policy violation, to be sure, but not exactly scandalous or meriting imprisonment. Worse, the conflation of intimate relations between consenting adults, no matter how unprofessional, with serious offenses such as sexual assault, is perverse and misguided. Rapists belong behind bars for their truly heinous crimes – but can the same be said for instructors who hook up with former trainees, once these junior airmen have moved on to their next stage of training? The Air Force and other military services are investing a great deal of effort in sexual assault response and prevention, but such overgeneralizations – like the so-called "continuum of harm" between sexual harassment and sexual assault – misses the point, and does nothing to advance this much-needed effort.

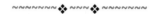

Unfortunately, the witch-hunt that began at Lackland has metastasized across the entire Air Force, making a mockery of the military justice system. Congressional pressure to correct the abuses at BMT, coupled with outrage over the handling of several other high-profile sexual assault cases – such as granting clemency to convicted offenders[530] – prompted concerted efforts by several Senators to strip military commanders of the ability to prosecute certain types of criminal offenses.[531] While many of these reforms have not yet been adopted, Air Force leaders have since gone out of their way to demonstrate how tough they are on crimes such as sexual assault.

This prosecutorial zeal too often manifests itself as injustice. Air Force Office of Special Investigations agents have repeatedly been implicated in abusive and unethical interrogation practices, as well as compelling reluctant witnesses to come forward with less-than-credible allegations. Rather than dispose of minor charges through nonjudicial punishment or administrative actions, commanders at all levels are now more likely to prefer charges against subordinates for trial at courts-martial.

---

[530] Craig Whitlock, "General's promotion blocked over her dismissal of sex-assault verdict," *The Washington Post*, May 6, 2013
[531] "Comprehensive Resource Center for the Military Justice Improvement Act," Senator Kirsten Gillibrand's official website

Prosecutors are prone to overcharging, while convening authorities routinely ignore pre-trial recommendations to proceed with caution. At Lackland, a "prosecution task force" was established without any corresponding plus-up to the area defense counsel staff, further tipping the scales of justice against the accused. All too often, acquittals seem contingent on how much money the accused can afford to spend on civilian attorneys to assist in their defense. Once convicted, their chances of receiving clemency are more remote than ever, as general officers are gun-shy about reversing or mitigating sentences handed down at court-martial, even in the most egregious cases. The wrongfully convicted must wait years in the often-vain hope that appeals courts will reconsider their fates.

But reconsider they must. The Air Force is prosecuting, convicting, imprisoning, and even discharging airmen, particularly for sexual-related offenses, at an alarming rate, yet at least some of these alleged felons do not appear to be guilty. The cases of MSgt Silva and Maj. Turpiano are but two examples of this sort of injustice in the wake of the Lackland sex scandal. Ironically, in an effort to keep Congress from stripping commanders of their prerogatives in such cases, the Air Force is instead demonstrating it can't ensure justice for all airmen. Tony Carr has called for Congress to "consider including in next year's defense authorization the requirement for a holistic review of the Air Force legal system by the Government Accountability Office."[532] In a blog post about the Turpiano case, *John Q. Public* went even further:

> *In current form, the Air Force disciplinary process is not about finding the truth or determining the right balance between punishment and rehabilitation. It's not about incapacitating offenders or affirming the dignity of victims. It's not even about discipline. It's about what most things in the Air Force are about: empowering a tiny number of senior bureaucrat-commanders as maximally as possible so they can reinforce institutional interests. Of late, those interests have to do with protecting the service's public image against an onslaught of criticism from a growing coalition of legislators, advocates, lawyers, airmen, and ordinary citizens who claim – credibly – that it doesn't know what the hell it is*

---

[532] Tony Carr, "Disgraced 2-star Sounds Off on Miley Gate, Raises New Questions," *John Q. Public*, January 18, 2016

*doing with its justice system. A few years ago, the complaint
was about sexual assault specifically. The response to that
criticism has now called the fundamental health of the
entire system into question.*

"There's a great irony at work here," the author continued. While
commanders need total authority over administering justice in
combat – "when the inability to control distraction, incapacitate a
troublemaker, or exact swift justice can create adverse
consequences measured in blood and harmful to the nation's
defense" – they have no need of such authority outside that context.
"By allowing them to hold on to it, Congress is allowing them to
undermine good order and discipline by continually injuring their
own credibility as they degrade the trust bond between themselves
and those they are charged to lead."

Because Air Force commanders perceive political disapproval is
their gravest risk, "they will tactically avoid it by exercising their
power to control processes and maintain stability. A justice system
in their hands will be governed accordingly, and will not remain a
justice system for long." Beyond the "disempowered and wretched
individuals" prosecuted by such a system, "our national defense
will also be a casualty when good people finally refuse to be part of
something manifestly unfair and morally wrong."[533]

A veteran Air Force attorney, writing under a pen name for
the *JQP* blog, noted the current sexual assault witch-hunt neither
helps victims nor commanders seeking to maintain good order and
discipline. First, the implication that alleged victims "must be
believed no matter the evidence" has single-handedly destroyed
the presumption of innocence for accused perpetrators. By
promoting the myth of the "always-truthful alleged-victim," the
sexual assault prevention and response program "ensures all
potential jurors are subject to persistent anti-defense propaganda
before they ever sit on an actual panel." Moreover, he felt "there
are zero consequences for a false accusation of sexual assault in the
military," since prosecuting false accusers for perjury would
presumably have a "chilling effect" on legitimate reporting of
sexual assault. Instead, "accusers are rewarded at every stage of

---

[533] John Q. Public, "How to Destroy an Air Force Officer With Four
Words: the Case of Maj. Michael Turpiano," *John Q. Public*, February
24, 2016

the process," while the accusation alone will destroy the defendant's career.

Second, military sexual assault cases lack common civilian procedural safeguards. Prosecutors need not prove probable cause before proceeding to trial, since few general court-martial convening authorities "are willing to risk the wrath of Senator Kirsten Gillibrand and others in Congress to save a potentially innocent soldier, sailor, airman, or Marine." Furthermore, potential military jurors are few in number and nominated by the command; only a two-thirds majority is required to convict at court-martial, except in death penalty cases; and military juries, rather than judges, control sentencing. Finally, military prosecutors are relatively inexperienced compared to their civilian colleagues, while alleged sexual assault victims "wield massively disproportionate power in a military context," including the provision of a dedicated victim advocate. This imbalance is dangerous, the author concludes: "there's a reason that it's *United States v. Defendant*, not *Angry Alleged Victim v. Defendant.*"[534]

This problem is not limited to the Air Force. In an unpublished manuscript, an Army judge advocate describes how soldiers accused of sexual assault and other sexually based offenses now face a system that is stacked unfairly against them. "Recent reforms to military law and practice have focused entirely on making it easier to convict Soldiers and providing comfort to the alleged victims of sexual assault, rather than ensuring impartial justice prevails." Noting that "the pendulum of justice does not seem likely to swing the opposite direction in the foreseeable future," the author focuses on practical suggestions which can lead to more just outcomes for law enforcement officers, prosecutors, and others.[535]

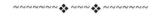

---

[534] "John Birdman" (pen name), "Air Force Insider: Overzealous Sexual Assault Prosecutions Threaten Our Justice System," *John Q. Public*, February 29, 2016
[535] Major Mason S. Weiss, "Defending the Indefensible? The Increasingly Difficult Job of Defending Soldiers Accused of Sexual Assault" (working draft), *Social Science Research Network*, February 29, 2016

The perversion of justice in the Air Force is not confined to the courtroom. My curious case reveals how commanders can ruin an officer's career without any semblance of due process. Nothing I was alleged to have done amounted to a crime punishable under the Uniform Code of Military Justice, and I was not offered nonjudicial punishment or taken to court-martial. Rather than allowing me to mount a proper defense, see the evidence against me, or confront my accusers, my wing commander subjected me to an amateurish inquiry that cast discredit on his handpicked investigating officer and the witnesses against me. Based on the results of this corrupt commander-directed investigation, Col. Camerer issued me a letter of reprimand; relieved me of command; opened an unfavorable information file; signed off on a referral officer performance report; petitioned to remove me from the senior developmental education list; filed this paperwork in my officer selection record for my upcoming promotion board; and attempted to ship me off to an undesirable assignment. This was clearly overkill, with no other purpose than to ruin my career and force me out of the Air Force.

There is no appeals process for any of the administrative actions taken against me, and none of the recourses I pursued – inspector general complaints, request for redress under Article 138, Congressional inquiries – was given proper consideration. Sadly, I am not alone. Other squadron commanders, including Lt. Col. Kaiser and Lt. Col. Annicelli, have been relieved without cause in recent years, their careers wrecked over dubious allegations while their chain of command closes ranks around the senior leaders responsible. Several former commanders were wrongly punished after the fact during the Lackland sex scandal, and even the favorable findings of the Air Force IG haven't been enough to get their careers back on track. The one bright spot in this dismal catalog – the exoneration of the "Molly Three" at Laughlin AFB – is the exception that proves the rule, requiring intense Congressional pressure and the personal intervention of the Chief of Staff of the Air Force to only partially correct the record.

It shouldn't be this easy for senior leaders to destroy an officer's career, but it is – in fact, it's written into Air Force instructions. While commanders have some latitude in handling LORs involving enlisted personnel, they are required to maintain officer LORs in unfavorable information files.[536] Mandating the inclusion of such derogatory paperwork in an officer's record, while offering no independent review or appeal mechanism for the punishment, breeds corruption and abuse of authority. Moreover, if a senior rater decides to file the LOR in the recipient's officer selection record as well, this decision is not subject to further review, and these documents must remain on file until after the next promotion board – unless removed early as an exception to policy by the wing commander or issuing authority (in the grade of O-7 or higher).[537] Of course, in each of the cases I've examined, it was the wing commander himself who issued the paperwork, so good luck getting him to reconsider his own decision, especially when his superiors refuse to question his actions.

"The power to end a career needs to be responsibly chained to a requirement to prove the action is justified," opined Tony Carr in *John Q. Public*, "and not the mistaken judgment or Caesarian fiat of an unduly empowered commander."[538] My career was ruined by a pair of officers who each had only five years seniority on me, yet their highly questionable actions were subjected to no scrutiny whatsoever. Meanwhile I was treated as if my decades of exemplary service and selection for command counted for nothing. As *JQP* argued in another post, "No matter how powerful the intangible and intrinsic incentives for command, they will be broadly and swiftly nullified if officers begin believing that an entire body of professional work can be obliterated, a reputation permanently tarnished, and future prospects dimmed at the whim of a disapproving boss." Sadly, with every case like this that goes unresolved, proposed Congressional reforms begin to look increasingly attractive.[539]

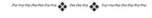

---

[536] AFI 36-2907, *Unfavorable Information File (UIF) Program*, November 26, 2014

[537] AFI 36-2608, *Military Personnel Records System*, October 26, 2015

[538] Tony Carr, "Ten (+1) Suggestions for a Resurgent Air Force in 2016," *John Q. Public*, December 31, 2015

[539] "Sidestepping Evidence, General Dismisses Fired Commander's Appeal," August 4, 2015

"It's one thing to fire a commander for an actual or claimed failure," Tony Carr wrote in the *John Q. Public* blog. "It's another thing altogether to inflict upon that relieved commander career-ending administrative punishments and performance appraisals. It's another thing still to affirmatively destroy that officer's future by having him stricken from the roster for developmental education that stands as an unwritten prerequisite for future advancement. Commanders in today's Air Force don't just get relieved . . . they get destroyed." This is not only immoral and unethical, he argued, it's counterproductive as well, since, as we learned during World War II, "sometimes, commanders relieved and given second chances were the best leaders of all."[540] What should the Air Force do to curb such wrongful relief of command? Mr. Carr proposed that, "four relatively straightforward actions, implemented together, would go a long way toward re-calibrating the service's power relationships such that toxicity would be systemically checked without unduly undermining command authority."

First, right certain wrongs. The Chief of Staff of the Air Force "should have the Air Staff glance backward a couple of years and collect information on fired squadron commanders. Each case should be evaluated carefully, and where relief was potentially unjustified, a full investigation performed to set things right." He suggested they might begin with my case, as my "sole misstep was failing to ingratiate himself to an unreasonable boss, as sometimes happens in any human activity. His reprimand and firing were based on hearsay evidence from biased sources who were co-opted to hound him over stylistic differences. In the legacy command system developed by Gen. George Marshall, which serves as the intellectual foundation of our modern system, Perry is *exactly* the kind of officer who would be put at the front of squadron again and given [...] another go, any past friction left squarely where it belongs."

Second, implement a two-tiered relief system. Sometimes philosophical or stylistic differences will manifest with superiors, which too often "results in the superior officer ejecting the junior from command as a matter of preference." But the Air Force doesn't allow firings without cause, so "senior officers routinely paper over firings to make a cause seem apparent even when there

---

[540] Tony Carr, "Betraying Marshall: Air Force Stands Idle Amid Toxic Destruction of Good Leaders," *John Q. Public*, July 23, 2014

wasn't one." Strong incentives exist to co-opt the tools of investigation and administration, leading to the false legitimation of firing decisions. To tame this impulse, Mr. Carr recommended the Air Force allow for firings *with* and *without* prejudice, distinguishing between misconduct or mission failure, on the one hand, and "an amicable dissolution of the command relationship for the good of the mission without the baggage of unjustly destroyed careers and reputations," on the other – a no-fault divorce, as it were.

Third, require evidence before making black marks permanent. "In today's Air Force, a commander can issue an administrative sanction for any reason and absent any standard of evidence." This is a perversion, Mr. Carr asserted, "violating several bedrock principles of any responsible administrative or judicial process. There is no presumption of innocence. There is no opportunity to confront witnesses. There is an opportunity for rebuttal, but it is notoriously perfunctory. There is no meaningful appeal. Power speaks, and its object is ruined. This reflects a corrupt system – one that has fed a fascist cultural movement in the ranks in recent years." The fix, however, is easy: require a "preponderance of the evidence" standard be met before entering such derogatory information in an officer's permanent record, and require commanders to submit their deliberations to independent review. "This reform would nullify the possibility of cheaply papered adverse actions. It would also provide a powerful incentive for constructive mentorship, rather than comfortably lazy disposal, when things aren't clicking between fellow leaders."

Fourth, collect and study data on fired commanders. In addition to giving the Air Force a better foundation to understand toxicity in its own ranks, there are three additional reasons to adopt this proposal: to pick up on trends that may be otherwise obscured; to impact the behavior of would-be abusive commanders; and to understand if the Air Force is hiring the wrong people and why. As Mr. Carr concluded, "Squadron commanders are selectively hired. They are the best-qualified officers available for arguably the most important roles in the Air Force, and have demonstrated sufficient leadership potential to earn the trust of the system and the officials who administer it. The process of removing one of these people from a position of special trust and responsibility should be a careful one that respects not only the broad discretion of the decision agent, but the dignity and presumptive honorability of the individual under review. Most importantly, such a process should be governed by what's best for the mission and people of the Air Force."[541]

Another author writing for the *JQP* blog offered his own proposed reforms for squadron commander relief. Noting the current process "results in significant human relations, talent management, and return on investment issues," he suggested the Air Force reform the squadron commander screening process, as well as group commander selection and training; reform human relations management; and create a firing process, allowing for "I don't like you" reliefs of command – similar to Mr. Carr's proposed two-tiered relief system. To eliminate unfair treatment, establish transparency, establish trust in the system, and improve support to airmen, the author recommended reforming the Article 138 process; establishing a review process for firings; eliminating redundancies in the Evaluation Reports and Appeals Board; allowing electronic applications to the Air Force Board for Correction of Military Records; revising the Developmental Education process; reforming the Area Defense Council system to pool experience with these types of issues; and ensuring family support for officers who are relieved. Finally, he recommended the Air Force establish some level of accountability at higher levels for improper firings; and root out toxic leadership by making it a command interest item, adding it as a category for IG complaints, and including it in climate assessments and surveys. The Air Force must "act before the ship sinks," while Congress should assert additional oversight.[542]

For most airmen, ours has become a one-mistake Air Force in recent years. Once upon a time, it was possible for junior officers to screw up, learn from their errors, and rehabilitate their reputations over time through hard work and superior performance. There are plenty of Chief Master Sergeants currently on active duty who did something stupid and even lost a stripe early in their careers, yet now take pride in having overcome

[541] Tony Carr, "Curbing Wrongful Termination in the Air Force: Four Common Sense Reforms," *John Q. Public*, June 17, 2015
[542] David R. Warren, "Firing an Air Force Squadron Commander, Part 3: Proposed Reforms," *John Q. Public*, July 21, 2015

adversity to reach the highest enlisted grade.   Such stories of redemption are inconceivable for airmen currently coming up through the ranks, however, as any blemish on their records is likely to set them so far behind their peers, they can never recover.

That is, of course, unless the airman is already a senior leader by the time he or she screws up. While the Air Force has very little tolerance for misconduct among the masses, once an officer pins on O-6 rank – or an enlisted member becomes a command chief – he or she is inducted into an exclusive club, where the prerogatives of rank extend beyond reserved parking spaces at the commissary and dedicated on-base housing. The Air Force invests an awesome amount of authority in such senior leaders, a testament to the impeccable records they've amassed over their years of service. They are, generally speaking, worthy of respect and deference by virtue of their rank and position.   However, although they remain only human, and they make mistakes like the rest of us, they are no longer held to the same standards as their subordinates.

Destroying the career of a "light" Colonel like me – or Lt. Col. Kaiser, or Lt. Col. Annicelli – is absurdly simple for a wing commander ... but try to hold "full-bird" Colonels accountable for their actions, and you've got another thing coming. There's a lot riding on the success of these senior leaders, which reflects on the general officers who endorsed their rise to prominence. Maintaining an aura of infallibility is considered a key component of this success, which is why the chain of command so often closes ranks around the questionable actions of its O-6 commanders. For example, when Col. Camerer indulged Col. Liddick's persecution of me, his superiors – Maj. Gen. Patrick, Gen. Rand, even Gen. Welsh – had no incentive to question his judgment or reverse his decisions, as this might undermine confidence in his leadership and cast doubt on their continued support for this wing commander. Even though he wasn't part of my chain of command, Col. Camerer's sponsor, Gen. McDew, apparently took a personal interest in the outcome of my case as well. The stars were literally aligned against me. "In the current Air Force system, someone at the level of squadron command or below who steps out of line is dealt with swiftly and severely, assumed to be both culpable and ill intentioned," Tony Carr noted. "By contrast, a colonel or general who creates systemic or climatic pathologies is given a weighty

461

presumption of honorability and handled with kid gloves."[543] This compulsive unwillingness to admit senior leaders can sometimes be wrong, or acknowledge even their most absurd decisions as misguided, ultimately discredits the entire corrupt enterprise.

Lord Acton famously noted that power tends to corrupt, and absolute power corrupts absolutely. Unfortunately, Air Force senior leaders are not immune from this maxim, as there are surprisingly few effective checks on their authority. Inspectors general, purportedly independent watchdog organizations, in fact "serve as an extension of their commander by acting as his/her eyes and ears to be alert to issues that affect the organization."[544] Complaints against general officers and selects are handled at the Air Force level, susceptible to internal Air Staff politics inside the Pentagon. The seemingly powerful Article 138 process depends on the chain of command to police itself, with predictable results. Inquiries about senior leader misconduct by members of Congress are almost always met with intransigence, unless these politicians are willing to aggressively press the issue. The Air Force often treats the media as the enemy, with public affairs officers fighting to shape the narrative and spin the debate rather than admit the truth. Requests under the Freedom of Information Act elicit only a bare minimum response, if that. In such an environment, is it any wonder that so many senior leaders act with impunity?

"From rot in the nuclear community to basic training abuses at Lackland, the Air Force clearly has a problem with the calibration of power in supervisory relationships," Tony Carr observed. "Abusive officers who find their way into leadership roles need to live in fear that they will be hunted, discovered, exposed, and upended," he continued. "They need to believe the big bosses at the very top are leading and sponsoring the effort to demand moral leadership and reject abuse, and that the chain of command is emboldened and enabled by support from senior management." Unfortunately, "When toxic officials are permitted to escape accountability time and again with no explanation, the effect is just the opposite." That problem won't be remedied "until

---

[543] Tony Carr, "Dishonor Roll: Documenting the Air Force Problem of Toxic Leadership," *John Q. Public*, June 1, 2015
[544] AFI 90-301, paragraph 1.2

it is acknowledged and denounced by top officials like Gen. Welsh," he concluded.[545]

While integrity is enshrined as the first Air Force core value, it does not seem to be a guiding principle at the highest levels of the military. The Secretary of Defense named my former boss, Rear Admiral Peg Klein, as his senior advisor for military professionalism in 2014, but so far the DoD has failed to follow through on several key initiatives designed to reduce ethics problems and poor professionalism in the military.[546] This must change, both for the good of the Air Force and the security of our country. If we cannot trust our military leaders to be honest, both with the American people and with those under their command, how can we be sure they will do the right thing when lives are at stake? And how can we expect those they lead to follow them into harm's way when they show so little regard for their subordinates?

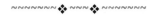

Centralized control and decentralized execution is a critical tenet of Air Force doctrine. Commanders at higher levels have a broader perspective to plan and direct operations, while front-line leaders require the flexibility to make tactical decisions as the situation warrants. However, the concentration of power among Air Force senior leaders in recent years has been accompanied by a corresponding decline in the importance of the squadron. Once the cornerstone of Air Force culture, this foundational unit has been progressively stripped of resources and authority, and subjected to an ever-more stifling bureaucracy and micromanagement by higher headquarters.

John Q. Public has been an outspoken advocate for the plight of Air Force squadrons. "As squadrons go, so goes the Air Force, and they are hurting. Losses in manpower and additions to workload have created a state of perpetual task saturation. This is exacerbated by a relentless tempo, asynchronous deployment routines that long ago outstripped roster depth while sending people running in multiple directions, and harebrained

---

[545] Tony Carr, "Flashback: Welsh Talks About Toxic Leaders," *John Q. Public*, April 20, 2015

[546] Andrew Tilghman, "GAO: Pentagon fails to address ethical problems," *Military Times*, September 3, 2015

reorganizations that have upended unity of command and unity of purpose at wing level and below in search of an imaginary oasis of new efficiency." Tony Carr traces this decline to around 2004, "when the manpower toll of concurrent wars started to fall due." The Air Force "had no plan for its role in the people-intensive, ground-centric, protracted wars that engulfed national defense after 9/11, and it had been burning through manpower margins for the previous dozen years as it remained on continual war footing while the other services generally found time to rest and reset" since the end of the first Gulf War, as airmen policed no-fly zones over Iraq and prosecuted an air war in the Balkans. "To compensate for all of this, the Air Force began a pattern of manipulating the basic formula that had long driven service life. It borrowed people from squadrons to fill unexpected new billets, borrowed even more to stand up and inflate new staffs, and then flat-out struck airmen from squadron rosters to support a massive drawdown designed to free up money for the F-22 and other modernization projects." Meanwhile, squadrons were stripped of experience and support staffs, "just as they began receiving an endless stream of new administrative bills to pay, and just as their missions grew more intense, dynamic, and enduring."[547]

As a result of these changes, squadrons now have less latitude and wherewithal to seize the initiative and provide innovative leadership, and instead are dependent on top-down direction for more and more functions. Not only does this jeopardize mission success, it unravels the very fabric of Air Force life. Most airmen are assigned to squadrons, and their commanders, superintendents, and first sergeants are periodically present in their work centers and involved in day-to-day operations. When these visible, local leaders routinely have their hands tied by higher headquarters, it undermines unit cohesion, esprit de corps, morale, and good order and discipline. The solution, of course, is to restore squadrons to their rightful place in the scheme of things. The Air Force must again return authority to the squadron level, establish reasonable expectations for unit performance, and restore modest unit support staffs to assist in mission execution.

---

[547] Tony Carr, "Problems with Finance Illustrate the Unraveling of Air Force Squadrons," *John Q. Public*, June 22, 2015

It is often said, the more things change, the more they stay the same. Since I was relieved of command in 2014, my former boss has retired, while several officers who wronged me have been promoted. Most of the personnel who worked with me at Lackland have moved on to other assignments, replaced by others of similar grade and background. Yet despite this constant turnover, the institution hardly changes, year after year. As much as I'd like to hold those individuals who wronged me accountable for their actions, this misses the point. The Air Force is more than just a collection of airmen and equipment; it's also the myriad interactions among these elements, and the purpose this complex system serves. As such, we must look beyond the players to the rules of the game. As the late Donella Meadows put it, once you begin thinking about such things properly, "You'll stop looking for who's to blame; instead you'll start asking, 'What's the system?'"[548] Sadly, the behavior of this Air Force system perpetuates a dysfunctional culture at odds with its mission.

The USAF purports to be "the world's greatest Air Force – powered by Airmen, fueled by innovation." The source of the global vigilance, global reach, and global power that defend our great nation is "the fighting spirit of our Airmen, and squadrons are the fighting core of our Air Force."[549] However, such noble sentiments are too often betrayed in actual practice. For all the talk by Secretary James and Gen. Welsh of treating airmen with dignity and respect, they have overseen a worrisome rise in toxic leadership and abuse of authority that undermines the very precepts they claim to hold dear. All too often, senior leaders place political expediency or professional advancement ahead of the true needs of their subordinates and the institution they serve. By leaving these airmen behind, they are putting the success of the Air Force at risk.

---

[548] Donella H. Meadows, *Thinking in Systems: A Primer*, Sustainability Institute, 2008
[549] Department of the Air Force, "The World's Greatest Air Force, Powered by Airmen, Fueled by Innovation: A Vision for the United States Air Force," January 11, 2013

Glossary of Air Force Terms & Acronyms

2 AF: *Second Air Force*, the AETC "numbered Air Force" responsible for BMT and non-flying technical training.

ABU: *Airman Battle Uniform*, camouflage utility uniform.

ADC: *Area Defense Counsel*, military defense attorney.

AETC: *Air Education and Training Command*, major command responsible for Air Force recruiting, basic and technical training, and developmental education.

AFB: *Air Force Base.*

AFI: *Air Force instruction*, regulatory guidance applicable to airmen; failure to follow such an order or regulation can be prosecuted under Article 92, UCMJ.

AFECD: *Air Force Enlisted Classification Directory*, catalog of enlisted career field requirements.

AFOSI: *Air Force Office of Special Investigations* (see: OSI).

AFPC: *Air Force Personnel Center*, provides centralized human resources management of active-duty airmen.

AMR: *Alleged Misconduct Report*, a 2 AF mechanism for reporting and investigating allegations of misconduct by instructors and staff.

Article 15: nonjudicial punishment under the UCMJ, which permits commanders to administer more serious discipline, including fines and loss of rank, in lieu of court-martial. Article 15s are typically offered only if the prosecution (judge advocate) has enough evidence to go to trial.

Article 32: Pre-trial preliminary hearing under the UCMJ, similar in some respects to a civilian grand jury.

Article 138: Complaint of wrongs under the UCMJ.

Blue Rope: Accouterment awarded to Master MTIs for wear on their campaign hats.

BMT: *Basic Military Training*, "boot camp" where all enlisted airmen undergo initial accession training while assigned to the 737th Training Group.

CDI: *Commander Directed Investigation*, internal investigation within command channels.

CGO: *Company Grade Officer*, junior officer in the ranks of Lieutenant through Captain.

CSAF: *Chief of Staff of the Air Force*, currently Gen. Mark A. Welsh III.

DoD: *Department of Defense.*

EFMP: *Exceptional Family Member Program*, medical program to assist families with special medical needs.

EPR: *Enlisted Performance Report*, a periodic formal evaluation by an enlisted member's rater and additional rater. Senior NCOs may also be eligible for senior rater indorsement. Under the system in place until 2015, members were evaluated in several specific categories of performance, and each rater issued an overall grade on a scale from 1 to 5. An EPR reflecting the highest marks in each of these sections was called a "firewall 5."

FAC: *Fitness Assessment Cell*, responsible for administering PT tests.

GCMA: *General Court-Martial Authority*, convening authority for military trials.

Group: The level of command above the squadron, usually led by a Colonel.

IG: *Inspector General*, the "eyes and ears" of the commander charged with investigating complaints of reprisal, abuse of authority, and other matters.

ISR: *Intelligence, Surveillance and Reconnaissance.*

JA: *Staff Judge Advocate*, legal advisors to commanders, who also prosecute criminal activity.

JBSA: *Joint Base San Antonio*, the largest single DoD installation incorporating the former Lackland AFB, including Kelly Field and Medina Annex; Randolph AFB; and Fort Sam Houston, including Camp Bullis. The JBSA commander also commands the 502d Air Base Wing, which manages most mission support functions across these posts.

LOA: *Letter of Admonition*, an intermediate form of administrative discipline; often issued to officers to punish more serious or repeated misconduct without the career-ending implications of an LOR.

LOC: *Letter of Counseling*, the lowest form of documented administrative discipline.

LOR: *Letter of Reprimand*, the most serious form of administrative discipline; for commissioned officers, an LOR has many of the same repercussions as an Article 15 for enlisted airmen.

MSG: *Mission Support Group.*

MTI: *Military Training Instructor*, the Air Force equivalent of a drill instructor or drill sergeant.

MTIS: *MTI School*, part of the 737 TRSS.

NCO: *Noncommissioned Officer*, an enlisted airman with the rank of Staff Sergeant (E-5) or higher. Master Sergeants (E-7) and above are considered senior NCOs.

Numbered Air Force: The level of command above the wing, usually led by a Major General or Lieutenant General.

OPR: *Officer Performance Report*, a periodic formal evaluation by an officer's rater and additional rater, and reviewed by the senior rater. If an airman fails to meet standards in one or more areas, the OPR (or EPR for enlisted members) is "referred" to the ratee, who has three duty days to provide a response. A referral OPR typically spells the end of an officer's career.

OSI: *Office of Special Investigations*, the Air Force's major investigative service primarily responsible for criminal investigations and counterintelligence services.

OSR: *Officer Selection Record*, personnel information available to promotion boards.

PRF: *Promotion Recommendation Form*, used by senior raters to evaluate an officer's suitability for promotion, including one of three recommendations: Definitely Promote (DP), Promote (P), or Do Not Promote (DNP).

PT: *Physical Training*, e.g. push-ups, sit-ups, running.

RFIIC: *Recruit/Family Inprocessing and Information Center*, the newly constructed facility at JBSA-Lackland that replaced the old BMT Reception Center in 2014. This complex is dedicated to former Chief Master Sergeant of the Air Force Gary Pfingston, who once served as an MTI and MTI School commandant.

SecAF: *Secretary of the Air Force*, currently the Honorable Deborah Lee James.

SFOI: *Security Forces Office of Investigations*, a unit within the local law enforcement squadron responsible for investigating certain types of misconduct.

SNCO: *Senior NCO.*

Squadron: The basic Air Force unit, usually commanded by a Lieutenant Colonel and composed of various flights.

Trainee: A new recruit attending Basic Military Training at JBSA-Lackland. Once they graduate from BMT, most airmen proceed to technical training in their career field.

TRG: *Training Group*, composed of one or more training squadrons.

TRS: *Training Squadron*, responsible for day-to-day training operations.

TRSS: *Training Support Squadron*, supports training operations.

TRW: *Training Wing*, composed of one or more training groups.

UCMJ: *Uniform Code of Military Justice*, legal framework for military members.

UIF: *Unfavorable Information File*, an official collection of derogatory information on an airman.

Wing: The level of command above the group, usually led by a Colonel or Brigadier General. Wing commanders have a wide range of prerogatives and authorities.

AIR FORCE RANKS

ENLISTED PAY GRADES:
- E-1: Airman Basic (AB)
- E-2: Airman (Amn)
- E-3: Airman First Class (A1C)
- E-4: Senior Airman (SrA)
- E-5: Staff Sergeant (SSgt)
- E-6: Technical Sergeant (TSgt)
- E-7: Master Sergeant (MSgt)
- E-8: Senior Master Sergeant (SMSgt)
- E-9: Chief Master Sergeant (CMSgt)

OFFICER PAY GRADES:
- O-1: Second Lieutenant (2d Lt)
- O-2: First Lieutenant (1st Lt)
- O-3: Captain (Capt)
- O-4: Major (Maj)
- O-5: Lieutenant Colonel (Lt Col)
- O-6: Colonel (Col)
- O-7: Brigadier General (Brig Gen)
- O-8: Major General (Maj Gen)
- O-9: Lieutenant General (Lt Gen)
- O-10: General (Gen)

About the Author

Craig M. Perry was born in raised in San Antonio, Texas, the child of Air Force brats. After graduating at the top of his class from Brown University, he joined the Air Force in 1994. During his distinguished career, he was the first airman to study as an Olmsted Scholar in Russia, and led the inaugural deployment of Air Force weapons intelligence teams in Iraq. In the wake of the Lackland sex scandal, Lieutenant Colonel Perry was selected to command a Basic Military Training squadron in his hometown, where he quickly gained a reputation as an engaged and effective leader – that is, until his chain of command rather arbitrarily fired him. He retired from active duty in 2015, determined to expose the truth about his curious case – and those of his fellow airmen left behind by the Air Force.

51005008R00261

Made in the USA
Lexington, KY
08 April 2016